Troubleshooting Linux® Firewalls

Troubleshooting Linux® Firewalls

Michael Shinn
Scott Shinn

⋏⋎Addison-Wesley

Upper Saddle River, NJ · Boston · Indianapolis · San Francisco
New York · Toronto · Montreal · London · Munich · Paris · Madrid
Capetown · Sydney · Tokyo · Singapore · Mexico City

The publisher offers excellent discounts on this book when ordered in quantity for bulk purchases or special sales, which may include electronic versions and/or custom covers and content particular to your business, training goals, marketing focus, and branding interests. For more information, please contact:

> U. S. Corporate and Government Sales
> (800) 382-3419
> corpsales@pearsontechgroup.com

For sales outside the U. S., please contact:

> International Sales
> international@pearsoned.com

Visit us on the Web: www.awprofessional.com

Library of Congress Catalog Number:
2004111873

Copyright © 2005 Pearson Education, Inc.

ISBN 0-321-22723-9

Text printed in the United States on recycled paper at RR Donnelley, Crawfordsville, IN.
Second printing, *May 2005*

Contents

SECTION I	GETTING STARTED	I
Chapter I	Introduction	3
	Why We Wrote This Book	3
	How This Book Is Organized	4
	Goals of This Book	5
	The Methodical Approach and the Need for a Methodology	6
	Firewalls, Security, and Risk Management	8
	How to Think About Risk Management	9
	Computer Security Principles	12
	Firewall Recommendations and Definitions	15
	Why Do I Need a Firewall?	16
	Do I Need More Than a Firewall?	17
	What Kinds of Firewalls Are There?	17
	Firewall Types	17
	The Myth of "Trustworthy" or "Secure" Software	19
	Know Your Vulnerabilities	20
	Creating Security Policies	21
	Training	21
	Defense in Depth	21
	Summary	21
Chapter 2	Getting Started	23
	Risk Management	24
	Basic Elements of Risk Management	24

Seven Steps to Managing Risk   25
Phase I: Analyze   26
    Inventory   26
    Quantify the Value of the Asset   28
    Threat Analysis   29
Phase II: Document   29
    Create Your Plan   30
    Create a Security Policy   33
    Create Security Procedures   34
Phase III: Secure the Enterprise   34
    Implement Policies   35
    Implement Procedures   35
    Deploy Security Technology and Counter Measures   35
    Securing the Firewall Itself   36
    Isolating Assets   36
    Filtering   39
    Ingress/Egress Filtering   39
Phase IV: Implement Monitoring   40
Phase V: Test   40
Phase VI: Integrate   41
Phase VII: Improve   41
Summary   41

Chapter 3   **Local Firewall Security**   **43**
The Importance of Keeping Your Software Up to Date   44
    yum   45
    red carpet   46
    up2date   47
    emerge   47
    apt-get   49
Over Reliance on Patching   50
Turning Off Services   50
    Using TCP Wrappers and Firewall Rules   51
    Running Services with Least Privilege   55
    Restricting the File System   56
Security Tools to Install   57
    Log Monitoring Tools   57
    Network Intrusion Detection   58
    Host Intrusion Detection   58

Remote Logging 60

Correctly Configure the Software You Are Using 60

Use a Hardened Kernel 61

Other Hardening Steps 62

Summary 62

Chapter 4 **Troubleshooting Methodology** 63

Problem Solving Methodology 64

Recognize, Define, and Isolate the Problem 65

Gather Facts 66

Define What the "End State" Should Be 67

Develop Possible Solutions and Create an Action Plan 67

Analyze and Compare Possible Solutions 68

Select and Implement the Solution 68

Critically Analyze the Solution for Effectiveness 68

Repeat the Process Until You Resolve the Problem 69

Finding the Answers or…Why Search Engines Are Your Friend 69

Websites 69

Summary 70

SECTION II **TOOLS AND INTERNALS** 73

Chapter 5 **The OSI Model: Start from the Beginning** 75

Internet Protocols at a Glance 76

Understanding the Internet Protocol (IP) 77

Understanding ICMP 79

Understanding TCP 82

Understanding UDP 88

Troubleshooting with This Perspective in Mind 89

Summary 92

Chapter 6 **netfilter and iptables Overview** 93

How netfilter Works 93

How netfilter Parses Rules 94

Netfilter States 100

What about Fragmentation? 101

Taking a Closer Look at the State Engine 102

Summary 107

Chapter 7	**Using iptables**	**109**
	Proper iptables Syntax	109
	Examples of How the Connection Tracking Engine Works	120
	Applying What Has Been Covered So Far by Implementing Good Rules	121
	Setting Up an Example Firewall	122
	Kernel Options	123
	iptables Modules	129
	Firewall Rules	130
	Quality of Service Rules	130
	Port Scan Rules	132
	Bad Flag Rules	134
	Bad IP Options Rules	135
	Small Packets and Rules to Deal with Them	135
	Rules To Detect Data in Packets Using the String Module	136
	Invalid Packets and Rules to Drop Them	139
	A Quick Word on Fragments	140
	SYN Floods	140
	Polite Rules	142
	Odd Port Detection and Rules to Deny Connections to Them	142
	Silently Drop Packets You Don't Care About	143
	Enforcement Rules	144
	IP Spoofing Rules	145
	Egress Filtering	145
	Send TCP Reset for AUTH Connections	146
	Playing Around with TTL Values	146
	State Tracking Rules	147
	STEALTH Rules	147
	Shunning Bad Guys	148
	ACCEPT Rules	149
	Summary	150
Chapter 8	**A Tour of Our Collective Toolbox**	**151**
	Old Faithful	151
	Sniffers	155
	Analyzing Traffic Utilization	157
	Network Traffic Analyzers	159
	Useful Control Tools	160
	Network Probes	161
	Probing Tools	162
	Firewall Management and Rule Building	163
	Summary	166

Chapter 9	Diagnostics	169
	Diagnostic Logging	169
	Scripts To Do This for You	170
	The catch all Logging Rule	172
	The iptables TRACE Patch	173
	Checking the Network	173
	Using a Sniffer to Diagnose Firewall Problems	179
	Memory Load Diagnostics	182
	Summary	186
SECTION III	**DIAGNOSTICS**	**187**
Chapter 10	Testing Your Firewall Rules (for Security!)	189
	INSIDE->OUT Testing with nmap and iplog	190
	Interpreting the Output from an INSIDE->OUT Scan	194
	Testing from the OUTSIDE->IN	195
	Reading Output from nmap	197
	Testing your Firewall with fragrouter	200
	VLANs	201
	Summary	202
Chapter 11	Layer 2/Inline Filtering	203
	Common Questions	205
	Tools Discussed in this Chapter	206
	Building an Inline Transparent Bridging Firewall with ebtables (Stealth Firewalls)	207
	Filtering on MAC Address Bound to a Specific IP Address with ebtables	211
	Filtering Out Specific Ports with ebtables	211
	Building an Inline Transparent Bridging Firewall with iptables (Stealth Firewalls)	211
	MAC Address Filtering with iptables	213
	DHCP Filtering with ebtables	214
	Summary	215
Chapter 12	NAT (Network Address Translation) and IP Forwarding	217
	Common Questions about Linux NAT	218
	Tools/Methods Discussed in this Chapter	219
	Diagnostic Logging	219
	Viewing NAT Connections with netstat-nat	220
	Listing Current NAT Entries with iptables	221
	Listing Current NAT and Rule Packet Counters	222
	Corrective Actions	232
	Summary	240

Chapter 13   **General IP (Layer 3/Layer 4)**   **241**

Common Question   243

Inbound: Creating a Rule for a New TCP Service   243

Inbound: Allowing SSH to a Local System   246

Forward: SSH to Another System   248

SSH: Connections Timeout   253

telnet: Forwarding telnet Connections to Other Systems   253

MySQL: Allowing MySQL Connections   253

Summary   255

Chapter 14   **SMTP (e-mail)**   **257**

Common Questions   257

Tools Discussed in this Chapter   258

Allowing SMTP to/from Your Firewalls   258

Forwarding SMTP to an Internal Mail Server   258

Forcing Your Mail Server Traffic to Use a Specific IP Address with an SNAT Rule   260

Blocking Internal Users from Sending Mail Through Your Firewall   261

Accept Only SMTP Connections from Specific Hosts (ISP)   262

SMTP Server Timeouts/Failures/Numerous Processes   264

Small e-Mail Send/Receive Correctly—Large e-Mail Messages Do Not   265

Summary   265

Chapter 15   **Web Services (Web Servers and Web Proxies)**   **267**

Common Questions   267

Tools Discussed in this Chapter   268

Inbound: Running a Local Web Server (Basic Rules)   269

Inbound: Filter: Incoming Web to Specific Hosts   270

Forward: Redirect Local Port 80 to Local Port 8080   271

Forwarding Connections from the Firewall to an Internal Web Server   272

Forward: To Multiple Internal Servers   273

Forward: To a Remote Server on the Internet   275

Forward: Filtering Access to a Forwarded Server   278

Outbound: Some Websites Are Inaccessible (ECN)   278

Outbound: Block Clients from Accessing Websites   279

Transparent Proxy Servers (squid) on Outbound Web Traffic   279

Summary   281

Chapter 16	File Services (NFS and FTP)	283
	Tools Discussed in this Chapter	283
	NFS: Cannot Get NFS Traffic to Traverse a NAT or IP Forwarding Firewall	284
	FTP Inbound: Running a Local FTP Server (Basic Rules)	290
	FTP Inbound: Restricting Access with Firewall Rules	291
	FTP Inbound: Redirecting FTP Connections to Another Port on the Server	293
	FTP Forward: Forwarding to an FTP Server Behind the Firewall on a DMZ Segment	293
	FTP Forward: Forwarding to Multiple FTP Servers Behind the Firewall on a DMZ Segment	295
	FTP Forward: From One Internet Server to Another Internet Server	297
	FTP Forward: Restricting FTP Access to a Forwarded Server	298
	FTP Outbound: Connections are Established, but Directories Cannot Be Listed, and Files Cannot Be Downloaded	299
	Summary	301
Chapter 17	Instant Messaging	303
	Common Questions/Problems	303
	Tools Discussed in This Chapter	304
	NetMeeting and GnomeMeeting	304
	Connecting to a Remote NetMeeting/GnomeMeeting Client from Behind an iptables Firewall (Outbound Calls Only)	304
	Connecting to a NetMeeting/GnomeMeeting Client Behind a netfilter/iptables Firewall (Inbound/Outbound Calls)	305
	Directly from the GnomeMeeting Website's Documentation	307
	Blocking Outbound NetMeeting/GnomeMeeting Traffic	308
	MSN Messenger	309
	Connecting to Other MSN Users	309
	Blocking MSN Messenger Traffic at the Firewall	310
	Yahoo Messenger	311
	Connecting to Yahoo Messenger	311
	Blocking Yahoo Messenger Traffic	311
	AOL Instant Messenger (AIM)	314
	Connecting to AIM	315
	Blocking AOL Instant Messenger Traffic	315
	ICQ	317
	Connecting to ICQ	317
	Blocking ICQ	317
	Summary	319
	Recalling Our Methodology	319

Chapter 18	**DNS/DHCP**	**321**
	Common Questions	321
	Tools Discussed in this Chapter	322
	Forwarding DNS Queries to an Upstream/Remote DNS Server	322
	DNS Lookups Fail: Internal Hosts Communicating to an External Nameserver	324
	DNS Lookups Fail: Short DNS Name Lookups Work—Long Name Lookups Do Not	325
	DNS Lookups Fail: Nameserver Running on the Firewall	325
	DNS Lookups Fail: Nameserver Running on the Internal and/or DMZ Network	326
	Misleading rDNS Issue: New Mail, or FTP Connections to Remote Systems Take 30 Seconds or More to Start	326
	DHCP: Dynamically Updating Firewall Rules with the IP Changes	327
	Blocking Outbound DHCP	328
	DHCP: Two Addresses on One External Interface	329
	DHCP: Redirect DHCP Requests to DMZ	330
	Summary	333
Chapter 19	**Virtual Private Networks**	**335**
	Things to Consider with IPSEC	335
	Common Questions/Problems	336
	Tools Discussed in this Chapter	338
	IPSEC: Internal Systems—Behind a NAT/MASQ Firewall Cannot Connect to an External IPSEC Server	338
	IPSEC: Firewall Cannot Establish IPSEC VPNs	340
	IPSEC: Firewall Can Establish Connections to a Remote VPN Server, but Traffic Does not Route Correctly Inside the VPN	342
	PPTP: Cannot Establish PPTP Connections Through the Firewall	345
	Running a PPTP Server Behind a NAT Firewall	347
	PPTP: Firewall Cannot Establish PPTP VPNs	347
	PPTP: Firewall Can Establish Connections to a Remote VPN Server, but Traffic Does not Route Correctly Inside the VPN	348
	Using a free/openswan VPN to Secure a Wireless Network	351
	Summary	358
	Index	**361**

SECTION I
GETTING STARTED

Introduction 1

WHY WE WROTE THIS BOOK

There are a lot of security books—books about risk management, cryptography, cracking, hacking, and writing better software, along with many firewall "cookbooks" and "bibles." We wrote this book because there are not many books out there that focus specifically on what to do when something goes wrong with your firewall or that explain how to fix errant firewalls. We wanted to put together a book that would combine the practical elements of fixing specific and common problems with Linux firewalls, along with how to figure out what might be causing a problem we might not have foreseen when we set out to write this book. In our exploration, we found that there was no book that did these things. Nothing existed that reduced all these disparate pieces of knowledge, the Tao of firewall security, the Zen of troubleshooting, and the nitty-gritty, step-by-step instructions to fix a problem. We hope you will agree that this book presents a simple and easy-to-follow methodology for solving problems, along with a practical manual that will give you the tools and the knowledge to fix some of the most common problems users experience when building and maintaining Linux-based firewalls.

When reading this book, realize that our intent is to first provide a methodology that can serve as the baseline for solving problems. We believe that having a good mindset is the most critical tool you can have at your disposal when addressing firewall issues. We cannot cover every possible problem, but we have combed our resources to provide as many common problems encountered with Linux netfilter-based firewalls and the solutions to those problems. We arrived at this list of common problems by researching all of the public Linux firewall mailing lists, by speaking with several large Linux customers, and by reflecting on our own experiences with Linux firewalls spanning over a decade of experience working with Linux. Hopefully we will have covered any problems you might have, but if not, we present our methodology for solving problems in Chapter 5, "The OSI Model: Start from the Beginning."

We have several goals in writing this book, but our chief intent is to make sure you can solve your firewall problems quickly and safely. Plans, strategies, and methodologies, while useful, are no replacement for cold, hard execution. With that intent in mind, this book is really two books. The first book teaches methods, concepts, and abstract ideas to help you learn how to diagnose a problem, to collect information about it, to arrive at a root cause, as well as what tools you can apply to that problem. The second book is a "grab it off the shelf," skim the Table of Contents, find the system/problem, flip to the appropriate page, follow the instructions, and fix the firewall type of book. We want to make sure you can pick this book up and flip to the troubleshooting chapters without having to read the entire book. We're all busy people, and we want to help you—not create more work for you.

In short, this book seeks to make engineers into mechanics with a whole tool box full of tools, a shelf full of easy to read manuals, and a mind filled with the necessary knowledge and scientific thinking to fix any problem a firewall might have. If you don't want to take the time to fully understand the mechanics of a problem, it's possible we have the solution already documented in this book. If you want to understand more, you can read the first half of the book.

How This Book Is Organized

This book is organized into three sections. Section 1 is a brief introduction to our principles of security and risk management in which we explain how firewalls work, how they should be set up, and some sample recipes for various firewall configurations. If you're new to firewalls or need a refresher, this is a good section for you to read. If you're an old hand with firewalls, you can probably skip this section and move on to Sections 2 and 3.

Section 2 is about troubleshooting and diagnostic methodologies. The intent here is to pass on troubleshooting methods and tools to reduce the amount of effort involved with troubleshooting and implementing a solution. The goal for this section is to teach you how to figure things out for yourself, to do it quickly, and to be able to repeat that process in the future. In Section 2 we explain how the key element to solving problems is to methodically reduce variables and to start with the simplest explanation first.

Section 3 contains the specific troubleshooting chapters in the book. This is where the troubleshooting guides reside. It should be possible to just flip open the book to any part of Section 3 and follow the instructions to diagnose and fix the problem. The goal of the section is to be a fix-it manual for even the least technically adept user. We believe this gradual procession to the final section of our book provides enough background information to make the process of troubleshooting second nature to the reader.

With regard to the issues of making this material as approachable as possible, we make no assumption about the reader's knowledge about good firewalling, risk management, and computer security practices. An important thought hopefully not lost on the reader is that firewalls and other security devices should be managed with a great deal of forethought and knowledge. Failure to understand a protocol or the consequences of allowing it through your firewall could have disastrous consequences.

However, we do understand that time is short, and sometimes you have to fix the problem and come back to it and understand what effect it has later. Nevertheless, with that said, along with our deepest empathy for all the overworked systems engineers out there, it is very easy to make changes to security models, firewalls, and other security technologies that can have profound and dangerous implications on the security posture of your network if you do not understand what those changes do. This book is not meant to be a replacement for competent technical security advice. There is much to be said for understanding how the products you support work, and firewalls are all the more important to fully grasp. If you're having trouble understanding the guts of your firewall, you could be in for trouble. When in doubt, you can never know too much, so avail yourself of all the information you can get your hands on about information security principles, risk management, and specifically firewall fundamentals. Given the propensity of organizations to rely solely on their firewalls for the lion's share of their security needs, it's critical that the firewall be configured in the most secure manner possible—it could be all that stands between your network's continued normalcy and high-pressure down time.

GOALS OF THIS BOOK

It is our sincere hope that that we accomplish three goals with this book:

1. To teach you, the reader, that security is not really the goal of computer security. As strange as that might sound, the only truly realizable goal of computer security is to manage risk. It's essentially impossible to avoid all the risks out there, so you need to learn to manage the consequences of those risks, while applying reasonable and effective countermeasures to help mitigate those risks. Sometimes, all you will ever be able to do is recover from a risk. The point is to change your mindset and to look at the problem through a different lens: risk management.

2. To teach you how to approach and solve problems in a scientific and methodical manner, using a well-known and widely used problem-solving methodology.
3. Finally and simply, to provide you with a book that contains specific information about how to solve your Linux firewall problem.

We can't cover every possible problem in this book, so as we've already alluded, we will have to show you how to troubleshoot and solve unforeseen problems on your own. To help with this process and to provide access to your peers, we have included numerous references to other websites, mailing lists, and forums where you might be able to seek help from the Linux community, and we've also set up our own website (`www.gotroot.com`) to further assist with the process of documenting new problems and to provide a forum for the community to discuss them and share information.

THE METHODICAL APPROACH AND THE NEED FOR A METHODOLOGY

Oh no you say—not more management speak! Please, I get enough of that already! Fear not; we promise that we won't waste your time with YAUM (Yet Another Useless Methodology). We want you to find your problem and fix it quickly. So you can call this a process, a method, a way, or if you like, call it a methodology—whatever works for you. What we don't want to do is fill your head with some useless babble. This methodology is hard won from years of solving problems.

It all started many years ago. Painted on the wall of our parents' garage was a slogan: "1st law of wrenchin': always check the spark plugs!" Scott painted this on the wall as a reminder of a valuable lesson we learned as teenagers. You need a plan for fixing things, and you need some "laws" to make sure you don't waste a lot of time figuring out what your problem is when it's staring you in the face.

As it was, we had cars, as many young men do in high school, which were the primary focus of our budding engineer minds. They were complex, they were fun, they took us places to have fun, and they were essential parts of teenagers' social lives. Without a car, life was a little less fun, and things were much farther away. However, our cars were used and needed work—sometimes a lot of work—to keep running. So we learned to take care of our cars, to fix them when they broke down, and to modify them to make them better. After all, what kind of engineer is happy with something as it is out of the box? Everything could be a little better, couldn't it? All of this meant that we had to figure out what was wrong with them while not wasting too much time doing so. We paid for those muscle cars, and we wanted to drive them! Enter the first law of wrenchin'.

The first law of wrenchin' was the result of a marathon session of trying to figure out what was wrong with one of our cars (Mike had a 1972 Pontiac GTO; Scott still has a 1970 Oldsmobile 442). For days we struggled to figure out why the motor wasn't performing as it should. We changed the timing, retuned the carburetor, drained the gas tank, uncorked the headers, and so on. We did everything we could think of…except check the spark plugs. That was too easy! It couldn't be the spark plugs, we told ourselves. Five minutes after we stopped convincing ourselves it wasn't the spark plugs, we pulled them out. They were covered with soot. The result of all our other twiddling had made already fouled plugs an absolute mess. In short, the problem was absolute—there was no way we could have gotten that GTO to run correctly, and the only solution was possibly the simplest and easiest to execute. After we had that figured out and had replaced the spark plugs, a five-minute job, we had that 1972 GTO running perfectly. What was really galling about this experience was that we knew better! Of course it could be the spark plugs; we just didn't check them, even though all the signs that this was the root cause were staring us in the face, as it were. The idea that the spark plugs were the cause of the problem just seemed too simple. We thought, wrongly, that it had to be something more complex.

Back then, our problem was caused by the lack of a clear system for problem solving or a mechanism for working through the problem to rule things out before leaping to what we might have thought was the root cause. We needed to work our way up the motor, ruling things out before moving on to the next component, and we had to learn to start with the simple things first. From that moment on, we decided that we wanted to spend more time using our cars as opposed to fixing them. So the journey started toward putting a plan in place to help prevent those forays into endlessly searching for the root cause of a problem. Over the years, we learned to work through the problem carefully, and we discovered that other people had come up with well thought out means of troubleshooting as well. It is that hard won experience and knowledge that we present here to help you to troubleshoot more effectively.

With Linux firewalls, this need for specific steps and a clearly defined approach is no different. There are so many variables in a modern firewall that it's easy to overlook the real source of any problem. For instance, we once had a big high-end SMP DEC Alpha Linux box that we used as a high-end packet switch and firewall. It worked perfectly in our lab in Virginia. We shipped it to our ISP, and all the network cards simply stopped working. We were puzzled, so we got on the box from a console and found that the network cards were up, that they had IPs, but that they simply could not talk to anything.

The NIC driver module was loaded, and the machine had worked without any problem for weeks on our lab's network. The co-location facility's network should have been no different, except for one small change: The ISP's network was Ethernet, and our lab was FastEthernet. We didn't expect that this would create any problems. After all, the network cards were designed to support both types of network, Ethernet and FastEthernet, and we had worked with these drivers before on both mediums. Our network was faster, and all we did was put the box on a slower network. Stepping down, as it were, shouldn't have made any difference. We were flummoxed. Why would that seemingly insignificant difference cause the cards to stop working?

The simple reason was that we were running the wrong driver. This might seem obvious now, but the cards we were using were DEC cards, and the wrong drivers would load and work with the wrong card, and they would work on a FastEthernet network! In our case, the system thought the card was Tulip FastEthernet card, when the cards were really DE500s. To make matters worse, they even look the same.

So back in our lab, the Tulip driver worked fine at FastEthernet speeds and never once complained about the fact that the card was not a Tulip. Couple this with the fact that we only stocked DEC NIC cards, Tulips, and DE500s, and you can see how this mistake was made. They look the same, and even the OS thought they were the same when it detected them. Fortunately, we had a simple process that we will illustrate here to work through this problem quickly, and we had the system up in short order. Total time to debug this problem and fix it was under five minutes.

The point here is that the best and quickest way to arrive at the root cause of your firewall problem is through the application of a well thought out process of elimination. It's very tempting sometimes to leap to a conclusion about what's causing the problem with your firewall, but unless you're lucky, you can actually make the problem worse. Take our word for it…relax, sit down, and work through the problem step by step. Stick with the approach we have outlined in this book, and you'll soon be tackling the thorniest firewall problems like a guru!

FIREWALLS, SECURITY, AND RISK MANAGEMENT

We believe it's important to discuss the topics of security and risk management, as they relate to firewalls, before we can jump into the process of troubleshooting. After all, your firewall problem might be something fundamental, as opposed to just a misconfiguration that's affecting your security in a very negative way. We strongly believe that you cannot manage a firewall without first thoroughly understanding risk management and computer security.

To begin, it's important to define what security is. Security is defined in some places as "freedom from risk." Some people would perceive this to mean "absence of risk," but we prefer to see it as freedom from its negative effects. The risk might still exist, but you are free to act (or not act) in spite of that risk. In some cases, you can even eliminate specific risks; in others you cannot but must still act with that risk looming, if you will, over your head. The bottom line is that you properly manage the risks around you so that you can reach a state of being "secure enough." That's what security really is. You can't make all the risks go away—that's impossible—but it doesn't stop people from trying to do it or simply telling themselves those risks don't exist. This is where the problem begins for too many organizations, but given that you are reading this book, you're already on your way to doing better. Learning to accept that risk is a part of life. You have to learn to manage the risks in your life to be "secure enough."

With that said, we are principally concerned with what is referred to as *effective security*—that is, the effort undertaken to manage risk in a calculated, economically feasible and tolerable manner to achieve some goal or set of goals. In a more practical sense, it's useful to think of security as those actions you take to protect yourself from risks that are preventing you from taking certain other actions. To be more succinct, security is everything you do to make it possible to do the things you do.

For example, if you wanted to go for a ride in a car but were concerned with safety, you might wear your seatbelt. You might also want to know how to drive that car and that the weather conditions outside were good enough to make your trip as safe as you wanted it to be. Or you might be a risk taker and be perfectly happy jumping out of an airplane with nothing but altitude and a parachute between you and certain death. In both cases, you might feel totally "secure." For each person, the decisions you arrive at that tell you have achieved that state of "security" are different. They are each dependent on how much risk you are willing to accept and how much you can afford at that particular moment given the information at your disposal.

The bottom line with security is this: Security is not a set of products, technologies, patches, or anything else technical, written, or dictated. It's a process. Security doesn't exist in nature—only the process of becoming "secure enough." Security is about managing your risks and taking actions that allow you to move ahead without getting eaten. When designing your firewall, keep this in mind. You can't stop everything, but you can keep the risks within your range of acceptance.

HOW TO THINK ABOUT RISK MANAGEMENT

There are some core concepts that we should cover first. The first concept to consider is threats. A *threat* is defined as an attacker or any person, trusted or mistrusted, who wants to break into, steal, cause damage, manipulate, or deny access to your information assets.

In Information Warfare parlance, there are three general classes of threats. They are unstructured, structured, and highly structured threats. Briefly, these are defined as

- **Unstructured:** A non-funded adversary with no specific organization or long term planning. *Example: disgruntled employee or a lone "cracker."*
- **Structured:** A funded attacker or group of attackers with some organization and funding with generally longer term planning. *Examples: organized crime or well-funded "cracker" organizations.*
- **Highly Structured:** A highly funded attacker or group of attackers, usually with national state assets. *Examples: national intelligence agencies or terrorist organizations.*

These are general classes of threats, and there are certainly overlaps between them, so don't think of them as hard and fast rules. These are generalizations of all the "bad guys" out there to help you think about who might want to cause harm to your assets, to "steal" them so they can use them for their own purposes or even just to deny you access to your assets. It's folly to try and divine the motivations of a threat. You'll never really know what your attacker is thinking, so don't get caught up in trying to convince yourself that some attacker won't be motivated to do something. People do things for all sorts of irrational reasons, and computer crackers are no exception.

The point here is that understanding the threat is only part of the process of managing risk. You should consider the threats against your assets, but you will also need to consider the second concept at the same time: value. It is not only important to define how valuable your assets are *to you*, but also to understand who might be willing to spend some of their own assets to steal or "borrow" yours and what those assets might be worth *to them*. The secretary's computer might seem unimportant in the grand scheme of things, but maybe your attacker just wants to use her drive space to store something on, or perhaps the attacker needs the secretary's computer to break into the network at large and then break into something far more important. Keep this in mind when analyzing threats and value in your organization.

In economic terms, it's also useful to remember that assets are not only monetary. An asset's value could simply be the time needed to break into your system, or perhaps something more abstract, the opportunity cost of breaking into your system versus some other organization's systems. The bottom line is that value goes beyond just putting a price on an asset; an attacker might not have money in mind at all when breaking into a network.

Consider this example: An unstructured threat, a bored student, decides to try and break into your network. The student might have no funding at all to attack your assets but is simply curious and motivated to see if he can break into a highly secure facility.

Time, for that threat, might be also be a low value asset because the student is on summer break and has free time in extreme abundance. Not all threats are so pedestrian; there are also highly funded and highly motivated organizations that have all the resources necessary to penetrate even the most well guarded assets. The point here is not to underestimate the resources at the disposal of a particular class of threats you might be attempting to defend against. Even though you will never truly be able to read the mind of someone who wants to beak into your computers, it can help to try to think like your opponent. Try to imagine what your enemy might do and, if possible, attempt to break into your own networks from the perspective of those various threats you are attempting to defend against. Just try not to underestimate your threats. A lack of imagination has been the undoing of more than one organization.

With those two critical concepts out of the way, the next core concept to cover is protection or to simply answer the question: What is it exactly that you want to protect? And within that question lies another: What is it about that asset you want to protect? One useful way to answer that question is by considering the following acronym: CIA. It stands for confidentiality, integrity, and availability. This defines what it is about the asset that is important.

For instance, if the asset has to be kept secret, then confidentiality is the goal. Is it critical that the asset not be altered or tampered with? If so, then integrity is a protection goal. And finally, must the asset be available, to whom, and under what circumstances? None of these goals are mutually exclusive; they are simply another means of determining what is important in a security model. You can have an asset that needs all three of these protection goals accomplished—and another with only one.

It's critical that you consider what it is, out of the CIA acronym, that you want to protect within each asset. If your goal is to make sure your website stays up and all the information on your site is public, then IA is important for that system. For e-mail perhaps you are only concerned with confidentiality, or perhaps your company is a health care provider and has a legal requirement to maintain the confidentiality of its customers' information. For each asset, the goals are different, and the reasons for those goals are going to be different.

The next concept to consider is means. How will you accomplish your risk management goals? With any risk management problem, you have three options, which also have their own acronym—AMR: avoid, mitigate, recover.

Specifically with avoidance you can try to prevent or avoid the worst case, with mitigation you attempt to mitigate or manage your risk, and with recovery, you simply plan how you will recover from that risk. As with CIA, none of these are inherently mutually exclusive. You must consider which of these options is acceptable to you before proceeding with your risk management plan.

Above all else, it's important to keep these elements in mind when designing a security model. One example of a "simple" attack on an electronic infrastructure would be to use explosives to destroy the systems. This concept, while far-fetched for our unstructured threat, is not outside the realm of possibility for the structured threat and is part and parcel for the highly structured threat. If you consider how inexpensive explosives are and that they could be placed inside a server, and then that server could be placed inside the co-location facility your systems are located in, the capacity for causing tremendous damage becomes shockingly clear. It's a far simpler solution than a complicated electronic attack when the goal is simply to cause destruction. That's why it's critical to really consider all of these elements when thinking about the risks your systems might face. Your system could simply be in the wrong place at the wrong time. It's a complicated world, and it takes some careful thought to put together a good plan.

Just remember, risk management is a process, not a silver bullet. You cannot "engineer" your way into being secure. Security can only be accomplished by practicing risk management, and that's what this material is all about. With all of this said, this book is not intended to be a comprehensive risk management tome, but merely a guide to the subject to help you think about how to build secure firewalls as part of the process of troubleshooting them. We recommend that if you find these risk management concepts to be new, you read up on risk management before embarking on a new or improved security plan.

COMPUTER SECURITY PRINCIPLES

Computer security, a subset of risk management, is about facilitating activity while minimizing unnecessary exposures that activity creates—in a way that makes it possible for users to still get work done. The bad news is that it's a pretty darn subjective process, and what makes one person feel secure might make another cringe. You can't please everyone. But you can construct a very solid security model by sticking with this simple and powerful premise: Unless we allow the system or network to do something, we will always deny it. The default state of all systems is to deny. Again, the rule is: unless allowed, deny. This is the golden rule for all well-designed firewalls.

This runs counter to the way some people choose to go about creating computing systems and networks. They build a system to do something, and if security is a criteria, they come back to the system after it's built with a set of rules defining what they do not want someone to do. That is the wrong way to go about it, and it also can be a painfully tedious process, even if you do it before you start to build a system. If you want to build a truly secure system, do what you do best—design your system and define what you want your users to do. From there, you construct a security model that opens those capabilities in your firewall. What you don't want to do is add a bunch of rules to your firewall, defining (exclusively) behavior that your users cannot do. You're bound to miss something that the highly imaginative human mind will come up with. The only thing you want to concern yourself with is what the users need to be able to do. Because your firewall is configured by default to deny everything, you don't run the risk of missing something. You're only allowing things through your firewall that you know about.

Let's explore this further. Think of a firewall as a totally closed system, in essence a "cut" in the wire between two networks through which no traffic at all flows. There are no holes in real firewalls, that is, the physical kind that protect buildings, and we want to keep it that way unless we can prove that there is a need for a hole or service to be opened and that we know we can do it in a way that doesn't introduce fire into the rest of the building. There is a reason firewalls, the networking kind, got their name. A long time ago, that's how most of them were configured—with no holes at all. They were just application proxies that moved data from one domain to the next, and in classified environments there were even firewalls that could only move data one way through a firewall where literally no traffic could flow back in the opposite direction. The point is, firewalls need to be built in as paranoid a manner as you can because with today's demanding networks and customer needs, we have to open a lot of holes in firewalls, and this is where we need to be especially careful. A firewall is not a silver bullet. Allowing traffic through a firewall, sometimes referred to as opening a hole in the firewall, is the same as putting that system out on the Internet with no firewall in front of it!

Remember, the firewall isn't going to magically strip away all the attacks that someone might launch through your firewall. Use the firewall as one of many mechanisms to protect the system or systems behind it. You need to look at things like Intrusion Detection, Protocol analyzers, Intrusion Prevention Systems, classic system hardening, the venerable method of keeping your system patched, cryptography, authentication, software security, and above all else real risk management before you can even begin to say that your system is "secure." Firewalls are only one slice of the security spectrum. You need all the elements of the visible light spectrum to get white light, so it is with security; you need the whole spectrum of methods, procedures, technologies, and management practices to make something "secure."

With that said, here's the bad news…there is no such thing as a "secure" system, which is why we put this word in quotes. The term, secure, is subjective and means different things to different people at different times. For example, your system might be patched up today, so you tell yourself it's "secure," but when you head off for a much earned vacation this weekend, a new vulnerability is published, and you can't get to your system to patch it. And along comes an attacker that uses that vulnerability to break into your, now, insecure systems.

It's also important to keep in mind that with all these measures taken, it is still possible that your system might be broken into or that some other calamity might destroy or make the system unavailable. A flood for instance, an earthquake, or a just plain old hardware failure could be far more damaging than a hypothetical attack. That's why it's important to recognize that there is more to risk management than just securing a system from attacks.

That's the real business that every security professional is really in—managing risk. With risk, as we stated before, you can do three things to manage it: you can avoid it, mitigate it, or recover from it. Sometimes you can do several of theses things; other times you can do only one; and sometimes you can do none of the above. It's important to understand this. This point is critical, and it bears repeating. All security is really about is managing risk. Sometimes you can do something because the risk is acceptable, and sometimes you cannot. This point causes much grief for many security professionals, their customers, users, and bosses when security is confused with some mythical state of being absolutely secure. All you can ever do is manage your risk in a manner that meets your criteria for acceptable risk and loss. You're happy jumping out of the airplane with a parachute; your buddy is not.

Also, to review, threats are a critical competent of risk analysis. To determine if your efforts are necessary or if they are enough, you must consider what threats are going to try to compromise the system(s) you are protecting. For instance, if you are running a simple website with nothing of interest or value to terrorists or organized crime, you might not need to consider those threats. If you're the CIA, you need to consider those threats.

One other thing to keep in mind with threat analysis is that the system you are running might not be the attacker's real target. Your system might be broken into by a highly structured threat to attack the real target or perhaps another "zombie" along the way, which in turn might be used to break into the real target, or your system could just be broken into by a worm, virus, or bored cracker.

The bottom line is that there are some very odd people out there who want to break into systems for all sorts of reasons. It's critical to understand that there are many reasons your system might be broken into, some of which might never have dawned on you. Many a poor system owner has found their "unimportant" system broken into by persons that could care less about what that system had been used for. The attackers now "own it," and they're using it for their own ends. Sometimes, all an attacker really wants is the virtual real estate your systems occupy.

FIREWALL RECOMMENDATIONS AND DEFINITIONS

A firewall is a device that provides secure separation of one or more networks from each other. In the ideal case, a firewall should provide physical separation between all networks. Virtual networks have become very popular, and there is a tendency to create "separation" between networks by using virtual abstractions. This is not a recommended configuration. One error in the configuration, a flaw in the software or hardware, or some other problem can cause your security to fail dramatically and completely with purely virtual network separation.

The best rule of thumb, especially given the availability of free firewalling technologies such as **iptables** and **ipchains**, is to always separate networks in a manner that you can physically verify. Color-coded wires running to networks on physically separated, not virtually or VLAN separated, switches and hubs is a wise investment. Nothing beats physical separation.

We also recommend that your routing scheme be organized in such a manner that if your firewall is misconfigured or fails for some reason, that traffic would not normally move from one domain of your network to the other. This might sound like common sense, but some commercial firewalls have been known to fail "open" and forward all traffic between networks.

For example, we were asked to look at a customer's network that was experiencing some "strange" behavior. After quickly looking at the company over the Internet, it was determined that their entire corporate network, every server and workstation, was completely exposed to the Internet. We knew that they had a firewall, and it was a reliable commercial grade product that should not have allowed this to occur. However, we also knew that they had been issued an Internet routable network by their ISP and were using that IP space for their internal network as well. When we arrived, we were amazed at what havoc a simple mistake could make. Our customer had installed their firewall on a switch and had plugged BOTH their internal and external interfaces into the same unmanageable switch! From their perspective, everything was working perfectly. They could get out to the Internet, mail worked, and everything was as it should be. You see, it turns out that they never bothered to check to see if anyone could get in! Sadly, this turns out to be the case with many organizations, which is why we recommend that your networks be configured in such a way as to make sure this is unlikely to occur if your firewall fails. One simple way to do this is to never, under any circumstances, use Internet routable IPs behind your firewalls. Thankfully, there is an entire IETF RFC dedicated to this, RFC 1918, and there are network blocks set aside for everyone to use for their internal use.

Briefly, they are:

```
10.0.0.0       -   10.255.255.255  (10/8 prefix)
172.16.0.0     -   172.31.255.255  (172.16/12 prefix)
192.168.0.0    -   192.168.255.255 (192.168/16 prefix)
```

If you use these addresses for your internal networks, they will not easily route over the Internet if you start to experience problems with your firewall.

You should also test your firewall—not to see if you can get out, but rather, start by testing to see if you can keep the bad guys out. We can't stress the importance of this enough. It's very easy to misconfigure a firewall and never know about it until it's too late.

Equally, this example serves to illustrate the value of using a private network for your internal and, where possible, DMZ networks. This is not a fool-proof solution, but it adds another layer of security to your risk management program.

WHY DO I NEED A FIREWALL?

If it's not already clear, there are many reasons, but the two really big ones are that there are bad people in the world who want to get in to your networks and that your network depends on millions of lines of buggy, imperfect software, usually filled with really big security holes that can compromise your assets, which no one seems to know about until it's too late.

If this doesn't sound like a problem for you, then you don't need a firewall. In practical terms, it's the very rare case when a firewall would not be helpful, especially with Linux, where we have access to many powerful and free, as in beer and speech, firewall tools. Given the tremendously powerful firewall tools included with Linux, it would be foolish not to use them. And because these tools are free, we strongly recommend that you not only build a network firewall, but that you also use **iptables** or **ipchains** on all your workstations, laptops, servers, devices, and anything else running Linux.

Thankfully, many Linux vendors have made the process of configuring desktop and server firewalls much easier by including firewalling tools that auto-magically configure **iptables** or **ipchains** on install, or any time you wish to change or install those firewall rules. And if your vendor doesn't include tools to do that, there are dozens of tools that make configuring a Linux firewall a snap. Some of them are available at our website, www.gotroot.com.

Just remember, like everything else we've discussed so far, firewalls are not a silver bullet. Just because you installed one doesn't mean you're safe. A firewall is a compartmentalization tool with holes in it. If you let someone through to your web service port, it's not going to protect you from web attacks; if your browser has a flaw in it, it's not going to protect from spyware that leverages that hole to attack your computer. It takes more than a firewall to manage risk these days.

DO I NEED MORE THAN A FIREWALL?

Yes, always, without a doubt, you need more than a firewall. You will need tools to help you harden your system, to check the integrity of your files, binaries and drivers, intrusion detection and prevention tools, patch management technologies, and penetration testing tools. Sometimes you might even need military grade cryptography, security policies to describe what users can and cannot do, training for those users, and above all else, a certification program and even a risk management plan. A firewall is never enough by itself.

WHAT KINDS OF FIREWALLS ARE THERE?

There are four types of firewalls, which are all available on Linux platforms. These are, in order of complexity and features, packet filtering, application proxies, stateful inspection, and hybrid. There are, as we will explain, a few very specialized firewalls for extremely high security environments, trusted guards, and one way filters. Those types of firewalls are beyond the scope of this book, but if you are interested in learning more about them, we have a section on those types of devices at our website (`www.gotroot.com`).

FIREWALL TYPES

- **Packet Filtering:** These are the first generation of firewalls, generally what you see on modern routers these days. While useful, they are generally trivial to circumvent an attacker using a number of common attack methods.
- **Application Proxies:** This is the second generation of firewall technology, although it could be said this is actually the first in some ways. An application layer firewall is a proxy server, like the HTTP proxy server, Squid, for example. They also provide a layer of granularity into security policy that you won't find in stateful inspection or packet filtering firewalls.

Basically, an application proxy is an application that runs on your firewall or gateway that relays traffic between you and your destination. The added advantage here is that the traffic is being sent/received between both endpoints by a third-party application, meaning you can enforce very specific guidelines on the way the traffic is crafted between both points.

- **Stateful Inspection:** This would be the third generation of firewall technology, this is related to the packet filtering method, but it extends the capabilities of firewalling by continuing to inspect the packets as they pass through the firewall. Netfilter/**iptables** is a stateful inspection type firewall.

  Netfilter/**iptables**' main features are

  - stateful packet filtering (connection tracking)
  - all kinds of network address translation
  - flexible and extensible infrastructure
  - large number of additional features as patches

- **Hybrids:** Hybrids are the fourth generation. They are a combination of the previous three, giving the users more control of the methods they intend to employ to carry out their firewall policy.

As stated previously, there are two other types of firewalls that we are not going to cover in this book. Their use is very specialized, and it's not practical to construct them with **iptables** or **ipchains**. The other types fall into two categories, trusted guards and one-way firewalls. Trusted guards basically prevent data, in theory, from moving from one domain to another domain. Basically, they are designed to prevent "Top Secret" data, for instance, from moving into a domain that is only rated "Secret," and they accomplish this with specialized hardware and Multi Level Security (MLS) data labeling techniques. With commodity hardware, such as off-the-shelf PCs, it's not really possible to accomplish true compartmentalized security with trusted guards. You need some specialized hardware to protect the memory on the PC and even in some cases, specialized NIC cards. You can accomplish some less trusted attempts at MLS with commodity hardware if you want to tinker, but with that type of hardware the system will never really be "trusted" in the classical computer science sense of the term. Hence, we will not focus on these security models in this book. Regardless, MLS and its use with what are referred to as Compartmentalized WorkStations (CWS) is a really neat and useful concept. It has its uses, but these technologies are rarely used in the commercial world. And, as we alluded to earlier, the capacity to label the data in a manner that would make trusted guards possible without the use of commercial products has only recently entered the standard

Linux kernels, and the hardware to support it is not in high supply for the general public. As it is right now, there is no easy way to set up a trusted guard with Linux, but this is likely to change as demand increases. We are fascinated by the improvements in the Linux kernel in this area and are keeping a very close eye on developments. As before, if this topic interests you, feel free to visit our website (`www.gotroot.com`) and join in the forums there on this topic.

Aside from trusted guards, the other type of firewall we will not cover in this book is known as a "one way" firewall. This kind of firewall involves the use of specialized hardware that literally will only transmit data in one direction. This too is a highly specialized form of a firewall because it is designed to prevent a very unique form of attack through all modern firewalls called a "covert channel attack." Briefly, a "covert channel attack" is where someone behind a firewall is able to send data, or possibly to even construct a full data channel, through a firewall in spite of the firewall's policy. It's beyond the scope of this book to go into more detail on this type of attack, but it's a fascinating issue to consider as it may be relevant to your organization's risk management plan. Again, you can always check `www.gotroot.com` for information on this topic or to ask on our forums for more information.

Both of these types of firewalls are in response to risks that classic firewalls, all four of the types discussed at the first part of this section, cannot adequately protect against. We think it's good to point this out because your firewall can only protect against a finite range of risks. It alone cannot protect against all of the current known threats that networks face.

THE MYTH OF "TRUSTWORTHY" OR "SECURE" SOFTWARE

The goal of building secure and more reliable software can never be under-appreciated or over-emphasized in our opinions. We want to see vendors produce better software, but we do recognize that wanting something is very different from having something, and too many promise what they can't deliver. As it is, software is going to have flaws because it's very hard to write bug free and infallible software, and software is written by imperfect people. That's not to just pick on software; hardware is equally plagued with these issues. Computer hardware and software are complex systems, ever more complex everyday, and market forces sometimes dictate whether or not security will be the product's primary focus, or even if security will be get any attention at all. After all, as we already said, "secure" is a subjective concept that differs from party to party. What the builder envisions as "secure" might not be the ultimate case for every user. With that said, if you want to manage the security of your systems, you need to start with the cardinal rule:

People are not perfect. People make the things we use. Therefore those things we use will not be perfect.

To be more succinct, your software and hardware probably have bugs in them. They probably have a lot of bugs. Prepare for that, no matter how great your software or hardware vendor is or what they might say about the security of their products or their track record.

It's best to look at your systems as the flawed, imperfect and insecure things they probably are. If you start with this assumption, the task at hand can seem daunting. But don't fear! You've made it this far in life, and real life is no more certain, perfect, or secure than the computing world is. In nature, there is no such thing as total security. That concept does not exist. There is only risk management. Sometimes you crawl out of your hole to seek food, and something else eats you; other times you stay in your hole and starve; and other times, most of the time, you leave your hole, you find food, purpose, enjoyment, and everything turns out fine. It's balancing those risks, threats, and rewards that defines life.

With computers it's no different. Sometimes you have to take greater risks with your Information Technology systems to reach a new customer, to link with an important vendor, or to simply operate your business. If you have systems attached to the Internet, then you are taking a risk.

KNOW YOUR VULNERABILITIES

Continuing this thread, it's important to understand what your weaknesses and vulnerabilities are before you try to solve any security problem through improvement. After all, if you don't know what's broken, how can you fix it? As we mentioned before, the best way to learn what your adversaries can do and where you need to focus your efforts, is to look at your network and its assets from the perspective of an attacker in a brutally honest manner. You will want to attack your network or engage someone who can do it for you. The intent is to enumerate every known vulnerability in your organization so that you can make an informed assessment to manage the risks created by these vulnerabilities. We will explore this topic in more depth in later chapters. Just remember, it's not enough to secure your network. After you do that, you will want to try and break in. You can't know if your efforts are worthwhile without testing them.

CREATING SECURITY POLICIES

In addition to the technical methods used to secure networks and computers, via electronic rules, it's important to create rules for the people that will be using those computers and networks. Many times, you cannot engineer away the cause of the problem: the user. Having a clearly defined security policy is critical to the success of any risk management plan.

TRAINING

After you have your security model and policies in place, users will need to be trained on them. This can be something as simple as, for a home firewall, explaining to your spouse, roommates, or whomever that you now have a firewall in place and how it is configured.

For larger organizations, you will need to go a little further than this. Training your users can be the difference between a security plan that works and one that fails on the first day. For instance, your plan might be thwarted via something as simple as a social engineering attack. An employee or user is convinced to give someone else access to your systems or building.

DEFENSE IN DEPTH

We can't stress enough the need for Defense in Depth (DID). Computers, software, firewalls, and all the creations of man have one fundamental flaw: People created them, and people are not perfect; people make mistakes. You simply cannot rely on one thing to protect your network and computers. Firewalls are wonderful and powerful tools for protecting systems, but they are neither perfect nor complete solutions for the incredibly wide range of vulnerabilities and threats that modern networks and computers face.

SUMMARY

Even though this is a book specifically about firewalls, we would be remiss if we did not point out that security requires more than just deploying a firewall. A firewall will not protect your systems from many of the electronic threats they may face. Remember, a firewall is just one security tool; it's not a silver bullet! We'll discuss this in more detail in the next chapter, but suffice it to say that firewalls are over emphasized in many security plans. At the very least, plan for what you will do if your firewall fails you miserably. Create a plan to recover and build in additional layers of defense to protect your assets.

As to the purpose of this book and its goals, troubleshooting your firewall will require you to develop an approach to solve problems. In later chapters we describe the methodology we use, which also happens to be used by the U.S. Army, emergency medicine, and other high-pressure fields to quickly arrive at the root cause of a problem, to implement a solution, and to test the effectiveness of the implemented solution. You will find that this approach will not only save you time, but it also will save you the trouble of potentially making the problem worse.

Getting Started

2

Starting off this chapter, we're going to repeat a topic covered in Chapter 1, a topic that in our opinion can't be repeated enough. A firewall is never going to be enough to secure your network, your hosts, your data, or whatever else you are trying to protect; you must do more. It takes a lot more than one method, a firewall, or even technology alone to manage risk. Technology alone will not suffice. If you find yourself repeating it until you are blue in the face, you will understand why this is such a critical point to repeat. Risk management is more than technology and more than policies or any other single element. It takes the full spectrum of risk management solutions to truly address the problem.

In case the point wasn't clear the first time we said it, a firewall alone will not make your computer security problems go away. With that said, the goal of this chapter is to explore and expand on those concepts that can help you to protect your computing assets where a firewall cannot. The most important element of that total approach is to recognize that your goal is not to secure your assets, but to come up with a comprehensive risk management plan and to execute *that* to secure your assets.

In this chapter, we will explore the major elements of the risk management approach to computer security and present some basic concepts to get you started. It is not only important to ensure that your firewall is working and that it's doing its job of protecting your enterprise correctly, but also that you understand what a firewall cannot do for you. One of the worst trends we have seen in computer security is an over-reliance on firewalls and the false belief that a firewall can be relied upon to shoulder the lion's share of the work when securing a network and its assets. Too many organizations install a firewall and go no further. Firewalls are important and useful security tools, but they are not silver bullets, and they are becoming less and less effective against the growing range of threats and vectors used against protected systems.

RISK MANAGEMENT

As already stated, the key to any good computer security program is risk management. Nothing short of a comprehensive risk management program is going to suffice in the rapidly evolving world of computer security. New threats, vulnerabilities, counter measures, technologies, exploits, and products appear on the market everyday. Sooner or later, something will happen that your security model does not account for. Natural disasters such as fires and floods or physical theft of a laptop, and your data can be lost or in the hands of some hostile party. Without a comprehensive and holistic approach to security, you will always be playing catch up. The good news is that computer security is a subset of risk management, so our computer security problems fit nicely into a body of work that stretches back over centuries. There are even whole industries, of which you might already be aware, that cater directly to the risk market, such as insurance companies and underwriters. Risk, as we already mentioned, is a fact of life; you cannot build a perfect security model that will protect you from all possible threats. What you can do is build a good risk management model that accounts for the things you cannot control, the things you can, and how you will sort out the problems that crop up in between. Keep this in mind: It is possible to implement a risk management program that will address your worst-case scenario so that you can sleep at night. The best part is that your program only needs to be as complicated as you need it to be.

BASIC ELEMENTS OF RISK MANAGEMENT

There are three basic goals of computer security, which are broken down into the CIA acronym. Keep in mind we are not talking about the intelligence agency with the same acronym, but rather the three goals of computer security: protect the confidentiality, integrity, and/or availability of a computing asset. The goal of confidentiality is to prevent disclosure of information to unauthorized parties. Integrity is the goal of ensuring that the information or asset has not been tampered with, and availability is exactly what it sounds like—the goal of making sure that the information or asset is available to the parties that need access when they need access.

For any given asset, one or more of these goals might be more important than the other, and the extent to which that goal is achieved is entirely unique to that asset. What is secure enough for one system might not be for another. One simple example is to ask yourself if your home is secure enough. For some, simple locks will suffice for their assets and the threats they feel their home many be exposed to; for others an alarm system, dead bolts, and irons bars are sufficient. The point here is that the goals are always going to be different for each asset you choose to protect, as will the methods and the extent to which you protect that system.

Keep this in mind when evaluating your risk management processes. It will help to focus your efforts on those elements of your plan that will accomplish your goals in a customized manner for each asset.

SEVEN STEPS TO MANAGING RISK

We are firm adherents to the principle that risk management has to be an ongoing cyclical process. You cannot expect to respond to the ever-changing landscape of threats and vulnerabilities by relying on an old risk assessment or a one-time shot at developing a risk assessment program. For your risk management program to succeed, you have to re-evaluate your data, systems, and counter measures regularly. One way to accomplish this is to conduct regular vulnerability assessment and threat analysis of your organization. The vulnerability assessment should be conducted many times a year, and IT vulnerability assessment should be conducted as often as possible. With open source vulnerability assessment tools such as nessus (`www.nessus.org`), there is no reason why an organization could not schedule weekly vulnerability scans on their IT resources, and with the wide range of qualified firms to choose from, a third party assessment should be conducted on at least a quarterly basis for the entire organization. Why so often? Things change, and with IT, they change often and fast. With every new patch, piece of software, computer, or user, something has changed. The key element here is that your organization changes all the time, and you have to keep up with that dynamic element of life. One suggestion we make to all our customers is to always run a vulnerability scanner against any system that has changes made to it. Such is the case of installing a new patch or granting/removing a user's access. The following sections discuss seven phases of implementing a strong risk management program. The phases are

Phase I: Analyze
Phase II: Document
Phase III: Secure the Enterprise
Phase IV: Implement Monitoring
Phase V: Test
Phase VI: Integrate
Phase VII: Improve

PHASE I: ANALYZE

INVENTORY

The first step in any risk management process is to take stock of what you must protect and to not make the mistake of looking at just what you want to protect. This involves establishing what systems and networks you're working with and the way data flows between those systems, domains, or enclaves you're trying to compartmentalize by inventory of your systems, defining what they do, and detail regarding who should have access to what specific resources on those systems. This includes all the pieces to your system or enterprise that must be protected and how they are deployed today. This is a critical distinction because too often when constructing risk management programs, organizations become very myopic in their analysis of what they think they need to protect. Many organizations will zero in on only those assets that they want to protect, while ignoring all the other pieces of their network that might contribute to a reduced security posture for that asset. The problem becomes one of omission through ignorance.

For instance, we have seen customers overlook that modems are an easy vector of penetrating an organization's security perimeter (the proverbial Belgium to the firewall's Maginot Line). In these cases it was felt that the systems the modems were attached to were of low importance and, hence, not a high security priority. Further, there was a general lack of operational awareness of how these systems connected to the rest of the network.

The problem is that the low value or unimportant system with the modem connected to it was really just a vector into something far more valuable, the network itself. After you are inside an organization's network, you have free run of the place. In short, too many computer security models tend to look like an egg, hard on the outside, liquid on the inside. If you get past the shell, through a modem for instance, you can move around with impunity throughout the entire organization.

The point here is to recognize the dependencies in your organization's security plan. Just because your organization has an excellent Internet security plan provided by a state of the art Linux firewall does not mean that you do not have to consider other vectors into your security enclave. Look at everything and consider how it could be used to defeat a security counter measure. Laptops are another example. Assume for a moment that you have fantastic perimeter security and you have every way into your organization accounted for and properly compartmentalized, such as modems and wireless access points. However, the users on your network take their laptops outside your network, to their homes, school, or a coffee shop, and those laptops become infected with worms or Trojans while connected to the not so secure network they are temporarily attached to.

These users then reconnect their laptops to your network and without realizing it, unleash those worms on your network—defeating your perimeter security model.

You cannot manage these risks by only looking at what you want to protect. You have to expand your horizons, so to speak, and look at the whole picture. Be creative and think about the threats and vectors that bring those threats onto your network. If you have some critical assets in your network, then consider what it is that those assets trust and don't make assumptions about your security model that are not based on fact. A good rule of thumb: When in doubt, don't trust it.

To wrap up this thread, the first step is to take stock of what your network is composed. How is it laid out, what systems are connected to it, who runs those systems, and what are all the paths from outside the network to your critical assets? Then consider how much you can trust the assets inside your network. You might have to compartmentalize certain systems off from others by deploying internal firewalls. For more critical systems, you have to do more than that, such as isolating those systems so that they are not connected to your main network. Some organizations do this with their accounting systems, and the military is supposed to isolate classified systems onto their own networks, physically separated from the non-classified systems.

Another problem we have seen is organizations that look at what they want their networks to be or hope them to be. Reality, cold unfiltered reality, is the only ingredient that will work here. Don't assume that your roll out of that fancy new "secure" network will be deployed on time or that your wire or logic diagrams correspond to the physical layout of the network. In one fascinating example we ran into with a large organization, they had one of the most elaborate security models we had ever seen. This organization had seven separate networks, all separated by firewalls with Network-based Intrusion Detection Systems (NIDS) at each entry point. The products they chose were all top of the line, to include trusted Operating Systems and, at that time, brand new Host-based Intrusion Detection Systems (HIDS) products. Everything looked great on paper and even logical when mapped out with our tools. But when we did wire traces, we realized that they had hooked everything up to the same switch. They were relying on this one switch to create their carefully separated networks, to include having external networks plugged into the same switch! To their overall team, this was a perfectly reasonable solution—and this was far and away one of the more well read and intelligent customers we had encountered. The problem was that their networking team was not part of the security design team, and the security design team was not part of the deployment team. So, when all was said and done, the system in logical terms was exactly as the designers had said it should be, but in physical terms, it was a different story. The moral of the story is to assume nothing when taking stock of your assets. Documentation is useful only to get you started. Check everything manually and physically—and assume nothing.

QUANTIFY THE VALUE OF THE ASSET

As part of the process of taking stock of what you must protect in your organization, it's important to quantify what those assets are worth to your organization. How much would disclosure of that information cost? How much would loss of that asset cost? What if the data was simply tampered with? For each organization, and for each asset, the answers to these questions are different. A public web server might not be as important as the company's accounting system—or vice versa in some cases. Consider the asset, what it does, and what would happen if the asset couldn't continue in its current function.

As part of the analysis phase, conduct a vulnerability assessment of the entire organization to verify this data and help to find vulnerabilities. A vulnerability assessment is defined by the U.S. Government as

1. "An examination of the ability of a system or application, including current security procedures and controls, to withstand assault. A vulnerability assessment might be used to: a) identify weaknesses that could be exploited; and b) predict the effectiveness of additional security measures in protecting information resources from attack.
2. Systematic examination of a critical infrastructure, the interconnected systems on which it relies, its information, or product to determine the adequacy of security measures, identify security deficiencies, evaluate security alternatives, and verify the adequacy of such measures after implementation." (U.S. Government, CIAO)

In short, a vulnerability assessment is any means of testing your entire organization, its systems, controls, and personnel, to detect vulnerabilities and to determine if the controls are adequate to protect against threats to your organization.

One of the more critical elements in any risk management program is the vulnerability assessment. Only by critically and scientifically assessing the vulnerabilities and testing the controls in an organization can one hope to improve that organization's security posture, to develop an effective risk management program, and to truly understand the inter-relationships between the elements of an organization. Thankfully, vulnerability assessments have become part of the lexicon for IT and are commonplace across the industry, but they are still not conducted with as much regularity or vigor as we would like to see. For IT assessment, there are now open source tools, such as **nessus** (www.nessus.org), that make it possible to automate vulnerability scans for IT resources from Cron. We highly encourage you to do this wherever possible. Think of as a tripwire for your network.

THREAT ANALYSIS

The final step in the analysis phase is to analyze the threats that might want to gain access to, damage, or deny access to your assets. Recall from Chapter 1 that there are three general classes of threats that we can look at for quick reference. Not all threats fall into those three categories, but as a whole they tend to cover the threats most organizations will face. Different assets might be exposed to different threats; a low value asset might just be a stepping stone to a higher value asset for one class of threats. For instance, an unimportant public web server with no important data or accounts is allowed to connect back into the organization's internal network through a hole in the firewall so that it can authenticate to a Primary Domain Controller (PDC). The web server is broken into, and the attacker then uses the unimportant web server to break into the PDC through a vulnerability in the RPC services. The PDC is then used to break into all the critical systems on the internal network. In this example, the threats perceived to exist against the web server, unstructured threats, are not the full range of threats the system might experience—because of its relationship to a higher value target. This goes back to the issue of understanding the inter-relationships between systems, networks, assets, and even people. When analyzing for threats (i.e. who would want to break into this system?), consider the down stream effects of breaking into the assets. This also brings up an emerging risk to organizations that goes beyond the scenario painted here and is directly related to the problem of analyzing threats; that risk is down stream liability.

Down Stream Liability

A not so new concept that is garnering a good deal of attention is "down stream liability." This concept relates to the notion that your organization is liable for any damage done to a third-party system because your systems were used to effect this damage. For example, in the previous case, your unimportant web server is broken into and used to break into a bank. The bank could sue your organization for failing to take appropriate measures to properly protect your systems. In layman's terms, basically this means that you can be sued for failing to effectively manage the security posture of your systems.

PHASE II: DOCUMENT

Once you have determined what you must protect, what it's worth, and who might want to attack it, then it's time to document all of this along with some clear information about who manages the system, who they might work for, and what the system does. The primary reason for documenting these sorts of details is to take a snapshot in time of the enterprise and to protect your organization against loss of this knowledge should people leave the organization. In our experience, formal office documents for this sort of documentation might be necessary for legal and regulatory purposes. There are new federal laws that require companies to fully document their internal controls and for the senior management to literally sign off on the integrity of those controls. Imagine if you were held personally liable for the security of your entire company. You might want it in writing as well.

However, an electronic version of this information shouldn't conflict with this requirement, and we have found that having this information available to authorized parties through a web interface can be invaluable during a crisis. If your data changes frequently, you might consider using a wiki (`www.wiki.org`) or some other Content Management System (CMS) to help manage the dynamic flow of information into these documents. Finally, when you are constructing this documentation, online collaboration tools can really pay off. In a large multi-state or multi-national organization, it can be difficult to exchange documents with colleagues in different time zones. By making the documentation process as easy and accessible as possible, with the appropriate security controls of course, you can reduce the level of effort required to document systems and system changes. We believe that when creating these documents, it's helpful to keep the process as dynamic and flexible as possible. Formal controls on the documentation process can be put into place after you have collected the information you need to create the formal documentation.

There are three sub-phases within this phase:

1. Create your plan
2. Create a security policy
3. Create security procedures

CREATE YOUR PLAN

To secure an organization you need to create a plan. To start off with the plan, you need to consider the security models and approaches that are appropriate for your networks. There is a whole range of security models that are appropriate for one set of threats over another, and it is beyond the scope of this book to go into much detail on security models.

As to security approaches, there are currently two effective approaches to building the security plan: the classic and time proven method, Defense in Depth (DID), and the relatively new Holistic approach. We will explain these in detail here, but we consider the

Holistic approach to really be a natural extension of the DID approach into the entire enterprise and always recommend the Holistic approach over classic DID.

Defense in Depth

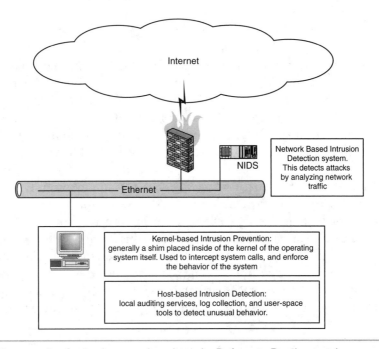

Figure 2.1   An example of a simple network applying the Defense-in-Depth principle.

Defense in Depth relies upon layers of security procedures, technologies, and policies to compensate for breaches to any one or more layers before it as part of a perimeter-based security model. Like an onion, this security approach is implemented by building in layer after layer of counter measures for each identified threat or class of threats around an asset or assets to be protected. For instance a very simplistic layering might look like this: firewalls Layer 1, Intrusion Detection Systems (IDS) Layer 2, systems hardening Layer 3, Host-based Intrusion Detection (HIDS) Layer 4, Kernel-based Intrusion Detection Systems/Kernel-based Intrusion Prevention Systems (KIDS/KIPS) Layer 5, systems backups Layer 6, and insurance Layer 7.

Again, this is just a simplistic example of layered security, which excludes many other elements of the model and assumes that only one technology might make up a layer. Defense in Depth is typically built backwards from a designated perimeter towards an asset or set of assets. This complicates matters tremendously when you start opening up your firewall to allow services into your networks and/or start connecting your networks with other organizations' networks; the perimeter essentially disappears.

In those cases, which are becoming the norm as opposed to the exception, it is very difficult to define what the perimeter is or even where it is. The class DID model is left wanting because the perimeter can, in essence, be bypassed. It's still a good model to keep in the back of your mind, building in layers to fall back on one another, but as a concept it isn't even remotely as effective as it once was. The network perimeter has almost disappeared with the introduction of wireless assets, laptops, VPNs, ASPs, virtual servers, shared hosting, and other technologies. It is our contention that the perimeter is really down at every desktop and server, and in some cases, it's down to the very applications themselves.

This leads to the holistic approach, which is essentially akin to pushing those perimeters straight down to each server and in some cases into each application. In short, it's like living in a world without firewalls, where the bad guys can communicate with every system and program in your network. In many cases, this is precisely the world that we live in now. None of this is to say that firewalls are not useful; that is far from the case. You don't want to get rid of your firewalls and other perimeter security devices, and you certainly don't want to stop creating security perimeters around an asset or set of assets. The point is to realize that this approach is not as effective as it might seem in most cases.

Holistic

The holistic approach makes risk management an integrated part of the organization's standard operating practices. As opposed to looking at risk management and its subset, security, as a perimeter issue or by securing assets via an after-the-fact approach, the holistic approach recognizes that perimeters generally do not exist in modern networks or are difficult to create and that an after-the-fact approach to security is not effective. For any risk management program to succeed, it has to be built into the way the organization functions in as seamless a manner as possible, where security is built into every system and application with the realities of modern computing firmly in mind.

This approach to information security is touted by some as a "new" approach. We disagree. It might be new in the sense that more organizations should be doing it and are not, but it's not new in the sense that it's an approach that the security community is just warming up to. The holistic approach is a logical extension of good risk management approaches. You cannot expect to understand the inter-relationships of your risks and exposures without looking at the whole picture.

This brings us to the issue of looking beyond just IT security. For any risk management program to be effective, all the organization's risks must be evaluated, from physical security, personnel issues, and IT security to legal liability, regulatory issues, and so on. It must all be integrated into the plan. The good news is that life is all about risk management already, so there is nothing unusual about this approach. It comes naturally when you start practicing it. Security has to be part of the whole process, not an afterthought or focused on an isolated element. As the old saying goes, you're only as strong as your weakest link.

Within the holistic approach, there are typically three critical elements to the risk management plan, which are protection, detection, and reaction, defined as follows:

- **Protection:** Counter measure that includes risk assessments, vulnerability assessments, threat analysis, policies, procedures, and technical controls to defend against all threats to the assets being protected.
- **Detection:** Elements that monitor for potential and real breakdowns in protections that could result in security breaches.
- **Reaction:** Those responsive mechanisms that will thwart attacks before damage can be done.

A holistic approach is incomplete and ineffective without all these elements. For instance, if the organization can only detect after the fact that a break-in has occurred, via a non-reactionary IDS for instance, then it lacks a try reaction capacity. Try to create a plan that is as fail safe as possible. Humans are always slower than computers, and any security plan that depends on a person to react to an attack is doomed to fail. You'll never win that race.

After you have settled on the security approach and model, document your plan and how you intend to approach securing your assets.

CREATE A SECURITY POLICY

Surprisingly, many organizations have security policies, which is a step in the right direction. Unfortunately, they tend to either be developed in a vacuum or are woefully out of date with the current technologies being used in an organization. One agency we worked with had a policy of virus scanning all floppy disks that physically came into their offices. This was a great idea—before laptops, modems, and the Internet and had little practical effect when it came to protecting their network and computers from viruses. Users simply took their laptops home and came back with a virus. The point here is that after you create a set of rules to define what is acceptable behavior on your networks and what personnel controls you will depend on to help control the security posture of your enterprise (such as shredding documents), it's important that the policy be kept up to date. An out of date policy is a liability. Users will recognize that the policy is out of date and will begin to disregard other rules that might still be useful and valid in the mistaken belief that those rules are also no longer pertinent.

CREATE SECURITY PROCEDURES

Security procedures are briefly defined as those documented steps and methods your organization will undertake as part of its normal operational procedures to manage the security posture of your enterprise. Some examples would be procedures for monitoring firewalls, installing patches, or deploying new systems. These are basically your cookbooks for securing your enterprise. Instead of requiring each member of the organization to work out the methods of implementing the policies and managing their security posture, the procedures break it down into that level of detail needed for that audience. In some cases, this might require significant automation; for instance, a good procedure for securing a Windows workstation, while valuable, might be far more time-consuming than creating a set of scripts that accomplish the same thing. It's still a good idea to document the script, but with a useful tool there is no need to produce a step-by-step guide for the end user.

PHASE III: SECURE THE ENTERPRISE

Ironically, this is usually the only phase that most organizations undertake and even then only partially. After you have completed Phases I and II, you can start to appreciate how hard it is to secure an asset without a thorough understanding of its value, purpose, and the threats arrayed against it. You wouldn't want to spend a million dollars defending something that is only worth a hundred, and vice versa.

Only when the first two phases are complete should an organization focus its energies on securing its assets. This is not to say that some emergency stop gap measures are not appropriate in the interim, but do not make the mistake some organizations have made of assuming these temporary measures are sufficient for a leisurely approach to Phases I and II. We have seen some government agencies that have given themselves years to complete Phases I and II with disastrous, highly public results.

There are three basic sub-phases to this phase:

1. Implement policies
2. Implement procedures
3. Deploy security technology and counter measures

IMPLEMENT POLICIES

This sounds like a simple step, but it's often overlooked. Policies are created but aren't effectively enforced or implemented in a meaningful manner inside an organization. If the policies don't make sense because the users don't understand them or know they exist, they won't be followed. Or if the managing authority lacks the authority to enforce the policies, they aren't worth the paper they're written on. The implementation phase involves dealing with all of these issues in a productive manner so that your security policies are actually effective. This can be one of the more time-consuming elements of bringing a risk management program into an organization, as typically the process starts from inside the IT group in a corporation, which does not have the authority to dictate policies to the entire rest of the organization. For any set of policies to be effective, the process will require full management support and buy-in, all the way up to the highest possible authority in the company. Otherwise, you are left not with policies, but with suggestions. Suggestions will not protect you from risk.

IMPLEMENT PROCEDURES

As with policies, put the procedures into regular daily use. A good practice is to make sure it's as difficult as possible to *not* follow the procedures. When there is a shortcut available that bypasses your security procedures, sadly, people will take it. Policies can help here by instituting sanctions for bypassing procedures—as can technical barriers. For instance, password strength checkers are an example of automating a policy and a procedure. The user is forced to follow good security procedures for creating that strong password.

DEPLOY SECURITY TECHNOLOGY AND COUNTER MEASURES

As this book focuses on firewalls, we will concentrate on how we can deploy security technology and counter measures using a firewall; however, keep in mind that this phase is absolutely not accomplished through the use of firewalls alone. There are a number of excellent books and resources that explain how to secure all the elements of an enterprise. We must stress that this phase is not complete until all the elements, not just the firewall and the network or networks it protects, are properly secured through the use of additional security technologies and counter measures, such as IDS, patch management, AAA, and so on.

SECURING THE FIREWALL ITSELF

More about how to accomplish this is detailed in Chapter 3, "Local Firewall Security." The key point to remember is that the firewall, as a trusted element of the security model, needs extra attention paid to securing it. A firewall should have as few functions as possible and should never be used for anything other than a firewall. When you run any service on a firewall, you are changing its function into a server that doubles as a firewall. If you have the extra resources, do not run any services on your firewall; run them on other systems.

ISOLATING ASSETS

Isolation or compartmentalization is the cornerstone of security and what firewalls are really good at implementing. The principle is simple—secure an asset so that it cannot be used to break into another asset regardless of how compromised that asset might have become. An example of this would be two servers, one on either side of a firewall, that have no means of communicating with each other through the firewall. In that sense, those servers are isolated and compartmentalized from one another, so if one is broken into, it cannot be used to break into the other. Typically with firewalls, this is accomplished with what are called DMZs or Demilitarized Zones. Basically, a DMZ is like a no man's land for systems that might be exposed to greater threats than other systems and have a higher probability of being broken into.

Another use of compartmentalization is through the use of internal network firewalls, isolating elements of an organization's networks from one another. An example would be firewalling off the accounting department from the rest of the company to prevent unauthorized users on the company's network from accessing the accounting network. Each separate isolated network is sometimes referred to as an *enclave* or *domain*. We prefer to use the term enclave, because domain has a different context with some systems, as with Microsoft products for instance, but you might see the term used interchangeably in this book.

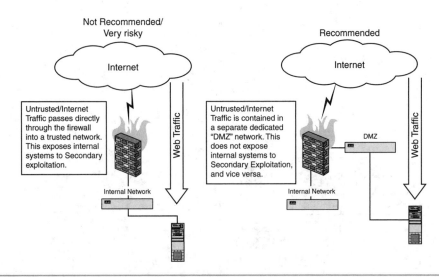

Figure 2.2 The wrong and right ways to forward traffic through a firewall.

For those systems that need to have presence in multiple enclaves, this is where DMZs come into effect. It's generally a bad idea to just allow traffic from a system in a less secure enclave (the Internet) to have direct access to a system on your more secure enclave (your internal networks). Moving systems into a DMZ segment that is isolated from both enclaves ensures a more secure design. A compromise on the system utilizing a DMZ will not allow an intruder to escalate access across the board on your internal network. This is known as *Secondary Exploitation*. Remember, the intent with compartmentalization is to isolate a system or systems so that if they are compromised, they cannot be used to break into other systems.

One bad trend we have seen recently is placing web servers on a DMZ and having them communicate to internal database servers back through the firewall. This is a recipe for disaster. A better model would be to set up a duplicate database server on the DMZ and to have the internal database server synchronize itself with the DMZ-ed copy. This way, if the DMZ database is compromised, the internal database server cannot be broken into and then used to break into other internal systems.

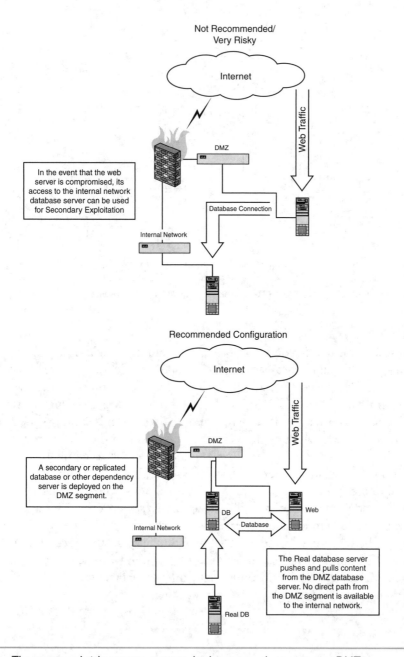

Figure 2.3   The wrong and right ways to connect databases to web servers on a DMZ.

FILTERING

As you are no doubt already aware, this is the bread and butter of what a firewall does—it filters traffic, or at least it tries to, and we hope that it does. The golden rule with firewalls is always this: unless allowed, deny it. Never under any circumstances attempt to build a firewall that is configured the other way around: allow everything; deny something. This is an approach doomed to fail. One additional advantage of the good approach, "unless allowed, deny," is that you learn very quickly what sort of traffic is traversing your firewall. This might produce time-consuming work determining what to allow in and out of your firewall, but it's an excellent invaluable tool for determining what's going on. This approach gives you visibility into your network and users that you would otherwise never see if your firewall were built only to block certain things.

Also keep in mind that ports alone do not a good firewall policy make. Do not assume that just because you only allow port 80 traffic into a network that the traffic will only be HTTP if you are using the Linux kernels packet filtering capabilities. By default, the kernel has no way of inspecting the traffic to ensure that it is HTTP traffic. Ports are no longer enough to define what the traffic is. If you want to filter the traffic into or out of a network by protocol, then you will need to use either an application proxy that understands the protocol (**squid**, **gatekeeper**, **reaim**, and so on) or utilize some of the **iptables** modules that can perform protocol inspection, such as ipp2p. We have had the unfortunate task of cleaning up security breaches of customers that failed to understand this distinction. A port is nothing but a number to an IP stack; it has no bearing on the protocol that might run over that port. Anything could be running on that port, not just the service that normally resides there.

INGRESS/EGRESS FILTERING

Filtering what goes out of your networks is just as important as filtering what is allowed to come in. This is easily one of most overlooked elements of firewall configuration. Too many organizations set up their firewalls to, essentially, allow anything out of their networks. We always recommend that you carefully control what traffic you allow out of your networks so that you can minimize the effects of internal security breaches, such as information leakage, deliberate or inadvertent exposure of sensitive data, worms and viruses and unauthorized VPNs, and other tunnels set up by your users to bypass your security controls.

PHASE IV: IMPLEMENT MONITORING

When all is said and done, you're going to need to develop a system to measure the quality of your efforts on an ongoing and regular basis. This is done through security metrics and improves with maturity of the security process within an organization. There are five levels of maturity of a risk management program:

1. Having well-defined security policies
2. Having well-defined procedures
3. Implementing those procedures
4. Testing compliance with and effectiveness of those procedures
5. Fully integrating those policies and procedures into the ongoing regular operations of the organization

Don't feel like you have to bite off the entire risk management approach in one step. It takes time, research, tact, patience, and persistence to collect all the data, to create coherent and balanced policies and procedures, and to get them integrated into an organization. It might take years for a large government agency or company to fully embrace these changes, and sadly it usually takes a major disaster for the process to really gain momentum. If you want to see fundamental changes in your organization's risk management process occur, it's going to take hard work. All the firewalls in the world can't replace the effect of having a Level 5 risk management program in place. It is well worth the effort.

PHASE V: TEST

During this phase, the organization should rigorously and skeptically test every assumption and system for weakness. Testing should also be built into the standard practices of the organization to occur on a regular basis. This phase is not only designed to determine if the effort at any one point is effective and where it can be improved upon, but also to create a regular and in-depth process for testing all policies, procedures, personnel, and controls for ongoing effectiveness. When first creating a risk management program, this can be accomplished by conducting another set of vulnerability assessments.

PHASE VI: INTEGRATE

Integrate all procedures, policies, and controls into the standard practices of the organization to occur on a daily basis. No really—we mean it. For the process to truly be integrated, and this is a very difficult thing to do we realize, it has to become part of the fabric of daily activities. Systems need to be patched quickly, passwords must be strong, policies must be followed, intrusions must be detected, and so on. The list goes on. The point is that you can't produce several policies and deploy some clever security controls, such as firewalls, and then forget about it all and hope that everything will be secure. All the former steps should lead to fundamental change in the organization.

PHASE VII: IMPROVE

The last phase of the process is to integrate all the lessons learned and any new information gleaned from all the other phases into improving the entire risk management program. This is basically a loop or a full life cycle approach. Phase VII leads back into Phase I, where the process is repeated again infinitely.

To close out this chapter, the overall security of your networks and organization will depend entirely on how robust your risk management process is and how well and sincerely it is implemented.

SUMMARY

Before you implement a firewall, first ask yourself what you are trying to defend—and from whom. Firewalls are only one part of the overall security strategy, one tool among many that will help you defend your network, systems, and ultimately your business from threats. It is not a replacement for diligent planning, nor is it a security "silver bullet." Its purpose is, above all, to serve as a mechanism for compartmentalization. It cannot protect your systems from what you allow in.

Local Firewall Security

As part of our goal of covering the larger security issues before moving on to the information about how to troubleshoot your firewall problems, we feel it's important to cover issues that affect the security of the firewall itself. Just because a system is a firewall will not imbue it with some inherent lack of susceptibility to being broken into.

A firewall is just like any other system; in fact, your firewall might be nothing more than a typical server with two or more Network Interface Cards (NICs) in it, running firewall rules, while doing double duty as your fileserver, firewall, and e-mail server. We've seen it done. The point here is that adding firewall rules alone will not protect your system completely. There are other actions you will need to take to ensure that your system is properly secured against the risks you have identified.

The local firewall security approach is broken into the following macro steps:

1. Patch your system and keep it patched.
2. Turn off services you can't prove you need.
3. Run services with the least amount of privileges needed.
4. Use **chroot** services. (This is the process of essentially putting the service into its own isolated file system that, if done properly, will be difficult for an attacker to escape from.)
5. Remove all unnecessary software.
6. Install security tools to help manage security posture and to help detect intrusions.
7. Log events remotely to a trusted system as well as to the local **syslog** subsystem.
8. Configure your software securely.

9. If you can, use a hardened kernel such as **grsecurity**, **openwall**, **SELinux**, **LIDS**, and other patches.
10. Test your system's security and improve it.

Keep in mind that these are general concepts, so if you have a better means of accomplishing these goals, stick with what works for you. Security is a complicated process, and people seem to have their own specific methods that work for them.

THE IMPORTANCE OF KEEPING YOUR SOFTWARE UP TO DATE

If you haven't already picked up on the importance of keeping your system properly patched and up to date from all the stories constantly in the media and on various mailing lists, then let us join the chorus. You must get into the habit of monitoring the latest patch releases from your vendors, and you must keep up to date with the various security lists for your products. There is a continuous daily deluge of new vulnerabilities being discovered, which might affect you. If you want to keep the probability of intrusion down, then you really need to make this a top priority in your Information Technology plan. As we already stated, computer products, hardware, and software are created by people, and people are not perfect creatures. They make buggy software, and they keep making buggy software, revision after revision. Hardware is no different. It's critical that you install vendor security patches, new security flash updates for your hardware, and other fixes as quickly as you can after they come out. In some cases we recommend installing them the day they are released. This isn't always practical, so you will have to weigh the risks associated with each new software change in your enterprise against what vulnerabilities they protect you against, if those vulnerabilities are exposed in your enterprise, the problems they fix, and if they introduce any new problems.

This isn't call to procrastinate. Waiting for your peers to show you the way is a recipe for disaster. The really bad news is that by the time a patch comes out, the bad guys are definitely on their way to writing an exploit for it that will be crawling around the Internet within days, if not hours. In some cases, the patch might fix a vulnerability that the bad guys found out about before the good guys did, and are already actively exploiting it. Every day the window of safety between when a patch is released and when it starts to become actively exploited shrinks, and, as stated, sometimes that gap does not exist at all. There are several security approaches that seek to address this "zero day" problem—that is, the notion that you have no time to keep your systems up to date and the assumption that your systems have additional, as yet undiscovered vulnerabilities. We will touch on some technologies available to Linux that can assist in this area. One of these is the new **SELinux** extensions in the 2.6 kernel. **SELinux** gives you the ability to define policies for software running on your systems and roles for users. Again, we will cover **SELinux** briefly in other chapters in this book. We also have a lot of material on **SELinux** and links to other sites about **SELinux** at our website (`www.gotroot.com`).

Returning to the issue of patching your systems and keeping your software up to date, outside of tools such as **SELinux** (and even with them), patching your systems rapidly is the best way to manage this risk. Even with **SELinux** and other hardening tools, you are still dependent on those tools to be as bug free as possible, and we already know that bugs are a fact of life. So you will still want to keep your systems up to date even with those tools.

The good news is that there are excellent tools for Linux to help automate the process of patch maintenance. Some of the more well-known ones are **apt-get, emerge, red carpet, open carpet, yum, up2date, autorpm** and others. Most of these tools can be set up as **cronjobs** or are already automated to download and to verify the cryptographic signature of and, optionally, install the latest updates. We have found all of these to be excellent tools that in most cases can be trusted to do the right thing automatically, but beware—sometimes a bad patch will make it into the mix. It's extremely rare that this happens. However, it's fair to point out this risk as well. You will need to be prepared for what to do if your patch management system installs an update that breaks something. We can recall one incident when a new version of **glibc** had a bug in it that prevented systems from booting. Bad things happen. Even patches can have bugs.

If you are unsure, back up your system first before running any of these tools in automated mode. As part of your risk management program, you should be backing your systems up on a nightly basis anyway. In the aforementioned **glibc** incident, we had a few systems affected by this bug, but fortunately all of them had been backed up the night before, and we simply rolled back to an old version and installed the fixed **glibc**.

Here are some instructions for using some of the more popular patch and software management tools for Linux:

YUM

yum is an automated package management tool that utilizes the system's existing rpm system to do the package management but provides for automated package downloading, integrity testing, fail over, and other useful networking features. **yum** was originally part of Yellow Dog Linux and is now used for many Linux distributions, including Redhat, Suse, Fedora and others. We especially like **yum** because it is very easy to use and to add new software repositories to its configuration. **yum** also includes gpg/pgp signature verification and download site fail over methods to ensure that patches are downloaded, in case a site is down, and that the patches have not been tampered with. You can run **yum** out of **cron**, or you can use some of the `init.d` scripts that some **yum** distributions include to add **yum** to the **cron** process automatically.

Here is an example **yum cron** process that would attempt to download and install any new updates to the system at 3:00 a.m. every night of the week. The `-y` switch simply tells **yum** to answer "yes" to any questions it might ask. The upgrade option tells **yum** to only update existing software and not to install any new packages that have been released.

```
0 3 * * *    /usr/bin/yum upgrade -y
```

You can find **yum** at the following websites: `http://www.gotroot.com` and `http://www.fedora.us`.

RED CARPET

red carpet was Ximian's, now Novell's, package management system. **red carpet** is a truly advanced package management system, leveraging the systems local package management system (rpm for instance) along with remote host management capabilities, a slick GUI, integrity verification, site fail over, and a true client/server model. This wonder package allows you to remotely control all your hosts running **red carpet** and to push/remove/install software on all those hosts. You can also run it in standalone mode if you do not need the remote control features, and it also works just as well from the command line as it does from the GUI.

For instance, from the command line you can instruct **red carpet** to upgrade all the software on a system:

```
rug up -y
```

or for the older **red carpet** client:

```
rc up -y
```

It's important to note though that **red carpet**, like **yum**, uses channels to control the software it will manage. You will need to configure **red carpet** to download and watch for software changes to the channels that matter to your system.

Also **red carpet** will not automatically install updates. You will need to setup a **cronjob** to do that for you. Here is an example of a **cronjob** we have used successfully:

```
0 */12 * * *    /usr/bin/rug up -y
```

This tells **red carpet** to run the update process every 12 hours and to download and automatically install all updates. This does not tell **red carpet** to remove anything; if anything needs to be removed, **red carpet** will not install any of the updates, so it's important to watch your e-mail for these sorts of errors. If you want to allow removals, just add the -r flag:

```
rug up -y -r
```

UP2DATE

up2date is part of Red Hat's patch management system. It too utilizes the underlying systems package management system, in this case rpm, to do the actual package management. **up2date** provides the networking infrastructure and channel management to download the necessary patches for your system. **up2date** is also a subscription-based system, and with previous versions of Red Hat, the system will stop working, without a subscription, after a short number of days.

The syntax for **up2date** is very similar to **yum** and **red carpet**. To install updates, you would execute this command:

```
up2date update
```

And as with the previous tools, you can also run this one from **cron**:

```
0 3 * * *    /usr/bin/up2date upgrade -y
```

EMERGE

emerge is part of the Gentoo system and is part of Gentoo's ports system, a system very similar to BSD's ports system. **emerge** is the package management, downloading, integrity checking, compiling, installing, whole ball of wax system for Gentoo. At present, it is only used on Gentoo systems, but we don't see why it couldn't be used on others. Also Gentoo currently works by downloading source files and compiling the updates on the fly for that specific system, so with **emerge** you will not be downloading precompiled binaries; you will have to compile everything. We do not recommend fully automating **emerge** unless you are comfortable with the ports system and your system is using up considerable cycles to compile the new updates. For our Gentoo systems, we only automate the synchronization phase of the **emerge** process so that we are notified of any changes in the Gentoo source code repositories. We then manually select the packages we want our Gentoo systems to download, compile, and install. This is not nearly as "hands off" as the other package management systems, so you will need to allocate resources and time to monitor any updates to the Gentoo source code repositories—and to then have someone review the updates and oversee the compiling process.

When using Gentoo, there are three critical commands for **emerge** that you will want to familiarize yourself with. The first is sync.

```
emerge sync
```

This tells **emerge** to synchronize the local portage tree to the remote source repositories tree. This will tell you if anything has changed and download **emerge** files that describe the patches to the **emerge** system and other information needed to download these updates. The sync process will also tell you about new code in the tree. Keep that in mind as well—just because it was added does not mean that it's worth upgrading. Some of the additions many not be stable patches or might be brand new higher revision code that you might not want to use (apache 1.x versus 2.x for instance).

```
emerge -up world
```

In this example, there are two new switches, -u and -p. -u tells the system to upgrade whatever the object is. In this case the object is the "world" or the entire system. The second switch, -p, tells **emerge** to upgrade the entire system. We like to use this step before upgrading anything so we can see all the new patches and software related to our system—and then make decisions about what we want to upgrade and/or install.

The final command is to actually tell **emerge** to upgrade/install the new package.

```
emerge <package_name>
```

For instance:

```
emerge openssh
```

emerge would then check its local portage tree, find the openssh entry, locate the latest revision, download it, check for dependencies in the system that might also need to be updated and downloaded, compile all the parts, remove the old ones, and install all the updated code. Unlike binary only installations, this process can be very time-consuming and bandwidth intensive.

There are, of course, many more things you can do with **emerge** and numerous commands, but these are the big three. As we already stated, we do not recommend automating this entire process. If you are going to automate anything, the sync is the only one we recommend. Also please do not set your **emerge** sync to run more than once a day, unless you have set up your own mirror of the latest Gentoo repositories.

```
0 4 * * *    /usr/bin/emerge sync
```

APT-GET

apt-get is part of Debian but is available for other platforms such as Red Hat and others. It's also very similar to **yum**, **up2date** and to a lesser extent, **red carpet**. It's network aware, will check gpg/pgp signatures, provides for fail over and other useful services.

You will notice that the syntax of many of these tools is very similar. With **apt-get**, if you want to update you system, you simply pass **apt-get** the update command:

```
apt-get update
```

And you can automate the process with **cronjobs** as well:

```
0 3 * * *    /usr/bin/apt-get update -y
```

As with **red carpet**, the -y switch tells **apt-get** to assume yes to any questions, such as should **apt-get** install a new update. **apt-get** comes with Debian, and rpms for **apt-get** are available for Red Hat, Fedora, and Yellow Dog Linux at `http://apt.freshrpms.net/` and `http://www.gotroot.com`.

There might be other patching tools, no doubt fantastic ones, which we might have failed to mention. If you have a patching system that works for you, then by all means stick with it. The intent is to make updating your system a regular part of your system's life cycle, and one easy way to do that is to automate the process. Computers don't forget, but people sometimes do. Use a **cronjob** to keep up with the latest updates, and you won't have to worry about missing anything.

OVER RELIANCE ON PATCHING

With all the talk about patching and the importance of doing it regularly, we must caution you that patching is not going to be a silver bullet either. Not only is it likely that your system will still have numerous security vulnerabilities in it that you will need to patch in the future, but also the programs you are using could have fundamental flaws in them that do not properly guard against the risks you wish to manage. For instance, if you are concerned with protecting the confidentiality of your e-mails, patching your e-mail clients is unlikely to accomplish that without some additional security measures, such as encrypting your e-mail. In short, just because the software is bug free and working properly does not mean that using it is risk free.

As we already alluded to in earlier chapters, there are now several examples of previously unknown vulnerabilities being discovered in widely used software by the "bad guys," months before the good guys, such as you the gentle reader, and vendors find out. For instance, several very high profile sites were broken into in early 2004 due to an undiscovered flaw in rsync. The only people that were likely patched against that flaw were the crackers that discovered the flaw and kept it to themselves! Just because a flaw is not known to exist in something does not mean that the flaw does not exist. As Carl Sagan said, "Absence of evidence is not evidence of absence." It's always wise to assume that when you patch you are only doing the bare minimum necessary to secure your system. It's just par for the course to patch.

TURNING OFF SERVICES

You have likely heard this one as well. If you don't need a service, turn it off. We have to add one thing to that—if you cannot prove that you need the service, turn it off. Many of the customers we have worked with insisted that they needed a service, or at least thought that they did. They assumed that they needed the server. After all, it was on, so it must be necessary. A lot of services are turned on by default on many products that are not necessary to most users. If you aren't sure if you need a service, turn it off. If it doesn't break anything, then you don't need it. We can't think of a better way to learn about a service than by turning if off. If no one complains about it being off, you can file it away as a service to learn about when you have free time and focus your efforts on the services that your users do need. When in doubt, turn it off.

USING TCP WRAPPERS AND FIREWALL RULES

What chapter on securing a system would be complete without a quick reminder that you should protect all your running services with TCP wrappers and firewall rules? For those who are not familiar with TCP wrappers, as this tool is referred to, this gives you the ability to monitor and filter TCP connections via IP address or hostname. For example, let's say that you want to allow SSH connections to your firewall but only from certain hosts. Of course, you could control this via firewall rules, but what if you don't have any firewall rules on your firewall yet or on the interface you want to filter out unwanted connections to the SSH port. The solution is simple—use TCP wrappers.

Before diving into how to do this with SSH, a quick review of TCP wrappers is in order. Traditionally, TCP wrappers were used in conjunction with a "super server" such as **inetd** or **xinetd**. These super servers handle all the inbound connections to the servers they manage, such as **telnet**, **ftp**, **gopher**, and other services. TCP wrappers filter these connections by being invoked by the super server before the actual service itself is invoked, hence the name "TCP wrapper." The wrapper was placed "around" the service it is configured to protect. Here is a quick look at one such example from **inetd.conf**:

```
telnet stream  tcp     nowait  root    /usr/sbin/tcpd  in.telnet
```

This describes how the **inetd** "super server" is to invoke the **telnet** daemon. The TCP wrapper is invoked first via the /usr/sbin/tcpd command. For **xinetd**, tcpd is called automatically for any TCP service, unless you disable this functionality explicitly in that service's **xinetd** configuration file.

For services such as **ssh**, support for TCP wrappers may or may not be compiled into the daemon. Never assume that it is. To determine if TCP wrapper support is available in your sshd binary, you can use this command:

```
ldd /usr/sbin/sshd
```

This command will tell you what libraries your sshd binary is "linked" against. What you will be looking for is the libwrap library, and the format of the ldd output will look something like this:

```
libwrap.so.0 => /usr/lib/libwrap.so.0 (0x20706000)
libutil.so.1 => /lib/libutil.so.1 (0x2070f000)
libz.so.1 => /usr/lib/libz.so.1 (0x20712000)
libnsl.so.1 => /lib/libnsl.so.1 (0x20720000)
libcrypto.so.4 => /lib/libcrypto.so.4 (0x20735000)
```

```
libcrypt.so.1 => /lib/libcrypt.so.1 (0x20827000)
libc.so.6 => /lib/tls/libc.so.6 (0x20854000)
libdl.so.2 => /lib/libdl.so.2 (0x2098a000)
libgssapi_krb5.so.2 => /usr/kerberos/lib/libgssapi_krb5.so.2 (0x2098e000)
libkrb5.so.3 => /usr/kerberos/lib/libkrb5.so.3 (0x209a1000)
libcom_err.so.3 => /usr/kerberos/lib/libcom_err.so.3 (0x209ff000)
libk5crypto.so.3 => /usr/kerberos/lib/libk5crypto.so.3 (0x20a02000)
libresolv.so.2 => /lib/libresolv.so.2 (0x20a12000)
/lib/ld-linux.so.2 => /lib/ld-linux.so.2 (0x206c8000)
```

Your output will probably look a little different, but don't worry about that. In this example, you can see on the first line that our sshd binary is linked against the libwrap library:

```
libwrap.so.0 => /usr/lib/libwrap.so.0 (0x20706000)
```

Therefore we can conclude that our sshd binary will be protected by TCP wrappers—if we configure it accordingly. The only point of this exercise, running ldd against your binary, is to determine if the service you want to use TCP wrappers with is linked against the TCP wrapper library. Without the libwrap library or something like **inetd** or **xinetd** to "wrap" the service, TCP wrappers will not work with your service.

Now that you know how to invoke TCP wrappers and to test to see if your service supports TCP wrapper lookups internally, it's time to move on to how to configure a service to use TCP wrappers. When a connection comes into a service that is protected by TCP wrappers, the wrapper will first look in two files to determine if the inbound IP is allowed to connect to the service. These files are **/etc/hosts.allow** and **/etc/hosts.deny**. The **hosts.allow** file lists services and then hosts, IP addresses, or networks that are allowed to connect to a service, and the **hosts.deny** service would include the same information, only for denying access. These files look like this:

```
# hosts.allow    This file describes the names of the hosts which are
#                allowed to use the local INET services, as decided
#                by the '/usr/sbin/tcpd' server.
#
in.telnetd: 10.10.10.100


# hosts.deny     This file describes the names of the hosts which are
#                *not* allowed to use the local INET services, as decided
#                by the '/usr/sbin/tcpd' server.
ALL:ALL
```

In the example here, we err on the side of caution and deny connections to *all* services from *all* hosts in case we forget to configure something correctly. Thankfully, TCP wrappers will allow for exceptions to the **hosts.deny** file if they are included in the **hosts.allow** file.

The format for any line in either of these files is simple:

```
<service name>:<IP, hostname, or network>,<IP, hostname, or network>,<IP, hostname, or network>
```

You can list as many records as you like after the service name. There is one reserved word, ALL, that bears pointing out in this chapter. Quite simply, it means what it says—*all* services or *all* hosts, depending on which position it's used in for either the **hosts.allow** or **hosts.deny** files. You can create a rule that relates to all services; for example, let's say you wanted to make sure that all TCP wrapped services were available to connections coming from 127.0.0.1. You would place in your **hosts.allow** file the following record:

```
ALL:127.0.0.1
```

Or if you wanted to make sure that all hosts could connect to the sshd service, you could use this record in the **hosts.allow** file:

```
sshd:ALL
```

As you can see, the format is thankfully very simple and easy for us humans to read. Even if you are using firewall rules, we suggest you also use TCP wrappers in case you make a mistake or for those times when you are doing maintenance on your firewall and might leave those services otherwise exposed. Remember that security done in layers is far more effective than relying on one line of defense.

Finally, if you use TCP wrappers, we don't recommend you filter by hostname, as DNS responses can be spoofed. Instead, when using TCP wrappers, try to use the IP addresses of the hosts you want to allow in to a service.

Because you are running a firewall, it probably seems silly to remind you that you need to apply firewall rules to protect the services running on your firewall. In a sense, it does seem a little redundant, but we'd like to point out a simple mistake we've seen people make with **iptables**-based firewalls—confusing INPUT and FORWARD rules. Simply put, with **iptables**, you have INPUT, OUTPUT, and FORWARD rules. We'll explore these in more depth later on in the book, but for our purposes here, the only types of rules we are interested in, to protect the firewall itself, are INPUT rules. FORWARD rules only apply to traffic moving "through" the firewall, and OUTPUT rules, while useful for protecting a firewall in other ways, only affect traffic moving out of the firewall itself. INPUT rules relate to traffic bound only to the firewall and to nothing else.

So, to protect the ssh service on the firewall and to only allow connections in from 10.10.1.100, you could use a simple rule like this:

```
iptables -A INPUT -p tcp  --dport 22 -s 10.10.1.100 -j ACCEPT
```

And then this rule to deny all other traffic to the firewall's ssh port:

```
iptables -A INPUT -p tcp  --dport 22 -j DROP
```

We'll explore the syntax of **iptables** in greater depth in Chapters 6 and 7. For this chapter, the only values you should be concerned with in these commands are:

```
-p tcp
```

This defines the IP protocol. In the present case for ssh, we're using the TCP protocol because ssh runs over the TCP protocol. The TCP protocol is covered in the next chapter.

```
-s 10.10.1.100
```

The -s switch defines the "source" of the connection, 10.10.1.100. This can either be an IP address or a network address, such as 10.10.1.0/24. If your intent was to allow all connections from any 10.10.1.0/24 address, such as 10.10.1.101, and 10.10.1.200 and any other IP address in the 10.10.1.0/24 network, you would use this instead:

```
-s 10.10.1.0/24
```

And finally, the destination port itself is defined with this switch:

```
--dport 22
```

This tells **iptables** to only apply this rule to connections bound to the destination port 22 on the firewall. Keep in mind that these are very simple rules and that you can expand greatly on these using the switches and techniques we describe in Chapters 6 and 7 and other chapters in this book. For instance, you could apply this rule to a specific interface, such as eth0 or eth1 to further control who has access to this rule by adding the -i <interface> switch for INPUT and FORWARD rules and for OUTPUT and POSTROUTING rules, the -o <switch>. The -i switch defines the incoming interface for a rule and the -o switch, the outgoing interface for a rule. So for the ssh rule described here, if you wanted to restrict ssh access not only to the 10.10.1.100 host, but also to ensure that those connections can only come in from the eth1 interface, you would add the -i eth1 switch to your ssh allow rule:

```
iptables -A INPUT -i eth1 -p tcp  --dport 22 -s 10.10.1.100 -j ACCEPT
```

We suggest that whenever possible you define all your rules and chains with their respective interfaces to add an extra layer of security into your security model. IP addresses can be spoofed, and people do make mistakes with rules. By adding in an additional layer of specificity to your rules, by defining the interface that rule specifically applies to, you can help yourself with debugging rules and by making your firewall and network more secure.

RUNNING SERVICES WITH LEAST PRIVILEGE

The next important step with any system is to ensure that the services running it are running with the least amount of privilege they need to work. That means, for most services, they should not be running as **root**. Thankfully, many Linux vendors have gotten better in the last few years about configuring services to run as non-privileged users and going the extra mile to configure them to run in restricted file systems, such as **chroots**.

Some examples of common services you can run as non-privileged users:

Service	Example of user to Run as	Method
sshd	sshd	Set in the sshd_config file
ntpd	ntpd	ntpd -u ntpd
dhcpd	dhcpd	dhcpd -u dhcpd
apache	apache	Set in the httpd.conf file
named	named	Named -u named

continues

Service	Example of user to Run as	Method
postfix	postfix	Set in the `main.conf` file
sendmail	sendmail	Set in the `sendmail.cf` file
squid	squid	Set in the `squid.conf` file

You'll notice that we recommend you run each service as a different user. In the past the practice was to run them all as one common non-privileged user, such as *nobody*. We do not recommend this approach. It's literally putting all your eggs into one basket. If someone breaks in as the *nobody* user, he might have access to everything else of importance on your system also running as *nobody*. The goal is to compartmentalize. Every service, where possible, should run as its own user. We have additional recipes and instructions about running services with least privilege, as always, at our website, www.gotroot.com.

RESTRICTING THE FILE SYSTEM

Aside from managing your file permissions and ensuring that you don't have certain critical files and directories set to be world or group -writable by untrusted groups and users, we also recommend isolating certain files and processes and mounting them within special file systems.

The first approach we recommend is the use of **chroots**, which is just short hand for "change root." A **chroot** simply changes the root directory for a process. For instance, if you create a directory named /chroot/named, and you **chroot** the named process to this directory, the named process will see the /chroot/named directory as its directory and should not able to reach any files outside of that directory. This essentially "traps" the named process inside the **chrooted** file system. We must pause at this point and warn you that the vanilla **chroot** in Linux kernels is not nearly as secure as our description implies. There are many known ways of escaping **chroots** under Linux with the vanilla Linux kernel.

The good news is that there are several security patches for Linux that close these holes, such as **openwall** (www.openwall.com) and **grsecurity** (www.grsecurity.net), but without these patches or other modifications to the kernel, the **chroot** is not as secure as it should be. With that said, even a vanilla kernel's **chroot** affords some security in the face of none, so do **chroot** your processes where you can and if you can patch your kernel, we recommend these patches. Also check with your Linux vendor to see if they have hardened the kernel to protect against **chroot** escapes.

The next element to securing your file systems is to move all your **suid** files to a special file system for **suid** files. If you do not know what **suid** and **sgid** files are, they are simply files set with a special file system bit that tells the Linux kernel to run that program with different or elevated privileges. For instance, the passwd command has the **suid** bit set on it, and the file is owned by **root**. This means that when you run the passwd command, the OS will "set the uid," or **suid**, of the process to **root**, the owner of the file. This means that passwd will now run as if **root** were running the command, which is what gives it permission to modify the **/etc/passwd** and **/etc/shadow** files. The security risk here is that if the passwd command or some other **suid** command has some flaw in it, you might be able to exploit that flaw with **root** privileges. **sgid** files are very similar; when the **sgid** bit is set on a file, it "sets the group" for the process. This means, similar to **suid**, that the process will then run with the group privileges of the group the file is owned by. In essence, every **suid** and **sgid** file is a potential hole in the system, so review those files carefully and only give access to **suid** and **sgid** files to trusted users, and remove those **suid** and **sgid** files you cannot prove that you need.

After you have isolated your **suid** and **sgid** files, move them to their own file system on which you can set the **suid** bit to active in **/etc/fstab**. Then set all your other mount points to **nosuid**.

```
cat /etc/fstab
/dev/hda3        /home        ext3    nosuid,nodev    1 2
/dev/hda1        /usr         ext3    nosuid,nodev    1 2
/dev/hda2        /trusted     ext3    suid            1 2
/dev/hda4        /tmp         ext3    nosuid,nodev    1 2
```

By doing this you can set the rest of your file systems not to allow **suid** and **sgid** files to run. This also helps you to evaluate which **suid/sgid** files you have on your system and to remove the ones you cannot prove you need, which brings us to the final point about **suid** and **sgid** files. You want to inventory all of these files on your system and remove the **suid** and **sgid** bits from any programs you do not use.

SECURITY TOOLS TO INSTALL

This is by no means an all-inclusive list—just a listing of general categories of tools we think you should be running and some examples of software that can fill this need.

LOG MONITORING TOOLS

These are tools that parse through the system logs on the firewall to detect events worthy of attention. Some of the better tools can categorize and prioritize the events to help you identify attacks or even just suspicious behavior.

Two of our favorites are **logwatch** and **logcheck**. You can find both of these at our website, `http://www.gotroot.com`. **logwatch** comes with many Linux distributions now, and it basically gives you a daily summary of activity on your system. **logwatch** depends on extensions that understand the log format of the various applications running on your system, such as `sudo` or `ssh`. If there is no extension on your system for the application you wish to monitor, **logwatch** might miss some important information about that application.

The other side of the coin is **logcheck**, written by a friend of ours, Craig Rowland. Craig's **logcheck** takes the approach that you should be notified of anything you haven't told **logcheck** to ignore. This can generate a considerable about of alerts, but it guarantees you will not miss anything, and by default **logcheck** comes with a number of regular expressions in its default install to reduce the volume to a useful amount of traffic.

NETWORK INTRUSION DETECTION

This might seem out of scope for a firewall, but we think a firewall is a perfect place to run an NIDS, or Network Intrusion Detection System, provided that your firewall has enough disk space for the logs and enough memory and CPU power to handle the extra overhead of the NIDS. Generally a firewall is a good choke point to see traffic from many networks as it flows through the firewall. For instance, many firewalls are built with at least three network interfaces to allow for an internal, external, and DMZ network. If you ran your NIDS on another system, you might need three NIDS boxes to see all this traffic. Also with the introduction of **snort** and other open source NIDS on the scene, it's now free to run a high quality NIDS on as many systems as you want.

As with other services, make sure your NIDS is running all of its components as a non-privileged user and that it's also properly **chrooted**. **snort** has these capabilities built in, as do some of the other open source NIDS. Just because it's an NIDS does not mean that it's free from possible security vulnerabilities. Many commercial and open source NIDS have had security flaws in them that could have led to the compromise of the system running the NIDS, so again, assume the worst, run them with the least privilege necessary, and stick them into a **chroot**.

You can find **snort** at the website, `http://www.snort.org`. And you can find information out about other intrusion detection packages at `www.gotroot.com`.

HOST INTRUSION DETECTION

These are tools that focus not on looking at what's going on with your network, but solely on what's going on with the local system. These tools might look at what modules are loaded on a system, the users logged in, when they logged in, and from where. Others crawl the file system looking for known signs of intrusion, files with bad permissions, misconfigured programs, and other behaviors or indicators of problems. You might have to run several of these to get the full range of features you want. Again, this is only a partial list to get you started. There are many excellent HIDS tools and products out there.

TIGER

TIGER is a set of Bourne shell scripts, C programs, and data files which are used to perform a security audit of Unix systems. The security audit results are useful both for system analysis (security auditing) and for real-time, host-based intrusion detection (`http://www.tigersecurity.org`).

rkhunter

This tool scans for rootkits, backdoors, and local exploits (`http://www.rootkit.nl/`).

chkrootkit

chkrootkit is a tool to locally check for signs of a rootkit. This tool can also integrate with later versions of **TIGER** (`http://www.chkrootkit.org/`).

TITAN

TITAN is a collection of programs, each of which either fixes or tightens one or more potential security problems with a particular aspect in the setup or configuration of a Unix system. Conceived and created by Brad Powell, it was written in Bourne shell, and its simple modular design makes it trivial for anyone who can write a shell script or program to add to it, as well as completely understand the internal workings of the system.

    TITAN does not replace other security tools, but when used in combination with them, it can help make the transformation of a new, out of the box system into a firewall or security conscious system into a significantly easier task. In a nutshell, it attempts to help improve the security of the system it runs on (`http://www.fish.com/titan/`).

samhain

samhain is an open source file integrity and host-based intrusion detection system for Unix and Linux (`http://www.la-samhna.de/samhain/index.html`).

tripwire

tripwire is a file integrity checking tool. It's probably one of the most well known HIDS tools. **tripwire** basically generates a hash, or checksum, of all the files on your system you tell it to monitor. If the file changes, **tripwire** will alert you to it. There are commercial as well as open source versions of **tripwire**. The commercial version can be found on tripwire's website, `http://www.tripwire.com/`.

The open source version is available, as with many other tools in this book, at our website, `http://www.gotroot.com`.

AIDE

AIDE (Advanced Intrusion Detection Environment) is a free open source replacement for tripwire. It's very similar to **tripwire** and is even included in some Linux distributions. As with **tripwire**, it's a tool for generating hashes and checksums on files, and then periodically checking those files for changes. You can download **AIDE** from either our website (`www.gotroot.com`) or from its official website, `http://sourceforge.net/projects/aide`.

REMOTE LOGGING

You also might want to keep a real-time copy of your firewall's logs on another system you can trust. This system shouldn't be used for anything else if you intend to use the logs for forensics or evidentiary purposes. Judges and lawyers are starting to catch up with technology and beginning to realize how fragile digital evidence can be. If you are relying on a copy of logs running on a system that has been compromised, you have a serious problem. The logs can easily be tampered with to remove information, plant false information, or anything else you can or cannot imagine. For some peace of mind, keep a separate copy of your logs on a separate system. One way to accomplish this is to set up a `loghost` in your `syslog.conf` and to configure the remote system to listen for these entries. For most Linux systems using classic `syslog`, the remote host will need to be running `syslogd` with `-r` switch to set `syslogd` to listen to UDP port 514 for `syslog` traffic.

CORRECTLY CONFIGURE THE SOFTWARE YOU ARE USING

Most software comes with too many features turned on and is rarely configured to operate in the most paranoid mode. Again, assume the worst—that all the services and software running on your firewall are configured to allow the world to have full access to the system without having to so much as have an account and password on the system. For instance, the venerable `sshd`, the stalwart tool of Unix administrators everywhere, is rarely configured out of the box to its most secure settings. Too often `sshd` is set to allow protocol 1 connections, which is known to have serious security flaws, to allow root logins, to not run as unprivileged user, and to honor user environment settings. All of these can spell bad news for your firewall. Make sure you understand what the software does, and that you are configuring it correctly. If you aren't sure, ask.

USE A HARDENED KERNEL

"The reality is that secure applications require secure operating systems, and any effort to provide system security that ignores this premise is doomed to fail," (P. A. Loscocco, S. D. Smalley, P. A. Muckelbauer, R. C. Taylor, S. J. Turner, and J. F. Farrell. "The Inevitability of Failure: The Flawed Assumption of Security in Modern Computing Environments," in proceedings of *The 21st National Information Systems Security Conference*, page 303-314, Oct. 1998).

The vanilla Linux kernel is a marvel of open source development but has traditionally been lacking in truly above and beyond security models. The security model, particularly in the 2.4 kernel, is only adequate for systems where security is not a primary concern and with a firewall that's the system's entire purpose: security. To rest easy, the security model of the vanilla kernel will not do.

With 2.6, these trusted enhancements, referred to as **SELinux**, or Security Enhanced Linux, are now available in the vanilla kernel. **SELinux**, according to the NSA, provides for a "...flexible mandatory access control architecture incorporated into the major subsystems of the kernel. The system provides a mechanism to enforce the separation of information based on confidentiality and integrity requirements. This allows threats of tampering and bypassing of application security mechanisms to be addressed and enables the confinement of damage that can be caused by malicious or flawed applications." You will have to check your system to see if these features are compiled in by default to use them. There are also **SELinux** patches for the 2.4. kernel, should you choose to use a 2.4 kernel.

In addition to **SELinux**, we are particularly fond of combining the **grsecurity** patches with a 2.6 kernel running **SELinux**, or when running 2.4, we always add in the **grsecurity** patches. **grsecurity**, another kernel security enhancement project run by Brad Spengler, includes **chroot** hardening, IP stack hardening, stack overflow protection, address randomization, trusted path execution, and a real RBAC and MAC security model. The combination of the two works wonderfully for us and provides for so many extra features, it's more than worth the effort to patch your 2.6 kernel with the **grsecurity** 2.6 features.

You can find the **grsecurity** patches at `http://www.grsecurity.net`.

We have also collected many essays and manuals on **SELinux** at our website (`www.gotroot.com`). You also can go straight to the source, the NSA, which funded the **SELinux** enhancements to Linux for the latest patches, documents, and for instructions on how to join the **SELinux** mailing lists at `http://www.nsa.gov/seLinux/`.

OTHER HARDENING STEPS

Remove any software you cannot prove that you need. One easy piece of software to remove is your compiler. Regardless of what you remove, getting rid of software you don't need will reduce the number of patches you have to install, and it will also lessen your exposure to unknown flaws. The less software you have, the fewer vulnerabilities to which you are exposed.

And finally, don't assume you got any of this right. Now is the time to test the system and see if you can break in. Never assume that you haven't missed something or incorrectly installed some useful security tool. If you really want to test your system, don't do the testing yourself. Have a trusted associate test the system or hire a security auditor to test the security posture of your system.

SUMMARY

As we mentioned in the previous chapter, a firewall alone might not be enough to secure your systems. We highly recommend the tools mentioned here for both the firewall and any Linux-based servers you have in your internal network or DMZs. A combination of Network and Host-based Intrusion Detection systems and kernel hardening (we cannot recommend **grsecurity** enough) can assist you in dramatically increasing the overall security posture of your network. If anything, this chapter should serve as a good basic checklist for any Linux-based server, or even desktop, you are using in your enterprise.

Aside from constructing good firewall rules, you will also need to secure the firewall itself to truly benefit from any increase in protection your firewall might be able to convey. If your firewall is vulnerable, then everything else that depends on it is equally vulnerable. Ensure that your firewall is the most secured system in your enterprise before focusing your efforts on anything else. As it is, in most enterprises, the firewall is the single most important and relied upon component in the security model. Even if your enterprise is different, always make sure your firewall's security posture sets the standard for everything else in your enterprise.

Troubleshooting Methodology

It's important to use a systematic approach to solving firewall problems, much in the same manner that a systematic approach to risk management or network engineering is helpful when building a firewall. When troubleshooting, this is especially important in dealing with the increasingly complex world of networking and computing technologies we are required to support today. If you don't rely on a logical method of isolating root causes and eliminating variables, you can find yourself wasting significant amounts of time repeating the same steps in your effort to resolve a troublesome issue, or you might even make the problem worse. The issue is further exacerbated by the increased dependency on networks over the years to perform critical tasks, which has increased the need to resolve problems with those networks quickly. Down time is tolerated less and less, and firewalls tend to be choke points and single points of failure in many networks. Firewall outages tend to have significant effects on an organization's operations.

In the heat of the moment and under pressure to make things happen quickly, it's very easy to make matters worse. Having a good problem-solving process can help you to "take a breath" and pull yourself out of the emotions of the moment to think about the problem more rationally. Problem-solving methodologies are also used in other fields, such as in emergency medicine and military combat operations, so you can see that its use is not merely an academic approach useful for paper only; it's useful in some truly high stress fields when seconds really do count. If it works for them, it can work for you!

As we begin, we would like to point out that we did not create the problem-solving process we present in this book. Instead, we have adapted problem-solving methods that we were exposed to in the past, such as Cisco System's troubleshooting methodology, the U.S. Army's Problem Solving Methodology from FM 22-100, and others.

In our experience, when you become accustomed to using the process, you will forget that you are even doing it, but it takes practice. The best time to use it is when the chips are down and you are up against a tight deadline. There is a saying in the military, "Train as you will fight because you will fight as you trained." The point of this phrase is that you don't want to do things differently when you are learning as opposed to when you are doing it for real. When the pressure is on, it's typical to fall back on your training, so push yourself to be actively methodical and systematic in your approach. If you do, you will operate that way instinctively and won't have to think about it in the pressure of the moment. In short, it will come naturally to you.

Even if you don't make this approach a regular part of your troubleshooting, we have found this approach to be extremely helpful when working on particularly troublesome issues when you do have more time. And lastly, if you are pressed for time, always check the documentation for your products first because your problem may be a common one, and the solution might be simply documented therein. To that end, we have included some of the more commonly reported problems users have encountered with Linux firewalls in Section 3 of this book, which we hope will directly cover a problem you are encountering.

For all those other cases where the solution is either not well documented, not clear what the problem is, or simply doesn't work, it is helpful to use the methodical approach we outline here to troubleshoot your problem.

PROBLEM SOLVING METHODOLOGY

I. Recognize, Define, and Isolate the Problem
- What is the problem?
- Isolate the problem.
- What is the scope of the problem?
- Can you duplicate the problem? This is a critical step; if you cannot cause the problem to occur again, you will not be able to test your solution.
- Prioritize the problem(s). Is this something you have to fix right now?
- If it's a particularly difficult, boring, or unpleasant problem to solve, try the "ten minute plan." Just tell yourself you'll work on it for ten minutes. For most people, after they start working on a task, even an unpleasant one, they will commit to it. It's getting started that is the chore, not continuing to work on it.

II. Gather All Pertinent Facts About the Situation
   - The Golden Question: What Changed?
   - What's common to this problem?
   - Does it happen from everywhere on the network?
   - Do all OSs seems to be affected by this problem?

III. Define What the "End State" Should Be
   - How should the system or systems behave normally? In other words, do you know what the correct behavior is? Make sure you clearly define that; otherwise, you will not be able to test the system to determine if it is functioning properly.

IV. Develop Possible Solutions and Create an Action Plan
   - Develop possible solutions.
   - Develop a plan for each solution.

V. Analyze and Compare Possible Solutions
   - Start with the simplest problem first.
   - Start with the simplest solution first.

VI. Select and Implement the Solution
   - Track changes and give yourself the ability to roll back.

VII. Critically Analyze the Solution for Effectiveness

VIII. Repeat Process Until You Resolve the Problem

RECOGNIZE, DEFINE, AND ISOLATE THE PROBLEM

This is the simplest but most overlooked step in the problem-solving process. This is largely due to the perceived obviousness of what the problem is. People assume that the problem they are experiencing and reporting is the actual problem. More often than not, there are key details missing from the problem narrative. For instance, a user might report that he cannot log into a server the firewall is protecting, when in reality the user is trying to log into another server. The user is confident that he is logging into the server your firewall is protecting, but someone made a typo in the DNS server, and the IP address now points to a different system where the user does not have an account.

1. What is the problem exactly? Before even touching your firewall, consider that the problem may not be related to the firewall at all. As a central component in most

organizations' network architectures, the firewall tends to be blamed for everything and typically only when someone cannot get "out" to the Internet. It's useful to determine if the problem lies elsewhere—before starting in on such a complex task as troubleshooting your firewall.

2. Can you duplicate the problem and cause it to occur when you want to? This is essential when troubleshooting. The problem may no longer exist, and if you cannot duplicate the problem, you will have tremendous trouble testing your solution.

3. Ask the most important question of them all: What changed? We recommend you print these two words out and put them up over your desk, because in our experience these two words have solved more problems than everything else combined. In short, if the system was working correctly at some point, what has changed between now and then? Never assume that changes have not occurred, or that the changes that did occur would not have caused the problem you are trying to solve. Sometimes the problem is simpler than we imagine.

4. What happens if you revert the system back to its original state? Did that solve the problem? This is a critical step that helps to quickly eliminate the root cause of a problem. If rolling the system back to its original state does not solve the problem, you can rule out that change completely.

5. What is the scope of the problem?

   - Isolate the problem.
   - Where is it?
   - Does it affect one system, many systems, one protocol, or all of them?
   - Which ports are involved, and what time of day does the problem occur?
   - Which OSs is it affecting in your organization?
   - If the problem is big, break it into smaller problems and tasks that are easy to manage.

6. Prioritize the problem(s). Is this something you have to fix right now?

GATHER FACTS

1. Gather all pertinent facts about the situation:
   - Where does this happen?
   - When does this happen?
   - Who does this happen to?
   - What components are involved? (load balancers, switches, desktops, routers, and/or servers)

2. What's common to this problem?

- Does it happen from everywhere on the network?
- Do all systems and/or OSs seem to be affected by this problem? For example, turning ECN on under Linux can make it hard for a Linux box to connect to some systems that drop packets with "undefined" header options. Because ECN is an optional setting not defined in earlier RFCs, some paranoid firewalls and routers will assume the packet is bogus and drop it. In these cases, only the Linux systems with ECN turned on would be experiencing network problems, whereas all other systems would be functioning correctly. The point is to determine the scope of the problem rather than assuming it's universal.

DEFINE WHAT THE "END STATE" SHOULD BE

This is a simple one—basically define as specifically and precisely as you can how the system should be normally, optimally, and so on. In other words, how should the system or systems behave in the best case? Make sure you know what the correct behavior is; otherwise, you will not be able to test the system to determine if it is functioning properly.

DEVELOP POSSIBLE SOLUTIONS AND CREATE AN ACTION PLAN

In the case of simple problems, your plan could literally spell itself out, but for more complex problems where the stakes are high, it pays to take some time and lay out your plan. This way, you can look at all the consequences created by the different solutions and work out which parties this might affect. For a large organization, this can be a critical step to ensure that all the necessary parties have approved the plan before executing. It's also an exercise in good communication if the problem requires more than one party to execute. Documenting complex action plans in a typed form will help reduce the probability of miscommunication or misunderstood steps, which can result in disaster. Remember, even something as subtle as the order of your firewall rules can cause sweeping changes to all your other rules and might lock you out of the very systems you are trying to fix. Planning pays off in the end.

ANALYZE AND COMPARE POSSIBLE SOLUTIONS

1. Start with simplest problems first. Make a checklist and run down it from top to bottom. Generally it's a good idea to start with the standard network engineering problems before delving into more complex rule tracking. The rule of thumb is to test the easy stuff first!
2. Start also with the simplest solution first. For example, check for loose or bad cabling, DNS issues, or if the systems being affected are even available before investing a great deal of time debugging the firewall itself. More often than not, problems blamed on the firewall actually have nothing to do with it.
3. The OSI model, which is explained in the next chapter, is good to use here as a checklist of sorts. You work your way up the OSI model, ruling out dependencies that might be creating symptoms higher up in the OSI model. This further reinforces the process of working on the simplest problems first before moving onto the next complex problem.

SELECT AND IMPLEMENT THE SOLUTION

Put your plan into action. This is where you do all the work. Before this step, all you should have done is collected information about the problem and developed your plan of action.

CRITICALLY ANALYZE THE SOLUTION FOR EFFECTIVENESS

At this point, you will want to test your solution against the End State that you defined earlier. Is everything performing exactly as expected? Does the diagnostic data support the solution? Does this solve the entire problem or merely a symptom of the problem? The fact that you're in there changing things might be making things worse, so above all else, take the time to track what you're changing in the process of solving the problem, you may have to "undo" those changes.

REPEAT THE PROCESS UNTIL YOU RESOLVE THE PROBLEM

If none of this works, start over from the beginning. Maybe you're trying to solve the wrong problem. For example, you think it's the DNS that is preventing correct lookups for a website, but really it's the client's DNS settings. Perhaps you have the IP hard-coded into your /etc/hosts file—or maybe you're logging into the wrong box. When all else fails, go back to the beginning.

FINDING THE ANSWERS OR...WHY SEARCH ENGINES ARE YOUR FRIEND

Sometimes the solution is as close as your fingertips. When in doubt, look it up and save yourself a lot of time, energy, and headache. One great tool the Internet has brought us all is the concept of search engines. Before spending a great deal of time on a problem, try looking it up in a search engine first. It's amazing how often the problem you have encountered has been run into by dozens of folks before, and someone has taken the time to document the solution fully on a mailing list or website. While researching this book, we found that with most of the Linux firewall mailing lists, the vast majority of problems users reported had been answered many times before on that same mailing list, only months earlier. We're not going to expand on the finer points of mailing list etiquette—that's not our point here. The point here is that before you waste your time asking someone for the answer, try looking for it via a search engine.

WEBSITES

As the old saying goes, read the friendly manual. Sometimes the problem is as simple as not understanding the syntax of the command or how to use the command or tool correctly. Before spending a lot of time pulling your hair out, make sure you know that you're using your firewall correctly by checking the documentation or examples online. Some useful sites are the netfilter website, some firewall guru sites, and when all else fails, try our website (www.gotroot.com). If you have some favorite sites that help you with your problems, go there. Never be afraid to look for help elsewhere, but when posting to mailing lists or forums, it's usually good etiquette to check mailing list and forum archives first to see if anyone else has asked this question before and if they received an answer. Besides, it will save you time to look at it as opposed to waiting for an answer. Further, if someone already answered the question you are about to ask, try that information first before you ask the same question again. You may find yourself "shunned" by some of the more outspoken members of the list or forum if you waste the community's time. This is not to discourage you from asking "dumb" questions. The worst that can happen is no one answers, but if you want to be taken seriously in the future, check the archives first. No matter what, if the information is already in the archives, as we already said, you will have saved yourself a lot of time by not having to ask and wait for an answer!

- `http://netfilter.org/` This is the netfilter website, which obviously is the home for all that is netfilter.
- `http://iptables-tutorial.frozentux.net/` This site is probably the most fantastic tutorial about using **iptables**. It's very direct and straightforward and is constantly being updated. We cannot recommend this tutorial enough.
- `http://www.Linuxguruz.com/iptables/` Your one-stop shop for the **iptables/** netfilter "cheat sheet." This site contains numerous, well documented **iptables** scripts for all manner of configurations.
- `http://www.gotroot.com` Our one-stop shop for all things sysadmin related, from firewalls to system management. Our website includes all the tools in this book, along with example firewall scripts, forums, mailing lists, RFCs, and anything else our users and readers ask us to cover.
- `http://lists.netfilter.org/mailman/listinfo` This is the main mailing list for all things netfilter related and its archives. Although the archive is not searchable directly, the archives are downloadable.
- `http://marc.theaimsgroup.com/` The mother load of mailing lists. MARC stands for Mailing list ARChives, and it's a huge database of hundreds of mailing lists, including the netfilter lists, which are searchable even within the body of messages posted to the list. By far this is one of the most powerful tools on the Net for technical mailing lists, and we cannot recommend this site highly enough.

SUMMARY

Owning a book that contains specific solutions that aid you in solving problems is only going to be valuable for a finite period of time. If there is one thing we hope you walk away with after reading this book, it is that it is infinitely more important to have the mental tools to solve problems on your own than just to have the answers at your disposal. Sooner or later, you're going to encounter something no one else has, and you're going to have to figure it out yourself. This chapter should serve as an aid in creating a problem-solving process that should span far beyond just diagnosing firewall problems. The methodology described here is applicable to a number of problems even beyond IT problems. In later chapters we will get into specific solutions. However dull a chapter like this might be, the processes described here will be infinitely more valuable than any solutions we can outline in this or any other book. Sooner or later, things will change, and this book will no longer be relevant to the technologies in use. What will stay eternal, however, is the problem-solving process in this chapter. This one solution will help you when nothing else will.

SECTION II
TOOLS AND INTERNALS

The OSI Model: Start from the Beginning

So now that you know how to use a systematic method for solving problems, it's time to apply that knowledge to a well-understood model of networking behavior, the Open System Interconnection (OSI) model. The OSI model, in case you are not familiar with it, is composed of seven layers that describe all the elements in a networked connection. Think of it like building a house: To paint the outside of the house, you've got to have walls. To have walls, you've got to have a floor, and to have a floor, you need a foundation. The OSI model describes the layers of abstraction you need to create interconnected systems.

We have found that when you really don't know where to start, looking at the problem through this lens can be very helpful to quickly rule out elements and find the root causes of a tricky problem—without having to resort to more complicated methods. This approach might seem a bit condescending, but we aren't trying to insult anyone's intelligence with this approach. There are plenty of really sexy and complicated solutions provided later on in this book, but they won't help you diagnose some of the simpler problems as easily as we think this method will.

Expanding on the house example here, to create a network, you must have electrical (or optical) connections between devices by plugging them in (Layer 1). Adjacent Network Interface Controllers, in turn, can now communicate with each other (MAC addresses, Layer 2). IP addresses start at Layer 3; services that receive connections are at Layer 4. Layer 5 handles the session information such as an interrupted login attempt due to a network failure in the layers below. Layer 6 translates the information to and from the end user application and the network, and Layer 7 is the User Interface itself (web browser).

Physical Layer 1	Electrons, radio or light signals are all conveyed into a usable stream of data at this layer in order to form the most basic layer of sending or recieving data in a network.
Data Link Layer 2	This layer consists of two sub-layers, the Local Link Control (LLC) sub-layer, and the Media Access Control sub-layer. LLC is responsible for error correction, transmission of "frames" which are basically blocks of data MAC is responsible for determining how the device accesses the data, and the permission to transmit it.
Network Layer 3	Network routing information. The first layer of the Internet, IP (Internet Protocol) starts here.
Transport Layer 4	End to communication control. End to communication control.
Session Layer 5	Handles problems which are not communication issues.
Presentation Layer 6	Converts the networking information, into information usable by the application, and vice-versa.
Application Layer 7	The User interface.

Figure 5.1   The OSI model.

Remember the OSI model because we will be referencing it again as part of our troubleshooting system. The OSI model can help to quickly work upwards through the layers to rule out other problems that might be causing problems at a higher layer. For instance, a website could be slow due to a physical problem with the Fast Ethernet switch it is plugged into.

INTERNET PROTOCOLS AT A GLANCE

There is no way that we could hope to cover IPs completely in a book about firewall diagnostics. It's a huge subject and has been covered in absolutely fantastic detail by the late great W. Richard Stevens in the books, *The Protocols TCP/IP Illustrated Volume 1* and *The Implementation (TCP/IP Illustrated, Volume 2)*, coauthored by Gary R. Wright. A basic understanding of TCP/IP and how it fits with the concept of firewalling, however, is within the scope of this book. If you want to know more about TCP/IP, please check out the fine books mentioned here, and if you already have a firm grasp of this subject, then you can skip over some of this material. We provide it here as a brief introduction for the reader.

Understanding the Internet Protocol (IP)

IP is a Layer 3 protocol (Network Layer) and is documented fully in RFC 791. IP traffic contains routing and address information and is the medium by which packets traverse the Internet—hence, the rather obvious name, "Internet Protocol." This, combined with the Transmission Control Protocol (TCP), forms the backbone of how most services on the Internet function. Aside from IP's routing duties, this is also where the reassembly of packets (which is what we call a single unit of IP, TCP, ICMP, or UDP data) occurs when IP traffic moves through devices that dictate the Maximum Transmission Unit (MTU) size.

Briefly, the MTU defines how big of a packet a particular device can handle. With fast connections, this value isn't nearly as important because it's almost always set to the maximum size possible. MTU is mostly an issue with slower connections, such as modems, where the maximum packet size is much smaller. MTUs become important when packets are lost and have to be retransmitted. If a packet is very large and only a tiny portion of the packet was really lost, the entire packet must be retransmitted. The idea behind smaller MTUs is to help prevent resending too much data.

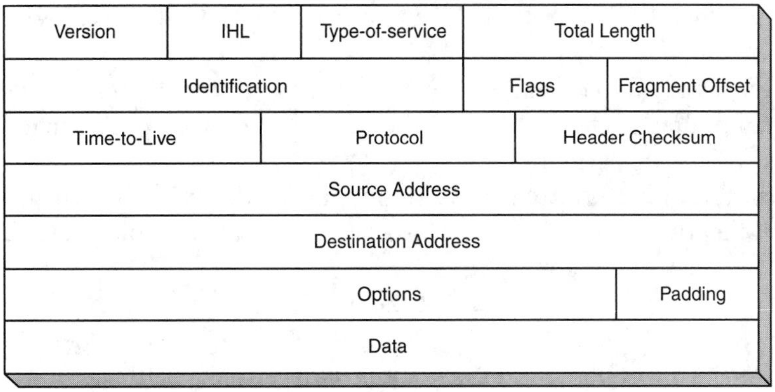

Version	IHL	Type-of-service	Total Length	
Identification			Flags	Fragment Offset
Time-to-Live		Protocol	Header Checksum	
Source Address				
Destination Address				
Options				Padding
Data				

Figure 5.2   The Internet Protocol Packet.

What an IP Packet Looks Like

There are 14 fields in an IP packet. They are (from left to right):

1. **Version:** The version of the IP packet, currently either IPv4 or IPv6.
2. **IP Header Length (IHL):** The datagram header length, in 32-bit words.
3. **Type-of-Service (TOS):** Specifies how an upper layer protocol (Layer 4+) should handle the packet and the importance of the packet.
4. **Total Length:** The length of the IP packet in bytes.
5. **Identification:** An integer that identifies the datagram, used for fragment reassembly.
6. **Flags:** 3-bit field, which designates the fragmentation information. The first bit specifies if the packet can be fragmented. The second bit specifies the last fragment in a series of fragments. The third bit is unused.
7. **Fragment Offset:** Specifies what position the fragment is in relation to the beginning of the datagram.
8. **Time-to-Live (TTL):** This is a counter that as the traffic moves between IP devices is decremented. When this counter reaches zero, the packet is discarded. The TTL counter is used to prevent IP traffic from looping.
9. **Protocol:** This designates what upper layer protocol this packet is destined to after the IP layer routing information has been processed.
10. **Header Checksum:** This is used to ensure that the IP packet has not been damaged in transmission.
11. **Source Address:** Referred to as SRC in many netfilter/**iptables** logging rules and sniffers like tcpdump and ethereal. This is the address field in the packet that designates what system sent the packet.
12. **Destination Address:** Referred to as DST in many netfilter/**iptables** logging rules and sniffers like **tcpdump** and **ethereal**. This is the address field in the packet that designates where the packet is going.
13. **Options:** Allows IP to support options like IPSEC.
14. **Padding.**
15. **Data:** Contains the upper layer information, like a TCP or UDP packet.

A word of caution—all of the headers in an IP packet can more or less be manipulated by any party between two points. This means that you shouldn't trust the fields in an IP packet arbitrarily. You can attempt to encrypt the traffic between two points, but if those two points are using IP, the headers on those packets can still be changed by an attacker. The bottom line is not to trust the headers of a packet by themselves.

UNDERSTANDING ICMP

The Internet Control Message Protocol (ICMP) is a quasi Layer 3 protocol (Network), documented by RFC 792 and RFC 1700. ICMP is used to pass IP packet error and processing information between IP devices. We call this information an "ICMP Message." A common ICMP packet is the "ping" packet, but there are many others. Some of them are not necessary anymore, and some are really critical to a healthy network.

ICMP packets are somewhat unique in the world of TCP/IP. Because ICMP cannot live in Layer 3 all by itself, it's actually contained inside of an IP packet as documented here, much like the Layer 4 TCP and UDP packets documented in the following sections. Also unique to the ICMP packet is that the data portion of the packet does not contain the "ICMP Message." Rather, the "Message" component is in the Type and Code fields as documented in Table 5.1.

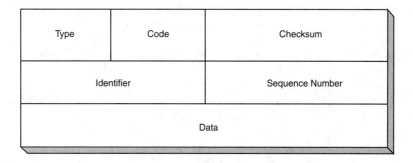

Figure 5.3   The ICMP Packet.

What an ICMP Message Looks Like

The two fields of real importance with ICMP are the Type and Code fields. There are technically 255 ICMP message types, although presently only 34 are used, of which there are also several sub-types or codes for each of those 34 types. To put it succinctly, there are many ICMP messages out there. As stated previously, only some of them are necessary to keep your network healthy; the others you can and probably should learn to live without.

Table 5.1   Referenced from `http://www.onlamp.com/pub/a/bsd/2001/04/04/FreeBSD_Basics.html?page=1`

Type	Name	Code	Note
0	Echo Reply	0 - none	Ping reply
1	unused		
2	unused		
3	Destination Unreachable	0 - Net unreachable	
3	Destination Unreachable	1 - Host unreachable	
3	Destination Unreachable	2 - Protocol unreachable	
3	Destination Unreachable	3 - Port unreachable	
3	Destination Unreachable	4 - Fragmentation needed and DF bit set	
3	Destination Unreachable	5 - Source route failed	
3	Destination Unreachable	6 - Destination network unknown	
3	Destination Unreachable	7 - Destination host unknown	
3	Destination Unreachable	8 - Source host isolated	
3	Destination Unreachable	9 - Communication with destination network is administratively prohibited	
3	Destination Unreachable	10 - Communication with destination host is administratively prohibited	
3	Destination Unreachable	11 - Destination network unreachable for TOS	
3	Destination Unreachable	12 - Destination host unreachable for TOS	
4	Source quench		
5	Redirect	0 - Redirect datagram for the network	
5	Redirect	1 - Redirect datagram for the host	
5	Redirect	2 - Redirect datagram for the TOS and network	
5	Redirect	3 - Redirect datagram for the TOS and host	
6	Alternate host address	0 - Alternate address for host	
7	Unassigned		

Type	Name	Code	Note
8	Echo	0 - None	Ping packet
9	Router advertisement	0 - None	
10	Router selection	0 - None	
11	Time Exceeded	0 - Time to live exceeded in transit	
11	Time Exceeded	1 - Fragment reassembly time exceeded	
12	Parameter problem	0 - Pointer indicates the error	
12	Parameter problem	1 - Missing a required option	
12	Parameter problem	2 - Bad length	
13	Timestamp	0 - None	
14	Timestamp reply	0 - None	
15	Information request	0 - None	
16	Information reply	0 - None	
17	Address mask request	0 - None	
18	Address mask reply	0 - None	
19	Reserved (for security)		
20-29	Reserved (for robustness experiment)		
30	Traceroute		
31	Datagram conversion error		
32	Mobile host redirect		
33	IPv6 where-are-you		
34	IPv6 I-am-here		
35	Mobile registration request		
36	Mobile registration reply		
37-255	Reserved		

Understanding TCP

TCP stands for the Transmission Control Protocol and is situated in Layer 4 of the OSI model. It is a connection-oriented service and handles the transfer of data, flow control, reliability, and multiplexing all in one protocol. TCP is a very robust protocol and can handle most error conditions with automated recovery. TCP is a good protocol for higher-level protocols, such as HTTP and SMTP, which do not have built in error recovery and flow control capabilities. But TCP is not ideal for protocols that handle this internally, such as VPN protocols, which are tunneling TCP connections within. With VPNs, UDP is usually the better protocol to use. We discuss this in more detail later in this chapter when we cover UDP.

There are 13 fields in a TCP Packet. They are (from left to right):

1. **Source Port:** The port number the packet was sent from on the source machine.
2. **Destination Port:** The port number the packet is being sent to on the remote machine.
3. **Sequence Number:** Either an initial number sequence used in the upcoming transmission or the number assigned to the first byte of data in the current message.
4. **Acknowledgment Number:** The sequence number for the next byte of data.
5. **Data Offset:** The number of 32-bit words in the TCP header.
6. **Reserved:** Set aside for future use.
7. **Flags:** Control information for the packet. SYN, ACK, FIN, RST, URG, and PSH flags are part of this field.
8. **Window:** Size of the sender's buffer space available for incoming data.
9. **Checksum:** A checksum of the header to determine if it was damaged during transmission.
10. **Urgent Pointer:** Location of the first urgent data byte in the packet.
11. **Options:** TCP options.
12. **Padding:** The padding field is used when alignment is needed or sometimes when used with encryption, such as IPSEC.
13. **Data:** The actual message or content being sent by the TCP packet.

TCP provides many additional capabilities, such as reliability, efficient and varied methods of flow control (Linux has the capability to modify this further through **/proc** as detailed in later chapters), full-duplex communication, multiplexing, and streaming.

With streaming, TCP can deliver bytes in an unstructured form identified by sequence numbers. This is used when an application does not or cannot break data into blocks that fit efficiently on the network. TCP is left to work this out for the application. In these cases, TCP groups the packets together into what are called sequences, based on internally determined maximum sizes based on network conditions and the way the system is configured.

Reliability

TCP provides reliability to data through full duplex connections. Unlike UDP, TCP packets always receive acknowledgment from the receiver, or they are sent again until acknowledged. TCP accomplishes this by performing what is called "forward acknowledgment" by adding in an Acknowledgment number for the next byte of data the source expects the recipient to receive. A specified amount of time is tracked by the sender, and if the block of data is not acknowledged within that period of time, the packet is sent again to the receiver. This makes it possible for TCP to respond to lost or damaged packets reliably. The receiver may also request that a packet be resent.

Full Duplex and Multiplexing

TCP is truly full duplex, which means that the protocol can be used to both send and receive data at the same time. TCP also can be used to perform multiplexing, which means that many simultaneous connections and conversations can be conversing over one connection. This is accomplished via upper layers of the OSI model through higher-level protocols, such as SMTP and HTTP for instance.

Flow Control

Flow control is another feature of TCP. Flow control is defined as a technique used to stop the sender of data from sending more data than the receiver can accept. This is achieved through the use of sequence numbers, where the receiver sends back the highest sequence number it can receive without exceeding its receive buffers. The sender is supposed to transmit packets up to but not exceeding that sequence number, and then the sender is to wait until the receiver sends another ACK packet with a higher sequence number. There are a number of algorithms to achieve this, many of which are configurable through **/proc** under Linux. More detail on this is provided in later chapters.

Congestion Control

TCP also provides for what is called *congestion control* by adapting to network conditions to slow down or speed up the rate at which packets are sent. This is to respond to the "common" reality of IP networks, where guaranteed flow rates are difficult to accomplish and packets are lost due to overloaded routers, switches, hubs, hosts, and any other device in the path.

How TCP Connections Are Established

TCP, unlike UDP, is designed to operate via fully established connections. It is not a broadcast protocol, but a true three-way communications protocol. Nothing is assumed with TCP until both the receiver and sender acknowledge the communication. To do this, TCP uses a three-way handshake to establish a new connection and to synchronize the hosts on both ends to each other's capability to receive and send data. If you recall the sequence numbers discussed earlier, this is how TCP accomplishes flow control and readies both sides to send and receive data at that established rate. This helps to prevent unnecessary packet retransmissions.

As each host starts the process, it is supposed to randomly pick a sequence number. It's worth noting here that not all random number generators are the same. Some OSs, including some Linux kernels, may not pick sequence numbers that are truly random. This may seem unimportant, but there are a number of attacks on TCP streams that are accomplished by predicting the next sequence number and spoofing the next packet in a stream to "hijack" the stream. A good random number generator for your sequence numbers helps to protect against these sorts of attacks and also makes certain types of DoS and DDoS bounce attacks more difficult against your systems. Thankfully, there are patches for the Linux kernel that make the sequence numbers and other random numbers used by the IP stack truly random.

After the hosts have picked random numbers to use as their sequence numbers, the host that is initiating the connection, Bob, sends a TCP packet to the receiver, Alice, with the initial sequence number, XY, and the SYN flag set in the header of the packet. Alice, the receiver, then processes the packet, records the sequence number XY, and sends back a packet to Barrett with the acknowledgment field set to XY+1. The receiver increments the original sequence number by 1. Alice also adds its own initial sequence number to the packet, Z, and sets the ACK flag in the headers of the TCP packet. Each host then increments these sequence numbers by the number of bytes of data it has successfully received from the other host. This acts as a mechanism for each host to limit the amount of data sent in each packet to only the data the other party needs and can receive.

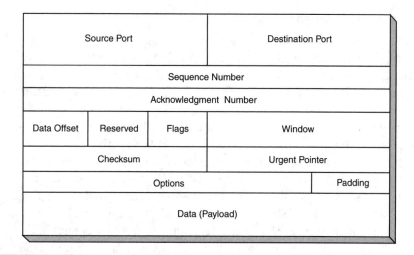

Source Port			Destination Port	
Sequence Number				
Acknowledgment Number				
Data Offset	Reserved	Flags	Window	
Checksum			Urgent Pointer	
Options				Padding
Data (Payload)				

Figure 5.4 The TCP packet.

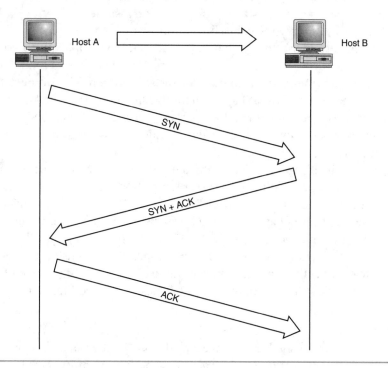

Figure 5.5 Three-Way Handshake (TWH).

How TCP Connections Are Closed

TCP is as equally methodical about closing down connections as it is about creating them. TCP sessions can be closed in two ways. The first is very similar to the way in which a connection is established, via a four-way handshake referred to as a "close." The second method is called a TCP abort and uses a special packet flag called the reset, or RST flag.

A close request using the four-way handshake method starts with the party that wants to close the connection by sending a FIN+ACK packet to the other party. This is the most graceful manner of closing a session and does not represent any sort of error state on the requester's end. We point this out because a TCP abort, the second method, is normally invoked when one of the parties experiences an error and wishes to close the connection in an error state. We have seen some vendors that use the RST method a little too prodigiously, which causes some high level applications that depend on this "niceness" to infer an error state from the state of the connection. If the close method is used, many programs assume the connection was successful; if the abort method is used, they infer, rightly in fact, that something went wrong. One fascinating example of this occurs with some high-level web applications that look for an error state from the TCP connect call, and when a TCP abort occurs, the web application assumes the entire HTTP connection failed and will simply retry the connection again. We found this problem at one large government customer of ours. They had an XML/HTTP application designed to send messages to another host running a web server. The client would send the data via an HTTP POST, the server would acknowledge the successful receipt of the data way up at Layer 7, and meanwhile down at Layer 3, a low balancing switch killed the session part way through the close process with an RST packet. The client inferred, incorrectly, that the server had not received the data correctly. Technically speaking, this was one correct manner of interpreting the TCP ABORT call.

Regardless, our client's application assumed it needed to resend all the data again because all the data it got back from the server saying that it successfully received the data was discarded due to an error state created by the TCP ABORT call. In fairness, the program on the client could have been better written to take these exceptions into account, perhaps by simply looking at the HTTP data and ignoring the TCP error state. Nevertheless, the problem was so low in the OSI model that our customer spent months trying to figure out why their application kept randomly attempting to resend the same messages over and over again when the server had acknowledged them already.

TCP CLOSE

The TCP CLOSE is accomplished, as we have already discussed, via a four-way handshake. Unlike establishing a connection, to close a session, both hosts must agree to the request.

One host cannot arbitrarily close the connection via this method. The process starts with the party that wishes to close the connection sending a FIN packet. The other host, if it agrees to close the session, sends back a FIN+ACK packet. The other host also must send its own FIN packet to the first host, which must also send back a FIN+ACK packet. The process is basically a complete mirror on both ends. This is done so that both sides can empty their buffers of any remaining data. Until the final FIN is sent, data can still flow from the party that did not initiate the CLOSE request. This means that connection can be half closed, meaning that one side has stopped sending data and is waiting for the other side to stop—while the other side is still sending data.

TCP ABORT

A TCP ABORT, or RST packet, is sent normally when data has been lost due to an unrecoverable error. This method of closing a TCP session can be used arbitrarily to shut a connection down. Both hosts do not have to agree to close the session.

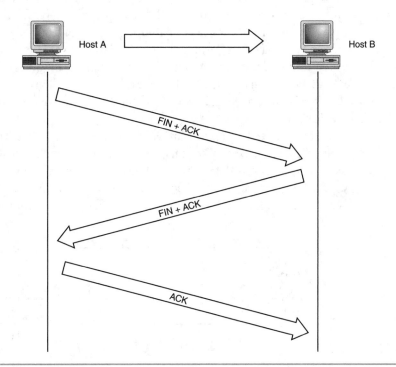

Figure 5.6 Three-way teardown.

There is much more to TCP than we have covered here, so don't consider this a complete explanation. For instance, we haven't covered the scenario of TCP windows or the various methods used to recover from packet loss. Other books cover those issues in wonderful detail; our objective is to briefly cover those aspects of TCP that are most important to troubleshooting firewalls. We also will assume, in later portions of the book, that the reader has a more in-depth understanding of TCP if the subject matter requires it. Where this assumption exists, we will point the reader to other books on the subject.

UNDERSTANDING UDP

User Datagram Protocol (UDP) is the other "big" protocol used on the Internet. Unlike TCP, it is entirely connectionless, but like TCP, it's also a transport layer protocol (Layer 4) and is part of the Internet Protocol. Also unlike TCP, UDP has no inherent flow control, error recovery, or reliability capabilities. If a UDP packet is lost, the receiving host has no way of knowing or reporting this as part of the native functionality of UDP. Because of this, some applications that use UDP have implemented their own internal functions to compensate. This is not to say that UDP is bad protocol—far from it. Sometimes a developer does not need the additional functionality of TCP, or the flow control characteristics of TCP may cause problems such as with VPNs. There are advantages to UDP because of its simpler design, as already indicated, but another is that because UDP packets tend to be smaller, they will use less bandwidth. This can be necessary for protocols that consume large amounts of bandwidth, such as file transfer protocols, VPNs, or voice-over IP.

UDP packets contain five fields, the first four of which are the UDP header. The header is made up the following fields: source and destination ports, length, and checksum. The body of the message, also known as its data or payload field, contains the actual message or data being sent via the UDP protocol. The checksum field is optional and can be used to provide some integrity check on the UDP header and data fields, but is not required.

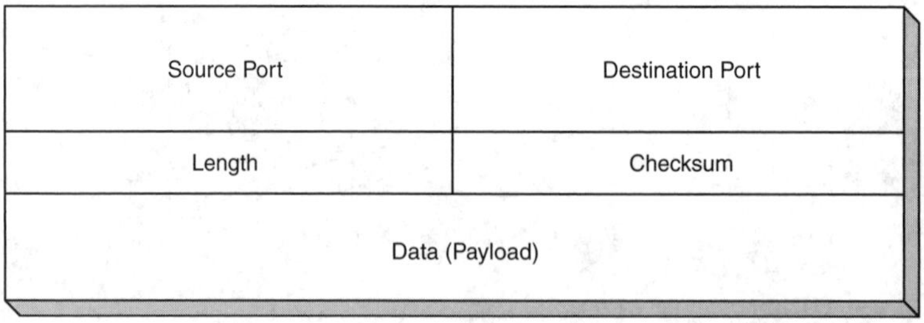

Source Port	Destination Port
Length	Checksum
Data (Payload)	

Figure 5.7   The UDP packet.

TROUBLESHOOTING WITH THIS PERSPECTIVE IN MIND

Aside from the obvious benefits of using this bottom-up methodology, we have found that when you don't really know where to start, that looking at the problem through this lens can be very helpful at quickly ruling out elements that may not be causing the problem. It's also amazing how often these simple problems end up being the cause of what appears to be a complex problem. Following are some undoubtedly oversimplified but really common problems we have seen happen far too often to people who should know better by now—to help illustrate the things to look for at these layers of the OSI model. The point being that sometimes, you're just over-thinking the problem. Also note how the "quick checks" get more complicated the farther you go down. Start with the simple things first! The following Scott one-liners on each layer help illustrate the point.

Layer 1: Test To Make Sure You Have Physical Connectivity

One-liner: "You kicked your patch cable out." —Scott

This is one of the simpler things to test but often goes overlooked. What you want to look for is not just that you have a link light, which is also important, but that the cable is properly terminated, is it in spec for the connection it's being used for (CAT3 when you need CAT6), and other physical problems. The following is a general list of things to look for; the key thing to keep in mind is that you want to rule out physical connectivity issues before you move on to more difficult problems.

1. Are you plugged in?
2. Is the cable actually any good? Is it in spec?
3. Is the port on the switch/hub working? Try another port to see if that fixes your problem.

Layer 2: Test Your Driver

One-liner: "That's not a Tulip card." —Scott

1. 10/100/1000/10000 issue—are you actually running the right one? Some cards use different drivers based on speed or need to be passed various switches to configure them to work at different speeds, full duplex, half duplex, etc.

2. Is the MTU size correct for your network? For instance, the MTU size on some DSL connections that use PPPoE actually matters to successfully process large packets. Hint—1500 is good for cable modems, Ethernet, and T1+ connections, but when you're dealing with VPNs (Virtual Private Networks) over DSL and ATM, you'll probably have to back this off in increments until you find the right setup for your network.
3. Is that network really Ethernet? Is it Token Ring? Is it something else?

Layer 3: Test IP Layer

One-liner: "That's not my IP." —Scott

1. Ping it first—from your box and another box.
    Traceroute.
2. Packet sniff it—are you getting packets back? Is anything going out? Are the IP addresses correct? For instance, NAT rules can change the IP addresses of the source and destination hosts. If this is done incorrectly, or not at all, the source address being sent out could be incorrect.

Layer 4: Test the TCP Layer

One-liner: "I'm not running a web server on that machine." —Scott

1. **Telnet** to the port, from in front of and behind the firewall. A great way to waste a lot of time is to diagnose a firewall by trying to connect to a service that isn't actually running on the other end. A simple "telnet somehost.com 25" (this would connect to the mail port) can help save you some time.
2. Test the service without the application. In other words, if you're testing a mail server rule, try testing the connection with a command line **telnet** before sending mail.
3. Test with the application last.

Layer 5: Test the Session Layer

One-liner: "Wait for the login prompt." —Scott

1. The session layer is responsible for coordinating the connection(s) from an application to a networked system and vice versa. Logins, Name resolution, etc. generally are depicted as happening at this level. So it helps sometimes to be patient. For example, some mail servers will do an **identd** request when you connect. Until they receive the response, they won't pass you up to the next layer. The connection will appear to stall. From your perspective it might appear as if something is wrong given that it's not responding right away—if you weren't running the **identd** service.

Layer 6: Test the Presentation Layer

One-liner: "That doesn't actually support your authentication system." —Scott

1. Test to make sure what you're using actually supports what you're trying to do when it comes to the presentation layer. A good example of this is the myriad IPSEC implementations. Generally getting them to communicate down in Layers 3 and 4 is pretty easy; it's when you get up to the authentication and encryption in Layer 6 that things get weird.

Layer 7: Test the Application Layer

One-liner: "Try using the right password." —Scott

1. Make sure you're actually entering the right login information or URL to that website you can't get to before you blame the firewall. Is that site even up?
2. Is the remote application working from somewhere else? Try connecting to the site from some host that is not affected by the firewall.

The lesson to take away from this approach is to conclusively eliminate dependencies. This isn't a complete list of things to check. It's just a set of examples to help remember the layers and what to look for as you work through them. The chapters in Section 3 of the book have more detailed lists of items to test at each layer for specific problems, but you may determine that there are others specific to your implementation that we may not cover.

Remember, if you cannot eliminate a layer and must move onto another layer, keep in mind the unresolved problems from the previous layers. It could be a more complex problem. The intent is to eliminate variables to make it possible to work on increasingly complex layers. As you move up the OSI model, the number of dependencies increases dramatically; if you don't rule out a layer, you're making it that much harder to diagnose the next layer. Repeat and live by the old adage, "keep it simple," when you're troubleshooting and you'll save yourself a lot of time by reducing the variables in your problem.

SUMMARY

As mentioned earlier in this chapter, we cannot hope to cover TCP/IP as well or as effectively as W. Richard Stevens and Gary Wright did in the *TCP/IP Illustrated* books. We used them before we wrote this book and have no doubt we will continue to use them after. So do yourself a favor and go pick up a copy; we cannot recommend them enough when it comes to a definitive guide on TCP/IP.

That being said, this chapter should serve as a very basic reference to the mechanisms by which the Internet Protocol will traverse a firewall at Layers 3 and 4. In later chapters we also cover firewalling at Layer 2 of the OSI model—to give a complete picture of the capabilities of netfilter and **iptables**.

netfilter and iptables Overview

The first thing to get out of the way is that netfilter and **iptables** are not the same thing. They are largely written by the same group of developers, but they are very different parts of a whole. netfilter comprises the kernel level code that Linux can use to conduct packet filtering, state management, NAT, packet mangling, QOS, and other neat tricks. **iptables** is the userland tool that can manipulate these kernel hooks to do these things for you. It's important to point this out because there are other userland tools that use netfilter as well and that also can accomplish some pretty neat tricks.

HOW NETFILTER WORKS

With this bit out of the way, we can move on with the discussion of how netfilter works. Starting with 2.4 of the Linux kernel, a complete rewrite of the "firewalling" code was undertaken. Because of this, 2.4 and greater kernels now have the ability to do stateful packet management. This means no more strange rules to prevent SYN packets from going the wrong way; the kernel will maintain state on outbound (or inbound for that matter) connections and open external ports for you as needed and only allow back the packets that it's supposed to for that specific connection. From this comes the term "connection tracking," which you will hear about frequently in later chapters.

It also means things completely changed from the old style of userland management tools, **ipchains**, to the new standard tool, **iptables**.

First, let's briefly discuss the differences between **ipchains** and **iptables**. **ipchains** is the userland tool used under 2.0 and 2.2 Linux kernels to manage firewall rules. It is not stateful but still allows one to set up some fairly strong firewall rules. It's important to note that without the ability to manage state, the 2.0 and 2.2 firewalling code is limited in terms of the traffic it can adequately and safely control. It is for this reason that we strongly advise that you use the newer netfilter firewalling capabilities in the 2.4, 2.5, and 2.6 kernels. netfilter is such a fantastic improvement that we can't recommend it enough.

Because the internal firewalling code between 2.0 and 2.2 kernels is different from 2.4 and 2.6 kernels, the use of **ipchains** on 2.4 and 2.6 kernels is largely an illusion. When **ipchains** is used with 2.4 and 2.6 kernels, it is through a compatibility layer that basically attempts to translate **ipchains** userland rules into the netfilter format. This doesn't always work correctly, which is yet another reason to not use **ipchains**. Even though the internals are different, once you get a feel for the new features in **iptables**, it is not difficult to convert **ipchains** rules to **iptables**. Also given some of the powerful new features, there is all the more reason to make the switch.

How netfilter Parses Rules

The value of understanding how netfilter parses rules can't be understated. The rules are parsed in different order depending on which chain you choose to use. For instance, the SNAT, DNAT, and FORWARD chains are part of a different path in the kernel. Traffic destined for the firewall versus being routed by the firewall takes two independent paths through the netfilter decision tree.

This last point is really the most critical one with **iptables**. INPUT rules and FORWARD rules are on two totally different paths, and they make up the key split in what rules will be triggered as a packet moves through your firewall. Let's take a look at some examples.

Our first case is what happens when a packet is sent from some remote host to some service running on our firewall. This is different from what happens when a packet is sent through the firewall and then sent on to some different system for processing.

Packet Sent to Service Running on Firewall from Remote Host (INPUT)

Steps:

1. Packet is sent from remote client.
2. Packet received by physical interface(s).
3. Packet is processed by the kernel driver.
4. Packet is processed by the networking protocol(s) layer(s).
5. Packet is processed by netfilter in this order.
6. PREROUTING mangle (TOS, etc.)
7. PREROUTING NAT
8. Routing decision: Is the packet for the local box, or is it to be forwarded to another system by us?

9. INPUT mangle
10. INPUT filter
11. Application on our system processes the packet.

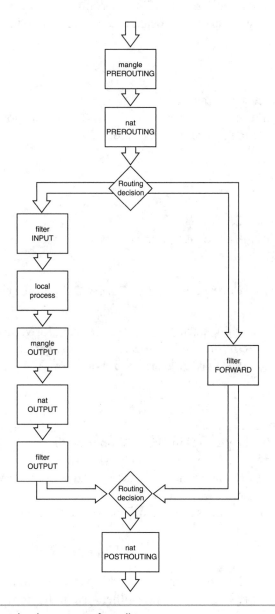

Figure 6.1 Packet sent to local process on firewall.

Packet Sent by Firewall from a Local Process to a Remote System (OUTPUT)

The next case covers what happens when a local process on the firewall tries to send a packet out. Such examples might be a DNS server running on the firewall or a proxy server. When a packet is generated by a local process, it follows a different and inverted path from the previous example.

Steps:

1. Local program/process generates packet.
2. The kernel makes a routing decision—where does this packet go?
3. The netfilter `OUTPUT` mangle chain is triggered.
4. `OUPUT: NAT`
5. `OUTPUT: filter`
6. `POSTROUTING: mangle`
7. `POSTROUTING: NAT`
8. Goes out firewall interface.
9. On the wire (might not get to destination).

Packet Our Firewall Is Forwarding for Some Other Host to Some Host (FORWARD)

Finally, the process for handling packets that are only being forwarded by the firewall is through yet another different branch in the packet processing tree. In this example, the firewall does not trip the `INPUT` or `OUTPUT` rules and only trips the `FORWARD` rules.

Steps:

1. Packet is sent by source to firewall.
2. Packet is received by the physical interface(s) on firewall.
3. Packet is processed by the kernel driver on firewall.
4. Packet is processed by the networking protocol(s) layer(s) on firewall.
5. Packet is processed by netfilter on firewall.
6. Any `PREROUTING` mangle rules are applied. This might change the TTL or TOS of the packet.
7. Any `PREROUTING` NAT rules are applied. This might change the source and/or destination of the packet.
8. Kernel makes routing decision—where does this packet go? In this example, it's destined not for the firewall, but for some other system the firewall forwards packets for.

9. Any FORWARD mangle rules are applied.
10. Any FORWARD NAT rules are applied.
11. Any FORWARD filtering rules are applied.
12. Kernel makes another routing decision—where does this packet go? In this example, the packet is destined for another host.
13. Any netfilter POSTROUTING mangle rules are applied; this might change TOS or TTL values in the packet.
14. Final netfilter step—any POSTROUTING NAT rules are applied.
15. Sent out of our interface(s) to destination.
16. On wire to destination (might not arrive).

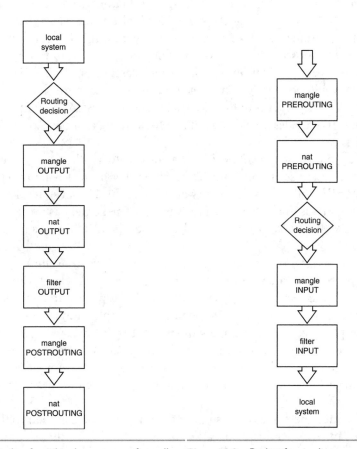

Figure 6.2 Packet from local process on firewall out to remote host.

Figure 6.3 Packet forwarding procedure.

Putting It All Together

Figure 6.4 shows what all of this looks like when put together. The important point in the decision-making process the kernel uses is the routing decision before either INPUT or FORWARD rules are used. Remember, INPUT rules do not affect packets that the firewall is forwarding to another host. If you want to deny a specific type of traffic and only apply that to the INPUT rules, then this traffic will continue to pass through your firewall to other hosts. When in doubt, do it twice—once for the INPUT rules and once for the FORWARD rules.

So to repeat, if a packet is being forwarded by our firewall, it will bypass the INPUT and OUTPUT rules. Remember this when you are constructing your rules and diagnosing problems with them. It also helps when creating logging functions, to detail if the rule set tripped was an INPUT, OUTPUT, or FORWARD rule. This is also where PREROUTING chains come into play. For instance, a packet might be destined for the firewall's external interface but is actually supposed to be sent to a host behind the firewall, and the PREROUTING rules change the packet's destination. NAT is one such case. In this case, the packet would be rewritten and would be sent down the FORWARD chains because the kernel would make a routing decision (this packet is not for us; it's for another system) and then try to route the packet. The netfilter rules would catch it as a forwarding event and process only FORWARD rules against it.

Another place you will see the opposite behavior is with application proxies. For instance, if you are using **squid** on your firewall, the FORWARD rules will not be called, even though your firewall is technically forwarding packets. However, it's the application, in this case **squid**, that is doing the actual forwarding. The kernel has no way of knowing this, so only the INPUT and OUTPUT rules will be tripped as **squid** is just a local process on the firewall.

netfilter maintains state on Packetsnetfilter, unlike previous firewalling systems in Linux, by having ability to track connections through their life cycles. It can automatically open ports on the firewall (if configured correctly) as needed to allow back dynamic protocols, such as FTP, without the need for complex and potentially dangerous rule sets that keep a "range" of ports open for such needs. It can track a session to ensure that an attacker cannot trick the firewall into passing traffic to a system. The connection tracking system can help to identify bogus or unclean packets that might be a result of an attack, and in general, the new statefulness of the Linux firewalling system can make your life much easier.

As the netfilter designers have been so kind to point out, you can refer to the elements of the Linux kernel that give us the ability to do this as either a connection tracking engine or a state engine. We, like the netfilter developers, will use both terms interchangeably.

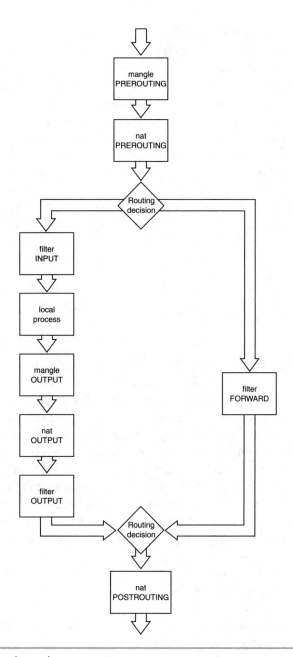

Figure 6.4 netfilter packet path.

The bottom line is that stateful firewalls are safer than non-stateful firewalls because we can write simpler and generally stricter rules. We don't have to open as much to get things to work. The firewall understands the lower-level protocols, and with the assistance of what are known as "helpers," can understand other higher-level protocols, such as FTP, IRC, and others. This allows the firewall to make decisions on the fly about its configuration based on its needs at the time. This also gives you greater control over the traffic moving through your firewall because instead of just trying to control things based on ports, you can now control them based on the protocol. For instance, if you wanted to block certain P2P traffic through your firewall you could do this using a helper module.

To accomplish all of these things, we need to understand the four states that the netfilter state engine recognizes. These are the states a packet is in based on the kernel's connection tracking capabilities. The four states are: NEW, INVALID, RELATED, and ESTABLISHED. At any given time a packet, when under the control of the state engine, is in one of these four states.

NETFILTER STATES

- **NEW:** A new connection. Only the first packet in a connection will meet this state. All subsequent packets, for that session, will not be considered NEW.
- **ESTABLISHED:** A session that has been established and is being tracked by the state engine. All packets that follow after a packet labeled as NEW in a single session.
- **RELATED:** A special state. A separate connection related to an ESTABLISHED session. This can happen when an ESTABLISHED connection spawns a new connection as part of its data communication process. An example of this is FTP-DATA connection spawned by an FTP connection. These types of connections are very complicated and almost always require a "helper" module that has been written to understand the underlying protocol. If there is no helper module to analyze a complex protocol that requires a RELATED connection to function, then that connection will not function properly.
- **INVALID:** A packet that is otherwise not identified as having any state. It is always a good idea to DROP, not REJECT, this packet.

A connection's state, however, can change based on what happens with future packets in that connection. An example of this would be a new telnet connection. When the first packet comes in, it would be in the NEW state; this would create a new connection for the state engine to manage. The proceeding packets that create the session would move the connection from the NEW state to the ESTABLISHED state.

The specific piece of the netfilter code that handles all of this magic is called conntrack. Its job is to watch each session and determine if the packets are part of an existing session or a related one and to enforce the rules supplied by the userland tools around that information.

All of this magic occurs in the PREROUTING chain. All connection tracking occurs there—except for any packets generated by the firewall itself. For instance, if you are running a name server on your firewall, and the firewall needs to lookup a host name, that packet's state would be handled in the OUTPUT chain.

For example, when a packet goes out of the firewall, its initial state is set to NEW in the PREROUTING chains; when the return packets arrive back at the firewall, the PREROUTING chain changes the connection's status from NEW to ESTABLISHED. This state is then passed up the chain to other rules. So if you had a rule that allowed ESTABLISHED packets through on your FORWARD target, the return packets would be allowed back to the client that initiated the connection.

WHAT ABOUT FRAGMENTATION?

netfilter and **iptables** have removed the need to muck around with turning fragmentation on or off, as with 2.0 and 2.2 kernels. Defragmentation, as it were, is always done when the state engine is used. The brief explanation for this is that the state engine could not work otherwise. Some packets simply lack enough context to tell the kernel enough about the connection it might be associated with. The fact that the kernel does this for us is a good thing. It makes the firewall more secure, the rules can be that much simpler because we don't have to worry about fragments anymore, and we can detect other problems with the packet before passing it on to a protected resource.

But because we are paranoid people and we like to be safe, it never hurts to add in a rule to catch any fragments and drop them if something were to go horribly wrong with all of this. We've never seen this happen, but it's such a trivially easy thing to add to your firewall rules that we don't see why it would hurt.

To catch any fragments that slip through, which, again, shouldn't occur if you are using the state engine, simply add these rules to the top of your rule sets:

```
$IPTABLES -N NOFRAGS
$IPTABLES -A OUTPUT -p ip -f -j NOFRAGS
$IPTABLES -A INPUT -p ip -f -j NOFRAGS
$IPTABLES -A FORWARD -p ip  -f -j NOFRAGS
$IPTABLES -A NOFRAGS   -m limit --limit 1/second \
-j LOG  --log-level info --log-prefix "Fragment \
-- DROP "  --log-tcp-sequence  --log-tcp-options  \
--log-ip-options
$IPTABLES -A NOFRAGS  -j DROP
```

Just to be clear, defragmentation happens automatically only when conntrack is used. If you are not using the state engine, then you have fragments aplenty to deal with. You also cannot turn this off if you are using conntrack. If you want fragments, then you cannot use the state engine.

TAKING A CLOSER LOOK AT THE STATE ENGINE

Now that we have a basic understanding of how the state engine works, let's take a look at what it's tracking. The first place to look is in the most powerful file system on a Linux system, **/proc**. In case you are not aware of what **/proc** is, it's a virtual file system that lets you look at the devices in your system, to reconfigure some of them, and even to modify the kernels' and networks' behavior on the fly. This is an extraordinarily powerful feature of Linux that we highly recommend you read up on if you are not already familiar with all the things you can do under **/proc**. It's beyond the scope of this book to spend too much time on the rest of **/proc**, so we will limit ourselves to those parts that relate to firewalls and, for now, just the state engine. Packets moving through the state engine are in one of four states.

As to the state engine, let's take a look at /proc/net/ip_conntrack. This lists all the current connections the kernel is tracking and any information the system has on those connections. A typical entry might look like this:

```
tcp    6 431890 ESTABLISHED src=68.100.73.75 dst=207.126.99.62 sport=47037 dport=80
src=207.126.99.62 dst=68.100.73.75 sport=80 dport=47037 use=1 bytes=3041
```

All the information needed to determine the current state of this connection is provided by looking inside this /proc entry, Table 6.1 contains a breakdown of all the fields. You can dump the real-time contents of this by simply typing this command:

```
cat /proc/net/ip_conntrack
```

Table 6.1   Connection Tracking Fields

Protocol	Decimal value for Protocol type	Time the connection has to live in the connection engine (*Note 1*)	Current state of this connection	Source IP	Destination IP	Key word: Expected source (*Note 2*)	Expected Destination (*Note 2*)	Expected source port (*Note 3*)	Expected source port (*Note 3*)

Note 1

This number is reset when a new packet arrives that is relevant to this connection. The value is then reset to the default value for this connection type.

Note 2

Depending on the direction of the connection—be it an SNAT, MASQ, or DNAT—one of these may be modified to the NAT-ed IP. See Table 6.1 for an explanation of these fields.

Note 3

Same as Note 2 except for port numbers that might be different depending on how your firewall is configured.

Breaking Down Some Examples

To get a sense of the wide range of connections you might see in /proc/net/ip_ conntrack, we will review some examples. In the next chapter we explore this system in even greater detail. The intent of this chapter is to cover broad concepts, so we will only cover two of the most common protocols, UDP and TCP.

The first example that follows is what an established TCP session for an HTTP server GET request might look like. The packet has also been mangled to allow the client, 172.31.254.2., to NAT its traffic through the firewall. The second hand of the IP pairs is the expected source and destination for any return packets.

```
tcp     6 271 ESTABLISHED src=172.31.254.2 dst=1.2.3.4 sport=2503 dport=80
src=1.2.3.4 dst=EXTERNAL_IP_FOR_NAT_CLIENT sport=80 dport=2503 use=1 bytes=118740288
```

This is what a fully TCP tracked NAT connection might look like. Before a TCP connection reaches the ESTABLISHED state, it has to go through the three-way handshaking process explained in Chapter 5. Within the netfilter state engine, this is reflected as part of three states: SYN_SENT, SYN_RECV, and ESTABLISHED. For example:

Step 1:

```
tcp     6 39 SYN_SENT src=172.31.254.2 dst=172.140.27.241 sport=1848
dport=3855[UNREPLIED] src=172.140.27.241 dst=EXTERNAL_IP_FOR_NAT_CLIENT sport=3855
dport=1848 use=1 bytes=144
```

Step 2:

```
tcp     6 29 SYN_RECV src=1.2.3.4 dst=1.2.3.5 sport=1855 dport=25 src=1.2.3.5
dst=1.2.3.4 sport=25 dport=1855 use=1 bytes=192
```

Step 3:

```
tcp      6 271 ESTABLISHED src=172.31.254.2 dst=1.2.3.4 sport=2503 dport=80
src=1.2.3.4 dst=EXTERNAL_IP_FOR_NAT_CLIENT sport=80 dport=2503 use=1 bytes=118740288
```

For UDP, the process looks a little different...

Step 1:

```
udp      17 26 src=10.10.10.8 dst=10.10.10.253 sport=40082 dport=53 src=10.10.10.253
dst=10.10.10.8 sport=53 dport=40082 use=1 bytes=255
```

Step 2:

```
udp      17 26 src=10.10.10.8 dst=10.10.10.253 sport=40082 dport=53 src=10.10.10.253
dst=10.10.10.8 sport=53 dport=40082 use=1 bytes=255
```

Step 3:

```
udp      17 0 src=10.10.10.8 dst=10.10.10.253 sport=40005 dport=53 src=10.10.10.253
dst=10.10.10.8 sport=53 dport=40005 [ASSURED] use=1 bytes=761
```

For a closed session, we will see a TIME_WAIT state. This is a post-closed state for this session. After a session has been terminated, the kernel waits, by default, for 180 seconds to ensure that any out-of-order packets that might have been part of this connection are properly sorted out and allowed to reach their destination. Once the timer reaches zero, the connection is removed from the state engine entirely. In this example, the connection has 45 seconds left.

```
tcp      6 32 TIME_WAIT src=172.31.254.2 dst=80.57.62.61 sport=1849 dport=2794
src=80.57.62.61 dst=EXTERNAL_IP_FOR_NAT_CLIENT sport=2794 dport=1849 use=1 bytes=956
```

You might notice that the states listed in these examples are sometimes different from the ones we explained in the first part of the chapter. This is because netfilter and **iptables** are different parts of the whole. **iptables** is a user interface to the netfilter code. Many of the internal netfilter states are not something the typical user will need to manipulate when using the state engine. For instance, when using **iptables**, we do not have to concern ourselves with the SYN_SENT and SYN_RECV states. They don't matter to us. We only care about the beginning or the end of that process. That is—a NEW,

ESTABLISHED, or RELATED connection. For almost every case, those three states are the ones you will use, but in case you want to manipulate packets at some other point along the way, you can use some of the more advanced features of **iptables** to grab these packets as they move through these intermediate states in the netfilter code. More about this subject is covered in Chapter 12, "NAT (Network Address Translation) and IP Forwarding."

There are also extension modules for conntrack that track even more states depending on the protocol. What has been covered here is only a partial list of all the internal states that can exist for the conntrack engine. The important thing to remember here is that for the most part, you don't need to worry about these netfilter internal states. The NEW, RELATED, and ESTABLISHED states will get the work done for you through **iptables**.

There is one other state that we only briefly touched on, the INVALID state. This state is supposed to catch all packets that don't easily fall into the other states; for instance, packets that are out of order or mangled somehow are supposed to be represented as INVALID packets. For the most part, this is true, but in practice it depends on the version of the kernel and the connection tracking code being used. To clarify, there are two different connect-tracking "engines" available for the netfilter subsystem in the Linux kernel. Most users will only use the standard engine, which comes by default in all Linux kernels. There is also an enhanced connection-tracking engine that implements and extends TCP connection tracking based on the article, "Real Stateful TCP Packet Filtering in IP Filter," by Guido van Rooij. This engine is also referred to as the tcp-window-tracking patch. We bring this up because it is possible that a packet might trick the default state engine into thinking it's valid, which is why there is a newer version of the state-tracking engine available as a patch for the kernel. If you are interested in using this patch, you will find information about how to patch your kernel in later chapters. If you have trouble patching your kernel, you can also visit our Web site (www.gotroot.com) for assistance.

On the surface, it appears that the NEW state should do some sanity checking of the packet to make sure it's a proper "new" connection. However, **iptables** has some useful features that make this more complicated than it seems. NEW does not check to make sure the packet is part of a NEW connection in the sense that it's a "new" TCP or UDP connection; instead, it will just assume that any packet that is not assigned to some other state is NEW. This means that for the unwary firewall administrator, the kernel will happily pass a packet that isn't either the beginning of a three-way handshake, a SYN packet, or part of an otherwise existing session. For the average firewall, this is a bad thing. We don't want any old packet coming along and getting passed through as a NEW connection. We usually want to see a three-way handshake or otherwise for our firewall to truly investigate the "newness" of a connection.

This is actually a feature of the firewall that has a practical use. And, no, this is a not a feature in the "it's a bug, but let's call it a feature" sense. It's a darn useful set of behaviors to have in a high-end firewall. For example, assume you have two firewalls for your network and one of them goes down. The one that went down is immediately replaced by the backup or secondary firewall; it simply changes its ips and spoofs its MAC to appear to be the firewall that died. This is called failover, and it's very handy. If **iptables** required a NEW session to fully negotiate its sessions, all the existing connections from the former now-dead firewall would die. They wouldn't work because the firewall would drop them as not being NEW, but as something else. So to give you the ability to do fancy things such as failover, the default behavior is to pick up sessions, midstream as it were, and continue on as if nothing happened.

However, if you don't have this sort of setup (and most people do not), and you are concerned about the sorts of packets that might slip through your firewall due to this feature, SYN-ACK packets for instance, then you obviously want to turn this off. And it turns out that it's a relatively simple thing to do. Just add these rules to the top of your firewall rules before any ACCEPT rules, and you're set.

```
$IPTABLES -N SYN_ONLY
$IPTABLES -A INPUT -p tcp ! --syn -m conntrack \
--ctstate NEW -j SYN_ONLY
$IPTABLES -A FORWARD -p tcp ! --syn -m conntrack \
--ctstate NEW -j SYN_ONLY
$IPTABLES -A SYN_ONLY  -m limit --limit 2/second \
-j LOG  --log-level info --log-prefix \
"SYN ONLY -- DROP "  --log-tcp-sequence  \
--log-tcp-options  --log-ip-options
$IPTABLES -A SYN_ONLY -j DROP
```

The behavior of the state tracking engine can be changed by installing a patch from the netfilter patch-o-matic archives called the "tcp-window-tracking extension." This change causes the tracking engine to maintain state by looking at the TCP window settings of the packet.

The tcp-window-tracking modification to netfilter/**iptables** expands the TCP connection tracking according to the article http://www.iae.nl/users/guido/papers/tcp_filtering.ps.gz by Guido van Rooij. In addition to the extended TCP connection tracking capabilities, it also supports TCP window scaling and SACK.

The next chapter will explore these behaviors and how to configure **iptables** in more depth.

SUMMARY

As you can see, netfilter has the capabilities to control traffic destined to, from, or through the firewall. Indeed, the capabilities extend far past basic firewalling. In later chapters we will discuss mechanisms to use **iptables** to implement anti-virus or intrusion detection rules inside of netfilter, creating DMZs, bridging Layer 2 capabilities, and VPN integration.

Using iptables

PROPER IPTABLES SYNTAX

In our experience, some of the problems with **iptables** that are more difficult to diagnose stem from a lack of proper understanding of **iptables** usage and syntax. As part of the troubleshooting process, make sure you double-check the proper syntax for **iptables** commands and that you understand how the commands are supposed to be used.

It is beyond the scope of this book to document all the switches for **iptables**; however, a few brief pointers should help with uncovering the proper manner in which a command should be executed. The first useful tool is **iptables** itself. **iptables** has a certain amount of built-in documentation that can be accessed by passing **iptables** the -h switch. When combined with module commands or targets, specific information about that module or target may be available. In this example, we are using a patched 1.2.9 **iptables** binary with the fake-source patch added. When the -h switch is passed, along with the specific commands and targets we are interested in seeing documentation about, we would use the following command to access the internal documentation:

```
iptables -j REJECT -h
```

Along with the normal **iptables** command help passed back, at the bottom of the list you may see some text like this:

```
Valid reject types:
    icmp-net-unreachable        ICMP network unreachable
    net-unreach                 alias
    icmp-host-unreachable       ICMP host unreachable
    host-unreach                alias
    icmp-proto-unreachable      ICMP protocol unreachable
    proto-unreach               alias
    icmp-port-unreachable       ICMP port unreachable (default)
    port-unreach                alias
    icmp-net-prohibited         ICMP network prohibited
    net-prohib                  alias
    icmp-host-prohibited        ICMP host prohibited
    host-prohib                 alias
    tcp-reset                   TCP RST packet
    tcp-reset                   alias
    icmp-admin-prohibited       ICMP administratively prohibited (*)
    admin-prohib                alias

--fake-source                   fake the source address with the destination
                                address of the matched packet (useful for
                                port unreachable ICMP message).
(*) See man page or read the INCOMPATIBILITES file for compatibility issues.
```

The proper syntax for this type of documentation request is

```
iptables <command switch> <target> -h
```

This can help with some of the more obscure options and with any custom patches to **iptables** that may not otherwise be documented by the netfilter project. With regard to the netfilter project, there is no better source of information than from the developers that created netfilter and **iptables**. The netfilter website (`http://www.netfilter.org`) contains the most complete set of documentation on **iptables** and netfilter available anywhere. The key lesson to take away from this section is that before you start digging deeper into a firewall problem, first make certain the syntax for **iptables** is correct.

Moving on, one of the more important set of switches to understand the differences between are the -I and -A switches. -I is used to insert a rule into the top of the current chain. The -A switch, unlike the -I switch, appends a rule to current chain. In other words, -A puts the new rule at the end of the chain, and -I puts it at the beginning.

The key thing to stress here is that -I puts rules in before all previous rules, and -A puts them in after. This is because the default behavior of -I is to insert the rule before all other rules in the chain, in what is referred to as "position 1." You can specify the exact position in the chain you want the rule inserted into with -I by passing it an integer with that location. But we really must advise against using the -I switch in this manner. There may be some unique circumstance when you need to do that, but it's a bad habit to get into, and with hard coded numbers, you run the risk of getting out of sync with your other rules. The better habit to get into is to use the -A switch and define your rules in the exact order in which you want the kernel to parse through them. From top to bottom you should have your default deny rules at the end of your list of rules and all your exceptions before these default deny rules.

Using -I prodigiously is a very common mistake made by those new to **iptables**. For instance, adding in a new global DROP rule with the -I switch to the INPUT chain would cause all packets to be dropped; whereas, using the -A switch would just drop any packets not otherwise addressed by your other rules in the INPUT chain before that DROP declaration. -I should only be used if you want to stick something in ahead of rules you have already placed on a system and only if you really know what you are doing. If you are creating a brand new set of rules, again we recommend you always use the -A switch. This will cause the rules to be added to the chain in the exact order in which they are executed whereas with -I, the exact opposite would be true!

With regard to defining a rules position by its number, you can also reference a rule by either its name—or by its number. As **iptables** is linear, each rule added into the kernel is assigned a number either in the order in which it was added, as with -A, or by the position dictated either by default with -I, which is in reverse order, or in explicit order as defined by the user. For instance, suppose you wanted to add a new rule at the top of the INPUT chain as the first rule in that chain and you wanted to reject all SYN packets sent to port 113 on the host. You would use the following syntax:

```
$IPTABLES -I INPUT 1 -p tcp -m tcp --dport 113 \
--syn -j REJECT
```

Because the default behavior of -I is used to insert the new rule into the chain at position 1, then the following command is the same as the previous example:

```
$IPTABLES -I INPUT -p tcp -m tcp --dport 113 \
--syn -j REJECT
```

If you only wanted to add this rule to the end of your current set of rules in your
INPUT chain, you would use this syntax:

```
$IPTABLES -A INPUT -p tcp -m tcp --dport 113 \
--syn -j REJECT
```

In addition to adding rules, it might be necessary to delete or replace a rule in its present location. Replacing a rule is done in a manner similar to the example here, where you
can either select the rule's name or number when replacing it.

```
$IPTABLES -R INPUT 1 -p tcp -m tcp --dport 113 \
--syn -j ACCEPT
```

And to delete the rule, the process is even simpler:

```
$IPTABLES -D INPUT 1
```

Aside from creating rules, you also can create your own chains with **iptables** by using
the -N command:

```
$IPTABLES -N my_chain
```

And much like rules, you also can delete, replace, or rename a chain. Deleting a chain
is accomplished by using the -X switch:

```
$IPTABLES -X my_chain
```

Renaming a chain is possible through the use of the -E switch, as in this example:

```
$IPTABLES -E my_chain new_name_for_my_chain
```

Finally, a default policy can be set for a chain with the -P switch. This allows for the
creation of default behaviors for a chain, perhaps to aid in debugging or to prevent mistakes that might lead to a security breach. For example, imagine that you do not want
your firewall to allow any inbound connections to the firewall itself. This is not to be
confused with forwarding connections, which are not to the firewall, per se, but rather to

some system on the other side of the firewall. To create a default policy to block packets to the firewall, the INPUT chain would have its policy changed to DROP or REJECT:

```
$IPTABLES -P INPUT DROP
```

A few administrative commands with **iptables** that are extremely useful are the list (-L) and zero (-Z) switches. List provides for a means to list the currently loading **iptables** rules on a system; the -Z switch will zero out the counters for each of the **iptables** rules. We will review counters in a moment, but first, to view all of the current rules on your system without counters, your **iptables** command would look like this:

```
iptables -L
```

And your output might look like this:

```
Chain INPUT (policy ACCEPT)
target        prot opt source                destination
RH-Lokkit-0-50-INPUT  all  --  anywhere              anywhere
SILENT       udp  --  anywhere            anywhere            udp
SILENT       tcp  --  anywhere            anywhere            tcp
SILENT       udp  --  anywhere            anywhere            udp
SILENT       tcp  --  anywhere            anywhere            tcp
SILENT       udp  --  anywhere            anywhere            udp
SILENT       tcp  --  anywhere            anywhere            tcp
SILENT       udp  --  anywhere            anywhere            udp
SILENT       tcp  --  anywhere            anywhere            tcp
LOG          all  --  anywhere            anywhere            limit: avg 1/sec burst 5
LOG level info tcp-sequence tcp-options ip-options prefix 'STEALTH -- DROP '

Chain FORWARD (policy ACCEPT)
target        prot opt source                destination
RH-Lokkit-0-50-INPUT  all  --  anywhere              anywhere

Chain OUTPUT (policy ACCEPT)
target        prot opt source                destination
TCPMSS       tcp  --  anywhere            anywhere            tcp flags:SYN,RST/SYN
TCPMSS clamp to PMTU

Chain RH-Lokkit-0-50-INPUT (2 references)
target        prot opt source                destination
ACCEPT       udp  --  localhost.localdomain  anywhere            udp spt:domain
dpts:1025:65535
```

```
ACCEPT     ipv6-crypt--  anywhere              anywhere
ACCEPT     ipv6-auth--   anywhere              anywhere
ACCEPT     61    --   anywhere        anywhere
ACCEPT     udp   --   anywhere        anywhere          udp dpt:isakmp
ACCEPT     udp   --   anywhere        anywhere          udp dpt:4500
ACCEPT     tcp   --   anywhere        anywhere          tcp dpt:ssh
flags:SYN,RST,ACK/SYN
ACCEPT     tcp   --   anywhere        anywhere          tcp dpt:6881
flags:SYN,RST,ACK/SYN
ACCEPT     udp   --   anywhere        anywhere          udp dpt:6881
ACCEPT     udp   --   anywhere        anywhere          udp spts:bootps:bootpc
dpts:bootps:bootpc
ACCEPT     udp   --   anywhere        anywhere          udp spts:bootps:bootpc
dpts:bootps:bootpc
ACCEPT     udp   --   anywhere        anywhere          udp spts:bootps:bootpc
dpts:bootps:bootpc
ACCEPT     udp   --   anywhere        anywhere          udp spts:bootps:bootpc
dpts:bootps:bootpc
ACCEPT     udp   --   anywhere        anywhere          udp spts:bootps:bootpc
dpts:bootps:bootpc
ACCEPT     all   --   anywhere        anywhere          state RELATED,ESTABLISHED
ACCEPT     all   --   anywhere        anywhere
ACCEPT     all   --   anywhere        anywhere
ACCEPT     all   --   anywhere        anywhere
ACCEPT     all   --   anywhere        anywhere
ACCEPT     udp   --   anywhere        anywhere          udp spt:domain
REJECT     tcp   --   anywhere        anywhere          tcp dpt:auth
flags:SYN,RST,ACK/SYN reject-with icmp-port-unreachable
DROP       tcp   --   anywhere        anywhere          tcp flags:SYN,RST,ACK/SYN
DROP       udp   --   anywhere        anywhere          udp

Chain SILENT (8 references)
target     prot opt source           destination
DROP       all   --   anywhere        anywhere
```

Should your **iptables** -L command "hang," it is because **iptables** is attempting to perform a hostname lookup of the IP addresses in your rules. In the example here, there are no IP addresses associated with any of the rules. If you have an IP address associated with your rules and your hostname lookups are hanging or taking too long for your purposes, add the -n switch to the **iptables** command. This switch will tell **iptables** not to do DNS lookups on IP addresses in the rulesets.

```
$iptables -L -n
```

Again, your output should look something like this, but with your rules:

```
Chain INPUT (policy ACCEPT)
target     prot opt source              destination
RH-Lokkit-0-50-INPUT  all --  0.0.0.0/0              0.0.0.0/0
SILENT     udp  --  0.0.0.0/0           0.0.0.0/0           udp
SILENT     tcp  --  0.0.0.0/0           0.0.0.0/0           tcp
LOG        all  --  0.0.0.0/0           0.0.0.0/0           limit: avg 1/sec burst 5
LOG flags 7 level 6 prefix 'STEALTH -- DROP '

Chain FORWARD (policy ACCEPT)
target     prot opt source              destination
RH-Lokkit-0-50-INPUT  all --  0.0.0.0/0              0.0.0.0/0

Chain OUTPUT (policy ACCEPT)
target     prot opt source              destination
TCPMSS     tcp  --  0.0.0.0/0           0.0.0.0/0           tcp flags:0x06/0x02 TCPMSS
clamp to PMTU

Chain RH-Lokkit-0-50-INPUT (2 references)
target     prot opt source              destination
ACCEPT     udp  --  127.0.0.1           0.0.0.0/0           udp spt:53 dpts:1025:65535
ACCEPT     esp  --  0.0.0.0/0           0.0.0.0/0
ACCEPT     ah   --  0.0.0.0/0           0.0.0.0/0
ACCEPT     61   --  0.0.0.0/0           0.0.0.0/0
ACCEPT     udp  --  0.0.0.0/0           0.0.0.0/0           udp dpt:500
ACCEPT     udp  --  0.0.0.0/0           0.0.0.0/0           udp dpt:4500
ACCEPT     tcp  --  0.0.0.0/0           0.0.0.0/0           tcp dpt:22 flags:0x16/0x02
ACCEPT     tcp  --  0.0.0.0/0           0.0.0.0/0           tcp dpt:6881
flags:0x16/0x02
ACCEPT     udp  --  0.0.0.0/0           0.0.0.0/0           udp dpt:6881
ACCEPT     udp  --  0.0.0.0/0           0.0.0.0/0           udp spts:67:68 dpts:67:68
ACCEPT     all  --  0.0.0.0/0           0.0.0.0/0           state RELATED,ESTABLISHED
ACCEPT     all  --  0.0.0.0/0           0.0.0.0/0
ACCEPT     udp  --  0.0.0.0/0           0.0.0.0/0           udp spt:53
REJECT     tcp  --  0.0.0.0/0           0.0.0.0/0           tcp dpt:113
flags:0x16/0x02 reject-with icmp-port-unreachable
DROP       tcp  --  0.0.0.0/0           0.0.0.0/0           tcp flags:0x16/0x02
DROP       udp  --  0.0.0.0/0           0.0.0.0/0           udp

Chain SILENT (8 references)
target     prot opt source              destination
DROP       all  --  0.0.0.0/0           0.0.0.0/0
```

The -L command also has the capability of reporting additional information about the rule, such as how much traffic is being processed by the rule, the aforementioned counters, the number of the rule, and in the most verbose mode very detailed information about the rule. The most common command to pass to your **iptables** is the -v switch along with -L, which will cause **iptables** to report the same information as in the preceding example, along with additional information about the amount of traffic processed by that rule or the rule's counters.

```
iptables -L -n -v
Chain INPUT (policy ACCEPT 78 packets, 4208 bytes)
 pkts bytes target        prot opt in    out   source          destination
 458K  277M RH-Lokkit-0-50-INPUT  all  --  *     *      0.0.0.0/0
0.0.0.0/0
    0    0 SILENT      udp  --  eth0   *      0.0.0.0/0          0.0.0.0/0
udp
    0    0 SILENT      tcp  --  eth0   *

   70 3536 LOG         all  --  *      *      0.0.0.0/0          0.0.0.0/0
limit: avg 1/sec burst 5 LOG flags 7 level 6 prefix 'STEALTH -- DROP '

Chain FORWARD (policy ACCEPT 0 packets, 0 bytes)
 pkts bytes target        prot opt in    out   source          destination
    0    0 RH-Lokkit-0-50-INPUT  all  --  *     *      0.0.0.0/0
0.0.0.0/0

Chain OUTPUT (policy ACCEPT 449K packets, 143M bytes)
 pkts bytes target        prot opt in    out   source          destination
10413  625K TCPMSS      tcp  --  *    ppp0   0.0.0.0/0          0.0.0.0/0
tcp flags:0x06/0x02 TCPMSS clamp to PMTU

Chain RH-Lokkit-0-50-INPUT (2 references)
 pkts bytes target        prot opt in    out   source          destination
12981 2380K ACCEPT      udp  --  *     *      127.0.0.1          0.0.0.0/0
udp spt:53 dpts:1025:65535
    0    0 ACCEPT      esp  --  *     *      0.0.0.0/0          0.0.0.0/0
    0    0 ACCEPT      ah   --  *     *      0.0.0.0/0          0.0.0.0/0
    0    0 ACCEPT      61   --  *     *      0.0.0.0/0          0.0.0.0/0
    0    0 ACCEPT      udp  --  *     *      0.0.0.0/0          0.0.0.0/0
udp dpt:500
    0    0 ACCEPT      udp  --  *     *      0.0.0.0/0          0.0.0.0/0
udp dpt:4500
    0    0 ACCEPT      tcp  --  *     *      0.0.0.0/0          0.0.0.0/0
tcp dpt:22 flags:0x16/0x02
    0    0 ACCEPT      tcp  --  *     *      0.0.0.0/0          0.0.0.0/0
```

```
tcp dpt:6881 flags:0x16/0x02
    0     0 ACCEPT     udp  --  eth0   *       0.0.0.0/0            0.0.0.0/0
udp spts:67:68 dpts:67:68 dpts:67:68
  433K  274M ACCEPT     all  --  *      *       0.0.0.0/0            0.0.0.0/0
state RELATED,ESTABLISHED
10931  676K ACCEPT     all  --  lo     *
    0     0 ACCEPT     udp  --  *      *       0.0.0.0/0            0.0.0.0/0
udp spt:53
    0     0 REJECT     tcp  --  *      *       0.0.0.0/0            0.0.0.0/0
tcp dpt:113 flags:0x16/0x02 reject-with icmp-port-unreachable
  494 23808 DROP       tcp  --  *      *       0.0.0.0/0            0.0.0.0/0
tcp flags:0x16/0x02
   14   979 DROP       udp  --  *      *       0.0.0.0/0            0.0.0.0/0
udp

Chain SILENT (8 references)
 pkts bytes target     prot opt in     out     source               destination
    0     0 DROP       all  --  *      *       0.0.0.0/0            0.0.0.0/0
```

When -vv is passed to **iptables**, the level of detail is simply increased. And a subset of what might be returned would look something like this:

```
iptables -L -n -vv
Chain INPUT (policy ACCEPT 79 packets, 4236 bytes)
 pkts bytes target     prot opt in     out     source               destination
 459K  277M RH-Lokkit-0-50-INPUT  all  --  *      *       0.0.0.0/0
0.0.0.0/0
    0     0 SILENT     udp  --  eth0   *               0.0.0.0/0                0.0.0.0/0
tcp
   71  3564 LOG        all  --  *      *       0.0.0.0/0            0.0.0.0/0
limit: avg 1/sec burst 5 LOG flags 7 level 6 prefix 'STEALTH -- DROP '

Chain FORWARD (policy ACCEPT 0 packets, 0 bytes)
 pkts bytes target     prot opt in     out     source               destination
    0     0 RH-Lokkit-0-50-INPUT  all  --  *      *       0.0.0.0/0
0.0.0.0/0

Chain OUTPUT (policy ACCEPT 450K packets, 143M bytes)
 pkts bytes target     prot opt in     out     source               destination
10414  625K TCPMSS     tcp  --  *      ppp0    0.0.0.0/0            0.0.0.0/0
tcp flags:0x06/0x02 TCPMSS clamp to PMTU

Chain RH-Lokkit-0-50-INPUT (2 references)
 pkts bytes target     prot opt in     out     source               destination
```

```
12985 2381K ACCEPT     udp  -- *     *     127.0.0.1         0.0.0.0/0
udp spt:53 dpts:1025:65535
    0     0 ACCEPT     esp  -- *     *     0.0.0.0/0         0.0.0.0/0
    0     0 ACCEPT     ah   -- *     *     0.0.0.0/0         0.0.0.0/0
    0     0 ACCEPT     61   -- *     *     0.0.0.0/0         0.0.0.0/0
    0     0 ACCEPT     udp  -- *     *     0.0.0.0/0         0.0.0.0/0
udp dpt:500
    0     0 ACCEPT     udp  -- *     *     0.0.0.0/0         0.0.0.0/0
udp dpt:4500
    0     0 ACCEPT     tcp  -- *     *     0.0.0.0/0         0.0.0.0/0
tcp dpt:22 flags:0x16/0x02
    0     0 ACCEPT     tcp  -- *     *     0.0.0.0/0         0.0.0.0/0
tcp dpt:6881 flags:0x16/0x02
    0     0 ACCEPT     udp  -- *     *     0.0.0.0/0         0.0.0.0/0
udp dpt:6881
    0     0 ACCEPT     udp  -- eth0  *     0.0.0.0/0         0.0.0.0/0
udp spts:67:68 dpts:67:68

 434K  274M ACCEPT     all  -- *     *     0.0.0.0/0         0.0.0.0/0
state RELATED,ESTABLISHED
10933  676K ACCEPT     all  -- lo    *     0.0.0.0/0            0.0.0.0/0
    0     0 ACCEPT     udp  -- *     *     0.0.0.0/0         0.0.0.0/0
udp spt:53
    0     0 REJECT     tcp  -- *     *     0.0.0.0/0         0.0.0.0/0
tcp dpt:113 flags:0x16/0x02 reject-with icmp-port-unreachable
  495 23856 DROP       tcp  -- *     *     0.0.0.0/0         0.0.0.0/0
tcp flags:0x16/0x02
   14   979 DROP       udp  -- *     *     0.0.0.0/0         0.0.0.0/0
udp

Chain SILENT (8 references)
 pkts bytes target     prot opt in    out   source            destination
    0     0 DROP       all  -- *     *     0.0.0.0/0         0.0.0.0/0
libiptc v1.2.8.  44 entries, 7776 bytes.
Table 'filter'
Hooks: pre/in/fwd/out/post = 0/0/2068/2364/0
Underflows: pre/in/fwd/out/post = 1920/1920/2216/2556/1920
Entry 0 (0):
SRC IP: 0.0.0.0/0.0.0.0
DST IP: 0.0.0.0/0.0.0.0
Interface: ''/...............to ''/...............
Protocol: 0
Flags: 00
Invflags: 00
Counters: 458725 packets, 277161237 bytes
Cache: 00000000
```

```
Target name: '' [36]
verdict=2880

Entry 1 (148):
SRC IP: 0.0.0.0/0.0.0.0
DST IP: 0.0.0.0/0.0.0.0
Interface: 'eth0'/XXXXX..........to ''/................
Protocol: 17
Flags: 00
Invflags: 00
Counters: 0 packets, 0 bytes
Cache: 00000624 IP_IF_IN IP_PROTO IP_SRC_PT IP_DST_PT
Match name: 'udp'
Target name: '' [36]
verdict=7304

[...]

Entry 43 (7600):
SRC IP: 0.0.0.0/0.0.0.0
DST IP: 0.0.0.0/0.0.0.0
Interface: ''/................to ''/................
Protocol: 0
Flags: 00
Invflags: 00
Counters: 0 packets, 0 bytes
Cache: 00000000
Target name: 'ERROR' [64]
error='ERROR'
```

A tangentially useful command to the -L command is the flush (-F) switch. Flush will simply delete a specified rule. If you do not select a rule, the -F switch will delete all the rules on the system. Keep in mind that deleting rules will not delete chains. Chains must be deleted with the -X switch as explained earlier. As with the -F switch, if you do not specify a chain to delete, -X will delete all the chains.

The last useful switch to understand with **iptables** is -j. This tells **iptables** to "jump" to another chain. This is extremely useful when constructing your own chains, as you can create some logic in your rulesets with different rules triggering different unique chains. For instance, if you created a chain called MY_LOG via this command:

```
iptables -N MY_LOG
```

and your intent was for that chain to log any packets associated with it, you would do this:

```
iptables -A MY_LOG  -m limit --limit 1/second -j LOG  --log-level info --log-prefix
"MY_LOG "
```

Notice that we are using the append command as opposed to the insert command. We could use the insert command here, but we prefer not to as it can create a dangerous habit when you get used to inserting as opposed to appending rules. Insertion can create strange behavior in your rule set, as the logic is inverted (each subsequent rule with -I places itself before all the previous rules). Stick with -A and, as they say, you'll be cream cheese.

Now that you have the MY_LOG chain, you can jump to it from other rules. For example, if you had a rule to detect every time someone SSH-ed into your system, you could jump to the MY_LOG chain to log the connection:

```
iptables -A INPUT -i eth1 -p tcp  -d <your firewalls IP>  --destination-port 22  -m
conntrack -j MY_LOG
```

There are many other switches available for **iptables**, some of which we will describe in greater detail later in the book. It is beyond the scope of this book to cover all of **iptables**, but additional information on this topic is available at our website, www.gotroot.com, at the www.netfilter.org website, and also if installed on your system, in the **iptables** man pages. You can access your **iptables** online documentation by simply running the command man iptables on the system where you have iptables installed.

EXAMPLES OF HOW THE CONNECTION TRACKING ENGINE WORKS

UDP

With the understanding in hand now as to how the netfilter engine specifically works and the proper manner in which to use **iptables**, let's take a look at how the engine works with specific protocols. The first protocol to look at is UDP, which is technically a connectionless protocol. Because UDP is connectionless, it would seem that the firewall would not be able to maintain state on these sorts of connections, but in a limited way it can. Let's take a look at an example.

Recall from Chapter 6 how netfilter tracks a UDP connection. In this example, a client has sent a DNS lookup request to a remote DNS server.

```
udp       17 20 src=10.10.10.2 dst=10.10.11.1 sport=5353 dport=53 [UNREPLIED]
src=10.10.11.1 dst=10.10.10.2 sport=53 dport=5353 use=1
udp       17 20 src=10.10.10.2 dst=10.10.11.1 sport=5353 dport=53  src=10.10.11.1
dst=10.10.10.2 sport=53 dport=5353 use=1
udp       17 20 src=10.10.10.2 dst=10.10.11.1 sport=5353 dport=53  src=10.10.11.1
dst=10.10.10.2 sport=53  dport=5353 [ASSURED] use=1
```

TCP

TCP connections, unlike UDP, are stateful. They consist of a predefined manner of establishing a connection and tearing it down. This mechanism is commonly referred to as the handshaking, which was covered in Chapter 5. Because of its connection-oriented status, a TCP connection has many more intermediate states before it reaches the ESTABLISHED state.

APPLYING WHAT HAS BEEN COVERED SO FAR BY IMPLEMENTING GOOD RULES

Now that we have covered risk management, securing the firewall, problem-solving methodologies, and how netfilter works, it's time to delve into some ideas about how to construct good files rules. One of the first tools you can use are **iptables** policies. **iptables** policies allow a user to set absolute and default rules for chains. For instance, if you set the policy for the INPUT chain to DROP, every packet going to the firewall's interfaces but not being FORWARD-ed by the firewall will be dropped unless you explicitly set up a rule to do otherwise. Policies are an excellent way of sanity checking your rules by defining a default behavior for all your rules—if no other conditions are met. For purposes of security, the default DROP rule for the INPUT, OUTPUT, and FORWARD rules is always recommended.

    iptables is linear—that is, rules are checked in a top to bottom, first inserted into the kernel order. If a rule exists to allow in all traffic to port 23, but a later rule says to block traffic from a specific host, that specific host will still be able to connect to port 23. It's critical then to structure your firewall rules in a carefully chosen order, putting all of your ACCEPT rules at the end of your rulesets so that any explicit and specific DROP or REJECT rules will be triggered before them. One note of caution—don't put your default DROP and LOG rules above your ACCEPT rules; otherwise, nothing will get through your firewall.

To keep it simple, we like to use this layout for our rules:

1. Kernel options
2. TOS rules (Type of Service)
   Examples:

   - MSS/MTU fixes (for DSL, PPPoE, and so on)
   - TOS settings for services such as telnet, ftp, VoIP, and others

3. Explicit drop rules
   Examples:

   - portscan detection
   - Bad packet detection (bad ports, options, and so on)
   - Drop fragments
   - SYN-Flood detection and protection
   - Silently drop packets that are unimportant (SMB broadcasts and so on)

4. Enforcement rules
   Examples:

   - SYN only packets establish NEW connections
   - IP spoofing protection
   - Egress filtering

5. Special rejection rules
   Examples:

   - Send TCP resets for AUTH requests
   - Three-way handshake politeness for spoofed packets

6. ESTABLISHED/RELATED ACCEPT rules
7. SHUN previously detected attack sources rules
8. ACCEPT rules
9. Default drop and logging rules

SETTING UP AN EXAMPLE FIREWALL

Next, we are going to create an example firewall with three interfaces. One, eth0, will be our Internet reachable interface; eth1, our internal interface; and eth2 will be the DMZ. We will document the kernel settings you should implement for this example firewall and will make suggestions on how you can apply these examples to your firewall. After we have finished with the kernel settings, we will move onto specific rules for a simple example firewall.

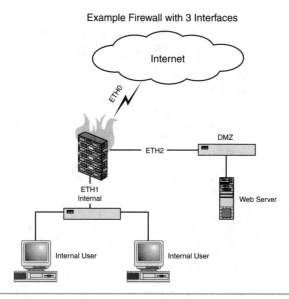

Figure 7.1 Example firewall with three interfaces.

KERNEL OPTIONS

The first task to undertake when configuring the firewall ruleset is to turn on all the options you would like the kernel to use when processing IP packets. The very first thing we recommend is that you turn `ip_forwarding` off. Don't worry—it will be turned on after everything is done. Of course, we will show you where we think it should be re-enabled as well. The point with turning it off is to make sure that nothing is flowing through your firewall when you are changing, flushing, and otherwise mucking with your rules. For extremely complicated rulesets, it can take a few seconds to load all the rules. We've even seen systems with thousands of rules that may take a minute to load. During that time period it's possible that something might slip through your firewall that you would not otherwise allow. The simplest way to prevent this is to turn `ip_forwarding` off while you are loading your rules and to turn it back on only when you are finished. To turn `ip_forwarding` off, change the boolean value from 1 to 0:

```
# Start Section 1
echo 0 > /proc/sys/net/ipv4/ip_forward
```

This next option is dependent on how your firewall gets its IP addresses. If one or more of the firewall's interfaces uses `bootp` or `dhcp` to configure its interfaces, then you need to turn the `ip_dynaddr` option on by passing it the integer value of 1:

```
echo 1 > /proc/sys/net/ipv4/ip_dynaddr
```

Should you require more verbosity with this option, you can pass the value 2 into `ip_dynaddr`:

```
echo 2 > /proc/sys/net/ipv4/ip_dynaddr
```

If all of your firewall's interfaces are assigned static IP addresses, you will want to set this variable to 0:

```
echo 0 > /proc/sys/net/ipv4/ip_dynaddr
```

This following script disables source routing. What is source routing? Well amongst other things, in terms of security, it's bad—really, really, bad. Most firewalls and routers ignore source routing requests these days, and your firewall should too. Source routing is basically a way of dictating what route the traffic will take from the origin of the packet as dictated by the client. This basically means that a client can dictate the specific route to a destination, subverting much of your firewall's purpose. To quote a line from the movie, *Spies Like Us,* "Guidance! Source programmable guidance!"

```
if [ -e /proc/sys/net/ipv4/conf/all/accept_source_route ]; then
  for f in /proc/sys/net/ipv4/conf/*/accept_source_route
  do
   echo 0 > $f
  done
fi
```

This next script will set the firewall not to respond to ICMP redirect requests. If you have multiple routers, or know that you need ICMP redirects, then don't use this script. If you are in doubt, try the script to see if everything still works for you; if it does, then continue to use it.

```
# Do not respond to 'redirected' ICMP packets from gateways
if [ -e /proc/sys/net/ipv4/secure_redirects ]; then
  echo 1 > /proc/sys/net/ipv4/secure_redirects
fi
```

This instructs the kernel not to send ICMP redirect requests—also a bad idea to set if your firewall is acting as a router. Unless your firewall has more than two NICs (Network Interface Card) in it, you are probably not acting as a router and can turn redirects off.

```
# Do not reply to 'redirected' packets if requested
if [ -e /proc/sys/net/ipv4/send_redirects ]; then
  echo 0 > /proc/sys/net/ipv4/send_redirects
fi
```

The other half of redirects is to accept them. That is, some resource on the network can send an ICMP redirect to your firewall telling it there is a new network route to some other device. If your routes are static and the devices handling the routing do not change, then you can safely turn accept_redirects off.

```
#Even more ICMP redirect suppression
# do not accept redirects
if [ -e /proc/sys/net/ipv4/accept_redirects ]; then
  echo 0 > /proc/sys/net/ipv4/accept_redirects
fi
```

We also may not want to respond to proxy ARP requests. Unless you know what these are, you probably do not need them and can use the example script that follows without any problems. Briefly, proxyarps are when a particular machine, in this case your firewall, will respond to ARP requests for other machines. In theory, this can make a firewall appear to disappear from a network. It's also a clever way of getting around to some daunting routing problems with subnetting and protocols that may not work well through the firewall. For most causes, you will not need to proxy ARP requests. Should you wish to learn more about this topic, you can look on our website (www.gotroot.com), or you can read this document, which has more information about the topic, http://www.sjdjweis.com/Linux/proxyarp/.

To turn proxyarp off, just use this script:

```
#Do not respond to a proxy arp  request.
#do  not reply to 'proxyarp' packets
if [ -e /proc/sys/net/ipv4/proxy_arp ]; then
  echo 0 > /proc/sys/net/ipv4/proxy_arp
fi
```

Spoof protection is something near and dear to the hearts of many in the network security world, and fortunately Linux gives us the ability to limit spoofed packets to some extent. The kernel includes a neat little /proc setting that basically tells the kernel not to respond to a packet out of a different interface than the interface from which it was received. This is basically a system for helping to prevent spoofed packets by looking at where, from the firewall's perspective, it expects the packet to come from. With this turned on, the firewall should reject packets that come from outside your protected network that pretend to come from inside. This will help to prevent an attacker from spoofing trusted systems in an attempt to circumvent your firewall rules.

```
echo 1 > /proc/sys/net/ipv4/conf/all/rp_filter
if [ -e /proc/sys/net/ipv4/conf/all/rp_filter ]; then
  for f in /proc/sys/net/ipv4/conf/*/rp_filter
  do
   echo 1 > $f
  done
fi
```

In addition to detecting and stopping spoofed packets, the kernel can also detect what are known as "martian" addresses. Simply put, martian addresses are invalid IP addresses that the firewall should never see. If you tell the firewall to, it will log all those invalid addresses it sees. This can be very useful when tracking down an errant piece of network or equipment or some strange attack on your firewall or the devices it's protecting. As with many of the examples of /proc entries, this one is a simple boolean. 0 turns the logging off, while 1 turns it on. You can enable or disable it for each individual interface, or you can simply use the command that follows to turn it on for all your interfaces. We recommend you use the example here on your firewall.

```
echo 1 > /proc/sys/net/ipv4/conf/all/log_martians
```

The next setting allows you to set the system to not respond to ICMP echo messages set to a broadcast address, otherwise known as a "smurf" attack. Unless you need to be able to ping broadcast addresses on your firewall, which you probably do not, just use the setting that follows. Failure to do so may cause your firewall to be used by an attacker to "amplify" an ICMP flood on another host.

```
echo 1 > /proc/sys/net/ipv4/icmp_echo_ignore_broadcasts
```

If you want your firewall to be stealthy to ICMP pings—that is, to ignore attempts to ping it, you could construct **iptables** rules to accomplish this, or you can use the /proc setting illustrated here to simply ignore all ICMP echo or ping requests. This can be somewhat handy if you don't want your firewall to be easy to find, but keep in mind there are other ways to detect a firewall besides ICMP echo requests. This may buy you some invisibility, if you will, from a less sophisticated attacker, but it's not going to make you completely invisible by any measure. Turning off the ability to respond to ICMP echo requests may also make some network diagnostics difficult and may also make your users more likely to call you with complaints that the firewall is "down" or not responding. Nevertheless, if you want to turn ICMP echo responses off, simply pass 0 into /proc/sys/net/ipv4/icmp_echo_ignore_all as detailed here:

```
echo 0 > /proc/sys/net/ipv4/icmp_echo_ignore_all
```

Sometimes devices like routers will send bogus responses to broadcast frames, which will be logged by the kernel. On a busy network this can quickly become annoying—or worse cause a DoS attack on your **syslog** daemon. Setting this to true (echo 1) will disable these messages from being logged. If you are experiencing a strange network problem, you may want to turn this back on, by passing 0 into

/proc/sys/net/ipv4/icmp_ignore_bogus_error_responses.

Again, to turn logging of these errors off, pass 1 into the same /proc entry:

```
echo 1 > /proc/sys/net/ipv4/icmp_ignore_bogus_error_responses
```

The final section to look at is the network performance settings in /proc. These are recommendations based on the firewalls we have built and should be adjusted, where needed, to fit your unique environment. As they say, your mileage may vary, and these settings are no exception. If you find yourself having trouble with any of these, please refer back to the descriptions in this chapter or, worst case, put these settings back to their default value and check the forums on our website to see what other users recommend (www.gotroot.com).

The first network setting of interest is the TCP FIN timeout setting. This defines the amount of time to hold a socket in the FIN-WAIT-2 status, if the socket was closed by our side. This is part of the final tear down part of TCP session where we send out FIN packet and are awaiting a response from the other side via an ACK response. If the host on the side is broken, is slow, or does not respond, the socket will be held open for a certain period of time to wait regardless of what happens. The usual value is 60 seconds for 2.4 and 2.6 kernel, and was 180 seconds for 2.2. We recommend you set this at 45 seconds, which means the socket will be killed off if the remote host does not finish the tear down in 45 seconds. If you find that you have too many open sockets in the FIN-WAIT-2 state, then you can try lowering this number further. The format for this setting is to pass in an integer value, as in this example:

```
echo 45 > /proc/sys/net/ipv4/tcp_fin_timeout
```

A similar setting worth tinkering with is the UDP connection timeout value. This defines how long the connection tracking engine will consider a UDP connection to be alive. If nothing else comes back within this timeframe, the connection will be removed from the state engine. Again, you can set this value to any integer you like; we recommend it be set to 60 seconds.

```
echo 60 > /proc/sys/net/ipv4/netfilter/ip_conntrack_udp_timeout
```

To help prevent SYN flood attacks, the 2.4 and 2.6 kernels, if compiled with this option, have the ability to send out what are referred to as "SYN cookies." These are basically ACK packets that contain a little cryptographic hash, which the responding client will echo back with as part of its SYN-ACK packet. If the kernel does not see this "cookie" in the reply packet, it will assume the connection is bogus and drop it. The kernel will only send SYN cookies if the SYN socket buffer is backlogged. The intent is to help protect the system against SYN flood attacks. We recommend this be turned on by passing 1 into the /proc/sys/net/ipv4/tcp_syncookies proc entry:

```
echo 1 > /proc/sys/net/ipv4/tcp_syncookies
```

ECN, or Explicit Congestion Notification, is a nifty little extension to IP that is still in the RFC phase and is not an official extension to IP. It basically allows for, as its name implies, a system to explicitly notify a peer that its connection is temporarily congested, which should help with dynamically reconfiguring timeouts, windows, and other aspects of network behavior to compensate for this. However, not all IP stacks know how to deal with this, so if you turn this on you may notice that you cannot connect to certain sites. For this reason, we recommend you turn this off on your firewall.

```
echo 0 > /proc/sys/net/ipv4/tcp_ecn
```

There are many other settings for the kernel—literally hundreds of them—that are documented in greater detail on our website (www.gotroot.com) and many others. Please feel free to visit our website or some of the following for information about other tweaks you can implement in your kernel to change the behavior of your IP stack.

iptables Modules

After the kernel is configured the way we would like, we can then start loading **iptables** modules we might want to use. There are two ways to do this: explicitly, which is the safer and more secure manner of doing this (we will have to decide for ourselves which modules we want the system to use), or we can simply load all the modules we have configured for this kernel. The latter can be just as safe and secure as the former if you know what modules you have loaded on your system. Here is a short little script to automatically load all the **iptables** modules on your system:

```
MODULE_DIR="/lib/modules/'name -r'/kernel/net/ipv4/netfilter/"
MODULES='(cd $MODULE_DIR; ls *_conntrack_*  *_nat_* | sed 's/\.o.*$//')''
for module in $(echo $MODULES); do
  if $LSMOD | grep ${module} >/dev/null; then continue; fi
  if [ -e "${MODULE_DIR}/${module}.o" -o -e "${MODULE_DIR}/${module}.o.gz" ]; then
    echo loading module ${module}
    $MODPROBE ${module} ||  exit 1
  fi
done
```

Otherwise, you will need to load each one explicitly that you want the system to use, for instance

```
modprobe iptable_nat
modprobe ipt_ROUTE
modprobe ipt_REDIRECT
modprobe ipt_stealth
[...]
modprobe ip_conntrack
```

This can be quite a long list (dozens of modules are available), which is why the easier option is to know what is compiled into your kernel and use a script to handle loading everything for you. Another upside to using the script is that it can prevent you from missing an important kernel module; the downside, of course, is that it might load a module you do not want loaded, such as ip_conntrack_tftp for instance.

The preferred method is to explicitly load your modules after you know which ones you need. Loading all the modules, either manually or via our script, can create numerous vulnerabilities for network by allowing certain types of traffic to flow through your firewall that otherwise may be too risky for you to allow.

FIREWALL RULES

After the kernel is properly configured and all the necessary firewall modules are loaded, you can start adding rules into the kernel. As with the order we defined at the beginning of this chapter, we will start with any special rules to affect the shape of packets for performance reasons. One example is to set up your MSS to PMTU clamp rules, as explained in later chapters in this book. We will only briefly touch on the problem they solve here, as it relates to an MTU problem typically encountered with PPPoE (PPP over Ethernet) connections, such as DSL. The symptom is that the connection will stall. We cover this in more detail in Chapter 12, "NAT (Network Address Translation) and IP Forwarding." The point is that you want to put these kinds of special purpose packet manipulation rules at the beginning of your firewall rules so they will always be used. Here is an example set of rules to fix an MTU problem on an example firewall, were it to be using a DSL connection on its Internet interface (eth0).

```
iptables -A OUTPUT -o eth0 -p tcp --tcp-flags \
   SYN,RST SYN -j TCPMSS --clamp-mss-to-pmtu
iptables -A FORWARD -o eth0 -p tcp --tcp-flags \
   SYN,RST SYN -j TCPMSS --clamp-mss-to-pmtu
```

This would "clamp" the Maximum Segment Size (MSS) to the path MTU. This would prevent unnecessary fragmentation in the connection that might cause it to stall.

QUALITY OF SERVICE RULES

Next, we will append our quality of service rules to establish the level of priority certain traffic will get for devices that honor what are referred to as Terms of Services (TOS) settings. These are just examples, but for our firewalls, we like to set telnet and the ftp command channel to Minimize-Delay, which should cause the telnet and ftp command sessions to be a little more responsive when dealing with a saturated network.

```
iptables -A PREROUTING -t mangle -p tcp --sport \
   telnet -j TOS --set-tos Minimize-Delay
```

```
iptables -A PREROUTING -t mangle -p tcp --sport \
  ftp -j TOS --set-tos Minimize-Delay
```

Then we will set the actual FTP-data traffic in such a way that the firewall will try to maximize the throughput of the FTP traffic. Delays are not at issue here; we can live with caching and other tricks that might otherwise make telnet or ftp command channels annoyingly slow or hard to use.

```
iptables -A PREROUTING -t mangle -p tcp --sport \
  ftp-data -j TOS --set-tos Maximize-Throughput
```

If your firewall calls for it, we also like to set up QOS rules for things such as VoIP protocols and any other specialty protocols from devices that need it. In this case, we return to the VoIP ATA. Our ATA uses a bunch of proprietary ports, along with TFTP, to carry out its function. We want everything but TFTP to have its TOS set to `Minimize-Delay`, except for TFTP. We don't mind if TFTP is slow, delayed, lagged, or otherwise adversely effected by other traffic, so we exclude it by using the "!" symbol.

```
iptables -A INPUT -i eth0 -t mangle -p udp    \
  -s 10.10.10.15 ! --dport 69 -d any/0 -j TOS \
  --set-tos Minimize-Delay
```

For the other traffic, you will notice that we explicitly set the destination ports to further refine the use of the TOS settings for this device.

```
iptables -A OUTPUT -o eth0 -t mangle -p tcp \
  -d 10.10.10.15 --dport 10000: -j TOS      \
  --set-tos Minimize-Delay
iptables -A OUTPUT -o eth0 -t mangle -p udp \
  -d 10.10.10.15 --dport 5060 -j TOS        \
  --set-tos Minimize-Delay
iptables -A OUTPUT -o eth0 -t mangle -p udp \
  -d 10.10.10.15 --dport 5061 -j TOS        \
  --set-tos Minimize-Delay
iptables -A INPUT -i eth0 -t mangle -p tcp  \
  -s 10.10.10.15 -d any/0 -j TOS            \
  --set-tos Minimize-Delay
```

We also can set a rule based on the MAC address of a host. In the following example, we are setting a mark rule for the MAC address of a Voice-over IP ATA (Analog

Telephone Adapter). We are setting this mark to be used later on in a QOS example, to allow the kernel to identify the VoIP traffic and other traffic from the ATA for traffic shaping purposes.

```
iptables -t mangle -I PREROUTING -m mac \
  --mac-source $VONAGE_MAC -j MARK --set-mark 1
```

PORT SCAN RULES

Sometimes you will want to detect what are referred to as port scans. These are either attempts to enumerate available services on your hosts or specially crafted packets to subvert your firewall rules to accomplish the same. The first set of rules will attempt to detect otherwise normal traffic that appears to be attempting to map out the services running on the hosts protected by your firewall. The following rules require the PSD (Port Scan Detection) module from patch-o-matic, as this module is not normally included in most Linux distributions.

After you have this module loaded, these rules will give your firewall the ability to detect certain types of port scans and, optionally, to take action when those port scans are detected.

```
  iptables -N PSD2
iptables -A INPUT -i eth1 -m psd -m limit \
  --limit 5/minute -j PSD2
iptables -A INPUT -i eth2 -m psd -m limit \
  --limit 5/minute -j PSD2
iptables -A INPUT -i eth4 -m psd -m limit \
  --limit 5/minute -j PSD2
iptables -A FORWARD -i eth1 -m psd -m limit \
  --limit 5/minute -j PSD2
iptables -A FORWARD -i eth2 -m psd -m limit \
  --limit 5/minute -j PSD2
iptables -A FORWARD -i eth4 -m psd -m limit \
  --limit 5/minute -j PSD2
iptables -A PSD2  -m limit --limit 1/second -j LOG   \
  --log-level info --log-prefix "PSD2 -- DROP SHUN " \
  --log-tcp-sequence  --log-tcp-options              \
  --log-ip-options
iptables -A PSD2 -m recent --set -j DROP
```

There are also types of port scans that are always indicative of malicious intent, as these packets cannot "normally" be produced through standard TCP communication practices. In essence, these are packets that contain bogus or illegal TCP flag combinations, such as a packet with the SYN and FIN flags set and other illegal combinations. First, we create the new chain, PORTSCAN:

```
iptables -N PORTSCAN
```

Then we detect any packets with the FIN, URG and PSH flags set, which is illegal and never happens with normal traffic. Because of this, we want to detect it and then do something about it.

```
iptables -A INPUT -i all -p tcp --tcp-flags ALL \
  FIN,URG,PSH -m recent --set -j PORTSCAN
iptables -A FORWARD -i all -p tcp --tcp-flags ALL \
  FIN,URG,PSH -m recent --set -j PORTSCAN
```

The same is true for other types of packets, such as SYN/RST, which is also bogus, along with SYN/FIN and FIN setting all the packet flags, setting none of the packet flags, and also the "xmas" tree packet flag combination or turning on the URG, ACK, PSH, RST, SYN, and FIN flags. All of these are illegal combinations we want to detect and correct. You also will notice that we are calling a new module, the -m recent module. This module, when used with the –set command, will record the IP address of the source (or destination if used with –destination-ip command) for use by the recent module. We will cover the recent module later on in this chapter, but briefly, it can allow us to temporarily block packets from those sources. If this is not something you want to try, just remove the -m recent –set from these lines.

```
# SYN/RST
iptables -A INPUT -i all -p tcp --tcp-flags SYN,RST \
  SYN,RST -m recent --set -j PORTSCAN
iptables -A FORWARD -i all -p tcp \
  --tcp-flags SYN,RST  SYN,RST -m recent --set \
  -j PORTSCAN

# SYN/FIN
iptables -A INPUT -i all -p tcp --tcp-flags SYN,FIN \
  SYN,FIN -m recent --set -j PORTSCAN
iptables -A FORWARD -i all -p tcp --tcp-flags SYN,FIN\
  SYN,FIN -m recent --set -j PORTSCAN
```

```
# NMAP FIN Stealth Scan
iptables -A INPUT -i all -p tcp --tcp-flags ALL FIN  \
  -m recent --set -j PORTSCAN
iptables -A FORWARD -i all -p tcp --tcp-flags ALL FIN\
  -m recent --set -j PORTSCAN

# ALL/ALL Scan
iptables -A INPUT -i all -p tcp --tcp-flags ALL ALL -m recent --set -j PORTSCAN
iptables -A FORWARD -i all -p tcp --tcp-flags ALL ALL -m recent --set -j PORTSCAN

# NMAP Null Scan
iptables -A INPUT -i all -p tcp            \
  --tcp-flags ALL NONE -m recent --set -j PORTSCAN
iptables -A FORWARD -i all -p tcp          \
  --tcp-flags ALL NONE -m recent --set -j PORTSCAN

#XMAS Scan
iptables -A INPUT -i all -p tcp  --tcp-flags ALL   \
  URG,ACK,PSH,RST,SYN,FIN -m recent --set -j PORTSCAN
iptables -A FORWARD -i all -p tcp  --tcp-flags ALL \
  URG,ACK,PSH,RST,SYN,FIN -m recent --set -j PORTSCAN
```

Now that we have detected all these types of port scans, we will want to do something about it, so we append to the PORTSCAN chain first a logging rule to capture all the information we can about the packet via the -log-tcp-sequence, --log-tcp-options, and --log-ip-options switches, and finally we discard these bogus packets via a stealthy packet DROP rule. Additionally, this rule will be logged to **syslog**, with the log level of info at the rate of one message per second.

```
iptables -A PORTSCAN  -m limit --limit 1/second \
  -j LOG  --log-level info --log-prefix         \
  "PORTSCAN -- SHUN "  --log-tcp-sequence        \
  --log-tcp-options  --log-ip-options
iptables -A PORTSCAN -j DROP
```

BAD FLAG RULES

These rules will drop packets with bad TCP flags, specifically any packets setting the TCP option 64 or 128 in the option field. The logging rule is identical to the rule here, with this being logged to **syslog**, with a log level of "info," and at a rate of no more than one message per second.

```
iptables -N BAD_FLAGS

iptables -A INPUT -p tcp --tcp-option 64 -m recent  \
  --set -j BAD_FLAGS
iptables -A INPUT -p tcp --tcp-option 128 -m recent \
  --set -j BAD_FLAGS
iptables -A BAD_FLAGS  -m limit --limit 1/second      \
  -j LOG  --log-level info --log-prefix              \
  "BAD_FLAGS -- SHUN "  --log-tcp-sequence            \
  --log-tcp-options  --log-ip-options
iptables -A BAD_FLAGS -j DROP
```

BAD IP OPTIONS RULES

This next rule is similar to the one just listed; however, we're looking at the options field in Layer 3 IP packets. This ruleset will drop and log those packets to **syslog** at the rate of no more than one per second. What we are looking for here are packets with either unused flags set or flags that might expose information about your network to an attacker. As with the port scan detector module, PSD, this module also may require you to modify your kernel.

```
iptables -N IPOPTS
iptables -A INPUT -m ipv4options --ssrr -m recent \
  --set -j IPOPTS
iptables -A INPUT -m ipv4options --lsrr -m recent \
  --set -j IPOPTS
iptables -A INPUT -m ipv4options --rr -m recent   \
  --set -j IPOPTS
iptables -A IPOPTS -j LOG --log-prefix          \
  "BAD IPOPTS SHUN " --log-tcp-sequence          \
  --log-tcp-options  --log-ip-options -m limit \
  --limit 1/second
iptables -A IPOPTS -j DROP
```

SMALL PACKETS AND RULES TO DEAL WITH THEM

This ruleset looks at the length of UDP, TCP, and ICMP packets. Packets under the specified length will be dropped. This is OK to do here and won't cause any issues with defragmentation, because real IP defragmentation happens before we get to these rules.

These are dropping intentionally broken packets used for a myriad of nefarious purposes (DoS attacks, and so on).

```
iptables -N SMALL
iptables -A INPUT -p udp -m length --length 0:27 \
  -m recent --set -j SMALL
iptables -A INPUT -p tcp -m length --length 0:39 \
  -m recent --set -j SMALL
iptables -A INPUT -p icmp -m length --length 0:27 \
  -m recent --set -j SMALL
iptables -A INPUT -p 30 -m length --length 0:31 \
  -m recent --set -j SMALL
iptables -A INPUT -p 47 -m length --length 0:39 \
  -m recent --set -j SMALL
iptables -A INPUT -p 50 -m length --length 0:49 \
  -m recent --set -j SMALL
iptables -A INPUT -p 51 -m length --length 0:35 \
  -m recent --set -j SMALL
iptables -A INPUT -m length --length 0:19 -m recent \
  --set -j SMALL
iptables -A SMALL -m limit --limit 1/second -j LOG  \
  --log-level info --log-prefix "SMALL -- SHUN "  \
  --log-tcp-sequence  --log-tcp-options  \
  --log-ip-options
iptables -A SMALL -j DROP
```

RULES TO DETECT DATA IN PACKETS USING THE STRING MODULE

This next rule set requires the string-matching module from patch-o-matic. This is specifically matching strings sent to the system containing known patterns of abuse. The first rule, for example, looks for connections on port 22 that send the string "Version_Mapper," which is a tool used to enumerate services. The second chain, STRINGS2, is applied against the OUTPUT chain. This prevents the firewall itself from sending packets that match these rules. Note that both rules also apply string matching against the FORWARD chains, which handle traffic forwarded through the firewall in a NAT configuration. String matching can be especially useful if you're dealing with some very specific patterns of abuse, such as Internet worms and viruses.

```
iptables -N STRINGS
iptables -A INPUT -p tcp --dport 22 -m string \
  --string '"Version_Mapper"' -j STRINGS
```

```
iptables -A FORWARD -p tcp --dport 22 -m string \
  --string '"Version_Mapper"' -j STRINGS
iptables -A INPUT -p tcp --dport 22 -m string \
  --string '"/bin/sh"' -j STRINGS
iptables -A INPUT -p tcp --dport 443 -m string \
  --string "TERM=xterm" -j STRINGS
iptables -A INPUT -p tcp --dport 53 -m string \
  --string "«Í .a" -j LOG --log-prefix " SID303 "
iptables -A FORWARD -p tcp --dport 53 -m string \
  --string "«Í .a" -j LOG --log-prefix " SID303 "
iptables -A STRINGS    -m limit --limit 1/second \
  -j LOG  --log-level info -log-prefix  \
  "STRINGS -- SHUN "  --log-tcp-sequence \
  --log-tcp-options  --log-ip-options
iptables -A STRINGS -m recent --set -j DROP
```

And now the STRINGS2 chain, which is applied against the OUTPUT chain to look for responses from our firewall in case it's being broken into and an attack has succeeded. The intent here is to block the destination of these packets to prevent an exploit from succeeding.

```
iptables -N STRINGS2
iptables -A OUTPUT -p tcp --sport 22 -m string \
  --string '"*GOBBLE*"' -j STRINGS2
iptables -A OUTPUT -p tcp --sport 22 -m string \
  --string '"uname"' -j STRINGS2
iptables -A FORWARD -p tcp --sport 22 -m string \
  --string '"*GOBBLE*"' -j STRINGS2
iptables -A FORWARD -p tcp --sport 22 -m string \
  --string '"uname"' -j STRINGS2
iptables -A STRINGS2    -m limit --limit 1/second \
  -j LOG  --log-level info --log-prefix "STRINGS2 \
  -- SHUN "  --log-tcp-sequence  --log-tcp-options  \
  --log-ip-options
iptables -A STRINGS2 -m recent --rdest --set -j DROP
```

Again, note that we also set the IP address via the -m recent module, but this time we used the -rdest switch, which records not the source of these packets, as in the previous example, but the destination. Later on in these rules, we'll use the information recorded by the "recent" module to temporarily block packets from this suspicious host.

These are just some simple examples of things you can do with string matching. The strings match is literal and, as of right now, does not understand the protocol it is working against. This means that for some protocols, the literal ASCII string will not work, or it may not even be possible to pull a string out of the communications stream for that protocol. Regardless, strings is a very useful tool for any firewall and because of this, some have even gone so far as to adapt **snort** signatures, an open source network intrusion detection platform (`www.snort.org`) to the **iptables** string format to give their Linux-based firewalls a true intrusion detection capability. One such site is `http://www.cipherdyne.org/fwsnort`.

The author of **fwsnort**, Michael Rash, even has some nifty string rewrite patches for **iptables** that allow you to rewrite the content of some packets on the fly. For instance, imagine you wanted to change every instance of the word foo in an HTTP session to bar. With his patches, you can do that. Here is an example ruleset using his patch:

```
iptables -A FORWARD -p tcp --dport 80 -m string \
   --string "/usr/bin/id" \
   --replace-string "/usr/ben/id" -j LOG \
   --log-prefix "nullify SID 1332"
```

In this case, this rule would rewrite traffic destined for a host on the other side of a firewall, notice the FORWARD rules, which would nullify a specific recon attack by changing the /usr/bin/id command to /usr/ben/id. As /usr/ben/id does not exist, the attack would do nothing, but might appear to otherwise work to the attacker. The attack would appear to complete successfully through the HTTP protocol, and there would be no source IP shunning or TCP resets which might otherwise give away the presence of an intrusion detection and response system, but the attack would still not work in a somewhat stealthy manner. The attack would essentially experience what is known as a "stealthy failure." The attacker or the attacker's program might conclude that the target is not vulnerable to this attack, regardless of what the attacker might infer from this action. The point is that this specific string would be rewritten by the firewall rendering this specific attack inert. As we mentioned, this is a clever and stealthy way of protecting a system without appearing to have done anything specifically to protect it or to have detected the attack. It's also good insurance against a range of known attack signatures. It's sort of a happy medium between just detecting an attack and doing nothing about it in realtime and blocking all the packets from the source of the attack for some period of time. The latter is difficult to implement for many organizations due to false positives, and the former is extremely ineffective when it comes to actually stopping an attack.

As we mentioned with the basic string module, this method, string rewriting, also suffers from the fact that the strings used are limited to protocols that literal strings can be constructed for. Protocol helpers coupled with this technology could help greatly with the translation of the user defined strings to the actual data structure and format for that protocol.

INVALID PACKETS AND RULES TO DROP THEM

As with the content of a packet, we might want to drop a packet because of its headers, because it doesn't match a known connection state, its checksum doesn't match, or something else is wrong with it. **iptables** gives us tools to help with this, the INVALID state and the unclean module. The INVALID state, described in earlier chapters, defines a packet that otherwise does not match the NEW, RELATED, or ESTABLISHED states. The unclean module, considered experimental and temporarily removed from the early 2.6 kernels, is supposed to detect packets with bad header options and other problems, such as bad ports. We don't recommend you use this module at this time.

```
iptables -N BOGUS
iptables -t filter -A INPUT -m conntrack \
  --ctstate INVALID -j BOGUS
iptables -t filter -A OUTPUT -m conntrack \
  --ctstate INVALID -j BOGUS
iptables -t filter -A FORWARD -m conntrack \
  --ctstate INVALID -j BOGUS
iptables -A BOGUS -m limit --limit 1/second -j LOG  \
  --log-level info --log-prefix "INVALID PACKET \
  -- DROP "  --log-tcp-sequence  --log-tcp-options \
   --log-ip-options

iptables -A BOGUS -j DROP
```

If you want to try the unclean module, here is a simple way to add it into your rule-sets. Remember that **iptables** is linear, so if you want the unclean module to check all of your packets, you will need to place this chain ahead of any ACCEPT rules you may have.

```
iptables -N DIRTY
iptables -A INPUT -m unclean   -j DIRTY
iptables -A OUTPUT -m unclean  -j DIRTY
iptables -A FORWARD -m unclean  -j DIRTY
iptables -A DIRTY -m limit --limit 1/second -j LOG \
  --log-level info --log-prefix "UNCLEAN PACKET \
  -- DROP "  --log-tcp-sequence  --log-tcp-options  \
  --log-ip-options
iptables -A DIRTY -j DROP
```

A QUICK WORD ON FRAGMENTS

With 2.4 and 2.6 kernels, fragment reassembly is automatic whenever you use the connection tracking engine or are doing NAT. For that reason, it is not generally necessary to concern yourself with fragments passing through your firewall. However, we all make mistakes, and it's possible the firewall could be started without the connection tracking engine properly initialized, compiled in, or even loaded. Because of this, we like to include a fragment sanity check ruleset to drop any fragments that might try to pass through the firewall. As already stated, this rule shouldn't be triggered if you are using connection tracking, as the state engine will handle fragment reassembly automatically.

The rules outlined as follows should never be triggered unless something has gone horribly wrong, which is why it might be useful to keep it in the rules in case you forget to load the conntrack modules or break your NAT rules. The bottom line is that it can't hurt you to add in these rules if you are doing NAT, connection tracking, or both; it can only help in the worst-case scenario. Remember, with security we are not interested in how a security technology works; we are interested in how it fails. We want to catch and stop the failures in a system, not assume that they won't occur.

```
iptables -N NOFRAGS
iptables -A OUTPUT -p ip -f -j NOFRAGS
iptables -A INPUT -p ip -f -j NOFRAGS
iptables -A FORWARD -p ip  -f -j NOFRAGS
iptables -A NOFRAGS   -m limit --limit 1/second \
  -j LOG  --log-level info --log-prefix \
  "Fragment -- DROP "  --log-tcp-sequence  \
  --log-tcp-options  --log-ip-options
iptables -A NOFRAGS  -j DROP
```

SYN FLOODS

Thankfully there are a number of ways to protect against SYN floods. One we already discussed, using SYN cookies, and the other is to use **iptables** to watch the rate at which SYN packets are flowing in or through the firewall and to throttle those SYNs accordingly. You also can use this method to control the flow of packets to host, to some extent, if your goal is to do more than just limit SYN floods.

```
iptables -N syn-flood
iptables -A INPUT -i eth+ -p tcp -tcp-flags \
  SYN,ACK,FIN,RST RST -j syn-flood
```

```
iptables -A FORWARD -i eth+ -p tcp -tcp-flags \
   SYN,ACK,FIN,RST RST -j syn-flood
iptables -A syn-flood -m limit --limit 75/s \
   --limit-burst 100 -j RETURN
iptables -A syn-flood -j LOG --log-prefix "SYN FLOOD "\
   --log-tcp-sequence --log-tcp-options -\
   -log-ip-options -m limit --limit 1/second
iptables -A syn-flood -j DROP
```

Let's break this chain down. The first part of this chain creates the new chain, syn-flood:

```
iptables -N syn-flood
```

The second and third statements define the specific packet circumstances under which this chain will be tripped. In both cases, the rules only apply to SYN, ACK, FIN and RST packets. And in each case, the chain is applied to both INPUT and FORWARD chains. You will also notice that the rules can only be applied to TCP, as there are no SYN, ACK, FIN or RST packets with UDP or ICMP traffic.

```
iptables -A INPUT -i eth+ -p tcp -tcp-flags \
   SYN,ACK,FIN,RST RST -j syn-flood
iptables -A FORWARD -i eth+ -p tcp -tcp-flags \
   SYN,ACK,FIN,RST RST -j syn-flood
```

Additionally, the interface selected in this example is the eth+ interface, which is a special shorthand for "all eth interfaces." We do not recommend you assign these rules to -i all, which would apply it to all your interfaces, including loopback. That would limit the flow of traffic on your loopback or localhost interface, which could cause problems with your firewall's proper operation. If you need to, you can create specific flow rates for individual interfaces by explicitly defining the interface.

```
iptables -A INPUT -i eth1 -p tcp -tcp-flags \
   SYN,ACK,FIN,RST RST -j syn-flood
iptables -A FORWARD -i eth2 -p tcp -tcp-flags \
   SYN,ACK,FIN,RST RST -j syn-flood
```

With this method, we are limiting the number of SYN packets to 75 per second. This is, admittedly, a very high flow rate, and we recommend you start with this flow rate and work backward until you reach a "low water" mark for your network. Then you can increase it until you are no longer getting any errors. To give yourself a little extra boost in case you underestimated the flow rate for your network, add in the `--limit-burst` <number> option, which gives you the ability to allow the network to burst above your flow limit.

POLITE RULES

This chain politely closes down the other half of a SYN scan and also SYN/ACK scans that might be directed against you. This is a trade-off because someone could portscan us with SYN/ACK scans and might gain some information on our firewall. So these rules incur some risk, and we leave it to the reader to decide if he or she wants to run them. We like to run these on our firewalls to help shut down spoofed connections from other hosts that might be using our IP as part of a SYN flood. It's not really specifically designed to help us, but rather, the victim of the SYN flood. This chain is all about being polite.

```
iptables -A INPUT -p tcp --tcp-flags SYN,ACK SYN,ACK \
  -m conntrack --ctstate NEW -j LOG -log-prefix \
   "reset spoof TWH"
iptables -A INPUT -p tcp --tcp-flags SYN,ACK SYN,ACK \
  -m conntrack --ctstate NEW -j REJECT \
  --reject-with tcp-reset
iptables -A FORWARD -p tcp --tcp-flags SYN,ACK SYN,ACK\
  -m conntrack --ctstate NEW -j LOG -log-prefix\
   "reset spoof TWH"
iptables -A FORWARD -p tcp --tcp-flags SYN,ACK SYN,ACK\
  -m conntrack --ctstate NEW -j REJECT \
  --reject-with tcp-reset
```

ODD PORT DETECTION AND RULES TO DENY CONNECTIONS TO THEM

This next chain requires that you apply the U32 patch from patch-o-matic to netfilter/**iptables**. It allows you to grab chunks of data from a packet and perform a comparison on it. This is similar to the strings module but focuses on the headers.

```
iptables -N ODDPORTS
```

As before, this simply creates the new chain ODDPORTS, which we can then set as a jump point or target for the **iptables** rule.

```
iptables -A INPUT -p udp --sport 2:21 -m recent \
  --set  -j ODDPORTS
iptables -A INPUT -p udp --dport 2:21 -m recent \
  --set  -j ODDPORTS
iptables -A FORWARD -p udp --sport 2:21 -m recent \
  --set  -j ODDPORTS
iptables -A FORWARD -p udp --dport 2:21 -m recent \
  --set  -j ODDPORTS
```

In the rules just listed, **iptables** is being told to detect all connections to ports 2–21 that occur over UDP on the INPUT and FORWARD chains and to jump to the ODDPORTS chain. For our firewalls, we have found that we have to leave port 1 available because some NTP (Network Time Protocol) servers will respond to port 1 with their NTP response.

```
iptables -A INPUT -p tcp --dport 0 -m recent --set \
  -j ODDPORTS
iptables -A INPUT -p tcp --sport 0 -m recent --set \
  -j ODDPORTS
iptables -A FORWARD -p tcp --dport 0 -m recent \
  --set -j ODDPORTS
iptables -A FORWARD -p tcp --sport 0 -m recent \
  --set -j ODDPORTS
```

This is the other half of the previous set of rules. These rules simply detect connections to port 0 and tell **iptables** to jump to the ODDPORTS chain when detection occurs. Finally, **iptables** is told to append the following rules to the ODDPORTS chain, which are to log the connections and finally to drop them.

```
iptables -A ODDPORTS -m limit --limit 1/second \
  -j LOG  --log-level info -log-prefix  \
 "ODDPORTS -- SHUN "  --log-tcp-sequence  \
  --log-tcp-options  --log-ip-options
iptables -A ODDPORTS -j DROP
```

SILENTLY DROP PACKETS YOU DON'T CARE ABOUT

We do this after the sanity checking because it's the "normal" packets we don't care about. A vanilla SMB broadcast, for instance, from a host we normally expect to see this behavior from is something we can safely ignore, but SMB traffic with strange packet flags and other suspicious behavior is something we don't want to ignore. Keep that in mind with these rules, as they will drop packets without logging them.

```
iptables -N SILENT
iptables -A INPUT -i eth2 -p tcp -d <DMZ_IP> \
  --destination-port 139  -j SILENT
iptables -A INPUT -i eth0 -p udp -d <EXTERNAL IP> \
  --destination-port 137 --source-port 137  -j SILENT
iptables -A INPUT -i eth2 -p udp -d <DMZ IP> \
  --destination-port 137 --source-port 137  -j SILENT
iptables -A INPUT -i eth1 -p tcp  \
-s <INTERNAL NETWORK> --dport 139 \
-d <INTERNAL NETWORK BROADCAST>  \
-j SILENT
iptables -A SILENT -j DROP
```

This is just to illustrate that you can "silently" drop packets without logging them—and where we think you should do this in your ruleset. Do it after you detect all the bad and suspicious traffic, or you could be missing something.

ENFORCEMENT RULES

Remember those rules to prevent the NEW state from forwarding packets that aren't technically new? Here are some rules to enforce that behavior:

```
iptables -A INPUT -p tcp ! --syn -m conntrack \
  --ctstate NEW -j LOG --log-prefix "New not syn:"
iptables -A INPUT -p tcp ! --syn -m conntrack \
  --ctstate NEW -j DROP

iptables -A FORWARD -p tcp ! --syn -m conntrack \
  --ctstate NEW -j LOG --log-prefix "New not syn:"
iptables -A FORWARD -p tcp ! --syn -m conntrack \
  --ctstate NEW -j DROP
```

Remember, without these rules it's possible that some traffic could slip through the firewall that you might otherwise want to drop. It is a useful feature that allows the firewall to gracefully pick up connections after a reboot of the firewall or when used in conjunction with another firewall to allow them to act as failover firewalls for each other. This might not be an important feature for your firewall, in which case you should not use these rules.

IP SPOOFING RULES

This rule applies the limit match against packets hitting the eth1 interface with the source IP address of the interface itself. We will log these packets at a maximum rate of one per second to **syslog** as an informational message that says "Spoofing DENY:." Then these packets will be dropped by the final rule.

```
echo prevent IP spoofing
iptables -N ANTI_SPOOF
# your IPs
iptables -A INPUT  -i eth1  -s <YOUR IP>  \
  -j ANTI_SPOOF

iptables -A ANTI_SPOOF    -m limit --limit 1/second \
  -j LOG  --log-level info --log-prefix \
  "Spoofing DENY: "  --log-tcp-sequence  \
  --log-tcp-options  --log-ip-options

iptables -A ANTI_SPOOF   -j DROP
```

EGRESS FILTERING

This ruleset that IP addresses are allowed out using the RETURN setting acts as an exception.

```
echo allow known IP packets out to enforce anti spoofing rules
iptables -N ALLOWED_OUT
iptables -A OUTPUT  -o eth1  -j ALLOWED_OUT
iptables -A FORWARD  -o eth1  -j ALLOWED_OUT
iptables -A OUTPUT  -o eth2  -j ALLOWED_OUT
iptables -A FORWARD  -o eth2  -j ALLOWED_OUT
iptables -A ALLOWED_OUT  -o eth0  -s <EXTERNAL IP>  \
  -j RETURN
iptables -A ALLOWED_OUT  -o eth0  \
-s <INTERNAL NETWORK>   -j RETURN
iptables -A ALLOWED_OUT  -o eth0  -s <DMZ NETWORK> \
  -j RETURN
```

SEND TCP RESET FOR *AUTH* CONNECTIONS

Many services out there will combine the inbound connection to the service with an outbound IDENTD/AUTH request. If we just drop this packet, the server on the other end will sit and wait for a response, thereby making your connections (FTP for example) appear to be slow. By returning a TCP RST/ACK response, you're telling the server making the auth request that you don't respond to AUTH. This should shut down the query on the other end and speed things up.

```
iptables -I INPUT -p tcp -s any/0 --dport 113 \
  -j REJECT --reject-with tcp-reset
iptables -I FORWARD -p tcp -i eth1 -s any/0 \
  --dport 113 -j REJECT --reject-with tcp-reset
iptables -I FORWARD -p tcp -i eth2 -s any/0 \
  --dport 113 -j REJECT --reject-with tcp-reset
```

PLAYING AROUND WITH TTL VALUES

This next example requires the TTL patch from patch-o-matic, which you can find at www.netfilter.org. This patch allows you to manipulate the TTL response values of your packets. This can be useful in doing things such as hiding your firewall from **traceroutes** or hiding the fact that you have hosts behind your firewall. For instance, to confuse classic **traceroute** by adding 1 to any TTL on the standard **traceroute** ports 333434-33542, you would use this rule:

```
iptables -t mangle -A PREROUTING -p UDP \
  --dport 33434:33542 -j TTL --ttl-inc 1
```

To briefly digress on the topic of fooling **traceroute**, there is also a user space program called **countertrace** that can create elaborate responses to traceroutes based on user defined configurations. The author's website said, "**countertrace** is a userland, **iptables** QUEUE target handler for Linux 2.4 kernels running netfilter, which attempts to give the illusion that there are multiple, imaginary IP hops between itself and the rest of the world. The imaginary hops that **countertrace** projects also have the ability to introduce accumulative, imaginary latency."

The URL for **countertrace** is http://michael.toren.net/code/countertrace/README.

If you just want a simple means of tricking **traceroute**, just rely on the rules detailed here. They work like magic.

STATE TRACKING RULES

Now you can add in your ESTABLISHED and RELATED rules. As most packets will fall into one of these categories, it makes sense to put these rules near the top of your firewall rulesets before your other ACCEPT rules. However, we prefer not to put these rules ahead of our sanity checking rules. Remember, **iptables** is linear. Rules are matched in the order from first added to last added, so if you have a rule to drop spoofed packets after your RELATED or ESTABLISHED rules, then spoof detection will not occur on ESTAB-LISHED or RELATED packets. To keep things simple, we prefer to set up our rules using a simple principle, DROP before ACCEPT. We do not set up any rules to ACCEPT packets until we are finished with all of our specifically defined DROP rules. Keep in mind, though, that we are not talking about your final DROP rules—those come last.

```
echo established and related
iptables -A INPUT   -m conntrack –ctstate \
   ESTABLISHED,RELATED -j ACCEPT
iptables -A OUTPUT  -m conntrack –ctstate \
   ESTABLISHED,RELATED -j ACCEPT
iptables -A FORWARD -m conntrack –ctstate \
   ESTABLISHED,RELATED -j ACCEPT
```

STEALTH RULES

This next ruleset uses the STEALTH module from http://www.grsecurity.net/download.php. From the STEALTH module documentation:

> *Enabling this option will drop all syn packets coming to unserved*
> *tcp ports as well as all packets coming to unserved udp ports. If*
> *you are using your system to route any type of packets (i.e., via*
> *NAT) you should put this module at the end of your ruleset, since it*
> *will drop packets that aren't going to ports that are listening on*
> *your machine itself. It doesn't take into account that the packet might*
> *be destined for someone on your internal network if you're using NAT*
> *for instance.*

Based on that documentation, that is why we place these kinds of rules after our state tracking rules. The ESTABLISHED and RELATED rules here will catch all of the NAT packets for us. Everything after that is an unused port and anyone hitting those ports is either confused, running a broken app, or up to no good.

```
iptables -A INPUT -p tcp  -i eth+ -m stealth \
  -j STEALTH
iptables -A INPUT -p udp  -i eth+ -m stealth \
  -j STEALTH
iptables -A STEALTH  -m limit --limit 1/second \
  -j LOG  --log-level info \
  --log-prefix "STEALTH -- DROP "  --log-tcp-sequence\
  --log-tcp-options  --log-ip-options
iptables -A STEALTH -j DROP
```

SHUNNING BAD GUYS

Remember all those rules with the "recent" switches? Well, as we touched on before, that module allows the kernel to remember an address for a period of time and then do something with it. A source or destination address can be added to this special list, which you can reference later on in your firewall rules. One useful trick you can do with this is to temporarily drop, or shun, packets from particular sources and destinations that you detect in other rulesets, such as with the port scan rules or string matching. This might allow you to respond to an attack and block all the packets from source or destination until you can investigate further—or simply for a small period of time, throw the attacker off. Here is an example of such a ruleset that blocks all packets from these recorded IPs for a period of 300 seconds:

```
iptables -N OFFENDER
iptables -A INPUT -m recent --rcheck --seconds 300 \
  -j OFFENDER
iptables -A FORWARD -m recent --rcheck --seconds 300\
  -j OFFENDER
iptables -A OFFENDER -m limit --limit 1/second -j LOG\
  --log-level info \
  --log-prefix "OFFENDER -- SHUN "  \
  --log-tcp-sequence --log-tcp-options  \
  --log-ip-options

iptables -A OFFENDER -j DROP
```

We recommend that until you are comfortable with shunning, you only add these rules after your ESTABLISHED and RELATED rules so that you don't accidentally shun yourself from your firewall or cut off already "trusted" traffic. With these rules added in after the ESTABLISHED and RELATED rules, only new traffic would be affected. In the previous example, as already explained, the shun period is set for 300 seconds—or 5 minutes. You can change this to whatever value you think is appropriate, 10 seconds or even an entire day (86400 seconds) or higher if you like. Our recommendation is not to get too crazy with these numbers; shunning is helpful in the short term, but not so useful in the long term. People can change their IP addresses, so the idea isn't to block someone forever—that would be impossible; they could just change their IP. The idea is to couple this with good signatures on your firewall and to shun the attacker long enough to fool their attack tools and to hopefully stop the attack. Human beings will never be faster than computers when it comes to responding to attacks; shunning buys you time to look into the attack and determine if further action is necessary or if a false alarm has occurred. We realize that for some organizations it might be difficult to trust a piece of technology, your firewall, to make these decisions for you. However, if you have a good response policy and some effective procedures in place so that you can review your shuns within a reasonable amount of time, it can become an extremely useful tool.

ACCEPT Rules

Only now can you add in all your ACCEPT rules. After you have finished with those rules, you will want to add in your default catch all DROP and LOG rule. Remember the cardinal rule, "unless allow, deny." This rule, which is put in at the end of all your rules, accomplishes that.

```
iptables -N FINAL_DROP
iptables -A OUTPUT  -j FINAL_DROP
iptables -A INPUT   -j FINAL_DROP
iptables -A FORWARD  -j FINAL_DROP
iptables -A FINAL_DROP   -m limit --limit 1/second \
 -j LOG  --log-level info --log-prefix "Final DROP "\
 --log-tcp-sequence  --log-tcp-options  \
 --log-ip-options
iptables -A FINAL_DROP  -j DROP
```

And finally, IP forwarding can be turned back on. We always like to turn forwarding off while we are loading new rules because sometimes you can get into a race condition where bad packets might slip through before your rules are fully in place.

```
echo 1 > /proc/sys/net/ipv4/ip_forward
```

SUMMARY

After reading this chapter, you should have a good understanding of the proper order of your firewall rules, some neat tricks you can implement to detect suspicious traffic and attacks through your firewall, and some useful kernel settings to help your firewall to perform more efficiently. Should you wish to explore any of the concepts in this chapter in greater detail, we will refer you again to our website (www.gotroot.com) and the documentation, tools, and forums there.

Finally, remember to construct your rules so that you deny everything by default and to only change your rules to allow traffic through that you can prove you need to let through. Never, ever try to build a firewall that explicitly denies certain things but otherwise allows everything else through. You can't even begin to imagine all the ways a firewall can be breached by applying this method. The golden rule is: "unless allow, deny." Stick with that, and as they say, you'll sleep well at night.

A Tour of Our Collective Toolbox

Every engineer needs tools to solve problems, and with firewalls there is no exception. Thanks to the wonders of open source development, there is a tremendous array of tools at your disposal to help test, debug, understand, and diagnose virtually any firewall problem. The purpose of this chapter is to review and present the tools that we use in this book to help identify and solve firewall problems. We have also included some other tools that we do not directly reference but should be of use.

OLD FAITHFUL

There are a number of tools we have already touched on that we consider to be basic but critical. Even though many readers are already well aware of them and how to use them, we would be remiss if we did not at least list them here. These tools, which have been in use for literally decades, fall into the category of "old faithful" because they can, in extremely short order and with little technical knowledge, tell you a lot about the state of affairs with your firewall and network.

The first is **telnet**. Certainly other tools such as **strobe, nc, nmap**, and others can initiate **tcpconnect** calls, but **telnet** tends to be simple, straightforward to use, and something we suspect many of our readers are already familiar with. If it's not already obvious for what you would use **telnet**, we recommend that you call on **telnet** to help you diagnose quickly if you can connect to a remote TCP server. Again, there are other tools such as **nmap** that can launch multiple connections, using different means of connecting and also can connect to UDP services, but **telnet** still remains the simplest to use in our opinion. No switches or knowledge is required—just the hostname or IP address and the port to which to connect, for example

```
telnet www.gotroot.com 80
Trying 205.241.45.98...
Connected to plesk.shinn.net (205.241.45.98).
Escape character is '^]'.
^]

telnet> quit
Connection closed.
```

This would connect to the HTTP port (80) on www.gotroot.com.

Our next "old faithful" tool is **ping**. If you are not already familiar with **ping**, this tool is used to generate ICMP packets to determine if a remote host is up and if packets to that host are being lost. For instance, as you may already know, to ping a host (in this case 10.10.10.192), you would first ping your own interface to make sure it is up:

```
ping 10.10.100.2
PING 10.10.100.2 (10.10.100.2) 56(84) bytes of data.
64 bytes from 10.10.100.2: icmp_seq=1 ttl=64 time=0.075 ms
64 bytes from 10.10.100.2: icmp_seq=2 ttl=64 time=0.060 ms
64 bytes from 10.10.100.2: icmp_seq=3 ttl=64 time=0.072 ms
64 bytes from 10.10.100.2: icmp_seq=4 ttl=64 time=0.054 ms

--- 10.10.100.2 ping statistics ---
4 packets transmitted, 4 received, 0% packet loss, time 3000ms
rtt min/avg/max/mdev = 0.054/0.065/0.075/0.010 ms
```

After you have determined that your network interface is functioning, you can proceed with pinging a remote host.

```
$ ping 10.10.10.192
PING 10.10.10.192 (10.10.10.192) 56(84) bytes of data.
64 bytes from 10.10.10.192: icmp_seq=1 ttl=59 time=288 ms
64 bytes from 10.10.10.192: icmp_seq=2 ttl=59 time=361 ms
64 bytes from 10.10.10.192: icmp_seq=3 ttl=59 time=321 ms
64 bytes from 10.10.10.192: icmp_seq=4 ttl=59 time=362 ms
64 bytes from 10.10.10.192: icmp_seq=5 ttl=59 time=257 ms
64 bytes from 10.10.10.192: icmp_seq=6 ttl=59 time=278 ms
64 bytes from 10.10.10.192: icmp_seq=7 ttl=59 time=328 ms
```

```
--- 10.10.10.192 ping statistics ---
7 packets transmitted, 7 received, 0% packet loss, time 6008ms
rtt min/avg/max/mdev = 257.770/314.176/362.035/37.688 ms
```

As you can see in the previous examples, the host's interfaces are up. In addition to that information, **ping** also tells us information such as the latency of the connection to the host's network interfaces. That information is provided in the time= field. Each iteration is a specific snapshot of the latency of the connection for that ICMP packet. In the present example, that latency changes slightly between each packet. To determine the total average latency of the connection, you would cancel the **ping** request by selecting Control-C, and **ping** would compute the average time for each packet in the summary statement upon exiting. An example of **ping** in action against the host 10.10.10.192 follows:

```
7 packets transmitted, 7 received, 0% packet loss, time 6008ms
rtt min/avg/max/mdev = 257.770/314.176/362.035/37.688 ms
```

ping can also be used to "flood" a network connection to determine what its network capacity is and to more thoroughly determine if the network is dropping packets, if it's overloaded, or if some piece of equipment along the way is problematic. This setting will send ICMP pings as fast as possible to the host, possibly saturating your network link— so use it with caution. It is, however, a useful tool for determining if you have some hardware or congestion problems that are causing packet loss. To use the flooding capabilities of **ping**, you will need to be **root**, or you can set the SUID bit on the **ping** binary, although we do not recommend doing this with **ping**. It may introduce a security vulnerability.

After you have **root** access on your system, you simply pass ping the -f flag as in the following example:

```
ping -f 10.10.10.192
PING 10.10.10.192 (10.10.10.192) 56(84) bytes of data.
..........................................................
--- 10.10.10.192 ping statistics ---
79 packets transmitted, 17 received, 78% packet loss, time 1204ms
rtt min/avg/max/mdev = 238.304/643.103/955.894/246.771 ms, pipe 62, ipg/ewma
15.446/722.229 ms
```

As you can see in this example, the target host 10.10.10.192 lost 78% of the packets sent to it. That tells us that something is wrong with the connection to that host, as 78% is an extremely high number of lost packets.

ping also can be used to determine the route a packet takes as it moves to its target. Again using 10.10.10.192 as an example, **ping** will be used to determine the route:

```
ping -R 10.10.10.192
PING 10.10.10.192 (10.10.10.192) 56(124) bytes of data.
64 bytes from 10.10.10.192: icmp_seq=1 ttl=59 time=225 ms
NOP
RR:     10.10.100.2
        10.10.10.253
        10.10.10.192

64 bytes from 10.10.10.192: icmp_seq=2 ttl=59 time=231 ms
NOP     (same route)
64 bytes from 10.10.10.192: icmp_seq=3 ttl=59 time=241 ms
NOP     (same route)
64 bytes from 10.10.10.192: icmp_seq=4 ttl=59 time=243 ms
NOP     (same route)
64 bytes from 10.10.10.192: icmp_seq=5 ttl=59 time=201 ms
NOP     (same route)
64 bytes from 10.10.10.192: icmp_seq=6 ttl=59 time=210 ms
NOP     (same route)
64 bytes from 10.10.10.192: icmp_seq=7 ttl=59 time=225 ms
NOP     (same route)
64 bytes from 10.10.10.192: icmp_seq=8 ttl=59 time=194 ms
NOP     (same route)

--- 10.10.10.192 ping statistics ---
8 packets transmitted, 8 received, 0% packet loss, time 7008ms
rtt min/avg/max/mdev = 194.399/221.710/243.789/16.886 ms
```

ping will also do some sanity checking on the reply packets for you. It will check for duplicate and damaged packets. If **ping** reports a duplicate packet, this might indicate that there is a link level problem somewhere in the route between your host and the remote host. Duplicate packets should never occur normally, but low numbers of them are not necessarily an indication of a serious problem. Unlike duplicate packets, damaged packets are always a sign of something serious being wrong in the network patch. Damaged packets only occur when a device is badly mangling the data moving through it. If you detect damaged packets, you should **traceroute** the connection and begin testing each device along the path, from multiple hosts, to determine which one is malfunctioning.

If you look at the main pages for **ping**, you will see a number of other switches for ping to control things such as the source IP address for ping, interval, padding, and other potentially useful options. **ping** is also discussed in more detail in the next chapter, "Diagnostics."

SNIFFERS

Sniffers are arguably one the most important tool sets in any network engineer's toolkit. Network sniffers are some of the first tools we use when we're debugging firewalls or just networks in general. They give visibility into the network itself in ways that host-based tools on the firewall or end nodes can't. You might read that your firewall rules are supposed to do one thing, but until you get down and look with a sniffer, there's no way to independently validate what your packets are doing. We can't tell you how many times by using a sniffer we've discovered some PEBKAC (Problem Exists Between Keyboard and Chair) that was being blamed on the firewall (that is, pointing to a nonexistent DNS server). We regularly use sniffers such as **tcpdump** and **ethereal** on both the firewall and client systems to watch sessions from source to destination and independently verify that our rules are, in fact, doing what we expect them to do. This is especially handy when attempting to debug bizarre VPN issues through NAT firewalls.

tcpdump is a command line network sniffer based on the **libpcap** library and is available for nearly every operating system under the sun. This is the defacto standard sniffer and comes with nearly every Linux distribution these days. Assuming, by some freak chance, that your distribution does not come with **tcpdump**, you can find it at `http://www.tcpdump.org/`.

Whereas **tcpdump** is nice, powerful, and comes with nearly every Linux distribution, **ethereal** (`http://www.ethereal.com`) is still our favorite network sniffer. It includes both a graphical and command line sniffer (`tethereal`), supports numerous protocol decoders, is available for both Windows and Linux, and can use data captured from **tcpdump**. One especially great feature with the command line version of **ethereal** (`tethereal`), is the ability to format the output like other command line sniffers, including **tcpdump** and Sun Microsystem's default sniffer, **snoop**.

For protocol level debugging, we highly recommend **ngrep** (`http://ngrep.source-forge.net/`), written by a good friend of ours, Jordan Ritter. **ngrep** is a network version of the Unix command, `grep`, which makes it very useful for debugging either protocol-level problems like you'd find in an instant messaging or our personal favorite, string matching firewall rules. We discuss string matching later in the book, but in essence, think about implementing Anti-Virus or Intrusion Detection rules in your firewall. **ngrep** is a good way to have an independent mechanism for debugging when those rules fire.

```
D</font></h3><font face="arial">.<H3>KIAD</H3>.<P>The most recent METAR obs
ervation from <B>KIAD</B> in our system was generated at the source at:</P>
.<P><FONT COLOR="#48D1CC"><B>.2004/04/19 19:51. UTC.</B></FONT></P>.<P>The
observation is:</P>.</font>.<font face="courier" size = "5">.KIAD 191951Z 2
1015G23KT 10SM FEW070 SCT100 BKN200 31/09 A2999 RMK A02 SLP151 T03110089..<
/font>.<hr>..</FONT></TT></P>.</td>.          </tr>.          </table>.</tabl
e>.<!-- footer -->.<table width="80%" cellspacing="2" cellpadding="2" borde
r="0">.  <tr>  .    <td colspan="3">  .        <hr>..    </td>.  </tr>.  <tr va
lign="TOP">  .    <td class="gray">  <a href="http://www.doc.gov"><span class
="gray">US Dept  .


T 205.156.51.200:80 -> 192.168.32.190:37002 [AFP]
of Commerce</span></a><br>.      <a href="http://www.noaa.gov"><span class=
"gray">National Oceanic and Atmospheric .      Adminstration</span></a><br>
..      National Weather Service<br>.      Office of the Chief Information
Officer (OCIO13)<br>..        1325 East West Highway<br>.      Silver Spring,
  MD 20910<br>.      Page last modified: May 23, 2003<br>.      Page Author:
  <a href="mailto:nws.isg.gov"><span class="gray">Internet .      Services G
roup</span></a></td>..    <td><a href="http://weather.gov/disclaimer.html">
<span class="gray">Disclaimer</span></a><br>.      <a href="http://weather.
gov/feedback.shtml"><span class="gray">Feedback</span></a> </td>..    <td a
lign="right"><a href="http://weather.gov/notice.html"><span class="gray">Pr
ivacy Notice</span></a><br>.      <a href="http://weather.gov/credits.html"
><span class="gray">Credits</span></a> </td>.  </tr>..</table>......</body>
```

Figure 8.1   A **ngrep** capture of a weather-reporting applet querying an external server for updates.

SSLdump (`http://www.rtfm.com/ssldump/`) is a network protocol analyzer that can decode SSLv3 and TLS connections and will display them in text form via **stdout**. This is handy because it allows you to pipe the rules to something else. We use **SSLdump** for breaking down SSL connections, whether for standard web traffic or other protocols we're encapsulating in an SSL session (SSL POP, SSL IMAP, etc.). Assuming you have the correct keys, you can also use **SSLdump** to look inside of an SSL encrypted session.

This is especially useful for debugging MTU issues that will pop up from time to time on DSL or multi-encapsulated sessions. **SSLdump** gives you visibility into the SSL session itself, to pick up potential error conditions that would not be visible through a regular sniffer.

```
root@winona:~
File   Edit   View   Terminal   Go   Help
sshinn@winona:~                              root@winona:~
3  2   0.3152 (0.2014)   S>C   Handshake
         ServerHello
           Version 3.1
           session_id[32]=
              3a 4c 58 81 5d 03 f2 55 6b ea 54 24 04 a1 ff d7
              b4 74 c8 5c 19 c8 82 92 d1 a1 2e cb 94 4c 1c 21
           cipherSuite            Unknown value 0x39
           compressionMethod                 NULL
3  3   0.3152 (0.0000)   S>C   ChangeCipherSpec
3  4   0.3152 (0.0000)   S>C   Handshake
3  5   0.3168 (0.0015)   C>S   ChangeCipherSpec
3  6   0.3168 (0.0000)   C>S   Handshake
3  7   0.3168 (0.0000)   C>S   application_data
2  8   0.5701 (0.2701)   S>C   application_data
2  9   0.5716 (0.0014)   S>C   application_data
2      0.5716 (0.0000)   S>C   TCP FIN
2 10   0.5767 (0.0051)   C>S   Alert
2      0.5771 (0.0004)   C>S   TCP FIN
3  8   0.4625 (0.1457)   S>C   application_data
3  9   0.4636 (0.0011)   S>C   application_data
3      0.4638 (0.0001)   S>C   TCP FIN
3 10   0.4642 (0.0004)   C>S   Alert
3      0.4644 (0.0002)   C>S   TCP FIN
```

Figure 8.2   An **ssldump** capture of an HTTPS connection to a website.

ANALYZING TRAFFIC UTILIZATION

Sometimes the problems in the network are not that you cannot get into or out of a network; rather, it's the performance. One of the most common issues we've found that cause this problem are systems that are consuming vast amounts of network resources, such as numerous streaming audio or video users, distributed denial of service attack zombies, or just a large download in progress. Finding the source of bandwidth consumption can be time-consuming, and if other firewalls or NAT devices are involved—like a great big game of network hide-and-go-seek.

etherape (`http://etherape.sourceforge.net/`) is a visualization tool for network data. It's a highly useful tool for looking at just how much and what kind of traffic systems are attempting to send information through your firewall. Unlike some of the other command line tools, **etherape** is entirely graphic, so piping anything from **etherape** to something else is out of the question. We're big CLI fans, but we like **etherape** because it's a good visualization tool—it's good for smaller networks or low traffic segments. If you are familiar with **etherman**, you will recognize **etherape** right away.

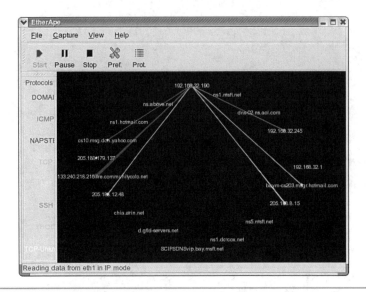

Figure 8.3   etherape in visualizing the traffic for the system 192.168.32.190.

We use **etherape** for a quick-and-dirty look at what kind of traffic is pulsing through the firewall and where. It's very easy to get an idea of what is going through the firewall in realtime. However, it's not very good for long-term trending. If you want to spot who's slowing down your network quickly, this is the first tool we'd try.

Like the process monitoring command, **top**, **iftop** (http://www.ex-parrot.com/~pdw/iftop/) monitors what systems are using the bandwidth on your system. To use **iftop**, you designate an interface for it to listen on, and **iftop** will display the current bandwidth usage by a pair of hosts in a **top**-like format. This can really help isolate network utilization problems.

iftop is the second line tool if you don't have an X11R6 Windowing system to run **etherape**, and you can handle finding a system by wading through a lot of output (don't worry—it does sort). **iftop** will help you find out just who is using the most traffic through your firewall.

tcprack (http://www.rhythm.cx/~steve/devel/tcptrack/) is also a sniffer, much like **iftop**. Its chief difference from **iftop** is that it displays the connection state information in a more "technically" friendly manner. **iftop** leans more towards the graphical. Each has its place, depending on what you are trying to accomplish. For instance, we like to use **iftop** to determine how much bandwidth a particular connection is using when doing "off the cuff" checks when we can't use **etherape**. An example might be the age old question, "Why is my connection so slow?" **iftop** can be really handy for this sort of quick visualization of a real-time connection; whereas, we tend to use **tcptrack** when we are interested in the state of a connection.

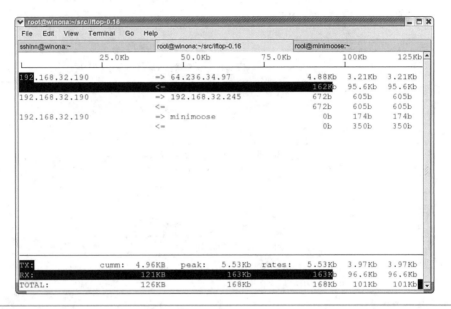

Figure 8.4   **iftop** displaying the traffic for the system 192.168.32.190 without host port information displayed. This is an aggregate display of the bandwidth used by the host pairs. If you want more detailed information, such as the ports in use, **iftop** can display that information as well.

NETWORK TRAFFIC ANALYZERS

When running a firewall(s) over time, good trending information will give you the visibility into identifying long-term problems. A really good example of this is an ISP where we had collocated some servers. Their network was misconfigured in such a way that other systems were dumping traffic onto the external segment on which our firewall was running, in turn charging us for traffic we weren't using. With accurate data from **vnstat**, we were able to demonstrate just how much traffic was really being consumed and were able to reap a considerable refund on our bill.

vnstat (`http://humdi.net/vnstat/`) is a trending tool. It will, when invoked, maintain a daily log of all the traffic it sees on a given interface. **vnstat** can, of course, look at more than one interface, but you have to designate the interface(s) to monitor. Unlike some of the sniffer tools that accomplish the same, **vnstat** works complete from /proc, meaning that it can be run as a nonpriviliged user, which is why we prefer this tool over other network traffic analyzers. Anytime you can get the same results without needing privileged access is a very good thing.

Here is an example of **vnstat** output from one of our firewalls. Run a 2.4 kernel with **openswan** installed and IPSEC in use:

```
$ vnstat
                   rx      /     tx     /    total   /  estimated
  eth0:
     yesterday   26.76 MB  /   56.04 MB  /   82.80 MB
         today   47.40 MB  /   21.87 MB  /   69.28 MB  /    140 MB

  eth1:
     yesterday   1,044 MB  /   96.68 MB  /   1,141 MB
         today  543.30 MB  /   79.83 MB  /  623.13 MB  /  1,295 MB

  ipsec0:
     yesterday      0 MB   /      0 MB   /      0 MB
         today      0 MB   /      0 MB   /      0 MB   /      0 MB

  ipsec1:
     yesterday   8.29 MB   /   34.99 MB  /   43.29 MB
         today   4.19 MB   /   10.48 MB  /   14.68 MB  /     28 MB
```

USEFUL CONTROL TOOLS

cutter (http://www.lowth.com/cutter/) allows you to abort connections routed over your firewall by using the FIN-ACK-RST technique to close connections. Let's say you want to cut off a specific SSH connection to a specific host—but not all traffic to the host. This tool will allow you to just shutdown the connection(s) that you want without affecting any other traffic to the host. **cutter** is purely an action-oriented tool. It will not tell you anything about a connection or your network, except to let you know that it sent the RST or if the connection does not exist.

Let's say we want to cut off all connections to the host 205.241.45.82. With **cutter**, this process is very simple and straightforward:

```
cutter 205.241.45.82
For connection 10.10.10.8:39010 -> 205.241.45.82:22
        sending RST from 205.241.45.82:22 to 10.10.10.8:39010
```

```
        sending RST from 68.100.73.75:39010 to 205.241.45.82:22
For connection 10.10.10.8:56690 -> 205.241.45.82:22
        sending RST from 205.241.45.82:22 to 10.10.10.8:56690
        sending RST from 68.100.73.75:56690 to 205.241.45.82:22
```

You also can be more specific, such as

```
cutter 68.100.73.75 205.241.45.82
```

which would only RST the connections between these two hosts. You also can specify the exact ports you want to target, further narrowing the scope of the connections you want to close down.

```
cutter 68.100.73.75 22 205.241.45.82 58099
```

In the previous example, only a very specific connection, that initiated from 205.241.45.82 to the SSH service running on 68.100.73.75, would be closed.

NETWORK PROBES

tcptraceroute (`http://michael.toren.net/code/tcptraceroute/`) is what its name sounds like, a **traceroute** that can use **tcp**. As a brief refresher, recall that regular **traceroute** sends out ICMP ECHO packets or UDP packets to determine the route a packet takes to get to a destination. Because many firewalls block ICMP and certain UDP ports, such as **traceroute** ports, there is a need for something that can probe the route of a packet despite these limitations…enter **tcptraceroute**.

Here is an example output:

```
tcptraceroute www.gotroot.com
Selected device ppp0, address 166.180.32.200 for outgoing packets
Tracing the path to www.gotroot.com (205.241.45.98) on TCP port 80, 30 hops max
 1  * * *
 2  * * *
 3  * * *
 4  * * *
 5  65.sub-66-174-104.myvzw.com (66.174.104.65)  148.481 ms  142.835 ms  137.663 ms
 6  sl-gw23-pen-1-0-1.sprintlink.net (144.228.179.73)  142.666 ms  130.920 ms  141.407
ms
 7  sl-bb25-pen-0-5.sprintlink.net (144.232.5.29)  105.704 ms  129.811 ms  132.654 ms
 8  sl-gw1-pen-10-0.sprintlink.net (144.232.5.6)  151.633 ms  137.984 ms  125.672 ms
```

```
 9  sl-twora-3-1.sprintlink.net (144.228.116.146)  137.638 ms
    sl-twora-3-0.sprintlink.net (144.223.22.62)  206.195 ms
    sl-twora-3-1.sprintlink.net (144.228.116.146)  343.609 ms
10  plesk.shinn.net (205.241.45.98) [open]  135.099 ms  183.420 ms  165.599 ms
```

The astute reader will note that in the previous example, a destination port was not set. The default is port 80, which, being one of the more common services running on the Internet, seems sane enough. You also can designate a source and/or destination port for **tcptraceroute** to further get around any firewall rules that may be preventing a successful trace of the packet's route. Here is a simple example:

```
tcptraceroute -p 1000 www.gotroot.com 22
Warning: --track-id implied by specifying the local source port
Selected device ppp0, address 166.180.32.200, port 1000 for outgoing packets
Tracing the path to www.gotroot.com (205.241.45.98) on TCP port 22, 30 hops max
 1  * * *
 2  * * *
 3  * * *
 4  * * *
 5  65.sub-66-174-104.myvzw.com (66.174.104.65)  100.426 ms  152.877 ms  274.671 ms
 6  sl-gw23-pen-1-0-1.sprintlink.net (144.228.179.73)  224.906 ms  238.076 ms  147.663
ms
 7  sl-bb25-pen-0-5.sprintlink.net (144.232.5.29)  123.684 ms  131.316 ms  129.185 ms
 8  sl-gw1-pen-10-0.sprintlink.net (144.232.5.6)  219.549 ms  132.361 ms  99.711 ms
 9  sl-twora-3-1.sprintlink.net (144.228.116.146)  156.652 ms
    sl-twora-3-0.sprintlink.net (144.223.22.62)  116.261 ms  132.005 ms
10  plesk.shinn.net (205.241.45.98) [closed]  107.728 ms  131.536 ms  158.638 ms
```

PROBING TOOLS

nmap (http://www.insecure.org) is a highly advanced port scanner with OS detection capabilities, banner grabbing, IDS evasion, and network discovery capabilities—among all the other wonderful features this tool provides. Besides being a nifty security tool, **nmap** is also a good network diagnostics tool. It gives the operator the ability to test remote connections via a number of different means, such as opening connections without normal three-way handshakes. We cover using **nmap** in more detail later in the book. Suffice it to say, a port scanner is the ideal tool to quickly verify what kinds of traffic can pass through firewall filter rules (in either direction!).

Following is a brief teaser on **nmap**. To quickly scan a system to determine if any ports are open, you can use this simple command:

```
nmap -sS <host name, IP, or network address>
```

This would launch what is referred to as a "SYN" scan against the host or network. This is basically a "half open" scan, if you recall from Chapter 5, "The OSI Model: Start from the Beginning." This would start the first part of the TCP connection by sending the SYN request to the host or hosts. If there were anything listening on that port, it would reply with an ACK. If nothing were there, the host could reply with an RST (this is what happens when you use a -j REJECT action with your rules), or it could simply not reply at all (such as what happens when you use a -j DROP action with your firewall rules). **nmap** then pulls all this information together and then tells you which ports are open.

Another simple and brief foray into **nmap** would involve how to test a specific port. You can do this with the following command:

```
nmap -sS -p 22 <host name, IP, or network address>
```

This would cause **nmap** to test only one port, 22, or the SSH port, to see if the service was open to the host doing the testing. You also can perform other types of tests with **nmap**, such as **tcp** connect scans, with the -sT switch instead of the -sS switch. This would carry out a full three-way handshake before reporting any port as being open—and other types of scans as well. We will explore the use of **nmap** with firewalls in Chapter 10, "Testing Your Firewall Rules (for Security!)."

FIREWALL MANAGEMENT AND RULE BUILDING

Of course when it comes to managing multiple or extremely complex firewall environments, some of the goals are automating away the drudgery and hopefully eliminating "fat-finger" mistakes in firewall rules. While not as flexible as creating your own rules by hand, these tools go a long way in abstracting away the vast majority of the situations you will run into when building and integrating several firewalls together.

ISCS, available from http://iscs.sourceforge.net/, is probably one of the more exciting open source projects we've run into in a while. ISCS (Integrated Secure Communications System) is a management infrastructure for firewalls, VPN's, PKI, and eventually IDS systems such as **snort**. When you're creating a large network of multiple VPN's, distributed DHCP servers, hundreds of firewalls, and a Public Key Infrastructure (PKI), this is the kind of tool you're not going to be able to live without.

If you're only running a single firewall, ISCS is not really going to be all that useful to you. However, if you're in a multiple firewall environment where you need to compartmentalize departments from one another (an environment where cheap Linux firewalls excel!) or perhaps a business with offices distributed all over a region or even the world, ISCS provides a great interface to create and manage a distributed infrastructure.

The following screenshot is just one example of a business with multiple departments and the access policies between each group, in this case, a default ALLOW policy. You can see how quickly you could use this system to compartmentalize different departments or regions from one another—or perhaps even just specific services, such as filtering common worm ports between departments, a dirt cheap and highly effective method of defending large networks against worm infections.

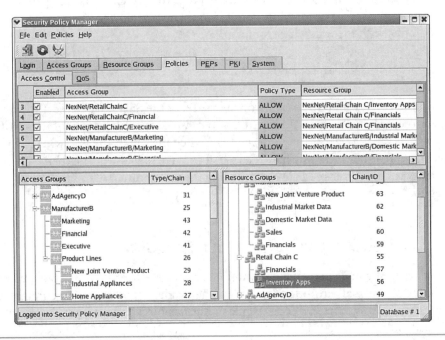

Figure 8.5   Graphic depicting the **iscs** interfaces' visualization of a default allow policy.

ISCS provides a very reliable mechanism for rolling out an initial deployment of internal firewalls into a business for the first time, and frankly this is probably one of the most important uses for low cost, highly configurable devices such as a Linux firewall. If you're in an environment where you're considering (or presenting!) the use of Linux firewalls, this is one potential way of demonstrating a low-impact rollout of firewall devices—for example, deploying multiple internal Linux firewalls as primarily a worm-defense system. Over time, more stringent firewall rules could be applied to restrict access between networks (or Quality of Service...ISCS does that too!). This is a far lower impact strategy than implementing a strict firewall policy from the get-go, which while more secure, is typically politically sensitive or even more likely, prone to cause issues with your users due to some unknown network behavior. This is just one example of where we used ISCS to save both time and money—and it worked.

Of course, you'll also run into environments where you have a mix of firewalls and don't need the management infrastructure of something as powerful as ISCS. That's where Firewall Builder (**fwbuilder**) comes in.

fwbuilder (`http://www.fwbuilder.org/`) is a firewall rule generation interface that supports both open source (Linux, BSD) and commercial firewalls (Cisco PIX). It's a graphical front end that allows you to quickly create complex firewall rule policies. Until we discovered ISCS, we used **fwbuilder** for large corporate rollouts, and we still do for what we call the "Diet-Coke" firewall implementations, "Just one firewall! Not enough for ISCS!"

Obviously, this tool is another X11-based interface for rule generation. It's absolutely fantastic when you're faced with the problem of creating and maintaining rules on a Linux firewall in conjunction with another firewall (like a PIX, they're everywhere). ISCS, like **fwbuilder**, can control the rules on multiple types of firewalls, not just Linux-based firewalls. This tool also includes a Druid, an open source speak for what Windows users would call a "wizard" for rapidly creating a basic firewall ruleset. In addition, there is a drag-and-drop interface for more common rules such as IPSEC or Voice-over IP, for example.

The open source community is not the only source of useful technologies to help you with the process of managing and troubleshooting your firewalls. However, we chose to cover only those technologies we felt would always be within the reach of all our readers, so the focus will be on open source tools. Additionally, we have not been found wanting for lack of commercial tools. We have not encountered any problem we could not diagnose and resolve through the sole use of open source tools.

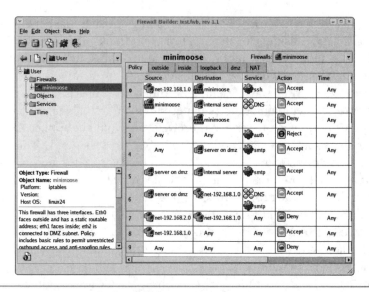

Figure 8.6   From the **fwbuilder** website documentation.

With that said, we don't want to diminish the efforts of the many fine companies out there that make useful tools that may assist you as well in your troubleshooting efforts. There are many excellent commercial software packages and tools that also can help in this regard, and we leave it as an exercise for the reader to explore these alternatives.

You can find all the tools we use in this book, plus some other useful tools for other system-related tasks, on our website (www.gotroot.com) and also on our FTP server, ftp.gotroot.com.

Summary

As we mentioned at the beginning of the chapter, your best tool for diagnostics is a good sniffer. About 80% of our firewall work is done with a sniffer, and even in those situations where the sniffer isn't germane to the topic (writing firewall rules, for example), it always shows up in the verification phase (you did remember to test those rules right?).

By no means is this a complete list of all the tools and gadgets that might assist you in your job. We are constantly seeking out newer, better applications to aid us in our security design work. Some are better than others, and they're constantly changing to keep up with the problems they're trying to solve. Just remember the best tool you have is between your ears—at least you know that one will have better documentation!

If you have alternatives to the tools we outlined in this chapter, and they work for you, please continue to use them. Always use the tools that help you to get your work done in the most effective manner possible. And if you have some thoughts you would like to share with other readers about how to use these tools, or even better tools that we have explored in this chapter, please visit the forums at our website (`www.gotroot.com`) and let the world know what you think!

Diagnostics

9

The intent of this chapter is to provide general technical guidance for troubleshooting firewall problems that this book does not directly cover in Section III. We have taken great pains in Section III to research some of the most common and not so common problems users have encountered with **iptables** firewalls, but we cannot cover every possible protocol or configuration—hence the purpose of this chapter. It is our hope that this chapter provides enough info about how we diagnose new and fabulously obscure problems with the firewalls we build. We've been able to solve every problem so far by applying a solid troubleshooting methodology and by using these techniques and tools.

DIAGNOSTIC LOGGING

This first trick to figuring out what's causing a strange problem with your firewall is to log everything netfilter is doing. Logging will help you to keep a record of how your rules are being executed, and a sniffer can give you visibility into the packets themselves to determine why a connection is behaving in a certain manner. As opposed to normal logging, which consists of logging behavior you want to know about, such as suspicious behavior or providing audit trails for certain connections, diagnostic logging is all about verbosity. You want to see things that you normally would not want to log, such as the execution of all your rules—even packets that you normally allow and do not care about. Naturally, this form of logging is not something you normally want to do with your logs, as it can fill them up with tons of information that you don't care about. Therefore, these techniques are only for diagnostic purposes and are not recommended for ongoing use with production firewalls. They can fill up your logs quickly and might also reduce performance on the firewall.

The goal with diagnostic logging is to see everything. You don't want to assume that something is working or that a packet is taking one route through one chain, INPUT for instance, when it's really being handled by the FORWARD chain. By logging everything, you can empirically ascertain the actual sequence of events.

SCRIPTS TO DO THIS FOR YOU

In classic engineer form, we prefer to use good scripts to add in and remove logging rules for us on-the-fly. You can always add in rules manually, but we prefer to have tools at our disposal to diagnose problems quickly so that we can start ruling out false root causes.

```
#!/bin/bash
# $Id: iptables-trace,v 1.14 2004/11/13 00:31:15 apc Exp $
# Tony Clayton <t ny-netfilter@clayt n.ca>

# You may use and edit this code freely.  If you make changes to
# it that are generally useful, please email them to me and/or
# post them on the netfilter mailing list.

LOGPREFIX='${table:0:1}:${chain:0:14}:$rulenum:${target:0:14}'

log_entry() {
  local action=$1
  local table=$3 chain=$5
  shift 5
  if [ "$last_chain" != "$chain" ]; then
    rulenum=1
  fi
  case $action in
  (skip) ;;
  (add)
    local rulespec
    while [ "$1" != "-j" ]; do
      rulespec="$rulespec $1"
      shift;
    done
    shift;
    target=$*
    eval prefix="${LOGPREFIX}"
    iptables -t $table -I $chain $rulenum $rulespec -j LOG \
        --log-level debug --log-prefix "*${prefix:0:27}:"
```

```
      let rulenum=$rulenum+1
      ;;
  (delete)
    iptables -t $table -D $chain $rulenum
    let rulenum=$rulenum-1
    ;;
  esac
  last_chain=$chain
}

start() {
  for table in $(cat /proc/net/ip_tables_names); do
    rulenum=1
    iptables-save -t $table | grep '^-' | \
      while read cmd; do
        log_entry add -t $table $cmd
        let rulenum=$rulenum+1
      done
  done
}

stop() {
  for table in $(cat /proc/net/ip_tables_names); do
    iptables-save -t $table | grep '^-' | \
      while read cmd; do
        echo $cmd | grep -q -e '--log-prefix "*'
        if [ $? -eq 0 ]; then
          log_entry delete -t $table $cmd
        else
          log_entry skip -t $table $cmd
        fi
        let rulenum=$rulenum+1
      done
  done
}

case "$1" in
  start) start
        ;;
  stop) stop
        ;;
  *) echo $"Usage: $0 {start|stop}"
     exit 1
esac

exit 0
```

When activated, the system will generate a log entry for each chain in the ruleset, prefacing these debugging rules with an asterisk "*" to help tell them apart from normal logging rules and also to make it easier to remove these rules via the **iptables**-trace script. The net field denotes the type of chain being logged, "m" for mangle, "f" for filter, and "n" for nat. Following that is the name of the chain, OUTPUT for instance, then the index number for the rule to tell you in what order this rule is triggered, and finally the target of the rule.

Like an init script, this one is invoked with a stop or start command. It then parses all the **iptables** rules and adds in a LOG target for that rule so that you can track the progress of a packet as it moves through the system. Tools like **fwbuilder** and others also can add in these sorts of diagnostic/debugging rules on-the-fly through their interfaces. The intent is to add in a logging rule for everything and to assume nothing is working correctly.

THE *CATCH ALL* LOGGING RULE

Another useful logging trick is to put in place at the end of all your firewall rules, before your final DROP or REJECT rule, a catch all logging rule. This will help you to diagnose packets that are dropped by the firewall because of a missing rule, typo, or other mistake. This is also a useful security measure because the firewall will now log all the packets you will reject as part of your "unless allow, deny" security philosophy.

```
# catch all dropped packets
$IPTABLES -A INPUT -p all  -m limit --limit 1/second \
-j LOG  --log-level info --log-prefix "FINAL -- DROP "  \
--log-tcp-sequence  --log-tcp-options -log-ip-options
```

Keep in mind that in our example we are limiting the number of packets that will be logged to one per second. This is to prevent the firewall logging system from being overwhelmed by either too much traffic or by a deliberate attempt by an attacker to overwhelm the system. This is just a suggestion, though. If you want to log every packet, your **iptables** command would look like this:

```
# catch all dropped packets
$IPTABLES -A INPUT -p all -j LOG  --log-level info \
-log -prefix "FINAL -- DROP "  --log-tcp-sequence \
--log-tcp-options -log-ip-options
```

THE IPTABLES *TRACE* PATCH

There is also a nifty little patch for **iptables** called TRACE. It is not presently part of the stock **iptables** binary or any stock kernels, so you will have to patch both to get this option. We provide instructions for patching on our website at http://www.gotroot.com. Where possible, we also provide links to and copies of some **iptables** binaries that include this option, and you will find it as a module in the kernels we provide on our website. The patch is also available from the netfilter website, http://www.netfilter.org. It's included in the patch-o-matic archives.

TRACE is a target, much in the same way that ACCEPT or DROP are. You mark a packet with TRACE, and the system will log its "flow" through the netfilter system via its table or chain name.

We think the -j TRACE target should be included in every **iptables** binary and kernel distribution. Although it can be slow, it's a useful tool designed specifically to help with diagnosing firewall rule problems.

Unfortunately, as TRACE is not included in any Linux distributions, we're not going to spend any time discussing it in this book, as it's not really available for most users. Our goal is to focus on tools that are in widespread use. If you are interested in using -j TRACE, please check our website (www.gotroot.com) for examples.

CHECKING THE NETWORK

Refer back to the troubleshooting methodology covered in Chapter 4 and the OSI model in Chapter 5. The first thing to check when diagnosing network problems is the arp cache to make sure that the problem with the firewall or host is not just related to a bad arp entry and a problem at Layer 2 of the OSI model. To view the arp cache, the command is very straightforward:

```
arp -n
```

```
Address            HWtype  HWaddress          Flags Mask   Iface
192.168.10.1       ether   00:00:12:34:56:78  C             eth1
```

Or in the Linux style:

```
arp -e
```

```
Address          HWtype  HWaddress              Flags Mask   Iface
foo.bar.edu      ether     00:00:12:34:56:78    C             eth1
```

In this example, there is just one host, our firewall, as seen from a client. Let's imagine that the arp entry is reporting the wrong hardware address for our firewall. You can flush this entry from the arp table with the -d switch:

```
arp -d 192.168.10.1
```

Then when viewing the arp cache on your host, you will see that it's empty:

```
arp -n
Address          HWtype  HWaddress              Flags Mask   Iface
```

Please check the arp man pages for information on other options for arp. The intent here is to show that you will want to work your way up from the OSI model, ruling out problems before moving on to more complex issues. When arp is ruled out, you can move on to IP and so on.

Next, we move on to **ping**. As the reader is no doubt aware, **ping** is one of the easiest to use tools for testing a connection and can help to determine if a host is up or if there is an outage between two hosts. Again, the intent is to rule out root problems at lower layers of the OSI model before moving on to higher levels. The standard **ping** included with Linux and other operating systems is largely limited in terms of what it can test for. With **ping**, you might be able, depending on your firewall rules, to help determine if a problem lies at a lower or higher level of the OSI model, indicating where you should start looking. The previous chapter included some examples of how to use **ping** to diagnose Layer 2 problems. Here we present some additional uses of **ping** to test more than basic connectivity between hosts. It can also be used to map out the route between two hosts by using the -R switch:

```
ping -R www.gotroot.com
PING gotroot.com (205.241.45.98) 56(124) bytes of data.
64 bytes from plesk.shinn.net (205.241.45.98): icmp_seq=1 ttl=50 time=92.7 ms
RR:     liberty.gmsociety.org (216.218.240.134)
        pos2-0.gsr12012.fmt.he.net (64.62.249.121)
        ix-4-0.core2.PaloAlto.Teleglobe.net (64.86.84.154)
        if-8-0.core2.PaloAlto.Teleglobe.net (207.45.222.26)
        sl-teleg-2-0.sprintlink.net (160.81.205.142)
        sl-gw28-ana-0-0.sprintlink.net (144.232.1.30)
        sl-bb21-ana-6-0.sprintlink.net (144.232.1.61)
        sl-bb25-ana-8-0.sprintlink.net (144.232.9.64)
        sl-bb24-fw-14-0.sprintlink.net (144.232.11.73)
```

The other switch we want to mention when using **ping** is the -s switch. This sets the size of the packet sent and can help with diagnosing MTU problems or other packet size problems with your firewall and the networks between your firewall and the target of your ping. If a normal ping, which is only 84-byte, gets through, and a large ping of 2000 bytes does not, the problem is most likely an MTU and fragmentation problem.

```
ping -s 2000 www.gotroot.com
PING gotroot.com (205.241.45.98) 2000(2028) bytes of data.
2008 bytes from plesk.shinn.net (205.241.45.98): icmp_seq=1 ttl=50 time=105 ms
2008 bytes from plesk.shinn.net (205.241.45.98): icmp_seq=2 ttl=50 time=153 ms
2008 bytes from plesk.shinn.net (205.241.45.98): icmp_seq=3 ttl=50 time=116 ms
2008 bytes from plesk.shinn.net (205.241.45.98): icmp_seq=4 ttl=50 time=183 ms
2008 bytes from plesk.shinn.net (205.241.45.98): icmp_seq=5 ttl=50 time=106 ms
2008 bytes from plesk.shinn.net (205.241.45.98): icmp_seq=6 ttl=50 time=117 ms

--- gotroot.com ping statistics ---
6 packets transmitted, 6 received, 0% packet loss, time 5008ms
rtt min/avg/max/mdev = 105.469/130.371/183.593/28.654 ms
```

nmap is another tool that can ping hosts, but unlike **ping**, it's not limited to using ICMP pings. To send an ICMP ping with **nmap**, you would use the -sP switches with **nmap** in this manner, replacing 10.10.10.192 with the IP address or hostname of the host you wanted to ping:

```
nmap -sP 10.10.10.192

Starting nmap 3.50 ( http://www.insecure.org/nmap/ ) at 2004-07-11 23:09 EDT
Host printer.int.shinn.net (10.10.10.192) appears to be up.
Nmap run completed -- 1 IP address (1 host up) scanned in 0.324 seconds
```

nmap also has the ability to "sweep" a network block, pinging all the hosts in that box, and then presenting information about which hosts responded to the ICMP pings. This can be useful to determine if a particular host is having a problem at a lower layer in the OSI model and ruling out a network-wide problem. Here is an example of using **nmap** in that manner:

```
nmap -sP 10.10.10.0/24

Starting nmap 3.50 ( http://www.insecure.org/nmap/ ) at 2004-07-11 23:12 EDT
Host a.foo.com (10.10.10.192) appears to be up.
Host x.foo.com (10.10.10.253) appears to be up.
Nmap run completed -- 256 IP addresses (2 hosts up) scanned in 294.960 seconds
```

nmap also can generate what is referred to as a `tcp ping`. This is basically accomplished by sending a `SYN`, `ACK`, `SYN+ACK`, or any other packet to a host and registering the response it gets back from the port that was "pinged." This is an excellent way of testing to see if a service is up, when you know the host is up. Keep in mind that this sort of a "ping" is occurring at Layer 4 of the OSI model and as such might not be an effective way of ruling out problems at lower layers.

If you can `ping` it with ICMP and you aren't losing any packets, including large packets, then you can rule out the problem as a Layer 2 problem. The problem lies somewhere in Layers 3 through 7.

```
nmap -sT -p 80 www.gotroot.com

Starting nmap 3.50 ( http://www.insecure.org/nmap/ ) at 2004-04-20 21:10 EDT
Interesting ports on www.gotroot.com (205.241.45.98):
PORT   STATE SERVICE
80/tcp open  http

Nmap run completed -- 1 IP address (1 host up) scanned in 0.715 seconds
```

The next tool, **traceroute**, is a key piece of any network diagnosis toolkit. **traceroute** can record the routes of a packet as it moves through the network. This is similar to using **ping** with the -R switch, but **traceroute** uses a different method for recording routes. There are two versions of **traceroute**—the venerable classic **traceroute**, which uses UDP and ICMP, and **tcptraceroute**, which uses TCP to trace out the routes of clients. Both of these tools have their place, so neither one is better than the other.

Classic **traceroute** uses UDP packets with an initial TTL of 1 set to determine the route to a host. **traceroute** sends out its first packet to the destination with its TTL of 1, causing the first machine or device it reaches along the way to send back an ICMP unreachable message because the message has "lived too long." TTL, or Time To Live, is a field in the IP headers that tells a compliant device along the way how much "life" is left in the packet. Each device in a route is required to reduce the TTL by one before passing the packet on to the next device in the route. **traceroute** uses this to record the route by sending multiple packets with increasing TTLs, starting at 1, and increasing from there.

A device is required to send back an ICMP unreachable packet anytime the TTL reaches 0. So, when **traceroute** sends out its initial packet, it's already stacked the deck so that the first hop will have to reduce the TTL to 0 by subtracting 1 from the initial TTL of 1. It's a pretty neat trick, and it does this for each step along the way. Each time, **traceroute** records this information as the next hop in the route by looking for those ICMP unreachable packets.

So, in our example, **traceroute** sends the initial packet with a TTL of 1, the first hop subtracts 1 and sends back an ICMP unreachable. Then **traceroute** sends another packet with the TTL set to 2, causing the first hop to decrease the TTL in the header field of the packet to 1 and then to send it on to the second hop in the route. This second hop decrements the TTL to 0, drops the packet, and sends back a destination unreachable message. This process keeps happening, with **traceroute** patiently adding 1 to the TTL, until it generates the final packet to the destination host.

This is where you can, with **iptables,** play some neat tricks on **traceroute** by using the **iptables** TTL target (`-j TTL –ttl-inc <value>`) to increase the TTL, without **traceroute**'s permission, by any value you like. This causes the packet to appear to bypass the firewall, whereby the firewall becomes "invisible" to **traceroute**. For example, this rule increases the TTL for UDP **traceroute** packets by one:

```
iptables -t mangle -A PREROUTING -p TCP \
--dport 33434:33542 -j TTL --ttl-inc 1
```

which causes this behavior to occur with **traceroute** when the packet is sent from behind the firewall to a host on the Internet:

```
traceroute to liberty.gmsociety.org (216.218.240.134), 30 hops max, 38 byte packets
  1  ip68-100-72-1.dc.dc.cox.net (68.100.72.1)  25.685 ms  12.024 ms  18.446 ms
  2  ip68-100-0-1.dc.dc.cox.net (68.100.0.1)  17.811 ms  12.891 ms  15.039 ms
  3  ip68-100-0-137.dc.dc.cox.net (68.100.0.137)  15.712 ms  18.692 ms  21.172 ms 5
68.1.1.4 (68.1.1.4)  16.610 ms  42.524 ms  17.100 ms
  4  68.1.1.3 (68.1.1.3)  16.699 ms  13.659 ms  15.814 ms
  5  ashbbbpc01pos0100.r2.as.cox.net (68.1.1.19)  16.710 ms  12.788 ms *
  6  ash-ix.he.net (206.223.115.37)  23.008 ms  18.023 ms  23.396 ms
  7  pos7-0.gsr12012.pao.he.net (216.218.254.205)  117.154 ms  104.813 ms  123.567 ms
8  pos2-0.gsr12012.fmt.he.net (64.62.249.121)  102.942 ms  106.383 ms  102.014 ms
11  * * *
[...]
21  * * *
[...]
```

And this is what the **traceroute** would look like without that rule:

```
traceroute to liberty.gmsociety.org (216.218.240.134), 30 hops max, 38 byte packets
1  192.168.10.1
2  ip68-100-72-1.dc.dc.cox.net (68.100.72.1)  25.685 ms  12.024 ms  18.446 ms
  3  ip68-100-0-1.dc.dc.cox.net (68.100.0.1)  17.811 ms  12.891 ms  15.039 ms
```

```
 4  ip68-100-0-137.dc.dc.cox.net (68.100.0.137)  15.712 ms  18.692 ms  21.172 ms 5
68.1.1.4 (68.1.1.4)  16.610 ms  42.524 ms  17.100 ms
 5  68.1.1.3 (68.1.1.3)  16.699 ms  13.659 ms  15.814 ms
 6  ashbbbpc01pos0100.r2.as.cox.net (68.1.1.19)  16.710 ms  12.788 ms  *
 7  ash-ix.he.net (206.223.115.37)  23.008 ms  18.023 ms  23.396 ms
 8  pos7-0.gsr12012.pao.he.net (216.218.254.205)  117.154 ms  104.813 ms  123.567 ms
 9  pos2-0.gsr12012.fmt.he.net (64.62.249.121)  102.942 ms  106.383 ms  102.014 ms
12  * * *
[...]
21  * * *
[...]
```

The astute reader will notice that in both cases the **traceroute** did not succeed because the ISP at the end of that route is filtering out normal **traceroute** traffic. We illustrate this to remind you that this is one of the downsides to using **traceroute**, many sites filter it. Nevertheless, you will find that vanilla **traceroute** is still an extremely valuable tool when diagnosing the path a packet is taking through a network, although it might not always work due to filtering.

In those circumstances where vanilla **tracetroute** does not work, in steps **tcptraceroute**. As you may have already guessed, **tcptraceroute** uses TCP to trace the route to a host. **tcptraceroute** can take advantage of the fact that it is much more difficult to filter legitimate connections to hosts on open ports, such as the tcp port 80 for a web server. And, much like vanilla **traceroute**, **tcptracroute** utilizes that same incrementing TTL trick to get back unreachable messages from intermediate hosts along the way. Here is the same example using **tcptraceroute**:

```
tcptraceroute liberty.gmsociety.org 22
Selected device ipsec0, address 192.168.10.12 for outgoing packets
Tracing the path to liberty.gmsociety.org (216.218.240.134) on TCP port 22, 30 hops
max
 1  192.168.10.1
 2  ip68-100-72-1.dc.dc.cox.net (68.100.72.1)  67.165 ms * 17.423 ms
 3  ip68-100-0-1.dc.dc.cox.net (68.100.0.1)  13.608 ms  12.317 ms  14.783 ms
 4  ip68-100-0-137.dc.dc.cox.net (68.100.0.137)  18.330 ms  11.879 ms  11.650 ms 5
68.1.1.4 (68.1.1.4)  13.771 ms  16.825 ms  12.600 ms
 6  68.1.1.3 (68.1.1.3)  12.492 ms  14.013 ms  14.942 ms
 7  ashbbbpc01pos0100.r2.as.cox.net (68.1.1.19)  14.581 ms  31.069 ms  13.775 ms 8
ash-ix.he.net (206.223.115.37)  13.028 ms  12.797 ms  12.083 ms
 9  pos7-0.gsr12012.pao.he.net (216.218.254.205)  101.619 ms  85.920 ms  106.626 ms
10  pos2-0.gsr12012.fmt.he.net (64.62.249.121)  104.472 ms  108.409 ms  109.053 ms
11  liberty.gmsociety.org (216.218.240.134) [open]  122.805 ms  113.582 ms  113.513 ms
```

This time, you will notice that **tcptraceroute** was able to defeat both our **iptables** -j TTL rule and it was able to get around the upstream ISP's **traceroute** filtering. The key with **tcptraceroute** is to find a port that will get through all the hops along the way, so keep in mind that if your **traceroute** is not working, it's possible that your packet is just getting filtered, so try another port. If you're having trouble finding a port to use, start with the most obvious services you might expect to be running on that system. If you are still having trouble finding an open port, try using a tool like nmap to scan the system for open ports.

The bottom line with using tools like **traceroute** and **tcptraceroute** is to determine if you have a route to the remote host in question. If the route is up and correct, then the problem lies farther up the OSI model.

USING A SNIFFER TO DIAGNOSE FIREWALL PROBLEMS

Many problems can be isolated by running a packet sniffer on your firewall. Our favorite is **tetheral**, a part of the **ethereal** package, because it will put the packets into a more readable form than **tcpdump**, which is another good option. **tetheral** is also handy for command line diagnosis work because it works without all the fuss of a GUI and all the "voodoo" of a more lower-level sniffer such as **tcpdump**. **tetheral** is slower than **tcpdump**, however. Here is an example of a connection from behind our firewall to one of our hosts on the Internet:

```
tetwthereal -i eth1 host liberty.gmsociety.org and port 22
Capturing on eth1
  0.000000 68.100.73.75 -> 216.218.240.134 TCP 47104 > ssh [SYN, ECN, CWR] Seq=0 Ack=0
Win=32440 Len=0 MSS=16220 TSV=31410938 TSER=0 WS=0
  0.128939 216.218.240.134 -> 68.100.73.75 TCP ssh > 47104 [SYN, ACK, ECN] Seq=0 Ack=1
Win=5792 Len=0 MSS=1460 TSV=523459383 TSER=31410938 WS=0
  0.135917 68.100.73.75 -> 216.218.240.134 TCP 47104 > ssh [ACK] Seq=1 Ack=1 Win=32440
Len=0 TSV=31411052 TSER=523459383
  0.243449 216.218.240.134 -> 68.100.73.75 SSH Server Protocol: SSH-2.0-OpenSSH_3.8p1
  0.246039 68.100.73.75 -> 216.218.240.134 TCP 47104 > ssh [ACK] Seq=1 Ack=23
Win=32440 Len=0 TSV=31411161 TSER=523459509
  0.246187 68.100.73.75 -> 216.218.240.134 SSH Client Protocol: SSH-2.0-NOYB
  0.359056 216.218.240.134 -> 68.100.73.75 TCP ssh > 47104 [ACK] Seq=23 Ack=14
Win=5792 Len=0 TSV=523459627 TSER=31411162
  0.361615 68.100.73.75 -> 216.218.240.134 SSHv2 Client: Key Exchange Init
  0.363396 216.218.240.134 -> 68.100.73.75 SSHv2 Server: Key Exchange Init
```

This example demonstrates how the sniffer caught the entire session and put it into an easier to read format for someone not familiar with raw packets. The three-way handshake is illustrated in this sniffer trace, and **tetheral** was even kind enough to translate the SSH protocol for users so you can see that the SSH connection is working correctly, what protocol it is using, and even what step in the SSH process is occurring. The observant reader might have also noticed the ECN flag, which is the explicit congestion notification flag. That system uses it because we don't have to worry about connectivity problems for that host with systems that do not understand ECN, as in the following example:

```
 0.000000 68.100.73.75 -> 62.172.198.77 TCP 39114 > http [SYN, ECN, CWR] Seq=0 Ack=0
Win=5840 Len=0 MSS=1460 TSV=19362375 TSER=0 WS=0
 0.086282 62.172.198.77 -> 68.100.73.75 TCP http > 39114 [RST, ACK] Seq=0 Ack=0
Win=5840 Len=0 MSS=1460 TSV=19362375 TSER=0 WS=0
 0.087204 68.100.73.75 -> 62.172.198.77 TCP 34000 > http [SYN, ECN, CWR] Seq=0 Ack=0
Win=5840 Len=0 MSS=1460 TSV=19362384 TSER=0 WS=0
 0.175656 62.172.198.77 -> 68.100.73.75 TCP http > 34000 [RST, ACK] Seq=0 Ack=0
Win=5840 Len=0 MSS=1460 TSV=19362384 TSER=0 WS=0
 0.176618 68.100.73.75 -> 62.172.198.77 TCP 40151 > http [SYN, ECN, CWR] Seq=0 Ack=0
Win=5840 Len=0 MSS=1460 TSV=19362393 TSER=0 WS=0
 0.263994 62.172.198.77 -> 68.100.73.75 TCP http > 40151 [RST, ACK] Seq=0 Ack=0
Win=5840 Len=0 MSS=1460 TSV=19362393 TSER=0 WS=0
```

This connection starts off innocently enough, with a standard SYN request but with the Explicit Congestion Notification (ECN) Echo flag set (ECE) and the Congestion Reduction Windows flag (CWR) set. There is some debate about what the right thing is for an IP stack that does not understand what ECN does—ignore the flags and carry on or for the paranoid, drop the packet? Unfortunately for ECN, some vendors to chose to do the latter. In our example, you can see that the connection was immediately reset (RST) by the destination. Without a sniffer, it would have been difficult to see what was going on here.

What happens when we turn ECN off? The connection goes through without a hitch.

```
0.000000 68.100.73.75 -> 62.172.198.77 TCP 60276 > http [SYN] Seq=0 Ack=0 Win=5840
Len=0 MSS=1460 TSV=19370810 TSER=0 WS=0
 0.094593 62.172.198.77 -> 68.100.73.75 TCP http > 60276 [SYN, ACK] Seq=0 Ack=1
Win=24616 Len=0 TSV=1381457590 TSER=19370810 WS=0 MSS=1460
 0.095037 68.100.73.75 -> 62.172.198.77 TCP 60276 > http [ACK] Seq=1 Ack=1 Win=5840
Len=0 TSV=19370819 TSER=1381457590
 0.096459 68.100.73.75 -> 62.172.198.77 HTTP GET / HTTP/1.0
```

```
   0.194562 62.172.198.77 -> 68.100.73.75 TCP http > 60276 [ACK] Seq=1 Ack=395
Win=24616 Len=0 TSV=1381457600 TSER=19370819
   0.198269 62.172.198.77 -> 68.100.73.75 HTTP HTTP/1.1 200 OK (text/html)
   0.198597 68.100.73.75 -> 62.172.198.77 TCP 60276 > http [ACK] Seq=395 Ack=384
Win=6432 Len=0 TSV=19370830 TSER=1381457600
   0.452280 68.100.73.75 -> 62.172.198.77 HTTP GET /index.jsp HTTP/1.0
   0.633635 62.172.198.77 -> 68.100.73.75 TCP http > 60276 [ACK] Seq=384 Ack=798
Win=24616 Len=0 TSV=1381457644 TSER=19370855
   1.079874 62.172.198.77 -> 68.100.73.75 HTTP HTTP/1.1 200 OK (text/html)
```

The moral of the story is to look at the connections with a close eye and check for odd flags in the packets, such as ECN, if a connection is not working, again, before moving up in the OSI model. Always rule out lower-level problems before hypothesizing about the root cause of your problem.

The example above was not meant to single out ECN as a problematic extension to IP as we use ECN for all of our servers. What we're showing is how a simple change to the session can cause what appears to be a higher level problem, the need to truly isolate the root cause of a problem, and the tools to do so.

With ECN, however, we like to use it on our internal and Internet reachable machine but not as often for our firewalls because there are still too many sites out there that do not support ECN correctly. The good news is that you can run ECN to your heart's content behind your firewall, turn it off on your firewall, and filter out ECN packets on your outbound interfaces without causing any problems, while gaining the advantages of better congestion control. If you use **squid** as an HTTP proxy on your firewall, either transparently or not, the packets will also pack the ECN flag.

Let's take a look at another example. We have a firewall with two outbound Internet interfaces connected to two different ISPs. We want SMTP traffic to go over one of the interfaces, while the rest of the traffic goes over the other interface. To accomplish this we use the ROUTE patch-o-matic netfilter/**iptables** patch to give us the ability to route arbitrarily by source, destination, source or destination port, MAC address, and so on. The following is what the pertinent rules look like:

```
iptables -A POSTROUTING -t mangle -s 192.168.10.0/24 \
-p tcp --dport 25 -j ROUTE --gw 1.2.3.4 --oif eth2   \
--continue
```

gw is our upstream gateway for the second ISP connection on this firewall. When we try to connect out to port 25 on one of our servers, the connection does not go through.

When we use a sniffer to look at the connection, we can see that the packets are not being NAT-ed:

```
tethereal -i eth2 host plesk.shinn.net
Capturing on eth2
  0.000000 192.168.10.12 -> 205.241.45.98 TCP 39945 > smtp [SYN, ECN, CWR] Seq=0 Ack=0
Win=32440 Len=0 MSS=16220 TSV=32726418 TSER=0 WS=0
```

What we need to add to our rules is a specific NAT rule for this route:

```
iptables -t nat -A POSTROUTING -o eth1 -p tcp  \
-s 192.168.10.0/24 --dport 25 -j SNAT --to-source 1.2.3.5
```

This then tells the firewall to rewrite the packet so that its source address is 1.2.3.5, which is an address our remote server can locate on the Internet. Again, the intent is to move on to the sniffer after you have moved up the OSI model and have ruled out lower-level problems.

MEMORY LOAD DIAGNOSTICS

Sometimes everything is right about the firewall—the rules are fine, the drivers are installed correctly, and in fact everything seems perfect with the firewall except that it is just not quite working properly. Often, these hard to pin down problems can stem from the firewall simply being overloaded and not having enough memory or the connection tracking settings not being optimized for the network or system on which the firewall is running.

The connection tracking engine requires a certain amount of RAM to function properly, and, probably not too obviously, it takes more RAM to track more connections. The more connections and the more users, the more memory the firewall needs. To determine if this might be part of the problem, let's start with the formula used to determine memory usage of the state engine:

(memory used per tracked connection×maximum number of tracked connections)

+

(memory used per buckets×number of buckets)=nonpagable memory needed by the connection engine

To figure out the solution to this formula, the place to look is /proc/slabinfo. This will show you the amount of memory allocated to elements of the connection tracking engine.

```
cat  /proc/slabinfo
slabinfo - version: 1.1
kmem_cache            93     93    124    3    3    1 :   252  126
ip_conntrack         322    570    384   47   57    1 :   124   62
ip_mrt_cache           0      0     96    0    0    1 :   252  126
tcp_tw_bucket        320    320     96    8    8    1 :   252  126
tcp_bind_bucket      226    226     32    2    2    1 :   252  126
tcp_open_request     169    295     64    4    5    1 :   252  126
inet_peer_cache      177    177     64    3    3    1 :   252  126
ip_fib_hash           56    226     32    2    2    1 :   252  126
ip_dst_cache         426    552    160   23   23    1 :   252  126
arp_cache            150    150    128    5    5    1 :   252  126
uhci_urb_priv          1     63     60    1    1    1 :   252  126
blkdev_requests     4096   4120     96  103  103    1 :   252  126
journal_head         352    858     48    8   11    1 :   252  126
revoke_table           2    253     12    1    1    1 :   252  126
```

For the state engine, the value we are interested in is ip_conntrack. For those readers not familiar with the layout of data in slabinfo, here is a quick tutorial:

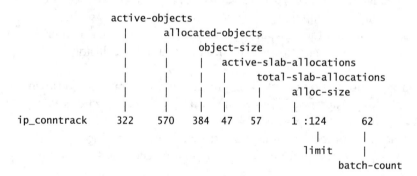

It's the object size that will start to tell us how much memory the state engine will be using to track connections. You also can use this shortcut to find this information:

```
grep ip_conntrack /proc/slabinfo  | tr -s " " | cut \
-d " " -f 4
```

The kernel will try to automatically set the maximum number of connections it can handle based on the amount of RAM in your system. You can see this by looking at your logs on bootup. If your machine has not been rebooted in a while, you might need to check messages.1, messages.2, and so on.

```
cat /var/log/messages | grep ip_conntrack

ip_conntrack version 2.1 (4095 buckets, 32760 max) - 360 bytes per conntrack
```

After you have this information, you can tell what the maximum recommended setting for your system should be and then compare that with what your system is set to support by looking once again in /proc:

```
cat /proc/sys/net/ipv4/ip_conntrack_max
32760
```

On our system, the value returned was "32760," which is exactly the "safe" limit. In reality, the system can handle significantly more than 32K connections with 512MB of memory. For 32,760 connections, with a connection size of around 360 bytes on our test system, that's only 11,793,600 bytes, or around 11.8MB of memory used. But that's just for the memory used per connection and the maximum number of connections. It might be tempting to change the value in /proc/sys/net/ipv4/ip_conntrack_max, but don't do this without reading on. Changing this value alone will only increase the number of connections to track but not the amount of buckets allocated for those connections. This will actually cause a decrease in performance by making the collision chains longer.

According to published information about the engine, the ultimate ratio for performance is 2:1 for buckets to connections. So if you want to track 32,760 connections, you need to increase the amount of buckets as well.

If you want to increase the number of connections the engine is managing, you can modify it by increasing the hashsize allocated for the module ip_conntrack.

```
modprobe ip_conntrack hashsize=16380
```

This will need to be run when the ip_conntrack module is first loaded. In 2.4 with a monolithic kernel (for example, a kernel without module support), the only way to change this value is by altering the kernel source. For 2.6, module parameters can be specified in a generic manner from the boot command line. Returning to the ip_conntrack_max variable, it adds the ip_conntrack_max value into /etc/sysctl.conf in this format so that the system is configured in this manner on its next boot.

```
#max connections
net.ipv4.ip_conntrack_max = 32760
```

In the short term you can also modify this value by echoing 32760 into

```
/proc/sys/net/ipv4/ip_conntrack_max
```

```
echo 32760 > /proc/sys/net/ipv4/ip_conntrack_max
```

We must also add in the memory used per bucket and the number of buckets. For a 32-bit system, each bucket uses eight bits of memory; for a 64-bit system, it's 16 bits. In our example, we have 16,380 buckets, which means the system is only using 131,040 bytes. It's not a whole lot in the grand scheme of things, but it can add up if you don't do your math. In total, the state tracking engine in this example is using just a little over 11.9MB of RAM.

In theory at least, this means that you could increase the number of connections the conntrack engine is managing pretty substantially, but this assumes that your firewall isn't using memory for much else. Also it's important to keep in mind the conntrack engine uses nonpagable memory, which also reduces the amount of memory available for other processes.

System memory is also used to handle things such as fragment reassembly, which might seem to be insignificant, but fragment reassembly on a network that is supporting clients with ever-changing MTU's can actually consume a substantially more significant amount of memory than the connection tracking engine. In earlier kernels, it was even possible to exhaust all of the system's memory by generating a flood of fragments and filling up the system's buffers while waiting for the rest of the fragments to arrive. This caused the kernel to start dropping connections, and in some cases could cause a DoS of the firewall's IP stack. The point here is that memory is quite important for a firewall, and because it's so cheap these days, there is great opportunity and need to increase the memory on a heavily used firewall. If your firewall is engaging in some extremely hard to diagnose problems, consider that it might simply be overworked and check the systems accordingly to determine if that is the case.

SUMMARY

Sometimes the problem you encounter will be outside the bounds of known documented problems. You might have a truly unique problem that this book and other sources will be unable to help you solve. That's where the use of the tools, techniques, and methodologies discussed thus far can help you. The last section of this book, Section III, contains some of the most commonly reported user problems with **iptables**-based firewalls, but we cannot cover every possible contingency. It is for this reason that we present you with the material in this chapter. We have also set up user forums on our website to help our readers get in touch with not only us, but with the wider community to help diagnose any new or unique problems you might encounter. By now you probably know where to go for more information, but just in case you need it again, our website address is `http://www.gotroot.com`.

SECTION III
DIAGNOSTICS

Testing Your Firewall Rules (for Security!)

Firewalls work both ways. You can use them to keep bad traffic from the outside coming in, as well as keeping bad traffic from the inside going out. Worms, mail connections, and X11 sessions are just a few examples of "bad traffic" depending on your security policy. But how do you test this quickly and consistently? Many times a change in the rules in one area can affect rules in other.

This is perhaps a good moment to talk about the concept of firewalls in general (we promise to be brief!) and why the very first diagnostic procedure we talk about is specifically the most important. A firewall is not a router; nor is it a gateway. It's a compartmentalization tool. If the whole reason you picked up this book is to make sure you can get your traffic out of your network, then this is probably the most important section for you to read. There are three types of firewalls:

1. Application Layer (proxy servers such as **squid**, **reaim**, or the TIS firewall toolkit)
2. Packet Filtering (routers, switches, and so on)
3. Stateful Inspection (netfilter/**iptables**)

Routers and other network gateways generally fall into the "packet filtering" category, which means that they look at the first packet in a session, match it to a rule, and then let the rest go with no further inspection. That means they are trivial to beat (and we'll show you how later in the chapter) using some very simple methods. Stateful inspection firewalls look at every packet as it goes by to ensure it conforms to the firewall policy you have created on the system. The methods used here *may* work on a stateful inspection firewall but generally only if you've done something horribly, *horribly* wrong.

So how do you beat packet filtering firewalls? Simple—fragment the packets. There are many ways to do this, either with userspace tools such as **nmap**, changing the MTU on your network card, or my personal favorite, a tool called **fragrouter** from the nids-bench toolkit (`http://packetstorm.widexs.nl/UNIX/IDS/nidsbench/nidsbench.html`) by Thomas Ptacek and T. Newsham. We will look at **fragrouter** later in the chapter to demonstrate weaknesses in packet filtering systems.

There are two types of tests you should perform on every firewall: an external scan against inside systems (`OUTSIDE->IN`), and an internal scan against systems on the outside (`INSIDE->OUT`). The first test is useful in occasions where you're dealing with address space reachable from outside your network through your firewall, such as on a DMZ network, or if you are in an environment where potential intruders can set your firewall as the gateway (think wireless networks or conference rooms if you put them in DMZs).

The `INSIDE->OUT` test verifies what kinds of traffic from your internal or DMZ networks can get across your firewall. This is a useful verification test if you are attempting to filter what types of traffic your DMZ systems can get through your firewall. If your DMZ hosts web servers, there really is no point in allowing them to send traffic out on the X11 port, SMTP, or frankly any traffic that is not coming from the source port of the web server itself (TCP ports 80 and 443, respectively). This is valuable from a security standpoint in that in the event the web server is compromised (through port 80—just because you have a firewall doesn't mean that your web server cannot be exploited on the ports you allow in!), it cannot be used as a platform to attack other systems through your firewall.

A good example of an `INSIDE->OUT` test discovering a weakness in firewall rules was when we were initially setting up IPSEC VPNs to secure our wireless networks (see Chapter 19, "Virtual Private Networks," for more information on this). Our firewalls were configured also to provide transparent proxies on web and IM traffic, so even though the firewalls were configured to block all outbound traffic not coming through the IPSEC VPN networks, the transparent proxy servers were redirecting the traffic outbound. This was discovered and corrected quickly by using an `INSIDE->OUT` scan.

INSIDE->OUT TESTING WITH NMAP AND IPLOG

Another way to test what can come in, or probably more interestingly, what can go out through a firewall is to use a combination of **nmap** and **iplog**. **nmap** (`www.insecure.org`) is a very popular userspace port scanner that comes bundled with most Linux distributions these days. **iplog** (`http://ojnk.sourceforge.net`) is a userspace port connection logger. You also could use **iptables**/netfilter rules to log these connections, but for the sake of testing, using **iplog** as an independent method for collecting diagnostic information is preferred.

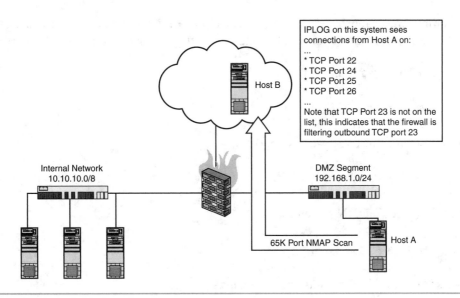

IPLOG on this system sees
connections from Host A on:

...
* TCP Port 22
* TCP Port 24
* TCP Port 25
* TCP Port 26
...

Note that TCP Port 23 is not on the
list, this indicates that the firewall is
filtering outbound TCP port 23

Host B

Internal Network
10.10.10.0/8

DMZ Segment
192.168.1.0/24

65K Port NMAP Scan

Host A

Figure 10.1   nmap INSIDE->OUT scan with **iplog**.

To test your outbound rules, you will need two systems—one behind your firewall running **nmap** and one on the outside running **iplog**. The idea here is that you're going to do full 65536 port TCP/SYN/FIN/UDP scans through your firewall to see what it allows outbound and log these connections on the **iplog** host. You will want to use this test method whenever you need to verify that you are filtering outbound connections successfully. (A very important test!)

The first system is your scanner system running behind your firewall, which we will call Host-A. The second system is the **iplog** system, Host-B.

Host-A:

This system will specifically need to be physically connected into the network on the same segment(s) containing the systems that you are testing your rules against. This is due to the nature of **iptables**/netfilter allowing you to assign rules based on the firewall's interface. Try and make sure that this system is as close to the "real thing" (a web server for example) as possible. Or barring that…use the real thing! In this first example we'll assume our scanner system is a Red Hat 9 web server called Host-A, sitting on the DNAT DMZ segment. From this system, we will perform our port scan against the system with Host-B on the opposite side of the firewall. From Host-A we will execute six types of test scans, a three-way-handshake `tcpopen()` scan, a `SYN only` scan, a `FIN only` scan, a `NULL` scan, an `XMAS` scan, and a `UDP` scan. The following is the syntax of the `tcpopen()` scan:

TCP Open (three-way handshake)

```
nmap -sT -P0 -p 1-65535 Host-B
```

SYN scan (sends the SYN packets only)

```
nmap -sS -P0 -p 1-65535 Host-B
```

FIN scan (sends the FIN packet only)

```
nmap -sF -P0 -p 1-65535 Host-B
```

NULL scan (sends TCP packets with NO flags set)

```
nmap -sN -P0 -p 1-65535 Host-B
```

XMAS scan (sends TCP packets with the X flag set)

```
nmap -sX -P0 -p 1-65535 Host-B
```

UDP scan (sends UDP packets only)

```
nmap -sU -P0 -p 1-65535 Host-B
```

ICMP scan

```
nmap -sP  Host-B
```

NOTE

The `-P0` flag instructs `nmap` NOT to use an ICMP or TCP ping to determine if the remote host is active. This ensures that your scan will work regardless of whether it is possible to ping or connect to a service on the remote system; otherwise, if ICMP were not allowed, `nmap` would exit, thereby ruining the value of this test. All we care about is the data!

Host-B:

This is your logging system, which should catch all the packets your firewall is allowing to pass through its rules. For this example, we will assume that Host-B is a Red Hat 9 server on the Internet with no filters or proxy servers other than the firewall being tested—between it and Host-A. This system is running **iplog** v 2.2.3, with the following options:

```
iplog -D -F -P -S -b -d -f -detect-syn-scan=true -n -p -w
```

Table 10.1 Options

-D	Logs the destination of traffic.
-F	Logs UDP scans.
-P	Log ICMP ping floods.
-S	Log smurf (These are attacks that involve pinging a system with a broadcast address in the response field. We're not testing this directly, but it comes in handy when playing with the mangle features in **iptables**.)
-b	Log bogus TCP flags.
-d	Ignore DNS traffic (from the local system, specified in /etc/resolv.conf).
-f	Log FIN scans.
--detect-syn-scan=true	(This keeps iplog from being overwhelmed if you're testing something like SYN flooding through the firewall.)
-n	Log NULL scans.
-p	Log port scans.
-w	Log the IP along with the hostname.
-t	Log traceroutes.
-x	Log Xmas scans.
-y	Log fragment attacks (ala fragrouter).

Once running, **iplog** will default to dumping its data to **syslog** on our Red Hat 9 system—this is the logfile **/var/log/messages**.

Interpreting the Output from an *INSIDE->OUT* Scan

This really depends on your rules, but to assume that you're following the basic "unless allow, deny" policy, you'll want to ensure that the data you see being allowed outbound is only to a valid policy. For example, a DMZ web server with a firewall policy configured to only allow traffic outbound in a response to web requests should never be allowed to connect outbound with source ports other than the ports the web server is running (default, port 80, and port 443 for HTTPS). The following output logged on Host-B shows this example policy in violation:

> **Note**
>
> **nmap** randomizes the ports it connects on—so don't be surprised when things are not sequential.

TCP Open scan: (nmap -sT -P0 -p 1-65535 Host-B)

```
Host-B iplog[26016]: TCP: port 834 connection attempt to Host-B from Host-A:42259
Host-B iplog[26016]: TCP: supfilesrv connection attempt to Host-B from Host-A:42260
Host-B iplog[26016]: TCP: port 428 connection attempt to Host-B from Host-A:42261
Host-B iplog[26016]: TCP: port 936 connection attempt to Host-B from Host-A:42262
Host-B iplog[26016]: TCP: gdomap connection attempt to Host-B from Host-A:42263
```

SYN scan: (nmap -sS -P0 -p 1-65535 Host-B)

```
Host-B iplog[26016]: TCP: SYN scan detected to Host-B [ports
691,654,689,140,288,889,918,115,151,917,...] from Host-A [port 39596]
```

FIN scan: (nmap -sF -P0 -p 1-65535 Host-B)

```
Host-B iplog[26016]: TCP: FIN scan detected to Host-B [ports
759,639,579,37,541,647,358,884,879,826,...] from Host-A [port 59479]
```

NULL scan: (nmap -sN -P0 -p 1-65535 Host-B)

```
Host-B iplog[14801]: TCP: null scan detected to Host-B (216.218.240.133) [ports
662,660,118,106,829,800,461,278,907,330,...] from Host-A [port 45662]
```

XMAS Scan: (nmap -sX -P0 -p 1-65535 Host-B)

```
Host-B iplog[26016]: TCP: Xmas scan detected to Host-B [ports
411,180,808,746,788,603,413,145,406,388,...] from Host-A [port 62702]
```

UDP scan: (nmap -sU -P0 -p 1-65535 Host-B)

```
Host-B iplog[14801]: UDP: dgram to Host-B:port 429 from Host-A (0 data bytes)
Host-B iplog[14801]: UDP: dgram to Host-B:port 338 from Host-A (0 data bytes)
Host-B iplog[14801]: UDP: dgram to Host-B:port 465 from Host-A (0 data bytes)
Host-B iplog[14801]: UDP: scan/flood detected to Host-B [ports
966,478,601,906,987,677,798,864,67,712,...] from Host-A [ports 49408,49409]
```

> **NOTE**
>
> UDP scans are highly unreliable. Sometimes you need to do these multiple times. This is due to a great many factors. In this particular example, UDP scans can miss open UDP ports due to timeout issues.

So the short-short version of reading this output is that if it looks wrong, it probably is. It's time to test your rules again.

TESTING FROM THE *OUTSIDE->IN*

Of course this is typically what a firewall is all about—making sure people cannot get back in. We use the exact same method as previously described in the INSIDE->OUT nmap scan but with the added dimension of looking at the **nmap** output itself. Obviously you need to have a host you can get to first, so if you're on the other side of the Internet, your options are limited. However, if you're on the same segment of the firewall, here is a neat trick that may help you identify weaknesses in your firewall. Set the firewall as your gateway. You'd be surprised at how many times we have managed to beat firewall rules by doing this. We realize it's a pretty brainless method, but it's often the simple things that get you into the most trouble.

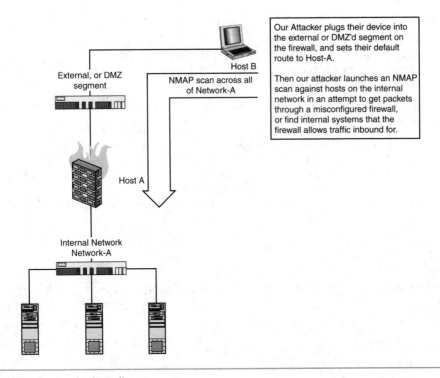

Figure 10.2   Setting the firewall as your gateway.

Host-A: Our firewall

Host-B: The attacker

Network-A: Internal Network

Host-B connects to the "hard" or externally facing network in your office building (perhaps from a conference room on a "DMZ" network or wireless network). Host-B sets the default route to Host-A. Then it starts using **nmap** to scan out nonroutable IP address space (RFC1918) and watching their logs for ICMP or UDP messages of interest, and ultimately it discovers what the IP space for Network-A is. Another method of discovering what this IP space is would be to send email messages to email addresses that do not exist and look at the IP information in the headers of the messages to determine the IP space of Network-A.

READING OUTPUT FROM NMAP

The reliability of data from **nmap** depends on the type of scanning being used and the types of systems you're scanning. Just remember, you can get false positives! If you're not sure, scan things more than once.

Personally, we favor TCP and SYN scanning; FIN and UDP scanning are unreliable when dealing with slow networks. Especially in the case of Microsoft-based systems, FIN scans are next to useless. UDP scanning is by nature very unreliable and time consuming. In general you'll find that doing full 65K port scans are not going to be fast unless you are on a very fast network. Let's look at some example firewall output:

TCP scan against the first 1024 ports (nmap -sT -P0 -p 1-1024 Host-B) to a DMZ web server from the outside. The firewall policy is flawed, so it's not really blocking things as it should.

```
Port         State        Service
21/tcp       open         ftp
22/tcp       open         ssh
25/tcp       open         smtp
53/tcp       open         domain
80/tcp       open         http
106/tcp      open         pop3pw
110/tcp      open         pop-3
143/tcp      open         imap2
443/tcp      open         https
465/tcp      open         smtps
466/tcp      open         digital-vrc
505/tcp      open         mailbox-lm
993/tcp      open         imaps
995/tcp      open         pop3s
```

Now what's interesting about this output is that the targeted system is actually running one more service, **RPC Bind** (**portmapper**, port 111), but is using local **iptables**/netfilter firewall rules to disallow access to that port (using REJECT, which returns an ICMP message). Let's see that output again, but using a SYN scan (nmap -sS -P0 -p 1-1024 Host-B):

```
Port         State        Service
21/tcp       open         ftp
22/tcp       open         ssh
25/tcp       open         smtp
53/tcp       open         domain
```

```
80/tcp      open        http
106/tcp     open        pop3pw
110/tcp     open        pop-3
111/tcp     filtered    sunrpc
143/tcp     open        imap2
443/tcp     open        https
465/tcp     open        smtps
466/tcp     open        digital-vrc
505/tcp     open        mailbox-lm
993/tcp     open        imaps
995/tcp     open        pop3s
```

Note that *this* time the SYN scan picked up the filtered port. This demonstrates the value of varying your scanning methods. TCP scans are by far the most accurate in terms of "can you get to the service," but SYN scans can show you more information. A FIN scan returns similar results (nmap -sF -PO -p 1-1024 Host-B):

```
Port        State       Service
21/tcp      open        ftp
22/tcp      open        ssh
25/tcp      open        smtp
53/tcp      open        domain
80/tcp      open        http
106/tcp     open        pop3pw
110/tcp     open        pop-3
111/tcp     filtered    sunrpc
143/tcp     open        imap2
443/tcp     open        https
465/tcp     open        smtps
466/tcp     open        digital-vrc
505/tcp     open        mailbox-lm
993/tcp     open        imaps
995/tcp     open        pop3s
```

However, let's try these same scans on a Windows PC, Host-C, first using a TCP scan(nmap -sS -PO -p 1-1024 Host-C).

```
PORT  STATE SERVICE

135/tcp open  msrpc
139/tcp open  netbios-ssn
445/tcp open  microsoft-ds
```

SYN scan (nmap -sS -P0 1-1024 Host-C):

```
PORT   STATE SERVICE

135/tcp open  msrpc
139/tcp open  netbios-ssn
445/tcp open  microsoft-ds
```

And finally a FIN scan (nmap -sF -P0 1-1024 Host-C)

```
PORT STATE SERVICE
```

As you can see, this scan returns no data on a Microsoft OS. We also have seen FIN scans return all ports as being open or sometimes just a few random ones. If you doubt the results, scan things multiple times. This doesn't mean that FIN scans are useless in terms of testing—quite the opposite. You might have configured your firewall to test for impossible TCP combinations, a FIN packet coming before a SYN packet for example. The iplog/nmap method is a very fast, reusable diagnostic procedure for testing all sorts of rules (the last thing you want to do is keep writing custom tools for custom rules!).

For the most accurate results, it's best if you can get on the systems and see what services those systems are running, first-hand, using the netstat command or a local nmap scan (we recommend both). Here is the output of the same system, Host-B just described, using netstat:

```
[root@Host-B root]# netstat -an
tcp        0        0 0.0.0.0:21          0.0.0.0:*          LISTEN
tcp        0        0 0.0.0.0:22          0.0.0.0:*          LISTEN
tcp        0        0 0.0.0.0:25          0.0.0.0:*          LISTEN
tcp        0        0 0.0.0.0:80          0.0.0.0:*          LISTEN
tcp        0        0 0.0.0.0:106         0.0.0.0:*          LISTEN
tcp        0        0 0.0.0.0:110         0.0.0.0:*          LISTEN
tcp        0        0 0.0.0.0:111         0.0.0.0:*          LISTEN
tcp        0        0 0.0.0.0:143         0.0.0.0:*          LISTEN
tcp        0        0 0.0.0.0:443         0.0.0.0:*          LISTEN
tcp        0        0 0.0.0.0:465         0.0.0.0:*          LISTEN
tcp        0        0 0.0.0.0:466         0.0.0.0:*          LISTEN
tcp        0        0 0.0.0.0:505         0.0.0.0:*          LISTEN
tcp        0        0 0.0.0.0:993         0.0.0.0:*          LISTEN
tcp        0        0 0.0.0.0:995         0.0.0.0:*          LISTEN
```

> **NOTE**
>
> A useful addition to this is the `netstat -pan` command, which will show you the process name associated with each port.

TESTING YOUR FIREWALL WITH FRAGROUTER

As we mentioned earlier, fragmentation attacks are a great way to beat packet filtering firewalls. This isn't normally an issue at all with **iptables**/netfilter; however, it can happen in certain conditions. And if you ever needed to assess the firewall capabilities of a piece of network gear in conjunction with your Linux firewalls, this is a great method to do it.

To test your firewall(s) using **fragrouter**, you will need two systems in addition to your firewall/packet filter. This is because **fragrouter** cannot by design be run on the same system from which you're testing (according to the documentation, this is to prevent abuse). In this example, we have three systems. The firewall, our scanner box called Host-A, the **iplog** machine called Host-B, and the **fragrouter** system called Host-C.

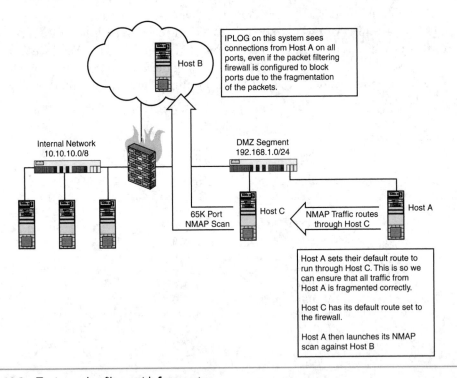

Figure 10.3   Testing packet filters with **fragrouter**.

We'll assume you've already set up Host-A and Host-B as outlined here. Our Host-C system is an aged Red Hat 7.2 system, and while this OS has been End-Of-Lifed (EOL) by Red Hat, security updates are still available from the FedoraLegacy.org project for at least another year and a half after the EOL date (at least). So it's a safe, supported OS that should not expose you to any additional unreasonable risk from using it in a testing environment. That long-winded startup aside, you'll need to install **fragrouter** on the system (which incidentally, we have only gotten to run on older Red Hat systems, which is why we brought all this up!).

On Host-A: Set the default route to Host-B using Host-C as the gateway:

```
[root@Host-A root]# route add host Host-B gateway Host-B)
```

On Host-C: Install and start **fragrouter**:

```
[root@Host-C root]# fragrouter -F1
fragrouter: frag-1 started
```

On Host-A, start your TCP connections, nmap attacks, and so on and watch the output on Host-B's **iplog** traffic. Additionally, return traffic from Host-B to Host-A will not pass through **fragrouter**, which is handy if you're also testing more advanced things such as combining your firewall with an IDS. In general, the output you're going to see on Host-B will be the same as the nonfragmentation tests. In fact, you can perform fragmentation tests using **nmap** with the -f flag. However, what's nice about **fragrouter** is that you're able to test any application you want in a fragmented state (web, NFS, mail, and so on). When it comes to demonstrating what the risk is from fragmentation attacks, this is a fantastic way to do it.

In closing, the scope of this test is specifically to verify that rules you know are in place and are not susceptible to fragmentation attacks. For example, you've already verified that outbound rules are working with your firewalls, and you're testing their ability to deal with complex packet fragmentation (or you just want to see if your packet filtering on the switch/router actually works!).

VLANs

VLANs are virtual LAN environments created logically (as opposed to physically) in network switching equipment. They are very common in modern networks and an absolutely fantastic way to improve quality of service in a big network. However, a VLAN is no substitute for real physical separation between firewalled segments. This is due to the fact that there are all sorts of different methods available to defeat the compartmentalization of a VLAN or switched network. One such tool is called **dsniff** (http://www.monkey.org/~dugsong/dsniff/), and we have used it many times to demonstrate how Layer 2 logical compartmentalization is not appropriate for firewall environments.

For example, we were performing a vulnerability assessment on a very large banking client. They had, by far, the most fantastic, heavily compartmentalized, paranoid wire diagram we had ever seen: multiple layers of firewalls, NIDS (network-based intrusion detection), and HIDS (host-based intrusion detection) all over the place, which looked absolutely fantastic on paper. However, what they failed to recognize was that the "compartmentalization" was really all logical. The entire five-layer (no joke—dual-connected, 10 firewalls protecting 20 systems) system was really two switches. We broke into their edge router, which was connected to the management network (also logical) and from there proceeded to spoof our way onto every VLAN, bypassing all five layers of firewalls. I doubt a single one of our packets ever even touched them. NIDS, of course, rarely can detect the symptoms of such an attack, and the HIDS…well, they all logged to the management system—which was the first system we were able to compromise.

As for a *How To* on how we did all of this…well, you'll have to wait for our next book!

SUMMARY

To repeat a theme, just installing a firewall is not going to secure your network. Testing the firewall rules, the placement of networks, and the physical infrastructure are all components in building an effective security model—along with other elements of security and risk management discussed throughout this book. If there is any theme you should take from this chapter, it's that you should always test everything rigorously whenever you make a change. Challenge your assumptions and whenever possible, use third parties to review your work!

Layer 2/Inline Filtering

In addition to Layer 3 (IP), and Layer 4(TCP/UDP) filtering capabilities as described in preceding chapters, **iptables**/netfilter also has the capacity to filter traffic at Layer 2. This is an especially useful mechanism in environments where you are attempting to build an inline transparent firewall, in the case of an IDS you would like to make capable of responding to attacks, performing filtering in a bridging environment, or adding in MAC address filter rules when dealing with wireless networks.

Bridging, simply put, is a method of joining two or more separate Ethernet networks together. From the perspective of the users on either side of the bridge, they are on the same network. This is because bridging happens at Layer 2 of the OSI model, which is the layer before IP (Internet Protocol). Because of this, firewalling in Layer 2 is considered "transparent" because no IP addresses are involved.

A transparent firewall is basically implementing a firewall inside of a bridge. The advantage of this is that it is a low-impact network topology change. If you have ever attempted to make topology changes in a large bureaucratic business or government agency, we are sure you can relate to the pain these changes cause. A transparent firewall is by its nature invisible—the fact that it's Linux-based means that it is low cost and can run on Legacy hardware. If you were ever looking for an ideal way to use Linux firewalls in a large enterprise, this is it. You can build them out of old gear you have lying around and deploy them throughout your network without having to change settings on other devices (routers, gateways, and so on). Best of all, your users will never even notice that they have been installed.

Figure 11.1 shows a 10.0.0.0/8 RFC1918 network running off of two separate switches. In this configuration, from the user's perspective on the 10.10.10.0/8 network and the 10.10.11.0/8 network, they are on the same network.

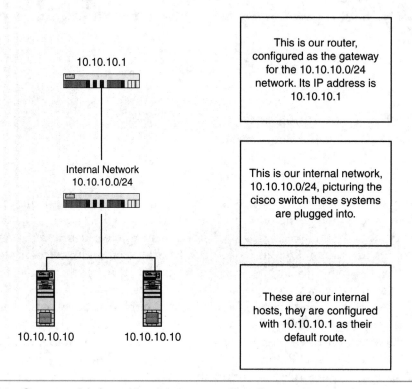

Figure 11.1   Our network before adding the transparent firewall.

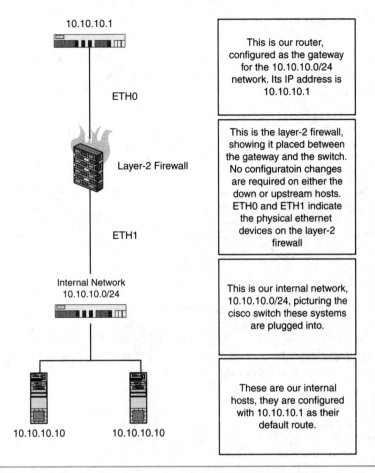

10.10.10.1

ETH0

Layer-2 Firewall

ETH1

Internal Network
10.10.10.0/24

10.10.10.10   10.10.10.10

This is our router, configured as the gateway for the 10.10.10.0/24 network. Its IP address is 10.10.10.1

This is the layer-2 firewall, showing it placed between the gateway and the switch. No configuratoin changes are required on either the down or upstream hosts. ETH0 and ETH1 indicate the physical ethernet devices on the layer-2 firewall

This is our internal network, 10.10.10.0/24, picturing the cisco switch these systems are plugged into.

These are our internal hosts, they are configured with 10.10.10.1 as their default route.

Figure 11.2 The same network with our transparent firewall installed.

COMMON QUESTIONS

Q: My bridge mode **iptables** rules such as the following don't work:

```
$IPTABLES -A INPUT...
```

A: Bridged traffic goes through the FORWARD chain. As you are bridging traffic, nothing is destined to the firewall itself. The right way to do the above rule is

```
$IPTABLES -A FORWARD...
```

Q: On a 2.6 kernel, how are the bridged interfaces different?

A: With 2.6, both the inbound and outbound network interface is the bridge interface, br0 for example. This means that when you are creating physdev rules, on connection tracking rules for example, you would use the br0 interface rather than the real interface, for example

```
# this configuration assumes that two interfaces, eth0 (external) and eth1(internal)
have
# been bound into one common bridging interface, br0
# traffic inbound, hitting the eth0 device, will be matched against this rule.
$IPTABLES -A FORWARD -i br0 -m physdev \
        -physdev-in eth0 -m state         \
        --state ESTABLISHED,RELATED -j ACCEPT
```

TOOLS DISCUSSED IN THIS CHAPTER

ebtables (http://ebtables.sourceforge.net) is a filtering tool for an **iptables**/netfilter firewall running in bridge mode. It also has the ability to alter MAC addresses and route traffic at Layer 2. From the website, **ebtables** supports the following features:

1. Ethernet protocol filtering
2. MAC address filtering
3. Simple IP header filtering
4. ARP header filtering
5. 802.1Q VLAN filtering
6. In/Out interface filtering (logical and physical device)
7. MAC address nat
8. Logging Frame counters
9. Ability to add, delete and insert rules; flush chains; zero counters
10. brouter facility
11. Ability to automatically load a complete table, containing the rules you made into the kernel
12. Support for user defined chains
13. Support for marking frames and matching marked frames

Building an Inline Transparent Bridging Firewall with ebtables (Stealth Firewalls)

As of the 2.6 Linux kernel, the ability to perform advanced bridge mode filtering using **ebtables** (`http://ebtables.sourceforge.net`) is supported by default. Patching the kernel or **iptables** is not required as of the 2.6 Linux kernel. 2.4.x Linux kernel users will first need to patch their kernel from the **ebtables** website using the `ebtables-brnf-5` patch. In addition, the user-space **ebtables** tool will be required on both kernels to manipulate the filtering rules.

In the following documentation we will assume that the system, minimoose, has two ethernet interfaces, `eth0` and `eth1`. This system will be inserted between two networks, 10.10.10.0/8 and 10.10.11.0/8, in such a way as the hosts on either side of these networks are not aware that a firewall has been put in place. This is outlined in Figure 11.3.

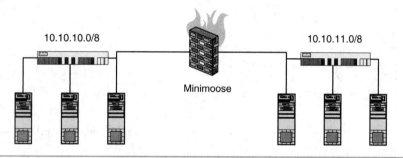

10.10.10.0/8   10.10.11.0/8

Minimoose

Figure 11.3   Inline transparent bridging firewall.

1. Configuring 2.4.x Kernels for **ebtables**. The latest version of this kernel patch is available from the **ebtables** website, at `http://ebtables.sourceforge.net/`. Download and patch your kernel with the appropriate version for your kernel release (example: `ebtables-brnf-5_versus_2.4.25.diff.gz` for Linux 2.4.25 kernels).

2. Configuring the kernel—code maturity level options:

```
[*] Prompt for development and/or incomplete code/drivers
```

Networking Options

```
IP: Netfilter Configuration
   (In addition to your regular options)
```

```
MAC address match support (NEW)
    <M>ARP tables support (NEW)
ARP packet filtering (NEW)
    <M>ARP payload mangling (NEW)
  <M>802.1d Ethernet Bridging
    <M>Bridge: ebtables (NEW)
     <M>ebt: filter table support
     <M>ebt: nat table support
     <M>ebt: broute table support
     <M>ebt: log support
     <M>ebt: IP filter support
     <M>ebt: ARP filter support
     <M>ebt: among filter support
     <M>ebt: limit filter support
     <M>ebt: 802.1Q VLAN filter support
     <M>ebt: 802.3 filter support
     <M>ebt: packet type filter support
     <M>ebt: STP filter support
     <M>ebt: mark filter support
     <M>ebt: arp reply target support
     <M>ebt: snat target support
     <M>ebt: dnat target support
     <M>ebt: redirect target support
     <M>ebt: mark target support
```

NOTE

The M flag means compile this option as a module. This assumes you have module support compiled into your kernel.

3. Install the user space **ebtables** utility from `http://sourceforge.net/project/ showfiles.php?group_id=39571`.
4. Compile a 2.6 Kernel for **ebtables**. As **ebtables** support is natively included in the 2.6 Kernel, there is no need to patch it. Let's move on to configuration you will need to select the following options:

```
Device Drivers
  Networking Support
    Networking Options --->
       <M> 802.1d Ethernet Bridging
```

```
[*] Network packet filtering (replaces ipchains)  --->
 [*]    Bridged IP/ARP packets filtering
  Bridge: Netfilter Configuration  --->
   <M> Ethernet Bridge tables (ebtables) support
    <M>    ebt: broute table support (NEW)
    <M>    ebt: filter table support (NEW)
    <M>    ebt: nat table support (NEW)
    <M>    ebt: 802.3 filter support (NEW)
    <M>    ebt: among filter support (NEW)
    <M>    ebt: ARP filter support (NEW)
    <M>    ebt: IP filter support (NEW)
    <M>    ebt: limit match support (NEW)
    <M>    ebt: mark filter support (NEW)
    <M>    ebt: packet type filter support (NEW)
    <M>    ebt: STP filter support (NEW)
    <M>    ebt: 802.1Q VLAN filter support (NEW)
    <M>    ebt: arp reply target support (NEW)
    <M>    ebt: dnat target support (NEW)
    <M>    ebt: mark target support (NEW)
    <M>    ebt: redirect target support (NEW)
    <M>    ebt: snat target support (NEW)
    <M>    ebt: log support (NEW)
```

5. Download and install the **ebtables** user space utility.

After your kernel has been built with **ebtables** support, you can move on to the next phase, which is to create the bridge interface on the kernel. There is an additional user space tool for this, which is included by most distributions by default, called **brctl**, which you can find in the bridge-utils rpm on rpm-based distributions (**red hat**, **mandrake**, **suse**, and so on). If you do not have **brctl** on your system, it is available at `http://bridge.sourceforge.net`.

In our example, we will assume that minimoose, our soon-to-be stealth firewall, has no IP addresses associated with it. This is a perfectly normal configuration for a stealth firewall, and provided you have physical console or serial console access, it is not difficult to maintain. You can, however, assign IP addresses to this firewall, provided you don't mind giving away its existence. If you're attempting to build a truly "stealth" firewall, you do not want this system to have any IP addresses assigned to where the systems on either side of the bridged networks can see the stealth firewall directly. That being said—on to creating our bridged interface...

A bridged network involves creating a third logical interface, which is a combination of the two (or more) bridged physical interfaces:

1. Create the logical interface in the kernel.

```
[root@minimoose root]# brctl addbr br0
```

2. Add the left interface, eth0 which connects to the 10.10.10.0/24 network.

```
[root@minimoose root]# brctl addif br0 eth0
```

3. Add the right interface, eth1 which connects to the 10.10.11.0/24 network.

```
[root@minimoose root]# brctl addif br0 eth1
```

4. Activate the bridged interfaces by bringing up the two real interfaces.

```
[root@minimoose root]# ifconfig eth0 0.0.0.0 up
[root@minimoose root]# ifconfig eth1 0.0.0.0 up
```

At this point your bridge will be active, and hosts between the two networks will be none-the-wiser. In this example we're splicing the transparent firewall in between two switches. You could, however, just as easily put this system up in between a router and a switch or even between the switch and a single host. This poses all sorts of useful configurations, transparent proxy servers, forensics logging hosts, network diagnostics/monitoring, IDS platforms, and of course "stealth" firewalls.

This then brings us to filtering traffic. Outlined in the following section are a few basic recipes for Layer 2 firewalls (this list is by no means complete).

FILTERING ON MAC ADDRESS BOUND TO A SPECIFIC IP ADDRESS WITH EBTABLES

The first example describes a rule only allowing a specific IP address, 10.10.10.12, to pass through the firewall if it is bound to the MAC address, 00:11:22:33:44:55. This is useful in the case of wireless networks (although not foolproof—MAC addresses can be spoofed, too!).

```
$EBTABLES -A FORWARD -p IPv4 --ip-src 10.10.10.12 \
      -s !  00:11:22:33:44:55 -j DROP
```

FILTERING OUT SPECIFIC PORTS WITH EBTABLES

The following rule demonstrates a more powerful target in **ebtables**, the BROUTING policy. The following example shows the **ebtables** rule being used to only allow port 25 traffic (SMTP) to the host at 10.10.10.12.

```
$EBTABLES -t broute -A BROUTING -p ipv4 \
      --ip-dst 10.10.10.12 -ip-proto tcp \
      -ip-dport 25  -j ACCEPT
$EBTABLES -t broute -A BROUTING -p ipv4 \
      --ip-proto tcp --ip-dport 25 -j DROP
```

BUILDING AN INLINE TRANSPARENT BRIDGING FIREWALL WITH IPTABLES (STEALTH FIREWALLS)

ebtables is a far more powerful interface for manipulating traffic at Layer 2; however, in environments where you do not need to control Layer 2 traffic with the granularity of **ebtables, iptables** can be used for handling firewall rules at Layer 3, implemented in a Layer 2 bridge.

An example of using **iptables** in a Layer 2 transparent firewall is as a worm defense system. As Figure 11.4 shows, we have several of these firewalls deployed throughout the network where we place restrictions on what kinds of traffic can come into and out of the networks. Our users are on the network 192.168.1.0, and we will use this firewall to block all NetBIOS traffic going into and out of this network.

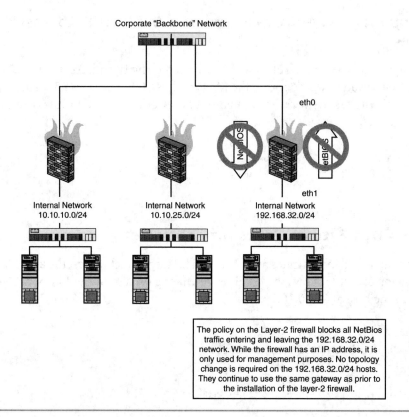

The policy on the Layer-2 firewall blocks all NetBios traffic entering and leaving the 192.168.32.0/24 network. While the firewall has an IP address, it is only used for management purposes. No topology change is required on the 192.168.32.0/24 hosts. They continue to use the same gateway as prior to the installation of the layer-2 firewall.

Figure 11.4   The use of inline Layer 2 firewalls.

The following script would be applied to each firewall, modifying the management IP and gateway variables as required.

```
#!/bin/sh

IPTABLES=/sbin/iptables
IFCONFIG=/sbin/ifconfig
BRCTL=/usr/sbin/brctl
ROUTE=/sbin/route

MANAGEMENTIP=192.168.1.51
MANAGEMENTGATEWAY=192.168.1.1

# shut down our Ethernet devices
$IFCONFIG eth0 down
$IFCONFIG eth1down
```

```
# bring the Ethernet devices back up with no IP addresses
$IFCONFIG eth0 up 0.0.0.0
$IFCONFIG eth1 up 0.0.0.0

# create our bridge device, and add our Ethernet devices
$BRCTL addbr br0
$BRCTL addif br0 eth0
$BRCTL addif br0 eth1

# add an IP address to the bridge device, this is for management purposes only
$IFCONFIG br0 $MANAGEMENTIP
$ROUTE add default gw $MANAGEMENTGATEWAY
# now for our firewall rules
# note that when bridging  these rules are applied against the FORWARD chain
$IPTABLES -A FORWARD -p all -sport 135 -j REJECT
$IPTABLES -A FORWARD -p all -dport 135 -j REJECT
$IPTABLES -A FORWARD -p all -sport 137 -j REJECT
$IPTABLES -A FORWARD -p all -dport 137 -j REJECT
$IPTABLES -A FORWARD -p all -sport 139 -j REJECT
$IPTABLES -A FORWARD -p all -dport 139 -j REJECT
$IPTABLES -A FORWARD -s 192.168.1.0/24 -j ACCEPT
$IPTABLES -A FORWARD -d 192.168.1.0/24 -j ACCEPT
```

MAC Address Filtering with iptables

In the Layer 2 world, systems are uniquely identified by their MAC addresses, which might look something like this: 00:90:F5:1E:30:D0. **iptables** can be used at Layer 2, just like **ebtables**, specifically for filtering out MAC addresses. You might want to do this because you are running a transparent firewall and your users have dynamically assigned IP addresses. Filtering purely on the IP address (Layer 3) might not be particularly effective due to the fact that these IP addresses are ever changing. (Note: MAC addresses can be changed too—this is *not* a silver bullet!)

In the event that you need to filter out MAC addresses either destined to or passing through the firewall (presumably in a bridging configuration), one recommended method is to combine your filter rules into one common user defined chain, as follows:

```
$IPTABLES -N MACFILTER
$IPTABLES -A MACFILTER -m mac \
        --mac-source 00:11:22:33:44:55 -j ACCEPT
$IPTABLES -A MACFILTER -m mac \
```

```
        --mac-source 00:11:22:33:44:11 -j ACCEPT
$IPTABLES -A MACFILTER -m mac \
        --mac-source 00:11:22:33:44:22 -j ACCEPT
$IPTABLES -A MACFILTER -m mac \
        --mac-source 00:11:22:33:44:33 -j ACCEPT
$IPTABLES -A MACFILTER -j DROP
```

To filter out MAC addresses destined to your firewall, you would apply this user-defined rule to the INPUT chain:

```
# eth0 assumes that the source of the MAC addresses being filtered are coming
#from the eth0 interface physically
$IPTABLES -A INPUT -i eth0 -j MACFILTER
```

To filter out MAC addresses passing through your firewall, you would apply this rule to the FORWARD chain:

```
# eth0 assumes that the source of the MAC addresses being filtered are
# coming from the eth0 interface physically
$IPTABLES -A FORWARD -i eth0 -j MACFILTER
```

> **NOTE**
>
> If you're trying to filter out DHCP requests, this is not the way to do it! See the next section.

DHCP FILTERING WITH EBTABLES

In this example, we are assuming that you are running a DHCP server on your **iptables**/netfilter system and are attempting to filter out incoming requests to the server using firewall rules. If you attempted the previous example, you've probably already noticed that this does not work. This is because DHCP acts at a much lower level than **iptables**/netfilter can process. This particular problem calls for using **ebtables** (http://ebtables.sourceforge.net) as the solution as outlined in the first section of this chapter.

Example rule:

```
$EBTABLES -A INPUT  -s 00:11:22:33:44:55 -j DROP
```

Note that this rule uses the INPUT chain. This is because the traffic is destined to the **iptables**/netfilter system itself. Applying the lessons learned from the simple **iptables**-based MAC filtering detailed previously, we can create a user-defined chain to filter out multiple MAC addresses.

Example:

```
$EBTABLES -N MACFILTER
$EBTABLES -A MACFILTER -s 00:11:22:33:44:55 -j ACCEPT
$EBTABLES -A MACFILTER -s 00:11:22:33:44:11 -j ACCEPT
$EBTABLES -A MACFILTER -s 00:11:22:33:44:22 -j ACCEPT
$EBTABLES -A MACFILTER -s 00:11:22:33:44:33 -j ACCEPT
$EBTABLES -A MACFILTER -j DROP
```

This would be followed by an INPUT chain rule to only allow MAC addresses listed in MACFILTER to communicate with the firewall.

eth0 is the physical interface that would be receiving the traffic.

```
$EBTABLES -A INPUT -i eth0 -j MACFILTER
```

Just like the MAC Filtering section here, if you only wanted to apply these rules on traffic passing through the firewall, you would use

```
$EBTABLES -A FORWARD -i eth0 -j MACFILTER
```

eth0 is the physical interface that would be receiving the traffic.

SUMMARY

As the **perl** motto goes, "There's more than one way to do it!" Firewalling can be done in such a way that it is transparent to the user and other components in the network. It really depends on the problem you are trying to solve. As mentioned before, we favor Layer 2 firewalls for internal use in environments where we need to have minimal impact on the users. As later chapters will show, it's not a one-size-fits-all process; there are times when using netfilter/ebtables will be the right solution, and other times when it would be better to use a netfilter/**iptables** as a Layer 3 device such as NAT, as the next chapter will discuss.

NAT (Network Address Translation) and IP Forwarding

By far perhaps the most common use of Linux firewalls these days are in SOHO (Small Office/Home Office) environments. NAT-ing, or setting up a firewall to perform Network Address Translation (NAT) services, is simply a method of translating one address space to another—or to be more specific in terms of SOHO users, a method of sharing a single network connection amongst multiple machines. NAT-ing is probably one of the most common uses of a firewall.

For more advanced installations, we can use NAT to create "DMZ" networks (short for De-Militarized Zones), which are networks that sit off to the "side" of the firewall so to speak. DMZs are dedicated to some specific task such as hosting corporate web, mail, DNS, and so on. A DMZ network would be used to provide limited access to/from those systems from other networks for the purpose of isolating those systems from the internal network and the Internet. The intent is to not only protect those servers, but also to protect the internal network from them. After all, they are exposed to some untrusted network, the Internet perhaps, and those servers have a higher probability of being broken into. But because they are isolated on a DMZ network, those servers cannot be used to break into the internal network if the firewall is configured properly. A word of caution: A DMZ is only a DMZ if the firewall is configured to isolate the systems on that DMZ network from some other network. If you punch holes in your firewall, allowing the DMZ servers to connect back into your Internet network(s), you're seriously weakening if not outright eliminating the protections you get by isolating your DMZ servers.

Some example uses of a DMZ network would be to create a DMZ for all your wireless access points (see the VPN chapter for more information on this) and to use that DMZ to limit what your wireless users can access on your internal "wired" network. Another use of a DMZ might be to allow access to your web or mail servers from networks outside of your control (like the Internet) or a partner's network. The value of such a configuration, as already described, is that if your mail or web servers are compromised, an intruder could not use access to those systems to leverage access into your internal network.

In this chapter we will cover diagnostic procedures for some of the most common NAT problems and provide examples of how to create specific types of firewalls. Specifically, debugging common DMZ mistakes, issues with the common network hardware, methods to aid you in debugging NAT or IP forwarding issues, and some frequently asked questions regarding Network Address Translation and IP Forwarding configurations will be discussed.

Recall that before starting on any of these steps, you will want to apply the troubleshooting methodology covered in Chapter 4, and the OSI model technique in Chapter 5 to rule out other root causes in lower parts of the OSI model (Layers 1 and 2) and also to correctly identify and recreate the problem before attempting any of these troubleshooting steps.

COMMON QUESTIONS ABOUT LINUX NAT

Q: What's the real difference between masquerading and SNAT?

A: Both are methods of moving traffic between networks through the firewall. In practice, masquerading is going to be the right choice when you're dealing with dynamic external IP addresses (Internet facing, and so on) on your firewall, and SNAT is going to be the right choice when that IP address is static and/or you're looking to allow connections back through your firewall to your internal network. Additionally the overhead of supporting SNAT connections is lower than that of supporting masqueraded connections.

Q: Can **iptables**/netfilter rules use hostnames for DNAT rules rather than IP addresses?

A: Yes and no. You can certainly use a hostname instead of an IP address in a firewall rule; however, when the rule is loaded, this is converted into an IP address. So if the intent is to get an effect like name-based virtual hosting in apache—where multiple hostnames point to a single IP address and you want to route those connections to different internal machines based on the hostname, **iptables** is not capable of doing this by itself. However the addition of a user space application-layer proxy, such as the http proxy, **squid** (http://www.squid-cache.org), or the user space utility, **iproute2** (ftp://ftp.inr.ac.ru/ip-routing/), would allow you to do this.

Q: My filter rules aren't working in a NAT environment!

A: One mistake you don't want to make is to use DROP/REJECT rules inside of a NAT table. This is because the NAT table makes heavy use of connection tracking, which simply put, means it's not going to see all the packets. If the firewall cannot see all the packets, then it's pretty likely that you're going to be leaking information—or worse, packets in and out of your network.

You'll also see this happen using the nmap tests discussed in Chapter 10 when your rules are out of order. Make sure you have your DROP rules before your ALLOW rules. A good way to do this is to set a global DENY ALL type rule first and then selectively allow what kind of traffic you want to allow through after that in each step.

TOOLS/METHODS DISCUSSED IN THIS CHAPTER

DIAGNOSTIC LOGGING

Probably one of the single most valuable diagnostic procedures in debugging firewall rules is a catch all logging rule, which was covered earlier in Chapter 9. In all of our following example rules, we will include that example of our diagnostic catch all rule. You may or may not want to keep this rule on in a production environment, especially if you are interested in seeing what your firewall is dropping from a security standpoint. However, bear in mind the additional disk space this might require for long-term use and potential I/O issues caused by excessive writes to the log file(s).

Example:

```
# catch all dropped packets
$IPTABLES -A INPUT -p all  -m limit --limit 1/second \
        -j LOG  --log-level info --log-prefix "FINAL -- DROP "\
        --log-tcp-sequence  --log-tcp-options --log-ip-options
```

Example output:

```
Jun 30 17:22:19 localhost kernel: FINAL -- DROP IN=eth0 OUT=
MAC=ff:ff:ff:ff:ff:ff:00:50:57:00:7d:b9:08:00 SRC=10.5.64.1 DST=255.255.255.255
LEN=328 TOS=0x06 PREC=0x00 TTL=16 ID=0 PROTO=UDP SPT=67 DPT=68 LEN=308
Jun 30 17:22:23 localhost kernel: FINAL -- DROP IN=eth1 OUT=
MAC=ff:ff:ff:ff:ff:ff:00:0a:e6:8d:ec:af:08:00 SRC=10.10.12.201 DST=255.255.255.255
LEN=153 TOS=0x00 PREC=0x00 TTL=64 ID=0 DF PROTO=UDP SPT=631 DPT=631 LEN=133
```

Line 1 shows the firewall is dropping a UDP port 67 (DHCP) packet being broadcast from the system 10.5.64.1 on the eth0 (external) interface. Line 2 shows a UDP port 631 (cups printer) packet being broadcast from the system 10.10.12.201 on the eth1 interface.

VIEWING NAT CONNECTIONS WITH NETSTAT-NAT

One highly recommended tool for viewing NAT-ed connections through a firewall is the user-space tool, **netstat-nat** available from: `http://tweegy.demon.nl/projects/ netstat-nat/index.html`.

This utility, which requires the kernel to be compiled with IP connection tracking, works similarly to the netstat command, but specifically displays NAT connection information.

Example diagnostic usage:

netstat-nat -S would display SNAT or masqueraded connections

netstat-nat -D would display DNAT connections

netstat-nat -L would display connections to the NAT system

Example output:

```
[root@minimoose root]# netstat-nat -S
Proto NATed Address          Foreign Address          State
tcp   10.10.12.201:59837     po:imaps                 ESTABLISHED
tcp   192.168.32.190:36340   server4:ssh              ESTABLISHED
```

This output shows that the system 10.10.12.201 has an open outbound SSL IMAP connection to the remote server "po" and that the system 192.168.32.190 has an open outbound SSH connection to the server "server4."

```
[root@minimoose root]# netstat-nat -D
Proto NATed Address          Foreign Address          State
tcp   10.10.12.201:37708.    10.10.12.1:http          ESTABLISHED
tcp   192.168.32.190:47775   192.168.32.1:5190        ESTABLISHED
```

This output demonstrates more advanced inbound connection data. Specifically, our firewall is running transparent application layer proxies, reaim (for IM traffic) and squid (for web traffic) on the firewall itself. Both of these proxies are discussed in later chapters, and the data here indicates that there is an open redirect from the systems

10.10.12.201 and 192.168.32.190 to the locally running proxy servers on the system. From the end user's perspective, they are using their applications as normal. Specifically the system at 10.10.12.201 has an open web browser on www.cnn.com, and 192.168.32.190 has an open AOL Instant Messenger client.

```
[root@minimoose root]# netstat-nat -L
Proto Source Address               Destination Address              State
raw   192.168.32.1:               192.168.32.190:                  REPLIED
tcp   192.168.32.190:59471        192.168.32.1:ssh                 ESTABLISHED
tcp   192.168.32.190:59590        192.168.32.1:ssh                 ESTABLISHED
tcp   192.168.32.190:58923        empire:ssh                       ESTABLISHED
tcp   ip68-98-150-6.dc.dc.cox.:41579 hal-d023e.blue.aol.com:5190   ESTABLISHED
```

This shows an even more advanced picture of the traffic being NAT-ed through our firewall. The output from this shows a "raw" connection from the firewall (192.168.32.1) to the system 192.168.32.190. In this case, this "raw" connection is an IPSEC VPN being used to secure a wireless network that has been configured as a DMZ. On lines 2 and 3, we also see two SSH sessions from the 192.168.32.190 host to the firewall. These are two separate SSH sessions being used to run the netstat-nat commands. The fourth line shows an open SSH session from 192.168.32.190 to the system named "empire," which in this case happens to be on the internal "wired" network. Line 5 shows the rest of the picture from the netstat-nat -D example here. This is the reaim proxy server making the connection to the AOL Instant Messenger on behalf of the host 192.168.32.190.

LISTING CURRENT NAT ENTRIES WITH IPTABLES

```
iptables -t nat -L
```

This command will show all your NAT rules on your system.

Example output:

```
[root@minimoose root]# iptables -t nat -L
Chain PREROUTING (policy ACCEPT)
target     prot opt source              destination
DNAT       tcp  --  anywhere            anywhere           tcp dpts:6881:6889
to:192.168.32.190
REDIRECT   tcp  --  anywhere            anywhere           tcp dpt:http redir ports 3128
REDIRECT   tcp  --  anywhere            anywhere           tcp dpt:5190 redir ports 5190
```

```
Chain POSTROUTING (policy ACCEPT)
target      prot opt source              destination
MASQUERADE  all  --  anywhere            anywhere

Chain OUTPUT (policy ACCEPT)
target      prot opt source              destination
```

The first line in the PREROUTING chain shows a DNAT rule on the firewall that redirects connections to the firewall on ports 6881 through 6889 to the system 192.168.32.190. This is specifically an example of getting the bittorrent file sharing protocol through a firewall. Line 2 shows the firewall is configured as a transparent proxy server—any outbound connections through the firewall on port 80 will be redirected to the local port 3128, which is running a squid proxy server. This is called a "transparent proxy" because from the user's experience, they do not even know the proxy server is there. Line 3 is a similar transparent redirect, but this time for the AOL Instant Messenger protocol. Again from the user's perspective, this is completely transparent.

The POSTROUTING chain shows that the system is configured to MASQUERADE connections from anywhere to anywhere. In this case our firewall has a dynamic IP address.

LISTING CURRENT NAT AND RULE PACKET COUNTERS

```
iptables -L -nvx
```

This command will show the packet counters on each one of your rules.

Example output:

```
[root@minimoose root]# iptables -L -nvx
Chain INPUT (policy DROP 2780 packets, 575124 bytes)
    pkts       bytes target     prot opt in      out     source          destination
 1844685 236055702 ACCEPT     all  --  *       *       0.0.0.0/0       0.0.0.0/0
state RELATED,ESTABLISHED
       3        180 ACCEPT     tcp  --  *       *       0.0.0.0/0       0.0.0.0/0
tcp dpt:22
       0          0 ACCEPT     tcp  --  !eth0   *       0.0.0.0/0       0.0.0.0/0
tcp dpt:53
      49       3196 ACCEPT     udp  --  !eth0   *       0.0.0.0/0       0.0.0.0/0
udp dpt:53
     124       6216 ACCEPT     tcp  --  !eth0   *       0.0.0.0/0       0.0.0.0/0
tcp dpt:3128
       8        480 ACCEPT     tcp  --  !eth0   *       0.0.0.0/0       0.0.0.0/0
```

```
tcp dpt:5190
    2794    577784 IPSEC     all  --  *       *       0.0.0.0/0           0.0.0.0/0
    2780    575124 XWIN      all  --  *       *       0.0.0.0/0           0.0.0.0/0
    2449    507425 LOG       all  --  *       *       0.0.0.0/0           0.0.0.0/0
limit: avg 1/sec burst 5 LOG flags 7 level 6 prefix `STEALTH -- DROP '

Chain FORWARD (policy DROP 0 packets, 0 bytes)
    pkts      bytes target     prot opt in     out     source
destination
 3619455 2438207911 ACCEPT     all  --  *       *       0.0.0.0/0           0.0.0.0/0
state RELATED,ESTABLISHED
     159     8513 ACCEPT     all  --  eth1   *       0.0.0.0/0           0.0.0.0/0
state NEW
       0        0 ACCEPT     all  --  ipsec0 eth0   0.0.0.0/0           0.0.0.0/0
state NEW
       0        0 ACCEPT     all  --  ipsec1 eth0   0.0.0.0/0           0.0.0.0/0
state NEW
    1219    77605 ACCEPT     all  --  ipsec2 *       0.0.0.0/0           0.0.0.0/0
state NEW
       0        0 IPSEC      all  --  *       *       0.0.0.0/0           0.0.0.0/0

Chain OUTPUT (policy DROP 0 packets, 0 bytes)
    pkts      bytes target     prot opt in     out     source
destination
 1895909 2414814203 ACCEPT     all  --  *       *       0.0.0.0/0           0.0.0.0/0
state NEW,RELATED,ESTABLISHED
       0        0 TCPMSS     tcp  --  *       eth0   0.0.0.0/0           0.0.0.0/0
tcp flags:0x06/0x02 TCPMSS clamp to PMTU

Chain IPSEC (2 references)
    pkts      bytes target     prot opt in     out     source
destination
       0        0 ACCEPT     udp  --  eth1   *       0.0.0.0/0           0.0.0.0/0
udp dpt:500
       0        0 ACCEPT     esp  --  eth1   *       0.0.0.0/0           0.0.0.0/0
      14     2660 ACCEPT     udp  --  eth2   *       0.0.0.0/0           0.0.0.0/0
udp dpt:500
       0        0 ACCEPT     esp  --  eth2   *       0.0.0.0/0           0.0.0.0/0

Chain XWIN (1 references)
    pkts      bytes target     prot opt in     out     source
destination
       0        0 ACCEPT     tcp  --  lo     *       0.0.0.0/0
0.0.0.0/0           tcp dpts:6000:6015
```

The output here shows the various packet counters for each default table (INPUT, FOR-WARD, and OUTPUT), as well as three user-defined tables, LOG, IPSEC, and XWIN. Packet counters are especially useful for debugging when your rules are being triggered.

Forward: A Basic Masquerading Firewall

Figure 12.1 is a basic firewall setup using IP masquerading. This type of configuration is suitable for environments involving dynamic IP addresses on the external interface. If you have a static IP address on your external interface, a SNAT configuration is going to be a more efficient choice. In this configuration, our firewall Host-A protects an internal network, 10.10.10.0/24, and is connected to the Internet through a cable or DSL connection. If you're trying to get a firewall set up quickly and aren't concerned about more complicated features, this is the section for you.

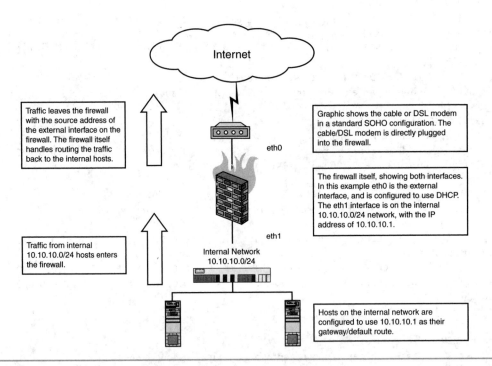

Figure 12.1   A masquerading SOHO firewall.

This example script is self-contained; it consists of a minimal filtering policy, purely allowing all traffic from the internal RFC1918 network to be masqueraded out through the external interface:

```
#!/bin/sh

IPTABLES="/sbin/iptables"
EXTERNAL="eth0"
INTERNAL="eth1"

# Flush our old rules
$IPTABLES -F
$IPTABLES -X



# load your connection tracking modules
modprobe ip_conntrack
modprobe ip_conntrack_ftp

# this next rule is mainly for PPPoE, VPN, and DSL users
$IPTABLES -A FORWARD -p tcp --tcp-flags SYN,RST SYN \
        -j TCPMSS -clamp-mss-to-pmtu


# these are our connection tracking rules
$IPTABLES -A INPUT  -m state \
        --state ESTABLISHED,RELATED -j ACCEPT
$IPTABLES -A OUTPUT -m state \
        --state NEW,ESTABLISHED,RELATED -j ACCEPT
$IPTABLES -A FORWARD -m state \
        --state NEW,ESTABLISHED,RELATED -j ACCEPT


# finally, we masquerade our traffic
$IPTABLES -t nat -A POSTROUTING -o eth0 -j MASQUERADE

# Enable IP Forwarding in the kernel
echo "1" > /proc/sys/net/ipv4/ip_forward
```

Note that we are binding this rule to our external interface, eth0. This is a good practice to get into because not specifying an interface will cause this rule to masquerade traffic across all interfaces. It doesn't really matter in a two-interface setup like our firewall here; however, if you were to add VPNs or other interfaces at a later date, this would cause problems.

Forward: A Basic SNAT Firewall

In a network where you have a static external IP, SNAT will provide you with better performance than a masquerading firewall. The following example demonstrates the same configuration as just detailed, where the firewall Host-A protects an internal network, 10.10.10.0/24, and has the static IP address 22.33.44.55 on its external interface. If you are in a SOHO environment with a dynamic IP address, you do not want to use SNAT.

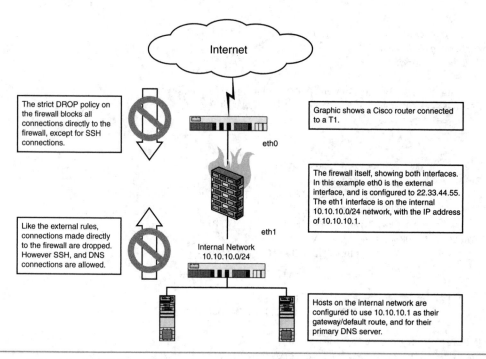

Figure 12.2   A basic SNAT firewall.

This example script is self-contained; it consists of a minimal filtering policy, purely allowing all traffic from the internal RFC1918 network to be NAT-ed out through the external interface. In addition, this example demonstrates a stricter "unless allow, deny" firewall policy, the rules required to allow SSH connections to the firewall, and a caching DNS server on the internal interface:

```sh
#!/bin/sh

IPTABLES="/sbin/iptables"
EXTERNAL="eth0"
INTERNAL="eth1"
EXTERNALIP="22.33.44.55"

# Flush our old rules
$IPTABLES -F
$IPTABLES -X

echo "Setting default filter policy"
$IPTABLES -P INPUT    DROP
$IPTABLES -P OUTPUT   DROP
$IPTABLES -P FORWARD DROP


# load your connection tracking modules
modprobe ip_conntrack
modprobe ip_conntrack_ftp
# this next rule is PPPoE, and DSL users
$IPTABLES -A OUTPUT -o eth0 -p tcp \
        --tcp-flags SYN,RST SYN -j TCPMSS \
        -clamp-mss-to-pmtu

# these are our connection tracking rules
$IPTABLES -A INPUT   -m state \
        --state ESTABLISHED,RELATED -j ACCEPT
$IPTABLES -A OUTPUT -m state \
        --state NEW,ESTABLISHED,RELATED -j ACCEPT
$IPTABLES -A FORWARD -m state \
        --state NEW,ESTABLISHED,RELATED -j ACCEPT

# Allow DNS queries on the internal interface
$IPTABLES -A INPUT -p tcp --dport 53 -i  eth1 -j ACCEPT
$IPTABLES -A INPUT -p udp --dport 53 -i eth1 -j ACCEPT

# Allow SSH
$IPTABLES -A INPUT -p tcp --dport 22 -j ACCEPT

# finally, we SNAT our traffic
$IPTABLES -t nat -A POSTROUTING -i eth1 -o $EXTERNAL\
        -j SNAT --to $EXTERNALIP
```

```
# Enable IP Forwarding in the kernel
echo "1" > /proc/sys/net/ipv4/ip_forward
```

Note how this final rule is applied to eth0, the external interface. This is because we want to match all traffic leaving our firewall and change its source IP to 22.33.44.55. This allows the flexibility of creating VPNs, as discussed in later chapters of the book.

Forward: A Basic DMZ

Figure 12.3 demonstrates taking the ruleset from the previous listing and adding a DMZ network, where we can support separate web and mail servers. Our firewall, Host-A, protects an internal network, 10.10.10.0/24, a DMZ network, 192.168.1.0/24, where we contain our web server Host-B with the IP address of 192.168.1.80 and our mail server Host-C with the IP address of 192.168.1.25. In addition, we will configure this DMZ so that it cannot access the internal network and that all hosts on both the Internet and the internal network can connect to our DMZ-ed web and mail servers using their hostnames, www.domain.com, and mail.domain.com, respectively. Creating DMZs around specific services is covered in more detail in later chapters.

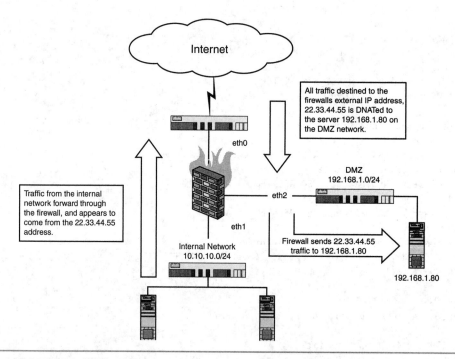

Figure 12.3 A basic DMZ network.

This example script is self-contained; it consists of a simple filtering policy allowing all traffic from the internal RFC1918 network to be NAT-ed out through the external interface and DNAT-ing all traffic from the firewall's 22.33.44.55 IP address to the DMZ server, 192.168.1.80:

```
#!/bin/sh

IPTABLES="/sbin/iptables"
EXTERNAL="eth0"
INTERNAL="eth1"
DMZ="eth2"
EXTERNALIP="22.33.44.55"

# servers
WEBSERVER=192.168.1.80

echo "Setting default filter policy"
$IPTABLES -P INPUT    DROP
$IPTABLES -P OUTPUT   DROP
$IPTABLES -P FORWARD DROP



# load your connection tracking modules
modprobe ip_conntrack
modprobe ip_conntrack_ftp
# this next rule is PPPoE, and DSL users
$IPTABLES -A OUTPUT -o eth0 -p tcp \
        --tcp-flags SYN,RST SYN -j TCPMSS \
        -clamp-mss-to-pmtu

# these are our connection tracking rules
$IPTABLES -A INPUT   -m state \
        --state ESTABLISHED,RELATED -j ACCEPT
$IPTABLES -A OUTPUT -m state \
        --state NEW,ESTABLISHED,RELATED -j ACCEPT
$IPTABLES -A FORWARD -m state \
        --state NEW,ESTABLISHED,RELATED -j ACCEPT

# Allow SSH to the firewall on the internal interface
# only
$IPTABLES -A INPUT -p tcp --dport 22 -i $INTERNAL \
        -j ACCEPT


# Forward traffic to our DMZ server, 192.168.1.80
$IPTABLES -A FORWARD -i $EXTERNAL -o $DMZ -p tcp \
```

```
        -d $EXTERNALIP -m state \
        --state NEW,ESTABLISHED,RELATED -j ACCEPT
$IPTABLES -A FORWARD -i $EXTERNAL -o $DMZ -p tcp \
        --dport $EXTERNALIP -m state \
        --state NEW,ESTABLISHED,RELATED -j ACCEPT
$IPTABLES -t nat -A PREROUTING -i $EXTERNAL -p tcp \
        -d $EXTERNALIP -j DNAT \
        --to-destination  $WEBSERVER

# finally, we SNAT our traffic
$IPTABLES -t nat -A POSTROUTING -o $EXTERNAL -j SNAT \
        --to-source $EXTERNALIP

# Enable IP Forwarding in the kernel
echo "1" > /proc/sys/net/ipv4/ip_forward
```

Note that we are sending all traffic hitting the firewall's external interface to the DMZ server. In later chapters we will discuss how to specify DNAT rules for specific services.

Troubleshooting: Internal Systems Cannot Communicate with External Systems—Packets Do Not Pass In or Out of the Firewall

Extended Description: You have created a NAT or masquerading firewall between an external network and one more internal networks. These networks cannot communicate with systems on the other side of the firewall. Packets do not pass through the firewall—either inbound or outbound.

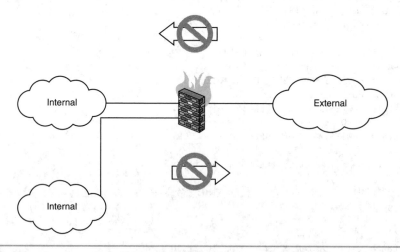

Figure 12.4   Graphic showing networks unable to communicate through a masquerading firewall.

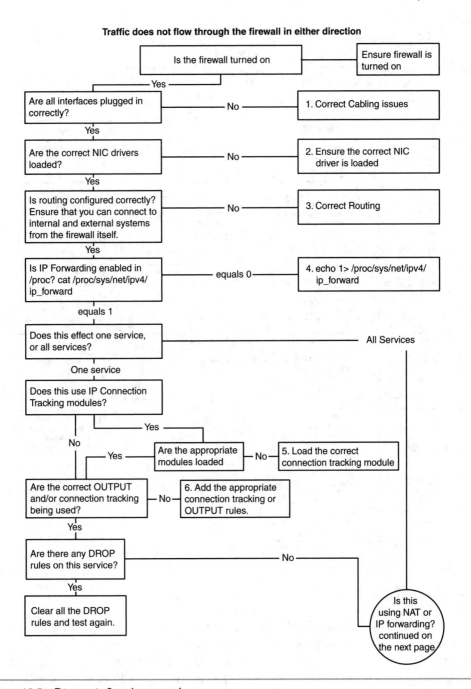

Figure 12.5 Diagnostic flowchart, part 1.

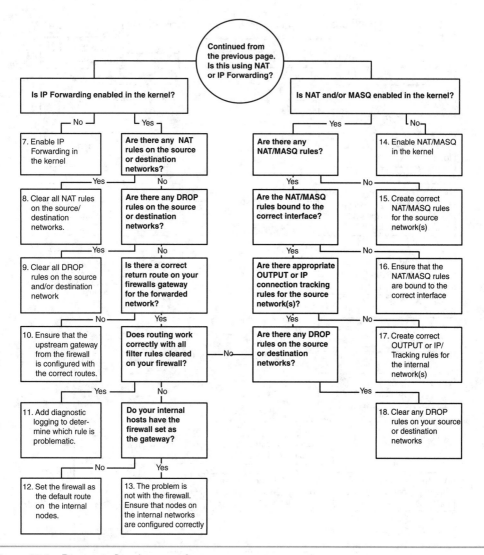

Figure 12.6   Diagnostic flowchart, part 2.

CORRECTIVE ACTIONS

1. Connect cabling—ensure that all cables are correctly wired and correctly plugged in. Loose or bad cabling can cause inconsistent operation.
2. Ensure that the network card driver you are using is the correct one for the device. Oftentimes drivers, such as the tulip chipset, will work on multiple tulip-based network cards.

3. Ensure that the correct default route and netmask is set on the gateway/firewall system. Ensure that the routes back to the internal networks are correct as well. Consider clearing all the firewall rules and testing basic access to external and internal networks from the firewall itself.
4. Enable IP forwarding: `echo 1 > /proc/sys/net/ipv4/ip_forward`.
5. Load IP connection tracking module `modprobe <modulename>`, where `<modulename>` corresponds to the `ip_tracking` module for the service you are using. Example:

```
modprobe ip_conntrack_amanda
modprobe ip_conntrack_ftp
modprobe ip_conntrack_irc
modprobe ip_conntrack
modprobe ip_conntrack_tftp
modprobe ip_nat_amanda
modprobe ip_nat_ftp
modprobe ip_nat_irc
modprobe ip_nat_snmp_basic
modprobe ip_nat_tftp
```

6. Enable connection tracking or output rules. Connection tracking rules:

```
$IPTABLES -A INPUT  -m state --state ESTABLISHED,RELATED -j ACCEPT
# Don't set NEW in here**
$IPTABLES -A OUTPUT -m state --state ESTABLISHED,RELATED -j ACCEPT
$IPTABLES -A FORWARD -m state --state ESTABLISHED,RELATED -j ACCEPT
```

7. Confirm that the kernel is actually compiled to support IP Forwarding and NAT For 2.4.x Kernels—if this is a custom compiled kernel, ensure that the following is set:

Make `menuconfig` for console
make `xconfig` for X11

** Setting NEW globally on the INPUT , FORWARD and OUTPUT chains effectively disables all your filtering.

Ensure the following is set:

```
Networking options   --->
  [*] Network packet filtering (replaces ipchains)
  IP: Netfilter Configuration   --->
    [*] Connection tracking (required for masq/NAT)
      [M]    FTP protocol support (** Only if you need FTP)
      [M]    Amanda protocol support (** Only if you need Amanda)
      [M]    TFTP protocol support (** Only if you need TFTP)
      [M]    IRC protocol support (** Only if you need IRC)
    [*] IP tables support (required for filtering/masq/NAT)
      [*]    Connection state match support
    [*]    Full NAT
      [*]       MASQUERADE target support (** Required for dynamic
                connections only)
```

For 2.6.x kernels—if this is a custom compiled kernel ensure that the following is set:

Make menuconfig for console
make xconfig for X11

Ensure the following is set:

```
Device Drivers   --->
  Networking support   --->
   Networking options   --->
   [*] Network packet filtering (replaces ipchains)   --->
     [*]    Bridged IP/ARP packets filtering (NEW) (if you are creating a
            briding firewall)

       IP: Netfilter Configuration   --->
         <*> Connection tracking (required for masq/NAT)
           [M]    FTP protocol support (** Only if you need FTP)
           [M]    Amanda protocol support (** Only if you need Amanda)
           [M]    TFTP protocol support (** Only if you need TFTP)
           [M]    IRC protocol support (** Only if you need IRC)
         <*> IP tables support (required for filtering/masq/NAT)
           [*]    Connection state match support
         <*>    Full NAT
         <*> MASQUERADE target support (** Required for dynamic
             connections only)
```

8. Clear all the NAT rules on the source or destination networks.

9. Ensure that any DROP rules do not match the traffic from your NAT-ed network(s). If the IP forwarding gateway system functions correctly with all firewall rules disabled, it's possible that there are issues with the order in which the firewall rules are set. Ensure that the ALLOW and session tracking rules come before any DROP rules that reference the internal network or services being accessed.

10. Ensure that the upstream gateway from the firewall is configured with the appropriate routes for the forwarded internal networks with the firewall set as the gateway for those networks.

11. Clear all the filter rules from your firewall. If one of these rules is having a conflict with the traffic routing through your firewall, consult the diagnostic logging section of this book for further information on how to determine which rule is being problematic.

12. Ensure that the nodes on your internal network are configured with the firewall set as their default route or gateway into those external networks.

13. The problem is most likely not in the firewall as at this point the system is configured as a basic IP forwarding gateway and contains no filtering rules at all. Possibly the problem is DNS related or is in the network (netmask, and so on) settings on the hosts themselves.

14. Enable NAT and/or MASQUERADE in the Linux kernel.

15. Enable NAT or MASQUERADE rules for the internal network. Example—MASQUERADE rule, where eth0 is the Internet or external network facing interface:

```
iptables -t nat -A POSTROUTING -o eth0 -j MASQUERADE
```

16. Ensure that the NAT or MASQ rule is bound to the correct interface. Failure to bind to the correct interface can result in traffic destined for non-masqueraded or NAT-ed network to appear to come from the NAT or MASQUERADED network(s), which may not be intended.

17. Enable connection tracking with the following rule:

```
$IPTABLES -A INPUT   -m state --state ESTABLISHED,RELATED -j ACCEPT     #
Don't set NEW in here**
$IPTABLES -A OUTPUT -m state --state ESTABLISHED,RELATED -j ACCEPT
$IPTABLES -A FORWARD -m state --state ESTABLISHED,RELATED -j ACCEPT
```

18. Clear DROP or OUTPUT filtering rules that may be interfering with the routing of traffic.

** Setting global NEW rules on the INPUT, FORWARD, and OUTPUT chains effectively disables all your filtering.

Troubleshooting: Internal Systems Can Communicate with External Systems—DMZ Systems Cannot Be Reached from the Outside

Extended Description: You have created multiple networks, including one or more DMZ networks. Both internal and DMZ networks can communicate with external systems, but external systems cannot connect to systems on the DMZ network.

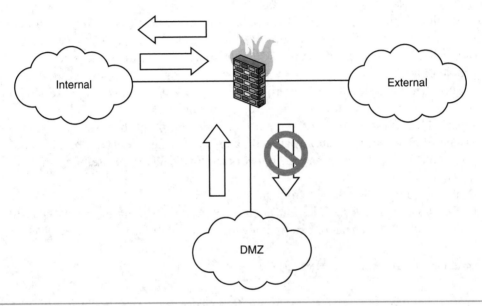

Figure 12.7   Internal traffic can communicate with external systems; DMZ systems cannot be accessed from the outside.

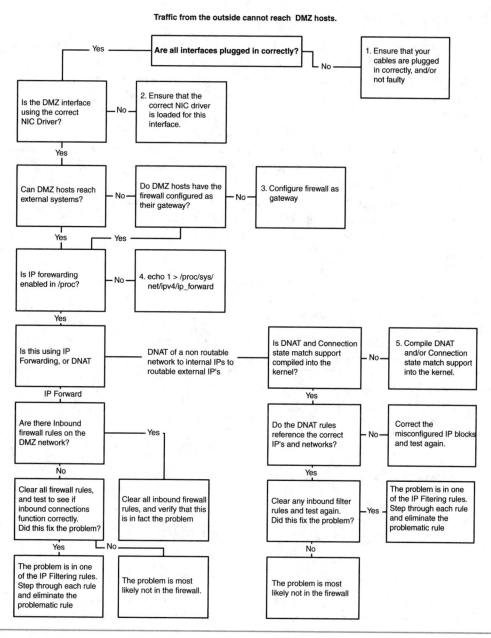

Figure 12.8 DMZ Diagnostic Flowchart.

CORRECTIVE ACTIONS

1. Connect cabling—ensure that all cables are correctly wired and correctly plugged in. Loose or bad cabling can cause inconsistent operation.
2. Ensure that the network card driver you are using is the correct one for the device. Oftentimes drivers, such as the tulip chipset, will work on multiple tulip-based network cards.
3. Ensure that the correct default route and netmask is set on the gateway/firewall system. Ensure that the routes back to the internal networks are correct as well. Consider clearing all the firewall rules and testing basic access to external and internal networks from the firewall itself.
4. Enable IP forwarding: `echo 1 > /proc/sys/net/ipv4/ip_forward`
5. Compile DNAT support into the kernel: 2.4.x Kernels:

```
Networking options  --->
  IP: Netfilter Configuration  --->
     <M>Connection tracking (required for masq/NAT)
        <M>   FTP protocol support
        <M>   IRC protocol support
Full NAT
           <M> MASQUERADE target support
           <M> REDIRECT target support
Device Drivers  --->
   Networking support  --->
     Networking options  --->
        [*] Network packet filtering (replaces ipchains)  --->
           IP: Netfilter Configuration  --->


<M> Connection tracking (required for masq/NAT)

FTP protocol support
<M>   IRC protocol support
<M> IP tables support (required for filtering/masq/NAT)
Full NAT
<M> MASQUERADE target support
```

6. Load IP connection tracking module: `modprobe <modulename>`, where `<modulename>` corresponds to the `ip_tracking` module for the service you are using, for example

```
modprobe ip_conntrack_amanda
modprobe ip_conntrack_ftp
```

```
modprobe ip_conntrack_irc
modprobe ip_conntrack
modprobe ip_conntrack_tftp
modprobe ip_nat_amanda
modprobe ip_nat_ftp
modprobe ip_nat_irc
modprobe ip_nat_snmp_basic
modprobe ip_nat_tftp
```

7. Enable connection tracking or output rules.

Connection tracking rules:

```
$IPTABLES -A INPUT  -m state --state ESTABLISHED,RELATED -j ACCEPT
# Don't set NEW in here**
$IPTABLES -A OUTPUT -m state --state ESTABLISHED,RELATED -j ACCEPT
$IPTABLES -A FORWARD -m state --state ESTABLISHED,RELATED -j ACCEPT
```

Internal Systems Can Communicate to External Systems Except to a Small Percentage of Systems

You have created internal and/or DMZ network(s). These systems can communicate with most systems in the outside world; however, a small percentage of systems that are otherwise accessible from other networks cannot be reached.

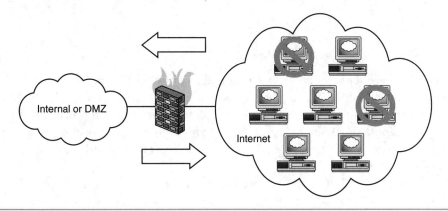

Figure 12.9 Internal systems cannot communicate with a small percentage of external systems.

** Setting global NEW rules on the INPUT, FORWARD, and OUTPUT chains effectively disables all your filtering.

This is most likely due to the Explicit Congestion Notification (ECN) feature in the Linux kernel. While a highly useful feature, some broken TCP/IP stacks cannot safely handle this traffic. Fortunately this is very easy to disable, using /proc:

```
# this will disable ECN
echo 0 > /proc/sys/net/ipv4/tcp_ecn

#this will enable ECN
echo 1 >/proc/sys/net/ipv4/tcp_ecn
```

Internal Systems Can Communicate with External Systems, but only with Small Packets—Large File Transfers Fail

You are configuring a network on a DSL and have created internal and/or DMZ network(s). Only small payload traffic, such as ping, will work inconsistently through the firewall. Large payload traffic fails to traverse the firewall 100% of the time.

Most likely this is due to an MTU mismatch when you're dealing with DSL, PPPoE, or VPN connections. Generally, the following rule should solve this problem:

```
$IPTABLES -A FORWARD -p tcp --tcp-flags SYN,RST SYN \
        -j TCPMSS –clamp-mss-to-pmtu
```

On VPN connections you might need to further reduce your MTU settings, due to the even higher overhead. Consult the VPN chapter for more information on this topic.

SUMMARY

As you can see, netfilter is capable of a considerable amount of granularity and flexibility, from creating a basic SOHO connection-sharing environment to complex DMZ configurations more in line with large enterprise deployments. This, combined with the Layer 2 functionality discussed in the previous chapter, shows the range of using Linux firewalls as a one-stop solution for solving complex corporate network configuration issues.

In later chapters we discuss how to specify using NAT rules both on source and destination addresses to create more complex rules that would allow you to break out destinations by the port as well as the IP, redirect traffic transparently into application layer proxies, and create multiple NAT configurations for VPN configurations.

General IP (Layer 3/Layer 4)

Whether you're running a host-based firewall and are only concerned about services connecting to your system or a multi-homed firewall handling VPNs, DMZs, and internal networks, knowing how to cleanly process basic protocols and services is imperative. This chapter should serve as a guide to creating rules for simple services that might not be covered in other chapters in this book and provides the basics to implement those rules effectively.

In nearly every rule we use in this section, you will note that we use "$IPTABLES" instead of "iptables." This is to ease the integration of these examples into scripts. The default on Red Hat systems is to place **iptables** in **/sbin/iptables**. You might or might not use this. Additionally you might have multiple versions of **iptables** installed on the system. Using $IPTABLES allows you to select which instance of **iptables** you want to use. As an example, the following setting at the top of your script will allow you to dictate which version of **iptables** you are going to use:

```
#!/bin/sh
IPTABLES=/sbin/iptables
```

Secondly, in addition to the three internally supplied chains, INPUT, OUTPUT, and FORWARD, there are user-defined chains. Depending on what you're doing, sometimes you'll want to create your own chain. In general you should create user-defined chains whenever you're doing something complicated. This reduces the chances that your user-defined chain is going to interact in a negative way with the other rules on the system.

Consider this a suggestion, rather than a hard and fast rule. Sometimes we create user-defined chains, and sometimes we do not in our examples. After you get the hang of creating your own and some of the more complex actions that you can perform in one, it will be very easy to convert our examples into your rules.

Finally, throughout this book we use the convention that eth0 is the external (or Internet facing) interface, eth1 is generally reserved for internal wired networks and eth2 for DMZ or wireless networks. We create these settings in all our scripts like this:

```
EXTERNAL=eth0
INTERNAL=eth1
DMZ=eth2
```

Figure 13.1 shows our firewall with three interfaces and how each device corresponds to each interface.

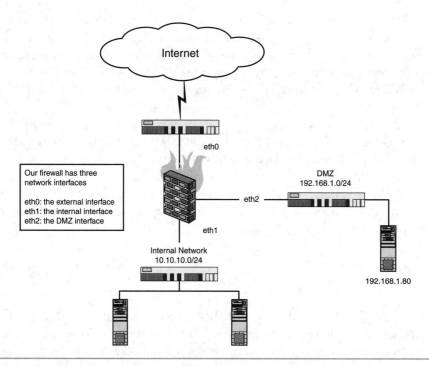

Figure 13.1   Firewall with three interfaces and their corresponding devices.

COMMON QUESTION

Q: How do I stop the network 169.254.0.0/16 from being added to my routes?

A: OK, this one is not firewall related, but we have been asked it enough that we promised to include it in the book. This is a DHCP thing, and it's called a "Zeroconf route." And we agree, it's annoying. If you are on a Red Hat box and want it to go away, comment out the following from /etc/sysconfig/network-scripts/ifup.

```
# Add Zeroconf route.
if [ -z "${NOZEROCONF}" -a "${ISALIAS}" = "no" ]; then
    ip route replace 169.254.0.0/16 dev ${REALDEVICE}
fi
```

INBOUND: CREATING A RULE FOR A NEW TCP SERVICE

Undoubtedly you're going to run into a situation where you need to create a rule for a new service. In this example, we have a system running a service called "turtled," which is responsible for controlling a 300-foot tall, fire-breathing rocket turtle named "Gamera." According to legend, he was made by Atlanteans, and because they're all gone, we don't have the documentation for turtled anymore. Even worse, because there's only one Gamera, you're not going to find any help on Google or a mailing list. Not to worry! First we need to determine what port turtled runs on. We can do that with the netstat -pan command:

```
[root@winona root]# netstat -pan |grep turtled
tcp        0      0 0.0.0.0:2212            0.0.0.0:*
LISTEN      3806/turtled
```

The first column tells us that this is a TCP protocol, and 0 0.0.0.0:2212 tells us that the service is listening on the port 2212. On a host-only firewall, the rule for this service would look like this:

```
$IPTABLES -A INPUT -p tcp -dport 2212 -j ACCEPT
```

If we wanted to limit connections to the turtled service, we could use the RETURN rule to create an exception to exclude hosts from a DROP rule. In this example, two users,

Asagi coming from the host 22.33.44.55, and Ayana coming from the host 11.22.33.44, need access to `turtled`:

```
$IPTABLES -N USERS
$IPTABLES -N GAMERA

$IPTABLES -A USERS -s 11.22.33.44 -j RETURN
$IPTABLES -A USERS -s 22.33.44.55 -j RETURN
$IPTABLES -A USERS -j DROP

$IPTABLES -A GAMERA -j USERS
$IPTABLES -A GAMERA -p tcp -dport 2122 -j ACCEPT
$IPTABLES -A GAMERA -j DROP
```

The first chain, USERS, contains a list of IP addresses we'll allow. The second chain, GAMERA, starts with a test against the first chain. This test matches the incoming rule against the IPs listed in USERS, if that rule is matched against the IP address 22.33.44.55—for example, we get an exception and RETURN to the GAMERA chain to process the next rule, which is to allow the connection to port 2122. If the IP address does not match anything in the USERS chain, the final rule is a DROP, which is matched, and terminates the rest of the GAMERA chain. As you can see, the use of RETURN in a firewall chain is very powerful. It allows you to quickly create groups of users and separate your rules more cleanly.

To continue with this example, let's assume that you are attempting to forward requests to `turtled` to an internal server. The firewall, Host-A, has three interfaces: external, internal (10.10.10.0/24), and DMZ (192.168.1.0/24). `turtled` runs on the system Host-B, located on the DMZ network with the IP address of 192.168.1.10. We will forward connections from Host-A's external IP address to Host-B:

```
# where eth0 is the external interface (Internet)
# where eth1 is the internal interface (10.10.10.0/24) with the IP 10.10.10.1
# where eth2 is the DMZ interface (192.168.1.0/24) with the IP 192.168.1.1

EXTERNAL=eth0
INTERNAL=eth1
DMZ=eth2

SERVER=192.168.1.10

$IPTABLES -A FORWARD -i $EXTERNAL -o $DMZ -p tcp \
     --dport 2122 -m state \
```

```
        --state NEW,ESTABLISHED,RELATED -j ACCEPT
$IPTABLES -t nat -A PREROUTING -i $EXTERNAL -p tcp \
      --dport 2122 -j DNAT --to-destination  $SERVER
```

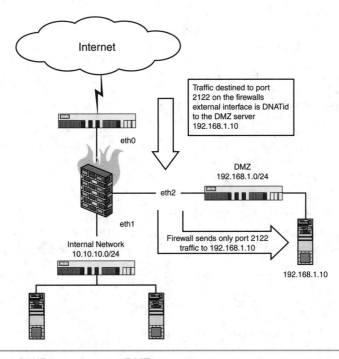

Figure 13.2 Using *DNAT* to connect to a DMZ server.

This would allow all connections to 2122 to be forwarded to 192.168.1.10. If we wanted to limit this to the same hosts, because let's face it, a 300-foot tall, fire-breathing rocket turtle is a dangerous thing, we would use a chain with exception rules (the -j RETURN flag). Asagi is coming from the host 22.33.44.55 and Ayana from the host 11.22.33.44—we will use the following to ensure only those addresses are allowed:

```
# where eth0 is the external interface (Internet)
# where eth1 is the internal interface (10.10.10.0/24)
# with the IP 10.10.10.1
# where eth2 is the DMZ interface (192.168.1.0/24) with
# the IP 192.168.1.1

EXTERNAL=eth0
INTERNAL=eth1
DMZ=eth2
```

```
SERVER=192.168.1.10

# Create our user defined chain for exceptions
$IPTABLES -N USERS
$IPTABLES -A USERS -s 11.22.33.44 -j RETURN
$IPTABLES -A USERS -s 22.33.44.55 -j RETURN
$IPTABLES -A USERS -j DROP

$IPTABLES -A FORWARD -i $EXTERNAL -o $DMZ -p tcp \
    --dport 2122 -m state \
    --state NEW,ESTABLISHED,RELATED -j USERS
$IPTABLES -A FORWARD -i $EXTERNAL -o $DMZ -p tcp \
    --dport 2122 -m state \
    --state NEW,ESTABLISHED,RELATED -j ACCEPT
$IPTABLES -t nat -A PREROUTING -i $EXTERNAL -p tcp \
    --dport 2122 -j DNAT --to-destination  $SERVER
```

This is the first time we demonstrate the use of -j RETURN. Basically this means when the rule is matched, stop parsing this chain and either return to the chain this rule was called from (which we are not doing in this example) or go to the next chain, in this case the line:

```
$IPTABLES -A FORWARD -i $EXTERNAL -o $DMZ -p tcp \
    --dport 2122 -m state \
    --state NEW,ESTABLISHED,RELATED -j ACCEPT
```

This allows our users to merrily resume wielding their 300-foot tall, fire-breathing rocket turtle. If you are familiar with the concept of groups in Unix, then this idea should not be too much of a stretch to grasp. We are basically creating a "group" of trusted IP addresses with the name "USERS." This way, we can reuse these IP addresses in other rules, thereby simplifying our overall ruleset.

INBOUND: ALLOWING SSH TO A LOCAL SYSTEM

Secure Shell (SSH) is the most common means out there of remotely administering a system. If you are in a situation where you have to explicitly allow an SSH session to your system, undoubtedly you have already grasped the concept of an "unless allow, deny" policy; however, as a recap, you would need to specify the following rule if your system was configured with a default -j DROP policy on the INPUT chain.

SSH, by default uses TCP port 22. To allow SSH connections to your system, you need to add the following rule:

```
$IPTABLES -A INPUT -p tcp -dport 22 -j ACCEPT
```

SSH supports userland connection filtering, using tcpwrappers; however, we recommend that you limit direct access to your services whenever you can because every service, including SSH, has had some type of remotely exploitable vulnerability that something like tcpwrappers would not save you from. The following example rule demonstrates a firewall set up to restrict access to only the SSH port from the hosts 22.33.44.55 and 11.22.33.44:

```
# where $DNSSERVER is your systems designated DNSSERVER
$IPTABLES -P INPUT -j DROP
$IPTABLES -A INPUT -s  11.22.33.44 -p tcp --dport 22 \
     -j ACCEPT
$IPTABLES -A INPUT -s  22.33.44.55 -p tcp --dport 22 \
     -j ACCEPT

# allow DNS
$IPTABLES -A INPUT -p udp -m udp -s $DNSSERVER \
     --sport 53 -d 0/0 -j ACCEPT
```

This last rule allows the system to make DNS lookups. The next example was generated by Red Hat's *Lokkit* utility and demonstrates using a user-defined chain to achieve the same:

```
#part 1
$IPTABLES -N SSHCLIENTS
$IPTABLES -A INPUT -N SSHCLIENTS
$IPTABLES -A FORWARD -j SSHCLIENTS
$IPTABLES -A SSHCLIENTS -p tcp -m tcp --dport 22 \
     -s 11.22.33.44 ---syn -j ACCEPT
$IPTABLES -A SSHCLIENTS -p tcp -m tcp --dport 22 \
     -s  22.33.44.55 --syn -j ACCEPT
$IPTABLES -A SSHCLIENTS -j ACCEPT

#part 2
$IPTABLES -A  SSHCLIENTS -p udp -m udp -s $DNSSERVER \
     --sport 53 -d 0/0 -j ACCEPT
```

```
#part 3
$IPTABLES -A SSHCLIENTS -p tcp -m tcp --syn -j REJECT
$IPTABLES -A SSHCLIENTS -p udp -m udp -j REJECT
```

In part 1 of these rules, we first create the user-defined chain, SSHCLIENTS with **iptables** -N SSHCLIENTS and then set the user define chain to be applied against the INPUT and FORWARD chains. This is so we can store our SSH rules in one chain and, if we were in a diagnostic mode, easily disable them. Also take note of the -syn flag—this means that the connection is to be accepted if it starts with a SYN packet. If it does not, the rule will not be matched and the traffic discarded by rules farther down.

Part 2 of this ruleset allows the system to make DNS queries.

Part 3 is where we set the deny policy. Any packets that do not match the ruleset in part 1 will be caught and dumped with a RST/ACK message from the server. The plus side to using -j REJECT is that it returns this response to the system originating the connection cleanly (in theory, there are a lot of broken IP devices out there) and shutting down the connection. The downside is that if you were trying to hide that you had an SSH service on this system, you just failed because you sent the bad guy an RST/ACK response. If you just want to drop the packets into the ether, use -j DROP.

FORWARD: SSH TO ANOTHER SYSTEM

In this example, we will assume that our firewall, Host-A, handles traffic for an internal network, 10.10.10.0/24, and a DMZ network, 192.168.1.0/24. On the DMZ network we have two servers, Host-B (192.168.1.10) and Host-C (192.168.1.11), that we will DNAT SSH sessions to. The first example assumes our firewall only has one IP address on its external interface, and the second example assumes that the firewall has multiple IPs.

When we only have one IP address, the only way to get this to work is to "run" SSH on a different port. This does not mean that we need to run sshd on different ports on our two DMZ hosts; rather we will demonstrate how to redirect ssh to different ports. Our firewall has the external IP address, 22.33.44.55. Port 2022 connections to this IP address will be forwarded to Host-B (192.168.1.10), and port 3022 connections will be forwarded to Host-C (192.168.1.11):

```
# where eth0 is the external interface (Internet)
# where eth1 is the internal interface (10.10.10.0/24) with the IP 10.10.10.1
# where eth2 is the DMZ interface (192.168.1.0/24) with the IP 192.168.1.1

EXTERNAL=eth0
INTERNAL=eth1
```

```
DMZ=eth2

HOSTB=192.168.1.10
HOSTC=192.168.1.11
# Host-B rules
$IPTABLES -A FORWARD -i $EXTERNAL -o $DMZ -p tcp \
      --dport 2022 -m state \
      --state NEW,ESTABLISHED,RELATED -j ACCEPT
$IPTABLES -t nat -A PREROUTING -i $EXTERNAL -p tcp \
      --dport 2022 -j DNAT --to-destination  $HOSTB

# Host-C rules
$IPTABLES -A FORWARD -i $EXTERNAL -o $DMZ -p tcp \
      --dport 3022 -m state \
      --state NEW,ESTABLISHED,RELATED -j ACCEPT
$IPTABLES -t nat -A PREROUTING -i $EXTERNAL -p tcp \
      --dport 3022 -j DNAT --to-destination  $HOSTC
```

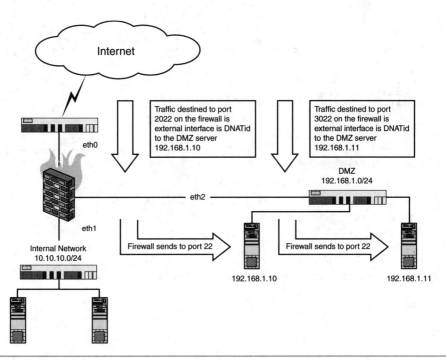

Figure 13.3 Graphic showing multiple DNAT rules to multiple DMZ servers.

This next example assumes that our firewall has three IP addresses, 22.33.44.55, 22.33.44.56, and 22.33.44.57. Connections on port 22 on the IP 22.33.44.55 will go to the firewall itself; connections to 22.33.44.56 will be forwarded to 192.168.1.10; and connections to 22.33.44.57 will be forwarded to 192.168.1.11 (see Figure 13.4).

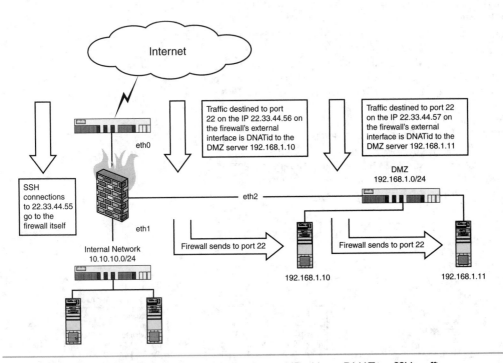

Figure 13.4   Graphic showing a firewall with three external IP address, DNAT-ing SSH traffic.

```
# where eth0 is the external interface (Internet) with the IP's
# 22.33.44.55 -> local
# 22.33.44.56 -> 192.168.1.10
# 22.33.44.57 -> 192.168.1.11
# where eth1 is the internal interface (10.10.10.0/24) with the IP 10.10.10.1
# where eth2 is the DMZ interface (192.168.1.0/24) with the IP 192.168.1.1

EXTERNAL=eth0
INTERNAL=eth1
DMZ=eth2

HOSTB=192.168.1.10
HOSTC=192.168.1.11

IP_HOSTB=22.33.44.56
IP_HOSTC=22.33.44.57
```

```
# Host-B rules
$IPTABLES -A FORWARD -i $EXTERNAL -o $DMZ \
     -d $IP_HOSTB -p tcp --dport 22 -m state \
     --state NEW,ESTABLISHED,RELATED -j ACCEPT
$IPTABLES -t nat -A PREROUTING -i $EXTERNAL -p tcp \
     -d $IP_HOSTB --dport 22 -j DNAT \
     --to-destination  $HOSTB

# Host-C rules
$IPTABLES -A FORWARD -i $EXTERNAL -o $DMZ \
     -d $IP_HOSTC -p tcp --dport 22 -m state \
     --state NEW,ESTABLISHED,RELATED -j ACCEPT
$IPTABLES -t nat -A PREROUTING -i $EXTERNAL -p tcp \
     -d $IP_HOSTC --dport 22 -j DNAT \
     --to-destination  $HOSTC
```

And finally, the previous examples using name-based chains to restrict access, we will only allow access to both systems from the IP addresses 33.44.55.66 and 44.55.66.77:

```
# where eth0 is the external interface (Internet)
# where eth1 is the internal interface (10.10.10.0/24) with the IP 10.10.10.1
# where eth2 is the DMZ interface (192.168.1.0/24) with the IP 192.168.1.1

EXTERNAL=eth0
INTERNAL=eth1
DMZ=eth2

HOSTB=192.168.1.10
HOSTC=192.168.1.11

$IPTABLES -N USERS
$IPTABLES -A USERS -s 33.44.55.66 -j RETURN
$IPTABLES -A USERS -s 44.55.66.77 -j RETURN
$IPTABLES -j DROP

# Host-B rules
$IPTABLES -A FORWARD -i $EXTERNAL -o $DMZ -p tcp \
     --dport 2022 -m state \
     --state NEW,ESTABLISHED,RELATED -j USERS
$IPTABLES -A FORWARD -i $EXTERNAL -o $DMZ -p tcp \
     --dport 2022 -m state \
     --state NEW,ESTABLISHED,RELATED -j ACCEPT
$IPTABLES -t nat -A PREROUTING -i $EXTERNAL -p tcp \
     --dport 2022 -j DNAT --to-destination  $HOSTB
```

```
# Host-C rules
$IPTABLES -A FORWARD -i $EXTERNAL -o $DMZ -p tcp \
    --dport 3022 -m state \
    --state NEW,ESTABLISHED,RELATED -j USERS
$IPTABLES -A FORWARD -i $EXTERNAL -o $DMZ -p tcp \
    --dport 3022 -m state \
    --state NEW,ESTABLISHED,RELATED -j ACCEPT
$IPTABLES -t nat -A PREROUTING -i $EXTERNAL -p tcp \
    --dport 3022 -j DNAT --to-destination  $HOSTC
```

And again, the same filtering method is applied against our multi-IP configuration:

```
# where eth0 is the external interface (Internet) with the IP's
# 22.33.44.55 -> local
# 22.33.44.56 -> 192.168.1.10
# 22.33.44.57 -> 192.168.1.11
# where eth1 is the internal interface (10.10.10.0/24) with the IP 10.10.10.1
# where eth2 is the DMZ interface (192.168.1.0/24) with the IP 192.168.1.1
EXTERNAL=eth0
INTERNAL=eth1
DMZ=eth2

HOSTB=192.168.1.10
HOSTC=192.168.1.11

IP_HOSTB=22.33.44.56
IP_HOSTC=22.33.44.57

$IPTABLES -N USERS
$IPTABLES -A USERS -s 33.44.55.66 -j ACCEPT
$IPTABLES -A USERS -s 44.55.66.77 -j ACCEPT
$IPTABLES -j DROP
# Host-B rules
$IPTABLES -A FORWARD -i $EXTERNAL -o $DMZ \
      -d $IP_HOSTB -p tcp --dport 22 -m state \
      --state NEW,ESTABLISHED,RELATED -j USERS
$IPTABLES -A FORWARD -i $EXTERNAL -o $DMZ \
      -d $IP_HOSTB -p tcp --dport 22 -m state \
      --state NEW,ESTABLISHED,RELATED -j ACCEPT
$IPTABLES -t nat -A PREROUTING -i $EXTERNAL -p tcp \
      -d $IP_HOSTB --dport 22 -j DNAT \
      --to-destination  $HOSTB
# Host-C rules
$IPTABLES -A FORWARD -i $EXTERNAL -o $DMZ \
      -d $IP_HOSTC -p tcp --dport 22 -m state \
```

```
        --state NEW,ESTABLISHED,RELATED -j USERS
$IPTABLES -A FORWARD -i $EXTERNAL -o $DMZ \
        -d $IP_HOSTC -p tcp --dport 22 -m state \
        --state NEW,ESTABLISHED,RELATED -j ACCEPT
$IPTABLES -t nat -A PREROUTING -i $EXTERNAL \
        -d $IP_HOSTC-p tcp --dport 22 -j DNAT \
        --to-destination  $HOSTC
```

SSH: Connections Timeout

This is a very common problem with secure shell, and is not normally firewall related—unless you have rules specifically set up to time out connections. Generally the way to fix this is on the SSH server itself by setting the following in the **sshd_config** file:

```
# this defaults to On
KeepAlive On
```

TELNET: Forwarding telnet Connections to Other Systems

This section is nearly identical to the setup of SSH, except that we absolutely, positively want you to stop what you're doing right now and ask yourself, "Why am I using **telnet**?" It's a very insecure, nonencrypted, trivially sniffable, and/or hijackable protocol. Only use this when SSH isn't available, and even then, be careful when, where, and how you use it.

Telnet uses TCP port 23, so for a shortcut you can just duplicate the SSH rules listed here, replacing references to TCP port 22 to TCP port 23.

MySQL: Allowing MySQL Connections

MySQL (http://www.mysql.com) is one of the most popular open source databases in use today. It uses the fixed TCP port of 3306 and as of MySQL 4.0.x, has started support-ing SSL encapsulation and x.509 authentication. Even with this added transport layer security, you'll want to protect your MySQL service from bad guys. However, you also might have a number of DBAs that will want to connect to this service, so a name-based allow chain would prove a good strategy to keep your administrative overhead from getting too out of control.

This first example assumes you're using host-based firewall rules and only want the systems 11.22.33.44 and 22.33.44.55 to be able to connect directly to your MySQL service:

```
$IPTABLES -N USERS
$IPTABLES -N MYSQLSERVER

$IPTABLES -A USERS -s 11.22.33.44 -j RETURN
$IPTABLES -A USERS -s 22.33.44.55 -j RETURN
$IPTABLES -A USERS -j DROP

$IPTABLES -A MYSQLSERVER -j USERS
$IPTABLES -A MYSQLSERVER -p tcp -dport 3306 -j ACCEPT
$IPTABLES -A MYSQLSERVER -j DROP
```

Assuming you're running MySQL on a server in the DMZ 192.168.1.0/24 with the IP address of 192.168.1.22 and using the previous allow list, you would use a ruleset like this:

```
# where eth0 is the external interface (Internet)
# where eth1 is the internal interface (10.10.10.0/24) with the IP 10.10.10.1
# where eth2 is the DMZ interface (192.168.1.0/24) with the IP 192.168.1.1

EXTERNAL=eth0
INTERNAL=eth1
DMZ=eth2

DBSERVER=192.168.1.22

$IPTABLES -N USERS
$IPTABLES -A USERS -s 11.22.33.44 -j RETURN
$IPTABLES -A USERS -s 22.33.44.55 -j RETURN
$IPTABLES -A USERS -j DROP

# Host-B rules
$IPTABLES -A FORWARD -i $EXTERNAL -o $DMZ -p tcp \
     --dport 3306 -m state \
     --state NEW,ESTABLISHED,RELATED -j USERS
$IPTABLES -A FORWARD -i $EXTERNAL -o $DMZ -p tcp \
```

```
        --dport 3306 -m state \
        --state NEW,ESTABLISHED,RELATED -j ACCEPT
$IPTABLES -t nat -A PREROUTING -i $EXTERNAL -p tcp \
        --dport 3306 -j DNAT --to-destination  $DBSERVER
```

SUMMARY

This chapter should serve as an introduction to simple Layer 4 DMZs and host-based firewall rule creation. Other protocols, such as FTP, Instant Messaging, or NFS are followed up in later chapters due to their more complex nature. We hope we have also demonstrated the use of the -j RETURN function in such a way that it will help to ease the administrative overhead of creating large complex exceptions to your rules and the process of creating user-defined chains in general. In addition, take note of the use of the -A flag when creating new firewall rules, as mentioned in previous chapters. -A appends rules to the end of the chain. Overuse of the -I flag, which inserts a rule at the beginning of a chain, will invert the rules and can be especially troublesome when combined with -j RETURN constructs.

SMTP (e-mail)

In this chapter we will cover some of the more common SMTP issues, including sending/receiving mail from the firewall, forwarding SMTP traffic to an internal mail server, and dealing with special circumstances to keep in mind when firewalling SMTP servers.

COMMON QUESTIONS

Q: Can **iptables**/netfilter alert via e-mail?

A: Natively, no, it cannot. There are numerous ways to add in alerting capabilities with user space tools such as the IDS **snort** (`http://www.snort.org`).

Q: Can firewall rules be used to route traffic based on the recipient?

A: The short answer is no. The (very) long answer is yes, but you would need to use something like **iproute2** (`ftp://ftp.inr.ac.ru/ip-routing/`) or an application layer proxy. It is also possible to use firewall rules to route SMTP traffic destined to one machine, to another machine using a redirect rule that can be used to do inline filtering (spam, scanning, and so on) on that traffic. It would be up to this third-party system to then send the processed SMTP traffic to the original destination.

TOOLS DISCUSSED IN THIS CHAPTER

snort, an open source Network-based Intrusion Detection System (NIDS), is covered in this chapter and can be found at `http://www.snort.org`.

ALLOWING SMTP TO/FROM YOUR FIREWALLS

In this configuration, our firewall (Host-A) is running a local MTA (Mail Transfer Agent). This MTA is responsible for sending and/or receiving of e-mail. It is assumed that you have correctly configured your MTA and that it functions when the firewall rules are not loaded. The following example rules should allow both host-based and network-protecting firewalls to allow the SMTP service on the firewall:

Receiving SMTP traffic on Host-A:

```
$IPTABLES -A INPUT -p tcp--dport 25 -j ACCEPT
```

This rule would allow inbound SMTP connections on all interfaces. If you wanted to limit this to a specific interface, say in the example of a firewall accepting mail only from an internal network, we would specify the interface with the following:

```
# where eth1 is the internal interface
$IPTABLES -A INPUT -i eth1 -p tcp--dport 25 -j ACCEPT
```

For allowing outbound SMTP traffic from the firewall, we would use a connection tracking rule as follows:

```
$IPTABLES -A OUTPUT -p tcp -sport 25 -m state \
    -state NEW,ESTABLISHED,RELATED -j ACCEPT
```

FORWARDING SMTP TO AN INTERNAL MAIL SERVER

In this configuration, our firewall, Host-A, receives and forwards SMTP connections on its external interface to an internal server using DNAT. Ideally in this configuration, you want your SMTP server (192.168.1.25) to exist on its own DMZ segment (192.168.1.0/24). Forwarding these connections directly to an internally hosted SMTP server, however common, is not recommended. It absolutely opens your internal systems to secondary exploitation through the SMTP server if/when it is compromised. The following illustration serves to show the recommended design.

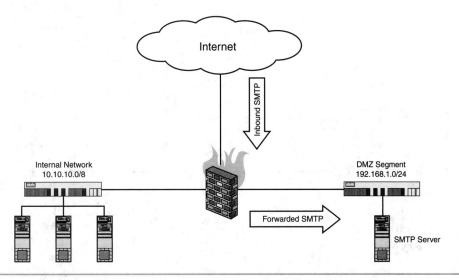

Figure 14.1 Demonstrates the logical layout of a mail server located on a DMZ segment.

This is accomplished through the following firewall rules:

```
# where eth0 is the external interface on the firewall
# where eth1 is the internal interface on the firewall  (10.10.10.0/24)
# where eth2 is the DMZ interface on the firewall (192.168.1.0/24)
EXTERNAL=eth0
INTERNAL=eth1
DMZ=eth2


MAILSERVER=192.168.1.25

$IPTABLES -A FORWARD -i $EXTERNAL -o $DMZ -p tcp \
     --dport 25 -m state \
     --state NEW,ESTABLISHED,RELATED -j ACCEPT
$IPTABLES -t nat -A PREROUTING -i $EXTERNAL -p tcp \
     --dport 25 -j DNAT --to-destination  $MAILSERVER
```

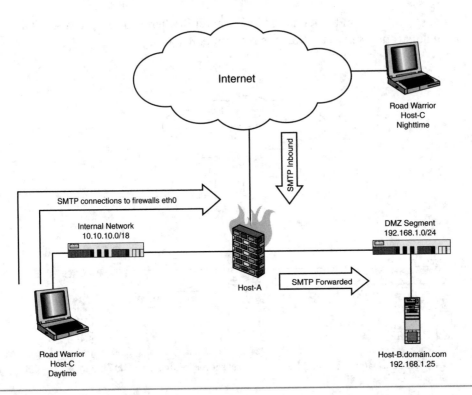

Figure 14.2   Outbound SMTP filter rules.

FORCING YOUR MAIL SERVER TRAFFIC TO USE A SPECIFIC IP ADDRESS WITH AN SNAT RULE

We run into this scenario frequently in the hosting business. These are servers with multiple IP addresses, sometimes two or three hundred, to a single machine, and the MTA is either incapable or too unfriendly when it comes to getting it to bind to a specific IP address. Other reasons to use this might stem from ending up with an IP address that is on one of the more difficult to remove real-time blacklists (RBLs). As such, you need to restrict your MTA to send mail from a specific IP address.

The following rule should do the trick:

```
# Where eth0 is your external interface
# Where $EXTERNALIP is the IP you'd like your MTA to
# send mail from
$IPTABLES -t nat -A POSTROUTING -o eth0 -p tcp \
     --dport 25 -j SNAT --to-source $EXTERNALIP
```

BLOCKING INTERNAL USERS FROM SENDING MAIL THROUGH YOUR FIREWALL

The following rule assumes that you have a fairly loose NAT/MASQUERADE policy on your firewall and have lately been posed with the problem of blocking your internal network users from sending mail out through your firewall. This could be because of a corporate information security policy change or perhaps more likely to prevent the spread of viruses and worms to systems outside of your network.

In our first example, the firewall Host-A protects the internal network, 10.10.10.0/24. Hosts on the internal network use the host, Host-B.domain.com, which is located on the Internet for mail. Connections to this server will be allowed; all other connections will be denied.

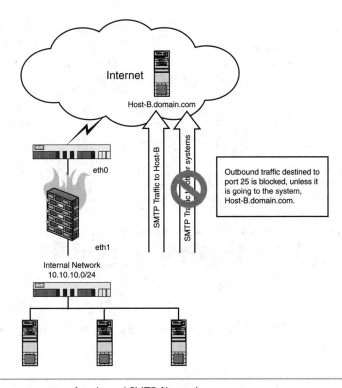

Figure 14.3   Demonstration of outbound SMTP filter rules.

```
# where eth0 is our external interface (Internet)
# where eth1 is our internal interface (10.10.10.0/24)
$IPTABLES -A FORWARD -p tcp -dport 25 -d host-b.domain.com -j ACCEPT
$IPTABLES -A FORWARD -p tcp -dport 25  -j REJECT -reject-with icmp-net-prohibited
```

First note that we apply this to FORWARD. This is because this applies to traffic passing through the firewall. Applying this same rule to OUTPUT would only affect mail originating on the firewall itself. Also note that we apply an ALLOW rule for our external mail server, Host-B.domain.com. We reject connections with the ICMP message icmp-net-prohibited for diagnostics purposes.

This next configuration assumes that the mail server, Host-B (192.168.1.25), exists on a DMZ segment (192.168.1.0/24) off the firewall.

```
# where eth0 is our external interface (Internet)
# where eth1 is our internal interface (10.10.10.0/24)
$IPTABLES -A FORWARD -p tcp -dport 25  \
      -s ! 192.168.1.25 -j REJECT \
      -reject-with icmp-net-prohibited
```

This final example is included for convenience, and while we do not recommend running your SMTP server along side your regular internal hosts, we recognize that sometimes security has nothing to do with it (it's still bad!). This configuration assumes the internal mail server, Host-B, is at the IP address 10.10.10.25:

```
$IPTABLES -A FORWARD -p tcp -dport 25 \
      -s ! 10.10.10.25 -j REJECT \
      -reject-with icmp-net-prohibited.
```

NOTE

This rule is not going to help you for users or malware sending mail out through other means, such as proxy servers on the other side of your firewall, exploitable web scripts, and so on.

ACCEPT ONLY SMTP CONNECTIONS FROM SPECIFIC HOSTS (ISP)

This configuration assumes that you are running an internal mail server, set up either internally or on a DMZ segment. This mail server is acting perhaps as a local mail spool only or smart host and only needs to send/receive mail to an upstream mail server—at an ISP for example.

The first example assumes that your firewall, Host-A, is only going to allow SMTP connections from the upstream ISP mail server, mailserver.isp.com. All other connections are to be rejected.

This example rule assumes you have a default DROP policy:

```
$IPTABLES -P INPUT DROP
# where eth0 is your Internet interface
$IPTABLES -A INPUT -i eth0 -p tcp -dport 25 \
     -s mailserver.isp.com -j ACCEPT
```

This second example assumes you have a firewall (Host-A) forwarding SMTP connections to an internal mail server (Host-B, 192.168.1.25) on the DMZ segment 192.168.1.0/24. The internal network address space is 10.10.10.0/24. We will only allow connections from mailserver.isp.com.

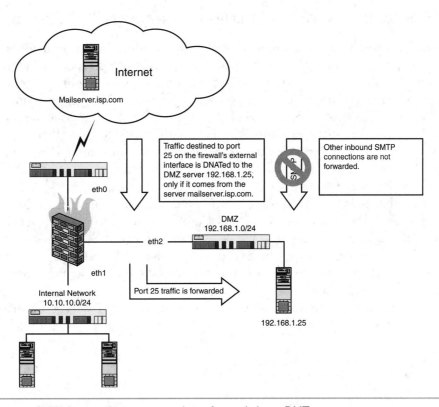

Figure 14.4   SMTP from mailserver.isp.com being forwarded to a DMZ server.

```
# where eth0 is your external Internet facing interface
# where eth1 is your internal network, 10.10.10.0/24
# where eth2 is your DMZ network, 192.168.1.0/24
EXTERNAL=eth0
INTERNAL=eth1
DMZ=eth2
MAILSERVER=192.168.1.25

$IPTABLES -A FORWARD -i $EXTERNAL -o $DMZ -p tcp \
     --dport 25 -s mailserver.isp.com -m state \
     --state NEW,ESTABLISHED,RELATED -j ACCEPT

$IPTABLES -t nat -A PREROUTING -i $EXTERNAL -p tcp \
     --dport 25 -j DNAT --to-destination  $MAILSERVER
```

SMTP Server Timeouts/Failures/Numerous Processes

In this scenario, you have just configured a mail server behind a Masquerading/NAT firewall, and now the mail server is manifesting issues with timeouts to some but not all external mail servers. Further, this issue might also result in an MTA with hundreds of open processes for incoming messages, running for several hours (reported on sendmail). When the server is connected directly to the Internet, these issues disappear.

Most likely this is an issue related to either an identd (AUTH) request, either from or to the server. A great many services, including SMTP, FTP, and POP3, use identd requests to query the remote server for the username initiating the connection. In this case, what is happening is that the identd (TCP Port 113) request is being dropped (-j DROP) at the firewall's external interface. The sending server (either your internal server or the remote one) in this case is not receiving a TCP RST packet, and as such, nothing is telling it to shut down the ident process, so it sits and waits until it times out. Your options here are either to allow the identd service, which we do not recommend, or change your rules on this service to a REJECT policy, which will return an RST/ACK, instructing the remote service to terminate the identd request.

This first rule assumes that the mail server is running on the firewall itself with a very restrictive "unless allow, deny" policy:

```
# where eth0 is our external interface
$IPTABLES -A INPUT -i eth0 -dport 113 -j REJECT
```

The following rule demonstrates how to achieve this, where Host-A is our firewall and Host-B (192.168.1.25) is our internal SMTP server, located on the DMZ segment 192.168.1.0/24:

```
# where eth0 is our external interface
# where eth1 is our internal network, 10.10.10.0/24
# where eth2 is our DMZ network, 192.168.1.0/24

$IPTABLES -A FORWARD -i eth0 -o eth2 -p tcp \
     dport 113 -j REJECT
```

SMALL E-MAIL SEND/RECEIVE CORRECTLY—LARGE E-MAIL MESSAGES DO NOT

In this example, our firewall is either operating an MTA or forwarding connections to a DNAT-ed SMTP server. Small e-mail messages can be sent and received correctly by the mail server; large messages repeatedly fail.

This is almost always caused by an MTU setting on the firewall, typically in DSL, or PPPoE environments where the overhead of this environment reduces the maximum unit size you can transmit over your upstream connection. This also can occur with VPN environments, such as PPTP. The fix for this situation is fairly straight forward, and we discuss it in more detail in the VPN chapter. For brevity's sake, here's the fix:

```
# where eth0 is the external interface
$IPTABLES -A OUTPUT -o eth0 -p tcp \
     --tcp-flags SYN,RST SYN -j TCPMSS \
     -clamp-mss-to-pmtu
```

SUMMARY

One thing we really did not touch on in this chapter is a set of firewall rules you can use to fight spam. This is a topic near and dear to us, as we are sure it is to you. Everyone hates spam, and there are more strategies for fighting spam than you can poke a stick at. We also are in the fight against spam, and you can see our anti-spam efforts at http://www.atomicrocketturtle.com.

Filter rules themselves, we feel, are not a realistic mechanism for dealing with spam; there are too many bad guys coming from too many IPs to realistically create a mechanism in **iptables**. A better option would be to use one of the RBL (`http://www.mail-abuse.com/`) services in your MTA itself. Even these services are not a silver bullet in fighting spam, which is why we opt for either content-filtering systems, such as **spamassassin** (`http://www.spamassassin.org`), a **DSPAM** (`http://www.nuclearelephant.com/projects/dspam/`), or challenge-response systems such as **TMDA** (`http://tmda.net/`).

This is a topic that really deserves its own book (or two...or three...).

That being said, this chapter should leave you with a good understanding on how to create host-based firewall rules or DMZs to contain your mail servers. The rules themselves are intended to be self-contained, so you should not have to reference other chapters to get something working on your firewall right away.

Web Services (Web Servers and Web Proxies)

In this chapter, we cover common firewall configurations for both network and host-only firewalls and web services. Specifically, we provide example configurations for "unless allow, deny" host-only firewalls, transparent web proxy servers, single and multi-IP forwarding configurations, filtering access to web servers and clients, as well as a typical road warrior forwarded configuration.

COMMON QUESTIONS

Q: I have a DMZ web server or one running on my firewall itself. I can see it at home but not from work. What is going on?

A: A great many ISPs filter out port 80 these days on their broadband networks. Before spending a great deal of time trying to debug your firewall, check with your ISP first and see if they are filtering this service out. If they are, your only option is to run your web server on another ISP that is not filtered or run your web server on a different port. A quick and dirty way to test this is with **telnet** and to issue an HEAD / HTML 1.0 \n\n.

Example:

```
[user@laptop tmp]$ telnet www.atomicrocketturtle.com 80
Connected to www.atomicrocketturtle.com (216.218.240.133).
Escape character is '^]'.
HEAD / HTML 1.0 \n\n
```

```
HTTP/1.1 403 Forbidden
Date: Wed, 15 Sep 2004 18:42:19 GMT
Server: Apache
Accept-Ranges: bytes
Content-Length: 2898
Connection: close
Content-Type: text/html; charset=ISO-8859-1

Connection closed by foreign host.
```

If you cannot connect, then it's a good indication that your ISP is filtering out port 80 into their network.

Q: I have one IP address—does netfilter support name-based hosting to route web traffic to two different web servers using the same port (80)?

A: No, netfilter operates at too low of a level to perform any kind of name-based hosting. You would need to use an application layer proxy on your firewall to do this.

TOOLS DISCUSSED IN THIS CHAPTER

squid: http://www.squid-cache.org/
From the **squid** website
squid is

- a full-featured web proxy cache
- designed to run on Unix systems
- free, open source software
- the result of many contributions by unpaid (and paid) volunteers

squid supports

- proxying and caching of HTTP, FTP, and other URLs
- proxying for SSL
- cache hierarchies
- ICP, HTCP, CARP, Cache Digests
- transparent caching
- WCCP (Squid v2.3 and above)
- extensive access controls

- HTTP server acceleration
- SNMP
- caching of DNS lookups

Inbound: Running a Local Web Server (Basic Rules)

In this, the most basic host-based firewall configuration, the system Host-A is running a web server. The only services you want to allow to this system are HTTP (TCP Port 80), HTTPS (TCP Port 443), and potentially SSH (TCP Port 22).

The first example ruleset shows how to configure your firewall rules with a very strict default policy:

```
# where $DNSSERVER is the IP address of your DNS server
$IPTABLES -P INPUT    DROP
$IPTABLES -P OUTPUT   DROP
$IPTABLES -P FORWARD DROP

$IPTABLES -A OUTPUT -m state --state NEW,ESTABLISHED,RELATED -j ACCEPT

$IPTABLES -A INPUT -p tcp --dport 22 -j ACCEPT
$IPTABLES -A INPUT -p tcp --dport 80 -j ACCEPT
$IPTABLES -A INPUT -p tcp --dport 443 -j ACCEPT

# this rule allows the server to perform DNS lookups
$IPTABLES -A INPUT -A INPUT -p udp -m udp \
     -s $DNSSERVER --sport 53 -d 0/0 -j ACCEPT
```

This next example is right from the Red Hat firewall rule generator; it demonstrates a completely different method with the same effect:

```
# where $DNSSERVER is the IP address of your DNS server.
$IPTABLES -N RH-Lokkit-0-50-INPUT
$IPTABLES -A INPUT -j RH-Lokkit-0-50-INPUT
$IPTABLES -A FORWARD -j RH-Lokkit-0-50-INPUT
$IPTABLES -A RH-Lokkit-0-50-INPUT -p tcp -m tcp \
     --dport 22 --syn -j ACCEPT
$IPTABLES -A RH-Lokkit-0-50-INPUT -p tcp -m tcp \
     --dport 80 --syn -j ACCEPT
$IPTABLES -A RH-Lokkit-0-50-INPUT -p tcp -m tcp \
     --dport 443 --syn -j ACCEPT
```

```
$IPTABLES -A RH-Lokkit-0-50-INPUT -i lo -j ACCEPT
$IPTABLES -A RH-Lokkit-0-50-INPUT -p udp -m udp \
      -s $DNSSERVER --sport 53 -d 0/0 -j ACCEPT
$IPTABLES -A RH-Lokkit-0-50-INPUT -p tcp -m tcp \
      --syn -j REJECT
$IPTABLES -A RH-Lokkit-0-50-INPUT -p udp -m udp \          -j REJECT
```

INBOUND: FILTER: INCOMING WEB TO SPECIFIC HOSTS

This next ruleset shows how to perform the same as the previous set but limiting the hosts that can connect to the web server. In our example, the web server Host-A is using host-based firewall rules to restrict the clients that can connect to it. The following networks are allowed to connect 10.10.10.0/24 and 192.168.1.0/24 to 80 and 443 only. SSH connections are only allowed from the host 172.16.32.32

Our first example is a very short, basic method:

```
# where $DNSSERVER is our DNS server.
$IPTABLES -P INPUT DROP
$IPTABLES -A INPUT -s 10.10.10.0/24 -p tcp \
      --dport 80 -j ACCEPT
$IPTABLES -A INPUT -s 192.168.1.0/24 -p tcp \
      --dport 80 -j ACCEPT
$IPTABLES -A INPUT -s  10.10.10.0/24 -p tcp \
      --dport 443 -j ACCEPT
$IPTABLES -A INPUT -s  192.168.1.0/24 -p tcp \
      --dport 443 -j ACCEPT
$IPTABLES -A INPUT -s  172.16.32.32 -p tcp \
      --dport 22 -j ACCEPT
$IPTABLES -A INPUT -A INPUT -p udp -m udp \
      -s $DNSSERVER --sport 53 -d 0/0 -j ACCEPT
```

This second example achieves the same effect with a bit more flexibility and overall network friendliness given that the REJECT will return an RST/ACK. The previous rule uses a DROP, which just tosses the packets to the side:

```
# where $DNSSERVER is the IP address of your DNS
# server.

$IPTABLES -N WEBCLIENTS
$IPTABLES -A INPUT -N WEBCLIENTS
$IPTABLES -A FORWARD -j WEBCLIENTS
```

```
$IPTABLES -A WEBCLIENTS -p tcp -m tcp --dport 80 \
     -s  10.10.10.0/24 --syn -j ACCEPT

$IPTABLES -A WEBCLIENTS -p tcp -m tcp --dport 80 \
     -s  192.168.1.0/24 --syn -j ACCEPT

$IPTABLES -A WEBCLIENTS -p tcp -m tcp --dport 443 \
     -s  10.10.10.0/24 --syn -j ACCEPT

$IPTABLES -A WEBCLIENTS -p tcp -m tcp --dport 443 \
     -s  192.168.1.0/24 --syn -j ACCEPT

$IPTABLES -A WEBCLIENTS -p tcp -m tcp --dport 22 \
     -s  172.16.32.32 --syn -j ACCEPT
$IPTABLES -A WEBCLIENTS -j ACCEPT
$IPTABLES -A  WEBCLIENTS-p udp -m udp -s $DNSSERVER \
     --sport 53 -d 0/0 -j ACCEPT
$IPTABLES -A WEBCLIENTS -p tcp -m tcp --syn -j REJECT
$IPTABLES -A  WEBCLIENTS -p udp -m udp -j REJECT
```

FORWARD: REDIRECT LOCAL PORT 80 TO LOCAL PORT 8080

In this scenario, our web server Host-A is not running on the standard HTTP port (TCP 80), so we will need to use a host-based firewall rule to forward queries to the port on which we're running the web server. In this case, Host-A is running a web server on port 8080.

This first example assumes that you have a restrictive policy, so our first rules are to allow connections to port 80 and 8080:

```
# Where $EXTERNALIP is the external IP Address on this
# server

$IPTABLES -A INPUT -p tcp --dport 80 -j ACCEPT
$IPTABLES -A INPUT -p tcp --dport 8080 -j ACCEPT
$IPTABLES -t nat -A PREROUTING -p tcp -dport 80 \
     -j REDIRECT -to-ports 8080
# This final rule ensures that port 80 connections that
# originate locally are redirected
$IPTABLES -A OUTPUT -t nat -p tcp -d $EXTERNALIP \
     --dport 80 -j REDIRECT --to 8080
```

Note that this final rule is applied to OUTPUT; this is because it's referring to traffic originating on the system itself.

FORWARDING CONNECTIONS FROM THE FIREWALL TO AN INTERNAL WEB SERVER

This configuration assumes that you have a front-end firewall (Host-A) and a web server (Host-B, 192.168.1.80) on a DMZ segment (192.168.1.0/24). Connections to Host-A on ports 80 and 443 (HTTP and HTTPS, respectively) will be forwarded to the web server Host-B on the DMZ segment. Figure 15.1 describes the design.

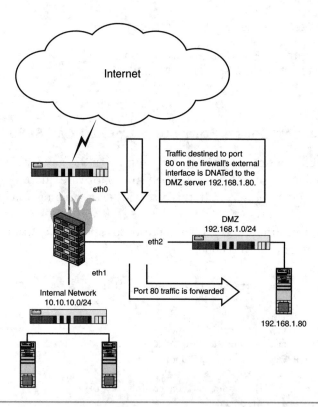

Figure 15.1   Demonstrating DNAT-ing HTTP and HTTPS traffic to a DMZ web server.

This first configuration demonstrates the rules in Figure 15.1:

```
# where eth0 is the external interface (Internet)
# where eth1 is the internal interface (10.10.10.0/24)
# where eth2 is the DMZ interface (192.168.1.0/24)


EXTERNAL=eth0
INTERNAL=eth1
DMZ=eth2

SERVER=192.168.1.80

# HTTP traffic, TCP port 80
$IPTABLES -A FORWARD -i $EXTERNAL -o $DMZ -p tcp \
     --dport 80 -m state –state \
     NEW,ESTABLISHED,RELATED -j ACCEPT
$IPTABLES -t nat -A PREROUTING -i $EXTERNAL -p tcp \
     --dport 80 -j DNAT --to-destination  $SERVER

# HTTPS traffic, TCP port 443
$IPTABLES -t nat -A PREROUTING -i $EXTERNAL -p tcp \
     --dport 443 -j DNAT --to-destination  $SERVER
$IPTABLES -A FORWARD -i $EXTERNAL -o $DMZ -p tcp \
     --dport 443 -m state –state\
     NEW,ESTABLISHED,RELATED -j ACCEPT
```

FORWARD: TO MULTIPLE INTERNAL SERVERS

This next example demonstrates the previous configuration, but with multiple web servers. The firewall, Host-A in this case, has multiple Internet IPs on its external interface, 11.22.33.44 and 11.22.33.45. These IP addresses are assigned to two separate internal web servers—Host-B (192.168.1.80) receives web traffic destined to 11.22.33.44, and Host-C (192.168.1.81) receives web traffic destined to 11.22.33.45.

```
# where eth0 is the external interface (Internet)
# where eth1 is the internal interface (10.10.10.0/24)
# where eth2 is the DMZ interface (192.168.1.0/24)
# where $EXTERNALIP is the external IP on your firewall
EXTERNAL=eth0
```

```
INTERNAL=eth1
DMZ=eth2

EXT_HOSTB=11.22.33.44
EXT_HOSTC=11.22.33.45

HOSTB=192.168.1.80
HOSTC=192.168.1.81

# HTTP traffic, TCP port 80 to HOSTB
$IPTABLES -A FORWARD -i $EXTERNAL -o $DMZ -p tcp \
     -d $EXT_HOSTB --dport 80 -m state \
     --state NEW,ESTABLISHED,RELATED -j ACCEPT
$IPTABLES -t nat -A PREROUTING -i $EXTERNAL -p tcp \
     -d $EXT_HOSTB --dport 80 -j DNAT \
     --to-destination  $HOSTB

# HTTP traffic, TCP port 80 to HOSTC
$IPTABLES -A FORWARD -i $EXTERNAL -o $DMZ -p tcp \
     -d $EXT_HOSTC --dport 80 -m state \
```

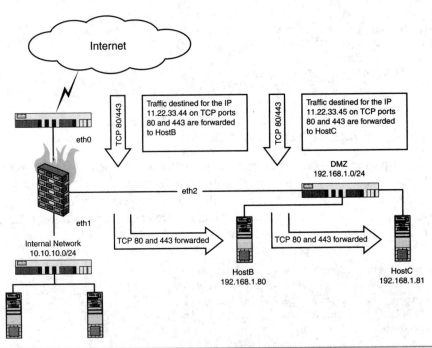

Figure 15.2   Multiple web servers on multiple DNAT-ed IP addresses.

```
        --state NEW,ESTABLISHED,RELATED -j ACCEPT
$IPTABLES -t nat -A PREROUTING -i $EXTERNAL -p tcp \
      -d $EXT_HOSTC --dport 80 -j DNAT \
      --to-destination  $HOSTC

# HTTPS traffic, TCP port 80 to HOSTC
$IPTABLES -A FORWARD -i $EXTERNAL -o $DMZ -p tcp \
      -d $EXT_HOSTC --dport 443 -m state \
      --state NEW,ESTABLISHED,RELATED -j ACCEPT
$IPTABLES -t nat -A PREROUTING -i $EXTERNAL -p tcp \
      -d $EXT_HOSTC --dport 443 -j DNAT \
      --to-destination  $HOSTC
```

FORWARD: To a Remote Server on the Internet

This particular scenario we see all the time when dealing with systems in the hosting
space. It's a fairly migratory business with servers moving frequently between the large
hosting providers or between IP space. The idea is to move your content and services to
the new system and set up firewall rules on the old system to DNAT traffic from the old
server to the new server. This is typically until all the content and users have been moved
to the new server and all the DNS and registrar records have been changed to point to
the new server. These rules work almost the same as a regular FORWARD rule. The main
difference is that our new server is only going to communicate back through the old
server when it sends traffic its way. Otherwise, it communicates as its normal IP address,
through its normal network, and with no NAT-ing.

In this example, we have two hosts, Host-A (11.22.33.44), which is our old server, and
Host-B (22.33.44.55), our new system. We add the following rules to Host-A:

```
#!/bin/sh

IPTABLES="/sbin/iptables"
EXTERNAL=eth0
OLDSERVER=11.22.33.44
NEWSERVER=22.33.44.55

# Enable connection tracking
$IPTABLES -A INPUT  -m state \
      --state ESTABLISHED,RELATED -j ACCEPT
$IPTABLES -A OUTPUT -m state \
      --state NEW,ESTABLISHED,RELATED -j ACCEPT
$IPTABLES -A FORWARD -m state \
      --state NEW,ESTABLISHED,RELATED -j ACCEPT
```

```
$IPTABLES -A FORWARD -i $EXTERNAL -o $EXTERNAL \
    -p tcp --dport 80 -d $OLDSERVER -m state \
    --state NEW,ESTABLISHED,RELATED -j ACCEPT
$IPTABLES -t nat -A PREROUTING -i $EXTERNAL -p tcp \
    --dport 80 -d  $OLDSERVER -j DNAT \
    --to-destination  $NEWSERVER
$IPTABLES -t nat -A POSTROUTING -p tcp --dport 80 -d $NEWSERVER \
                -j SNAT --to $OLDSERVER

# Enable IP Forwarding in the kernel
echo 1 > /proc/sys/net/ipv4/ip_forward
```

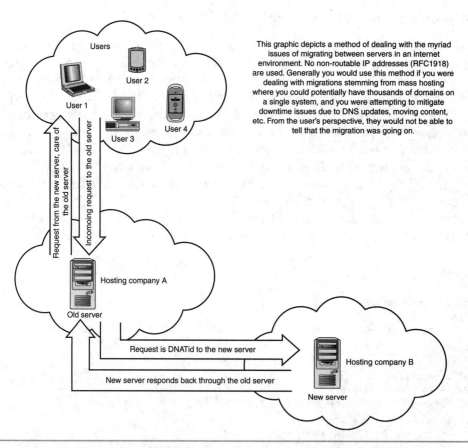

This graphic depicts a method of dealing with the myriad issues of migrating between servers in an internet environment. No non-routable IP addresses (RFC1918) are used. Generally you would use this method if you were dealing with migrations stemming from mass hosting where you could potentially have thousands of domains on a single system, and you were attempting to mitigate downtime issues due to DNS updates, moving content, etc. From the user's perspective, they would not be able to tell that the migration was going on.

Figure 15.3   DNAT being used to forward web traffic in a hosting environment.

The following script is a functional working example of the previous script, but one that forwards *all* traffic on the IP address to the remote server. This uses an external file called forwarded to list the source and destination IPs in this format: SOURCE-IP: DESTINATION-IP (i.e., 11.22.33.44:22.33.44.55).

```
#!/bin/sh

IPTABLES="/sbin/iptables"
CONFIG=/etc/rc.d/forwarded
EXTERNAL=eth0


# Enable connection tracking
$IPTABLES -A INPUT  -m state \
     --state ESTABLISHED,RELATED -j ACCEPT
$IPTABLES -A OUTPUT -m state \
     --state NEW,ESTABLISHED,RELATED -j ACCEPT
$IPTABLES -A FORWARD -m state \
     --state NEW,ESTABLISHED,RELATED -j ACCEPT


for i in `cat $CONFIG`; do
  SOURCEIP=`echo $i | awk -F: '{print $1}'`
  DESTIP=`echo $i | awk -F: '{print $2}'`
  echo "Forwarding $SOURCEIP to $DESTIP"
  $IPTABLES -A FORWARD -i $EXTERNAL -o $EXTERNAL \
        -d $SOURCEIP -m state --state \
         NEW,ESTABLISHED,RELATED -j ACCEPT
  $IPTABLES -t nat -A PREROUTING -i $EXTERNAL \
        -d  $SOURCEIP -j DNAT --to-destination  $DESTIP
  $IPTABLES -t nat -A POSTROUTING -d $DESTIP \
        -j SNAT --to $SOURCEIP

done

# Enable IP Forwarding in the kernel
echo "1" > /proc/sys/net/ipv4/ip_forward
```

In a hosting environment, it's very common to have multiple and sometimes hundreds of IPs on one interface. This method makes it possible to mitigate the outage time generally experienced while moving large numbers of virtual hosts between servers.

FORWARD: FILTERING ACCESS TO A FORWARDED SERVER

This next ruleset shows how to limit the hosts that can connect to the forwarded web server. In this example, our firewall, Host-A, forwards connections to the internal server Host-B (192.168.1.80). The following network is allowed to connect, 22.33.44.0/24 (Internet) to TCP ports 80 and 443.

This first configuration demonstrates the rules needed to achieve this type of configuration using DNAT rules:

```
# where eth0 is the external interface (Internet)
# where eth1 is the internal interface (10.10.10.0/24)
# where eth2 is the DMZ interface (192.168.1.0/24)
# where $EXTERNALIP is the external IP on your firewall
# where 192.168.1.1 is the internal IP address on the
# firewalls eth2 interface

$IPTABLES -A FORWARD -i eth0 -o eth2 -p tcp \
     -s 22.33.44.0/24 --dport 80 -m state \
     --state NEW,ESTABLISHED,RELATED -j ACCEPT
$IPTABLES -A FORWARD -i eth0 -o eth2 -p tcp \
     -s 22.33.44.0/24 --dport 443 -m state \
     --state NEW,ESTABLISHED,RELATED -j ACCEPT

# For our internet users from 22.33.44.0/24
$IPTABLES -t nat -A PREROUTING -i eth0 -p tcp \
     -s 22.33.44.0/24 --dport 80 -d $EXTERNALIP \
     -j DNAT --to-destination 192.168.1.80:80


$IPTABLES -t nat -A PREROUTING -i eth0 -p tcp \
     -s 22.33.44.0/24 --dport 443 -d $EXTERNALIP \
     -j DNAT --to-destination 192.168.1.80:443
```

OUTBOUND: SOME WEBSITES ARE INACCESSIBLE (ECN)

The symptoms of this problem are that in general, you can reach most websites with no performance or other issues; a small portion of websites, however, cannot be reached. This is a fairly common problem with the Explicit Congestion Notification (ECN) feature of the Linux kernel. If you have this compiled into your kernel and cannot connect to a small segment of non-Linux web servers, this is the most likely culprit. The fix is to disable ECN in your kernel.

To turn ECN off, as previously discussed in the book, you simply change the boolean value in

```
/proc/sys/net/ipv4/tcp_ecn:
echo 0 > /proc/sys/net/ipv4/tcp_ecn
```

OUTBOUND: BLOCK CLIENTS FROM ACCESSING WEBSITES

In this scenario you are in a position where you need to filter out access to specific websites by internal network systems traversing your firewall. This example really belongs in the NAT section of this book; however, given that this might only be related to a single service (web), we will address how to achieve this goal. In the following example, the firewall Host-A handles traffic for the internal network 10.10.10.0/24. Hosts on this network are only allowed to communicate with the web server at 11.22.33.44:

```
$IPTABLES -A PREROUTING -t nat -s 10.10.10.0/24 \
    -d 11.22.33.44 -dport 80 -j ACCEPT
$IPTABLES -A PREROUTING -t nat -s 10.10.10.0/24 \
    -d 0/0 -p tcp -dport 80 -j REJECT \
    -reject-with icmp-net-prohibited
```

The first rule allows the systems on the network 10.10.10.0/24 to access the web server at 11.22.33.44.

The second rule rejects traffic to any other web server, with the net-prohibited ICMP message. This is to aid in debugging and to cleanly reject the attempted connections to disallowed web servers.

TRANSPARENT PROXY SERVERS (SQUID) ON OUTBOUND WEB TRAFFIC

A transparent proxy server is a method of installing an application layer proxy server, such as **squid** (http://www.squid-cache.org), in such a way that the end users do not even know it is there by using REDIRECT rules on web traffic. This is useful because, amongst other things, traffic is cached on the proxy server, increasing performance and reducing bandwidth usage to oft-used websites.

In addition to the caching, using a transparent proxy server like **squid** in conjunction with an **iptables**/nefilter firewall brings other advantages. You can, for example, implement content filtering, ad-blocking, user authenticated web browsing, or provide much

more detailed browsing statistics from one of the many **squid** log analyzers listed at:
http://www.squid-cache.org/Scripts/.

In the following example, our firewall, Host-A (10.10.10.1), has an internal network,
10.10.10.0/24. This configuration demonstrates a transparent proxy rule to an instance
of **squid** running on the local firewall:

```
# where eth0 is the external (Internet) interface
# where eth1 is the internal (10.10.10.0/24) interface

$IPTABLES -A INPUT -p tcp --dport 3128 -i ! eth0 \
      -j ACCEPT
$IPTABLES -t nat -A PREROUTING -i eth1 -p tcp \
      --dport 80 -j REDIRECT --to-port 3128
```

The first rule allows port 3128 connections on all interfaces except for localhost.

The second rule dictates that all traffic passing through the firewall on port 80 will be
REDIRECTED to port 3128 (**squid**) on the server.

This next rule demonstrates the same configuration as the previous listing with an
additional external dedicated **squid** proxy server system, Host-B, with the IP address of
10.10.10.200:

```
$IPTABLES -t nat -A PREROUTING -i eth1 \
      -s ! 10.10.10.200 -p tcp --dport 80 -j DNAT \
      --to 10.10.10.200:3128
$IPTABLES -t nat -A POSTROUTING -o eth1 \
      -s 10.10.10.0/24 -d 10.10.10.200 -j SNAT \
      --to 10.10.10.1
```

The first rule redirects all www traffic on the internal network that is not from Host-B
(10.10.10.200), to Host-B.

The second rule rewrites all traffic passing through the firewall with the destination of
10.10.10.200 to appear to come from 10.10.10.1. This is so our redirected **squid** traffic
knows to come back to the firewall.

Sometimes it is necessary to exclude a host or a network from being cached by the
transparent proxy server. Excluding an IP or network from transparent caching can be
achieved with a user-defined chain. In the next example, our firewall Host-A runs a local

squid-caching server for the network 10.10.10.0/24. The system's Host-B (10.10.10.200), and Host-C (10.10.10.201) will be excluded from caching:

```
$IPTABLES -N SQUID
$IPTABLES -A PREROUTING -t nat -p tcp --dport 80 \
     -j SQUID
$IPTABLES -A SQUID -t nat -s 10.10.10.200 -j RETURN
$IPTABLES -A SQUID -t nat -s 10.10.10.201 -j RETURN
$IPTABLES -A SQUID -t nat -j REDIRECT --to-port 3128
```

The main difference here from the previous examples is that we use -j RETURN to match the hosts 10.10.10.200 and 10.10.10.201. This performs an exception when those IP addresses are matched against the rule and returns to the PREROUTING rule, passing the traffic from that host through the firewall without redirecting it to the **squid** port. All other traffic is not matched against those two exception rules, and will be processed by **squid**.

> **NOTE**
>
> The examples do not attempt to handle HTTPS traffic. This is because among other things, **squid** cannot really cache SSL encrypted traffic. But more importantly, using a transparent proxy with SSL traffic is a great example of a man-in-the-middle attack.

SUMMARY

Web server DMZs are probably one of the more common uses you will find for Linux firewalls these days. We run across people running NAT-ed web server clusters in the hosting business all the time using Linux boxes as front-end firewalls. Of course, one of the more common misconceptions we run into with these same users is that of surprise when a system is compromised—even though a firewall was being used (host-based or otherwise). A firewall is not a silver bullet, and while it can help protect your system from compromise, it cannot protect you from what you allow in. If you allow connections to your web server, the firewall does not really protect you from web-based attacks.

This is why we always recommend running web servers on dedicated DMZ segments. If and when your web server is compromised, it cannot be used to leverage access to your internal network.

File Services (NFS and FTP)

In this chapter, we will cover services used to share files, including NFS (Network File System) and FTP (File Transfer Protocol). Specifically, this chapter will cover configurations to apply firewall rules to an NFS file server, allow forwarded or DNAT style rules through a firewall using NFS and FTP, and rules to allow you to restrict access to these services—as well as troubleshooting steps for all of these.

More information on the NFS protocol can be obtained from RFCs 1094, 1813, and 3010. FTP is covered in RFC 959.

Recall that in earlier chapters, the problem-solving methodology we recommend requires that before moving on to a higher level in the OSI model, you must rule out any root causes in the preceding layers. If you have not already done so, please refer back to Chapter 5 for a discussion of the OSI model and how the problem-solving methodology is applied to it. Then work through and isolate the problem using the other chapters in this book before moving on to this one. The protocols in this chapter are somewhat complex and, as such, might prove to be difficult to troubleshoot without ruling out other root causes.

TOOLS DISCUSSED IN THIS CHAPTER

The website, `http://www.lowth.com/LinWiz/`, has an online scripting wizard for generating firewall rules for host-based firewall configurations. Additionally, this software package has absolutely fantastic documentation for getting a Linux-based NFS server to work with host-based firewall rules, and we recommend it highly.

NFS: CANNOT GET NFS TRAFFIC TO TRAVERSE A NAT OR IP FORWARDING FIREWALL

NFS is an RPC service that typically does not use predictable port numbers, which makes RPC services in general difficult to process effectively through netfilter. Fortunately, NFS is an exception. While it is an RPC service, it actually does use predictable port numbers, which makes it less of a chore to process through firewall rules.

In this configuration, you have an NFS file server (Host-B, 10.10.10.100) on one side of the firewall (Host-A) on the network 10.10.10.0/24 and one or more clients on the other side of the firewall in the network 192.168.1.0/24. Clients cannot successfully mount exported drives from the NFS server.

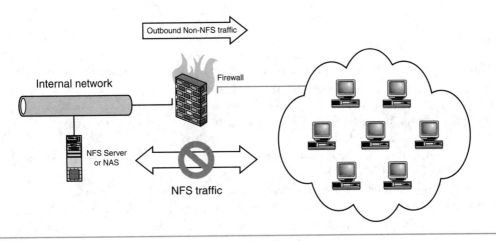

Figure 16.1   NFS traffic cannot traverse the firewall.

To forward or route to an NFS server firewall, we will first need to make some configuration changes to the NFS server itself to ensure that it is using the same consistent ports—due to the somewhat dynamic nature of RPC services port selection. Fortunately NFS is more "tame" than most other RPC services, so we will not need to make a great number of changes on the server itself to ensure consistent operation.

This example covers two types of complex configurations—the first assumes that the firewall is the destination for the NFS mount requests and forwards these connections to the real NFS server. The following documentation assumes you're using a Linux NFS server:

- **Portmapper, TCP/UDP ports 111:** No changes need to be made; this is the default port.
- `rpc.nfsd`, **TCP/UDP port 2049:** No changes need to be made; this is the default port.
- `rpc.statd`, **TCP/UDP port 4000:** On a Red Hat system, this is started from the **/etc/init.d/nfslock** script. Open this file in your preferred editor and change the following line:

```
daemon rpc.statd
```

to

```
daemon rpc.statd -p 4000
```

- `rpc.lockd`, **TCP/UDP port 4001:** On a Red Hat system, this is generally a kernel module, so we will need to modify the **/etc/modules.conf** file to pass in the parameters to this component. Open **/etc/modules.conf** in your preferred editor and set the following:

```
options lockd nlm_udpport=4001 nlm_tcpport=4001
```

For nonmodular kernels you will need to set this in your boot loader, **lilo** or **grub** with the following:

```
lockd.udpport=4001 lockd.tcpport=4001
```

- `rpc.mountd`, **TCP/UDP port 4002:** On a Red Hat system, this is configured from **/etc/sysconfig/nfs**. Load this file into your preferred editor and set the following:

```
MOUNTD_PORT=4002
```

- `rpc.rquotad`, **TCP/UDP port 4003:** On a Red Hat system, this is set from the **/etc/services** file. Load this file into your preferred editor and set the following:

```
rquotad 4003/tcp
rquotad 4003/udp
```

Assuming that the previous changes have been made and you are only attempting to set firewall rules on the NFS server itself, which has a default DROP policy, you will need to set the following:

```
# where eth0 is the systems only interface, with the IP address of 10.10.10.100
$IPTABLES -A INPUT -p tcp -m tcp --dport 111 -j ACCEPT
$IPTABLES -A INPUT -p udp -m udp --dport 111 -j ACCEPT
$IPTABLES -A INPUT -p tcp -m tcp --dport 2049 -j ACCEPT
$IPTABLES -A INPUT -p udp -m udp --dport 2049 -j ACCEPT
$IPTABLES -A INPUT -p tcp -m tcp \
                       --dport 4000:4003 -j ACCEPT
$IPTABLES -A INPUT -p udp -m udp \
                       --dport 4000:4003 -j ACCEPT
```

This would allow connections from all hosts to this system. However, if we wanted to limit these connections to specific hosts—192.168.1.5 and 192.168.1.6, for example—we could use the RETURN rule and user-defined tables to accomplish this:

```
# part 1
$IPTABLES -N NFSCLIENTS
$IPTABLES -N NFSSERVER
# part 2
$IPTABLES -A NFSCLIENTS -s 192.168.1.5 -j RETURN
$IPTABLES -A NFSCLIENTS -s 192.168.1.6 -j RETURN
$IPTABLES -A NFSCLIENTS -j DROP

#part 3

$IPTABLES -A NFSSERVER -j NFSCLIENTS
$IPTABLES -A NFSSERVER -p tcp -m tcp --dport 111 \
                          -j   ACCEPT
$IPTABLES -A NFSSERVER -p udp -m udp --dport 111 \
                          -j ACCEPT
$IPTABLES -A NFSSERVER -p tcp -m tcp --dport 2049 \
                          -j ACCEPT
$IPTABLES -A NFSSERVER -p udp -m udp --dport 2049 \
                          -j ACCEPT
$IPTABLES -A NFSSERVER -p tcp -m tcp \
                    --dport 4000:4003 -j ACCEPT
$IPTABLES -A NFSSERVER -p udp -m udp \
                    --dport 4000:4003 -j ACCEPT
$IPTABLES -A NFSSERVER -j DROP
```

The part 1 creates the user-defined chains, NFSCLIENTS, where we will stick all our allowed clients, and NFSSERVER, which is where we will contain our NFS server policy itself. part 2 defines the hosts that belong to the NFSCLIENTS allow list, using the RETURN flag. part 3 contains the policy that we're applying to the server itself. The first line in part 3 is to include the exception list of hosts from NFSCLIENTS and the ending DROP policy. Any hosts that do not match this list will be dropped by the final line in NFSCLIENTS before being processed by the remainder of the NFSSERVER chain.

This next configuration assumes that the firewall is located on an internal network with internal firewalls. The "external" interface in this configuration assumes the rest of the internal network. "Internal" is for clients in that particular department, and we still create a DMZ network to host our NFS server itself. The firewall is forwarding requests for a remote NFS server but will appear to be the NFS server itself to external clients. Client requests are directed to the firewall's eth0 interface with the IP address of 172.16.10.1. These are then forwarded to the internal NFS server, 192.168.1.100.

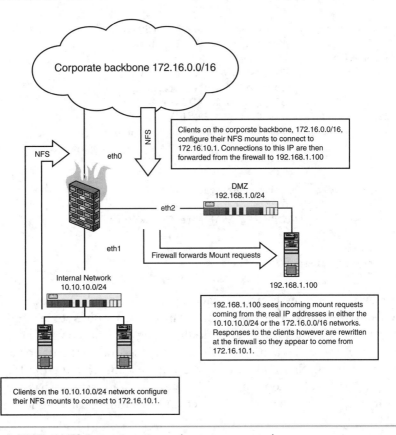

Figure 16.2 A DMZ-ed NFS server on an internal corporate network.

```
#!/bin/sh
IPTABLES=/sbin/iptables
#eth0 is the firewalls 172.16.10.0/16 network
#interface, 172.16.10.1
#eth1 is the firewalls internal 10.10.10.0/24 network
#interface, 10.10.10.1
#eth2 is the firewalls dmz  192.168.1.0/24, 192.168.1.1

EXTERNAL=eth0
INTERNAL=eth1
DMZ=eth2

EXTERNALIP=172.16.10.1
SERVER=192.168.1.100
NFSPORTS="111 2049 4000:4003"


# This example for loop runs through the array $NFSPORTS, for each port we need
# to allow. Otherwise, this script could be very long.
for i in $NFSPORTS; do
    $IPTABLES -A FORWARD -i $EXTERNAL -o $DMZ -p ALL \
                      --dport $i -m state –state \
                   NEW,ESTABLISHED,RELATED -j ACCEPT
    $IPTABLES -t nat -A PREROUTING -i $EXTERNAL \
                -p ALL  --dport $i -j DNAT --to-destination  \
                              $SERVER
done

# Final SNAT rule on our external interface
$IPTABLES -t nat -A POSTROUTING -i eth1 \
                   -o $EXTERNAL -j SNAT --to $EXTERNALIP


# enable IP Forwarding
echo 1 > /proc/sys/net/ipv4/ip_forward
```

Unlike many of our other examples where we use NAT to allow access to a device, in this example we will show the use of IP forwarding. This requires some minor upstream topology changes from the firewall, specifically setting your gateway to understand that the route to the network lies behind the firewall. This second configuration assumes that the firewall is not using NAT and is purely routing the traffic into the 192.168.1.0/24. Furthermore, the firewall is configured with an access list to restrict what networks can access this NFS server, specifically the network 192.168.2.0/24 and the host 192.168.3.100:

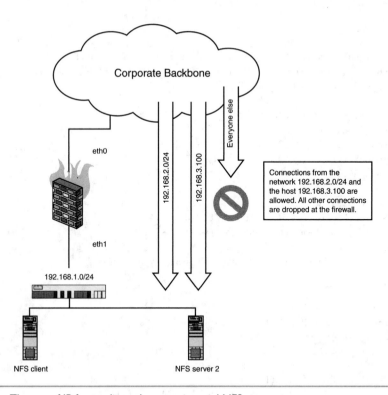

Figure 16.3 The use of IP forwarding rules to an internal NFS server.

```
#!/bin/sh
IPTABLES="/sbin/iptables"
#eth0 is the firewalls backbone interface, with the IP address 192.168.10.10
#eth1 is the firewalls 192.168.1.0/24 network interface, with the
#IP 192.168.1.1
EXTERNAL=eth0
INTERNAL=eth1
NFSPORTS="111 2049 4000:4003"



# clear legacy rules
$IPTABLES -F
$IPTABLES -X

# set default Deny ALL policy
$IPTABLES -P INPUT   DROP
$IPTABLES -P OUTPUT  DROP
$IPTABLES -P FORWARD DROP
```

```
# enable connection tracking
$IPTABLES -A INPUT  -m state --state ESTABLISHED,RELATED -j ACCEPT
$IPTABLES -A OUTPUT -m state --state NEW,ESTABLISHED,RELATED -j ACCEPT
$IPTABLES -A FORWARD   ESTABLISHED,RELATED -j ACCEPT

# create the user-defined access list
$IPTABLES -N NFSCLIENTS
$IPTABLES -A NFSCLIENTS -s 192.168.2.0/24 -j RETURN
$IPTABLES -A NFSCLIENTS -s 192.168.3.100 -j RETURN
$IPTABLES -A NFSCLIENTS  -j DROP

for i in $NFS_PORTS; do
  $IPTABLES -A FORWARD -i $EXTERNAL -p ALL -dport $i \
                        -m state -state NEW -j NFSCLIENTS
  $IPTABLES -A FORWARD -i $EXTERNAL -p ALL \
                --dport $i -m state -state NEW -j ACCEPT
done

# allow ssh to the firewall
$IPTABLES -A INPUT -p tcp --dport 22 -j ACCEPT

# final rule that lets 192.168.1.0/24 hosts communicate
# with the rest of the network
$IPTABLES -A FORWARD -i $INTERNAL -p ALL \
                -d 0.0.0.0/0 -s 192.168.1.0/24 -j ACCEPT

# enable ip forwarding
echo 1 > /proc/sys/net/ipv4/ip_forward
```

FTP INBOUND: RUNNING A LOCAL FTP SERVER (BASIC RULES)

In this, the most basic host-based firewall configuration, the system Host-A is running an FTP server. The only services you want to allow to this system are FTP (TCP Port 21), and potentially SSH (TCP Port 22).

The first example ruleset shows how to configure your firewall rules with a very strict default policy:

```
# where $DNSSERVER is the IP address of your DNS server
$IPTABLES -P INPUT   DROP
$IPTABLES -P OUTPUT  DROP
$IPTABLES -P FORWARD DROP
```

```
$IPTABLES -A OUTPUT -m state --state NEW,ESTABLISHED,RELATED -j ACCEPT

$IPTABLES -A INPUT -p tcp --dport 22 -m state \
                          --state NEW -j ACCEPT
$IPTABLES -A INPUT -p tcp --dport 21 -m state \
                          --state NEW -j ACCEPT


# this rule allows the server to perform DNS lookups
$IPTABLES -A INPUT -A INPUT -p udp -m udp \
                 -s $DNSSERVER --sport 53 -d 0/0 -j ACCEPT
```

This next example is right from the Red Hat firewall rule generator; it demonstrates a completely different method that achieves a similar effect. The key difference is that the former ruleset uses netfilter's stateful filtering to control new connection, whereas the following ruleset uses a simpler and somewhat less secure method of determining if a connection is new. Specifically, the following rules use the –syn rule to check the headers of the TCP packet to determine if it is part of an initial connection attempt. In theory, this would only allow new connections to the services allowed in these rules.

```
# where $DNSSERVER is the IP address of your DNS server.
$IPTABLES -N RH-Lokkit-0-50-INPUT
$IPTABLES -A INPUT -j RH-Lokkit-0-50-INPUT
$IPTABLES -A FORWARD -j RH-Lokkit-0-50-INPUT
$IPTABLES -A RH-Lokkit-0-50-INPUT -p tcp -m tcp \
                       --dport 22 --syn -j ACCEPT
$IPTABLES -A RH-Lokkit-0-50-INPUT -p tcp -m tcp \
                       --dport 21 --syn -j ACCEPT
$IPTABLES -A RH-Lokkit-0-50-INPUT -i lo -j ACCEPT
$IPTABLES -A RH-Lokkit-0-50-INPUT -p udp -m udp \
               -s $DNSSERVER --sport 53 -d 0/0 -j ACCEPT
$IPTABLES -A RH-Lokkit-0-50-INPUT -p tcp -m tcp \
                         --syn -j REJECT
$IPTABLES -A RH-Lokkit-0-50-INPUT -p udp -m udp \
                         -j REJECT
```

FTP Inbound: Restricting Access with Firewall Rules

This next ruleset shows how to perform the same as the previous section but limiting the hosts that can connect to the FTP server. In our example, the FTP server Host-A is using host-based firewall rules to restrict the clients that can connect to it. The networks 10.10.10.0/24 and 192.168.1.0/24 are allowed to connect to the FTP service on port TCP port 21. SSH connections are only allowed from the host 172.16.32.32.

Our first example is a very short, basic method:

```
# where $DNSSERVER is our DNS server.
$IPTABLES -P INPUT DROP
$IPTABLES -A INPUT -s 10.10.10.0/24 -p tcp \
                             --dport 21 -j ACCEPT
$IPTABLES -A INPUT -s 192.168.1.0/24 -p tcp \
                             --dport 21 -j ACCEPT
$IPTABLES -A INPUT -s  172.16.32.32 -p tcp \
                             --dport 22 -j ACCEPT
$IPTABLES -A INPUT -A INPUT -p udp -m udp \
                    -s $DNSSERVER --sport 53 -d 0/0 -j ACCEPT
```

This second example achieves the same effect with a bit more flexibility and overall network friendliness given that the REJECT will return an RST/ACK when a restricted host attempts to connect to the service, the previous rule uses -j DROP, which just tosses the packets to the side. While in effect this achieves the same thing, using a -j REJECT rule will make it easier to diagnose that they are being filtered out from the perspective of the client.

```
# where $DNSSERVER is the IP address of your DNS server.
$IPTABLES -N FTPCLIENTS
$IPTABLES -A INPUT -N FTPCLIENTS
$IPTABLES -A FORWARD -j FTPCLIENTS
$IPTABLES -A FTPCLIENTS -p tcp -m tcp --dport 21 \
                   -s  10.10.10.0/24 --syn -j ACCEPT

$IPTABLES -A FTPCLIENTS -p tcp -m tcp --dport 21 \
                   -s  192.168.1.0/24 --syn -j ACCEPT

$IPTABLES -A FTPCLIENTS -p tcp -m tcp --dport 22 \
                     -s  172.16.32.32 --syn -j ACCEPT
$IPTABLES -A FTPCLIENTS -j ACCEPT
$IPTABLES -A  FTPCLIENTS-p udp -m udp -s $DNSSERVER \
                    --sport 53 -d 0/0 -j ACCEPT
$IPTABLES -A FTPCLIENTS -p tcp -m tcp --syn -j REJECT
$IPTABLES -A FTPCLIENTS -p udp -m udp -j REJECT
```

FTP Inbound: Redirecting FTP Connections to Another Port on the Server

In this scenario, our FTP server Host-A is not running on the standard FTP port (TCP 21), so we will need to use a host-based firewall rule to forward queries to the port we're running the FTP server on. In this case, Host-A is running an FTP server on port 5050.

This first example assumes that you have a restrictive policy, so our first rules are to allow connections to port 21 and 5050:

```
$IPTABLES -A INPUT -p tcp --dport 21 -j ACCEPT
$IPTABLES -A INPUT -p tcp --dport 5050 -j ACCEPT
$IPTABLES -t nat -A PREROUTING -p tcp -dport 21 \
                        -j REDIRECT -to-ports 5050
# This final rule ensures that ftp connections that
# originate locally are redirected
$IPTABLES -A OUTPUT -t nat -p tcp -d $EXTERNALIP \
                     --dport 21 -j REDIRECT --to 5050
```

Note that this final rule is applied OUTPUT—this is because it's referring to traffic originating on the system itself.

FTP Forward: Forwarding to an FTP Server Behind the Firewall on a DMZ Segment

This configuration assumes that you have a front-end firewall (Host-A) and an FTP server (Host-B, 192.168.1.21) on a DMZ segment (192.168.1.0/24). Connections to Host-A on ports 21 will be forwarded to the FTP server Host-B on the DMZ segment. Figure 16.4 describes the design.

When working with this type of setup, one of the first things to keep in mind is that there are two separate netfilter kernel connection tracking modules that must be loaded to get this to work. They are

```
ip_conntrack_ftp
ip_nat_ftp
```

These modules are both configured by default on the commercial Linux distributions, like Red Hat and SuSE. If your system does not have these modules installed, or if you're using a custom kernel, ensure that you have the following configured in your kernel:

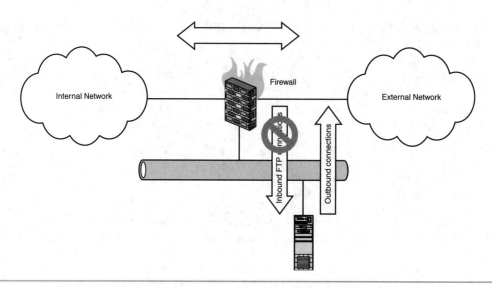

Figure 16.4   Forwarding to an FTP server on a DMZ segment through the firewall.

Kernels 2.4.x

```
Networking options   --->
  IP: Netfilter Configuration   --->
Connection tracking (required for masq/NAT)
      <M>FTP protocol support
```

Kernels 2.6.x

```
Device Drivers   --->
  Networking support   --->
    Networking options   --->
      Network packet filtering (replaces ipchains)   --->
        IP: Netfilter Configuration   --->
FTP protocol support
```

**Select M for modular support, or * to build this directly into the kernel.

This first configuration demonstrates the rules in the previous diagram using DNAT/SNAT rules, where the firewall's DMZ IP address is 192.168.1.1:

```
# where eth0 is the external interface (Internet)
# where eth1 is the internal interface (10.10.10.0/24)
# where eth2 is the DMZ interface (192.168.1.0/24)

EXTERNAL=eth0
INTERNAL=eth1
DMZ=eth2

SERVER=192.168.1.21

$IPTABLES -A FORWARD -i $EXTERNAL -o $DMZ -p tcp \
            --dport 20:21 -m state \
            --state NEW,ESTABLISHED,RELATED -j ACCEPT



$IPTABLES -t nat -A PREROUTING -i $EXTERNAL -p tcp \
            --dport 20:21 -j DNAT --to-destination  $SERVER
```

Note the use of –dport 20:21; this is specifying a range of ports, specifically ports 20 and 21.

FTP Forward: Forwarding to Multiple FTP Servers Behind the Firewall on a DMZ Segment

This next example demonstrates the previous configuration, but with multiple FTP servers. The firewall, Host-A in this case, has multiple Internet IPs on its external interface, 11.22.33.44 and 11.22.33.45. These IP addresses are assigned to two separate internal FTP servers. Host-B (192.168.1.80) receives FTP traffic destined to 11.22.33.44, and Host-C (192.168.1.81) receives FTP traffic destined to 11.22.33.45.

```
# where eth0 is the external interface (Internet)
# where eth1 is the internal interface (10.10.10.0/24)
# where eth2 is the DMZ interface (192.168.1.0/24)

EXTERNAL=eth0
INTERNAL=eth1
DMZ=eth2
```

```
HOSTB=192.168.1.10
HOSTC=192.168.1.11

IP_HOSTB=11.22.33.44
IP_HOSTC=11.22.33.45

# Host-B rules
$IPTABLES -A FORWARD -i $EXTERNAL -o $DMZ \
                -d $IP_HOSTB -p tcp --dport 20:21 -m state \
                --state NEW,ESTABLISHED,RELATED -j ACCEPT
$IPTABLES -t nat -A PREROUTING -i $EXTERNAL -p tcp \
                -d $IP_HOSTB --dport 20:21 -j DNAT \
                        --to-destination  $HOSTB

# Host-C rules
$IPTABLES -A FORWARD -i $EXTERNAL -o $DMZ \
                -d $IP_HOSTC -p tcp --dport 20:21 -m state \
                --state NEW,ESTABLISHED,RELATED -j ACCEPT
$IPTABLES -t nat -A PREROUTING -i $EXTERNAL -p tcp \
                -d $IP_HOSTC --dport 20:21 -j DNAT \
                --to-destination  $HOSTC
```

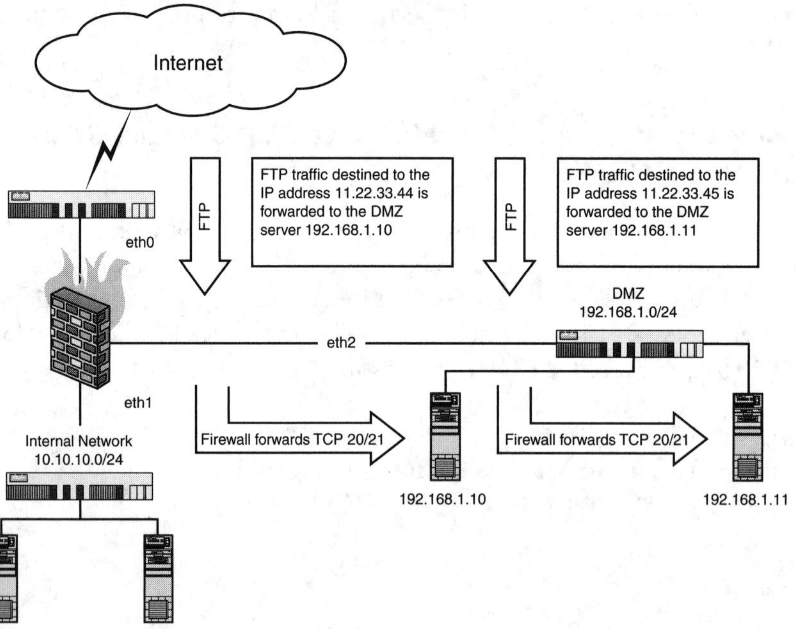

Figure 16.5   A multi-IP, multi-FTP server DMZ.

FTP Forward: From One Internet Server to Another Internet Server

We see this particular scenario all the time when dealing with systems in the hosting space. It's a fairly migratory business with servers moving between the large hosting providers or between IP space frequently. The idea is to move your content and services to the new system and set up firewall rules on the old system to DNAT traffic from the old server to the new server. This is the case typically until all the content and users have been moved to the new server and all the DNS and registrar records have been changed to point to the new server. These rules work almost the same as a regular FORWARD rule, the main difference is that our new server is only going to communicate back through the old server when it sends traffic its way. Otherwise, it communicates as its normal IP address—through its normal network with no NAT-ing.

In this example, we have two hosts, Host-A (11.22.33.44), which is our old server, and Host-B (22.33.44.55), our new system. We add the following rules to Host-A:

```
#!/bin/sh

IPTABLES="/sbin/iptables"
EXTERNAL=eth0
OLDSERVER=11.22.33.44
NEWSERVER=22.33.44.55



# load the ip_connection tracking modules for ftp
modprobe ip_conntrack_ftp
modprobe ip_nat_ftp

$IPTABLES -A FORWARD -i $EXTERNAL -o $EXTERNAL \
                -p tcp --dport 20:21 -d $OLDSERVER -m state \
                --state NEW,ESTABLISHED,RELATED -j ACCEPT

$IPTABLES -t nat -A PREROUTING -i $EXTERNAL -p tcp \
                --dport 20:21 -d  $OLDSERVER -j DNAT \
                        --to-destination  $NEWSERVER
$IPTABLES -t nat -A POSTROUTING -p tcp --dport 20:21 -d $NEWSERVER \
                -j SNAT --to $OLDSERVER

# Enable IP Forwarding in the kernel
echo 1 > /proc/sys/net/ipv4/ip_forward
```

If all this seems familiar, this is because this is exactly the same thing we did for web traffic in the previous chapter, with one exception—we have to add a ruleset for the FTP-data channel on port 20 and make sure the `ip_conntrack_ftp` and `ip_nat_ftp` modules are loaded.

FTP FORWARD: RESTRICTING FTP ACCESS TO A FORWARDED SERVER

This next ruleset demonstrates how to limit the hosts that can connect to the forwarded FTP server. In this example, our firewall Host-A forwards connections to the internal server Host-B (192.168.1.21). The following network is allowed to connect 22.33.44.0/24 (Internet) to the FTP TCP ports 20 and 21.

This first configuration demonstrates the rules needed to achieve this type of configuration using DNAT rules:

```
#!/bin/sh

IPTABLES="/sbin/sh"

# where eth0 is the external interface (Internet)
# where eth1 is the internal interface (10.10.10.0/24)
# where eth2 is the DMZ interface (192.168.1.0/24)
EXTERNAL=eth0
INTERNAL=eth1
DMZ=eth2

# Our internal DMZ servers
SERVER=192.168.1.21


# load the ip_connection tracking modules for ftp
modprobe ip_conntrack_ftp
modprobe ip_nat_ftp

# clear our old rules
$IPTABLES -F
$IPTABLES -X

# create our Allow lists
$IPTABLES -N FTPCLIENTS
$IPTABLES -A FTPCLIENTS  -s 22.33.44.0/24 -j RETURN
$IPTABLES -A FTPCLIENTS  -j DROP
```

```
$IPTABLES -A FORWARD -i $EXTERNAL -p tcp \
            --dport 20:21 --m state \
            --state NEW,ESTABLISHED,RELATED -j FTPCLIENTS
$IPTABLES -A FORWARD -i $EXTERNAL -p tcp \
            --dport 20:21 - -m state \
            --state NEW,ESTABLISHED,RELATED -j ACCEPT

$IPTABLES -t nat -A PREROUTING -i $EXTERNAL -p tcp \
--dport 20:21 - -j DNAT --to-destination  $SERVER

# Enable IP Forwarding in the kernel
echo 1 > /proc/sys/net/ipv4/ip_forward
```

The use of the user defined chain FTPCLIENTS allows the firewall administrator an easier method of modifying the allow list without having to customize a large number of rules. New users can be added to the FTPCLIENTS chain quickly.

FTP Outbound: Connections are Established, but Directories Cannot Be Listed, and Files Cannot Be Downloaded

In this example, internal systems on the network 10.10.10.0/24, behind the firewall Host-A, can successfully connect to FTP servers on the external side of the firewall. However, returning DATA port connections are not successfully transmitted through the firewall. The result is that commands in the FTP session appear to hang when performing commands that return data (1s, get, and so on).

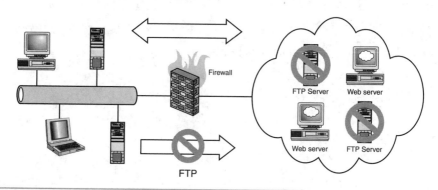

Figure 16.6 Outbound FTP connections are established, directories cannot be listed, files cannot be downloaded.

This is a very common problem that is indicative of the FTP connection tracking module either not being built into the kernel, or if this is a modular kernel—not loaded. Assuming you have a modular kernel, run the following command:

```
modprobe ip_conntrack_ftp
```

If you do not have this module or your kernel is compiled without module support, you will need to compile it in the following:

Kernels 2.4.x

```
Networking options  --->
  IP: Netfilter Configuration  --->
FTP protocol support
```

Kernels 2.6.x

```
Device Drivers  --->
  Networking support  --->
    Networking options  --->
      Network packet filtering (replaces ipchains)  --->
        IP: Netfilter Configuration  --->
FTP protocol support
```

**Select M for modular support, or * to build this directly into the kernel.

SUMMARY

FTP and NFS both demonstrate much more complicated firewall rule policies and module requirements due to their complex protocols. Fortunately they are very well understood and firewall-friendly protocols. Other methods of file sharing, such as **bittorrent**, or other protocols, such as Voice over IP H.323, can be considerably more difficult or limited in their ability to work in NAT environments.

Assuming that your problem isn't covered so far here, fall back on the methodology. For that matter, whenever you're making complex firewall changes such as supporting NFS, you probably want to follow through on this methodology anyway. It's a scary protocol in terms of security!

- **Define the Problem:** What is happening, and whom is it affecting? Is this affecting inbound or outbound traffic or every user or just a subset?
- **Gather Facts—Did anything change?** Are other systems on the internal network available that might indicate that this is a broader network outage? Don't forget to take a look with your sniffer!
- **Define the End State:** What is the goal—restoring file sharing through FTP for example? What components of your network does this affect, and what will/are they supposed to do?
- **Develop Possible Solutions and Create an Action Plan:** You've determined that you need to place your FTP server in a safer location, such as a DMZ network to provide access to internal and external users.
- **Analyze and Compare Possible Solutions:** What do you need, how long will it take to implement your plan, and will it solve the problem in the most efficient way? How long will it take you to create a DMZ or reuse an existing one? Will it expose other users or systems to risk?
- **Select and Implement Solution:** Make your plan and implement your solution.
- **Critically Analyze Solution for Effectiveness:** Did the system work? Test your firewall rules to verify that you haven't created other security risks and check with the users to make sure that they can access the system from where they need to.

We hope that you've finished this chapter understanding how to compile more complex, multi-port firewall rulesets and configuring your kernel to handle these more complex connection tracking issues before moving on to more sophisticated protocols. And don't forget to test your rules for security vulnerabilities! (See Chapter 10, "Testing Your Firewall Rules [for Security!])

Instant Messaging

Instant messaging (IM) is becoming an increasingly popular means of communication these days—for both personal and business traffic. In this chapter we cover some of the most common problems with supporting the myriad features of IM clients, as well as all the different protocols such as AOL's Instant Messenger (AIM), ICQ, Microsoft's MSN, Yahoo, NetMeeting, and the open source GnomeMeeting client. We will also touch on the subject of what to do when your policy dictates that you need effective ways of blocking IM traffic with your firewall.

COMMON QUESTIONS/PROBLEMS

Q: Should you be concerned about IM traffic in terms of security?

A: In a nutshell—yes, absolutely. It's a vector of data transmission just like e-mail, is generally sent in the clear and unencrypted, and allows the transfer of files, and the clients themselves have been subject to numerous security vulnerabilities in the past. Your own corporate information security policy will dictate whether the risk of using IM is acceptable or not. Personally, we feel it is and that IM is an excellent addition to any business that could use the added convenience for coordinating between coworkers, friends, and family that otherwise would have involved a phone call or face-to-face meeting (the social ramifications of this we do not feel we are qualified to comment on). The caveat here is that we also use encrypting IM plugins (**gaim-encryption**, `http://gaim-encryption.sf.net`) and definitely advise that other people do the same.

TOOLS DISCUSSED IN THIS CHAPTER

- **Sniffers:** As always, your best front line tool here is a good network sniffer. Ethereal (http://www.ethereal.com) specifically supports the ability to decode several of the more popular IM protocols.
- **Proxys:** ReAIM (http://reaim.sourceforge.net/) and GNU Gatekeeper Proxy (http://www.willamowius.de/h323develop.html)

NETMEETING AND GNOMEMEETING

NetMeeting (http://www.microsoft.com/windows/netmeeting/) is Microsoft's other "instant" messaging client (the main one being MSN, the messenger...not the ISP/Portal!). It's definitely not anything remotely in the same ballpark as the other clients when it comes to the prolific nature of its acceptance in terms of users. But in the case of business users, it's a fairly common application and lends itself to collaborative business needs, including the ability to do remote desktop sharing. Unlike the other IM services, NetMeeting does not require access to central servers on the Internet to function. Additionally, NetMeeting supports multiple complex protocols, including H.323, used for voice-over IP traffic.

GnomeMeeting (http://www.gnomemeeting.org) is the open source counterpart to Microsoft's NetMeeting, and is included by default with many Linux distributions these days, including Red Hat, SuSE, Mandrake, and Debian.

CONNECTING TO A REMOTE NETMEETING/GNOMEMEETING CLIENT FROM BEHIND AN IPTABLES FIREWALL (OUTBOUND CALLS ONLY)

Generally this is a fairly straightforward setup. Assuming you're running a standard masquerading or NAT firewall, no special settings are required. However, if you are experiencing difficulty establishing NetMeeting connections across your firewall, ensure that you have connection tracking enabled and that there are not any OUTPUT rules on the following ports:

TCP 1720

TCP 30000-30010

UDP 5000-5007

UDP 5010-5013

CONNECTING TO A NETMEETING/GNOMEMEETING CLIENT BEHIND A NETFILTER/IPTABLES FIREWALL (INBOUND/OUTBOUND CALLS)

There are two ways of allowing inbound Net/GnomeMeeting connections through a firewall, and it depends on the number of users that require Net/GnomeMeeting access. The first method is a Single-Use configuration, where only one system on the inside of the firewall can accept inbound connections. This is the most simplistic configuration and will cause the least amount of hassle on the part of the remote users attempting to communicate with you.

For users of GnomeMeeting, versions 0.94 have improved support for crossing NAT devices considerably. Specifically, you will need to reconfigure your GnomeMeeting client to be "NAT aware" by selecting the following under preferences:

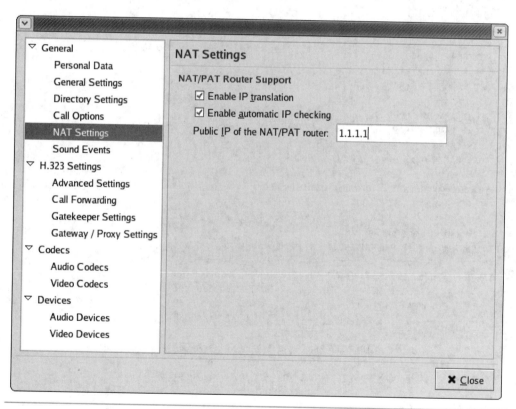

Figure 17.1 GnomeMeeting NAT preferences.

Single-Use configuration is as follows (this script was modified from the fantastic documentation provided by the GnomeMeeting developers):

```bash
#!/bin/bash

# = where resides the iptables binary (see "type -p iptables")
IPTABLES=/sbin/iptables

# = your public Internet-Device
OUT_DEV=eth0

# = your internal Internet-Device
IN_DEV=eth1
# = Host to which the incoming H323 is being forwarded
IN_HOST=192.168.70.18

TCP_PORT_RANGE=30000:30010
RTP_PORT_RANGE=5000:5007
TCP_LISTENING_PORT=1720
GK_PORT_RANGE=5010:5013

#TCP_PORT_RANGE - H245, if no tunneling is made
#RTP_PORT_RANGE - RTP connections (2 audio, 2 video - RTP and RTCP)
#TCP_LISTENING_PORT - H.323 port
#GK_PORT_RANGE - if external GK is used

# activate masquerading on public interface
$IPTABLES -t nat -A POSTROUTING -o $OUT_DEV \
                              -j MASQUERADE
# set incoming port forwarding...
$IPTABLES -t nat -I PREROUTING 1 -i $OUT_DEV -p tcp
          --dport $TCP_PORT_RANGE -j DNAT --to-dest $IN_HOST
$IPTABLES -t nat -I PREROUTING 1 -i $OUT_DEV -p udp \
          --dport $RTP_PORT_RANGE -j DNAT --to-dest $IN_HOST
$IPTABLES -I FORWARD 1 -p tcp -i $OUT_DEV \
          --dport $TCP_PORT_RANGE -d $IN_HOST -j ACCEPT
$IPTABLES -I FORWARD 1 -p udp -i $OUT_DEV \
          --dport $RTP_PORT_RANGE -d $IN_HOST -j ACCEPT
$IPTABLES -t  nat -I PREROUTING 1 -i $OUT_DEV -p tcp \
          --dport $TCP_LISTENING_PORT -j DNAT -to-dest \
                              $IN_HOST
$IPTABLES -I FORWARD 1 -p tcp -i $OUT_DEV \
          --dport $TCP_LISTENING_PORT -d $IN_HOST -j ACCEPT
```

```
# add port forwarding for external GK
$IPTABLES -t nat -I PREROUTING 1 -i $OUT_DEV -p udp \
            --dport $GK_PORT_RANGE -j DNAT --to-dest $IN_HOST
$IPTABLES -I FORWARD 1 -p udp -i $OUT_DEV \
            --dport $GK_PORT_RANGE -d $IN_HOST -j ACCEPT
$IPTABLES -I POSTROUTING 1 -t nat -o $IN_DEV \
              -d $IN_HOST -p udp --dport $GK_PORT_RANGE \
                        -j ACCEPT
```

For connecting to multiple Net/GnomeMeeting clients in through your firewall, you will be required to run the GNU Gatekeeper proxy (http://www.willamowius.de/h323develop.html).

DIRECTLY FROM THE GNOMEMEETING WEBSITE'S DOCUMENTATION

The latest versions of the gatekeeper have several possibilities that permit you to install it on your NAT/PAT gateway and configure it to act as a proxy. After it is installed and configured to act as a proxy (see the **config** file given below as example), you can go in the GnomeMeeting preferences and make GnomeMeeting register to that gatekeeper using a given alias (Directory section to register to the gatekeeper, Personal Data section to give the alias to use when registering).

Doing so, and provided that the correct ports are open on the firewall (read the previous section—but keep in mind that the gatekeeper can use other ports), you will be able to call registered and non-registered endpoints.

You can call a registered endpoint with GnomeMeeting using its registering alias (for example, the user e-mail address if it is what the external user chose to register on your gatekeeper).

You can also call an unregistered endpoint using an URL of the form @hostname (for example, @heraclite.be to call heraclite.be if that machine is not registered to the gatekeeper).

External users cannot call you except if they register to your gatekeeper installed on your gateway and if they know what alias you used to register to your gatekeeper.

The gatekeeper is able to work with H.245 Tunneling and without. It is automatic.

Here is the **config** file **gatekeeper.ini** to configure it as a gatekeeper/proxy:

```
[Gatekeeper::Main]
Fourtytwo=42
[RoutedMode]
GKRouted=1
AcceptUnregisteredCalls=0
```

```
SupportNATedEndpoints=1
[RasSvr::ARQFeatures]
CallUnregisteredEndpoints=1
[Proxy]
Enable=1
[GkStatus::Auth]
rule=allow
```

You also can more or less control the ports that are used using the following parameters in the **config** file:

```
[RoutedMode]
Q931PortRange=20000-20020
H245PortRange=30000-30010
[Proxy]
T120PortRange=40000-40010
RTPPortRange=50000-59999
```

We recommend the use of the gatekeeper. The gatekeeper will permit you to make calls from an internal GnomeMeeting to external GnomeMeeting and NetMeeting users. External GnomeMeeting and NetMeeting users will have to register to the gatekeeper to be able to call you using your alias.

BLOCKING OUTBOUND NETMEETING/GNOMEMEETING TRAFFIC

Blocking outbound Net/GnomeMeeting traffic is a fairly basic **iptables** filter rule:

```
# these rules will log attempts to use Net/GnomeMeeting
$IPTABLES -A FORWARD -p tcp  --dport 1503 -m limit \
                --limit 1/second -j LOG  --log-level info \
                        --log-prefix \
                "Policy Violation: Net/Gnome meeting: "
$IPTABLES -A FORWARD -p tcp  --dport 1720 -m limit \
                --limit 1/second -j LOG  --log-level info \
                        --log-prefix \
                "Policy Violation: Net/Gnome meeting: "

# and these will drop the connections
$IPTABLES -A FORWARD -p tcp -dport 1720 -j DROP
$IPTABLES -A FORWARD -p tcp -dport 1503 -j DROP
```

Ensure that these rules appear before any global ALLOW rules of course!

MSN MESSENGER

MSN is the other instant messaging client from Microsoft, available at `http://messenger.msn.com/`. Unlike NetMeeting, it's a much "lighter weight" client and uses basic TCP ports to communicate to its central servers. It also now includes the ability to handle voice and video traffic as well as transfer files.

CONNECTING TO OTHER MSN USERS

Text messaging is rarely an issue with MSN Messenger; it uses standard TCP ports, and provided you are not blocking anything outbound, it is a very simple connection that "just works" as long as your `NAT/Masquerading` rules are set up correctly.

File, video, and voice transfers are a completely different matter, however, and to get these to work consistently, we recommend the use of a transparent proxy like ReAIM (`http://reaim.sourceforge.net/`) on your firewall. After it is installed and running, you will need to add in some firewall rules to ensure that your MSN connections are being routed through the proxy server transparently. This ensures that your users will not have to make any configuration changes in their desktop MSN clients.

The following rules and documentation were copied from the ReAIM website:

```
# assuming eth0 is the external interface
# assuming eth1 is the internal interface

$IPTABLES -t nat -A PREROUTING -i eth1 -p tcp \
                --dport 1863 -j REDIRECT --to-ports 1863
$IPTABLES -A INPUT -i eth1 -p tcp --dport 1863 \
                                -j ACCEPT
```

The proxy will massage the redirected AIM and MSN messages and AIM Share so that direct connections appear to be from the external IP address, on the port range 40000-40099. However, this is not enough—the AIM software does not honor the overrides ReAIM uses, so we also listen to ports 4443 and 5566. For good measure, we listen to the MSN port too.

So, the very basic setup, in addition to your current ruleset, is to permit connections to these ports.

```
$IPTABLES -A INPUT -i eth0 -p tcp --dport 1863:1864 \
                                -j ACCEPT
$IPTABLES -A INPUT -i eth0 -p tcp --dport 4443 \
                                -j ACCEPT
```

```
$IPTABLES -A INPUT -i eth0 -p tcp --dport 5566 \
                                -j ACCEPT
$IPTABLES -A INPUT -i eth0 -p tcp --dport 40000:40099\
                                -j ACCEPT
```

BLOCKING MSN MESSENGER TRAFFIC AT THE FIREWALL

The standard MSN client uses TCP port 1863; however, it has been reported that some clients will also attempt to fall back on other standard ports such as 80 (http) and 443 (https) to reestablish connections. One strategy is to block access to the login servers themselves. At the writing of this book, this was messenger.hotmail.com, which maps to 207.46.104.20—although I suspect that MSN will have other login servers in that network space. Your approach here can be three-fold:

Log and Filter MSN port 1863:

```
$IPTABLES -A FORWARD -p tcp  --dport 1863 -m limit \
     --limit 1/second -j LOG  --log-level info \
                 --log-prefix "Policy Violation: MSN "
$IPTABLES -A FORWARD -p tcp -dport 1863 -j DROP
```

Log and Filter the login server:

```
$IPTABLES -A FORWARD -d 207.46.104.20 -m limit \
                 --limit 1/second -j LOG  --log-level info \
                 --log-prefix "Policy Violation: MSN "
$IPTABLES -A FORWARD -d  207.46.104.20 -j DROP
```

Log and Filter the messaging servers:

```
$IPTABLES -A FORWARD -d 207.46.110.0/25 -m limit \
                 --limit 1/second -j LOG  --log-level info \
                 --log-prefix "Policy Violation: MSN "
$IPTABLES -A FORWARD -d 207.46.110.0/25 -j DROP
```

YAHOO MESSENGER

Yahoo Messenger is the instant messaging client from Yahoo. It supports voice, video, and file transfers in addition to standard text instant messaging. It uses several TCP and UDP ports depending upon the services being used. The following page on Yahoo's site documents the ports and servers used by Yahoo Messenger: http://help.yahoo.com/help/us/mesg/twin/twin-15.html.

CONNECTING TO YAHOO MESSENGER

Yahoo has been by far the least problematic of all the IM services we have tested. It's extremely firewall friendly, even in the case of more complex services such as voice and video.

For login and text messaging connections, Yahoo Messenger will use the following TCP ports:

- 20 (generally reserved for FTP)
- 23 (generally reserved for telnet)
- 25 (generally reserved for SMTP)
- 80 (generally reserved for HTTP)
- 119 (generally reserved for NNTP)
- 5050
- Video traffic (Webcam) will use TCP port: 5100
- File Transfers use TCP port: 80 and the HTTP protocol (this is extremely trivial to get through firewalls)
- Voice communication uses TCP or UDP ports 5000-5010

If you experience difficulty in getting these services to traverse the firewall, the usual suspects would be DROP/REJECT rules on one or more (Yahoo is very difficult to block!) of the ports listed here.

BLOCKING YAHOO MESSENGER TRAFFIC

First and foremost, Yahoo has done a fantastic job at making their IM client firewall friendly (in terms of circumventing them, that is!), due to their copious use of "standard" services ports and literally hundreds of servers and IP addresses all over the place. This is by far one of the hardest IM clients to filter out. The most effective method we have used so far is to block the login servers; however, users clever enough to reconfigure their clients to use HTTP proxy servers can circumvent even these rules. As Yahoo changes these servers frequently, the first step is to check `http://help.yahoo.com/help/us/mesg/twin/twin-15.html` for the latest list of Yahoo servers. At the writing of this book, those were

* `scsa.msg.yahoo.com`
* `scsb.msg.yahoo.com`
* `scsc.msg.yahoo.com`
* `scs.msg.yahoo.com`

Example of extrapolating the IP addresses using the "host" command:

```
[user@firewall /tmp]$ host scs.msg.yahoo.com
scs.msg.yahoo.com  (an alias for scs-dcna.msg.yahoo.com)
  scs-dcna.msg.yahoo.com has address 216.155.193.128
  scs-dcna.msg.yahoo.com has address 216.155.193.129
  scs-dcna.msg.yahoo.com has address 216.155.193.130
  scs-dcna.msg.yahoo.com has address 216.155.193.131
  scs-dcna.msg.yahoo.com has address 216.155.193.132
  scs-dcna.msg.yahoo.com has address 216.155.193.133
  scs-dcna.msg.yahoo.com has address 216.155.193.134
  scs-dcna.msg.yahoo.com has address 216.155.193.135
scsa.msg.yahoo.com (an alias for scs.msg.yahoo.com)

[user@firewall /tmp]$ host scsb.msg.yahoo.com
scsb.msg.yahoo.com (an alias for scs-fooe.yahoo.com)
   scs-fooe.yahoo.com has address 66.163.173.8
   scs-fooe.yahoo.com has address 216.136.128.144
   scs-fooe.yahoo.com has address 216.136.227.23
   scs-fooe.yahoo.com has address 216.136.233.152
   scs-fooe.yahoo.com has address 216.136.131.64
   scs-fooe.yahoo.com has address 216.136.172.248
   scs-fooe.yahoo.com has address 216.136.173.180
   scs-fooe.yahoo.com has address 216.136.225.28
   scs-fooe.yahoo.com has address 216.136.226.13
   scs-fooe.yahoo.com has address 216.136.227.22

[user@firewall /tmp]$ host scsc.msg.yahoo.com
scsc.msg.yahoo.com (an alias for scsdcntest-b.msg.yahoo.com.)
   scsdcntest-b.msg.yahoo.com has address 216.155.193.147
   scsdcntest-b.msg.yahoo.com has address 216.155.193.148
   scsdcntest-b.msg.yahoo.com has address 216.155.193.149
   scsdcntest-b.msg.yahoo.com has address 216.155.193.150
```

```
scsdcntest-b.msg.yahoo.com has address 216.155.193.151
scsdcntest-b.msg.yahoo.com has address 216.155.193.152
scsdcntest-b.msg.yahoo.com has address 216.155.193.153
scsdcntest-b.msg.yahoo.com has address 216.155.193.154
scsdcntest-b.msg.yahoo.com has address 216.155.193.155
scsdcntest-b.msg.yahoo.com has address 216.155.193.156
```

As you can see, there are a lot of servers, and they change from time to time. So perhaps a more long-term option would be to use an IDS system, like **snort** (http://www.snort.org) for example, with Yahoo IM signatures tied into an auto-response system to shun (that is, reconfigure a filter on the firewall in realtime when a signature is fired) or a cron job to check for changes to the list of servers and to update the firewall rules. However, if none of these are an option, and you want to do this the hard way, the following firewall rules can be added to your system—but remember to replace these IPs with the IPs you enumerated using the host commands previously listed:

```
$IPTABLES -A FORWARD -d 216.155.193.128 -j DROP
$IPTABLES -A FORWARD -d 216.155.193.129 -j DROP
$IPTABLES -A FORWARD -d 216.155.193.130 -j DROP
$IPTABLES -A FORWARD -d 216.155.193.131 -j DROP
$IPTABLES -A FORWARD -d 216.155.193.132 -j DROP
$IPTABLES -A FORWARD -d 216.155.193.133 -j DROP
$IPTABLES -A FORWARD -d 216.155.193.134 -j DROP
$IPTABLES -A FORWARD -d 216.155.193.135 -j DROP
$IPTABLES -A FORWARD -d 66.163.173.8 -j DROP
$IPTABLES -A FORWARD -d 216.136.128.144 -j DROP
$IPTABLES -A FORWARD -d 216.136.227.23 -j DROP
$IPTABLES -A FORWARD -d 216.136.233.152 -j DROP
$IPTABLES -A FORWARD -d 216.136.131.64 -j DROP
$IPTABLES -A FORWARD -d 216.136.172.248 -j DROP
$IPTABLES -A FORWARD -d 216.136.173.180 -j DROP
$IPTABLES -A FORWARD -d 216.136.225.28 -j DROP
$IPTABLES -A FORWARD -d 216.136.226.13 -j DROP
$IPTABLES -A FORWARD -d 216.136.227.22 -j DROP
$IPTABLES -A FORWARD -d 216.155.193.147 -j DROP
$IPTABLES -A FORWARD -d 216.155.193.148 -j DROP
$IPTABLES -A FORWARD -d 216.155.193.149 -j DROP
$IPTABLES -A FORWARD -d 216.155.193.150 -j DROP
$IPTABLES -A FORWARD -d 216.155.193.151 -j DROP
$IPTABLES -A FORWARD -d 216.155.193.152 -j DROP
$IPTABLES -A FORWARD -d 216.155.193.153 -j DROP
$IPTABLES -A FORWARD -d 216.155.193.154 -j DROP
$IPTABLES -A FORWARD -d 216.155.193.155 -j DROP
$IPTABLES -A FORWARD -d 216.155.193.156 -j DROP
```

> **NOTE**
>
> You might want to replace the -j DROP rule for -j REJECT, as this will return an ICMP error. Some IM clients will honor this ICMP message immediately and stop reconnection attempts.

Obviously, maintaining a big list of firewall rules like the one just listed is a lot of overhead. The following script is for the more adventurous types who want to automate the filter generation:

```
#!/bin/sh

IPTABLES=/sbin/iptables
echo -n > /tmp/hosts

for i in scs.msg.yahoo.com scsa.msg.yahoo.com scsb.msg.yahoo.com  scsc.msg.yahoo.com;
do
  host $i |grep address|awk -Faddress '{print $2  }'\
        >> /tmp/hosts
done

for i in `cat /tmp/hosts`; do
    $IPTABLES -A FORWARD -d $i -j LOG
    $IPTABLES -A FORWARD -d $i -m limit \
        --limit 1/second -j LOG  --log-level info \
        --log-prefix "Policy Violation: Yahoo "
    $IPTABLES -A FORWARD -d  $i  -j DROP
done
```

AOL INSTANT MESSENGER (AIM)

AOL Instant Messenger (AIM) is probably one of the oldest and most widely used instant messaging clients in use today. It allows for text instant messaging, file transfers, and video (webcam) communication.

The ReAIM proxy (http://reaim.sourceforge.net/), discussed in the MSN section here applies directly to the AIM protocol as well.

CONNECTING TO AIM

AIM uses very basic TCP ports for connecting into their central servers, typically TCP port 5190. If you're using a standard NAT or Masquerading configuration, this won't be a problem for you. However, like MSN, file and video traffic can get confused when traversing NAT firewalls. To get these connections to work properly, you will need to install a transparent proxy on the firewall. We recommend ReAIM (`http://reaim.sourceforge.net/`), which after up and running on the firewall will require some transparent proxy rules to complete the configuration. After it is in place, your users will not need to make any changes to their AIM clients.

The following firewall rules will need to be added after the ReAIM proxy is running:

```
# eth0 assumes the external interface
# eth1 assumes the internal interface
EXTERNAL=eth0
INTERNAL=eth1

$IPTABLES -t nat -A PREROUTING -i $INTERNAL -p tcp \
      --dport 5190 -j REDIRECT --to-ports 5190

# this rule allows the firewall to accept the
# redirected connection, if you have a default DROP
# policy. And you do have one of those right?
$IPTABLES -A INPUT -i $INTERNAL -p tcp --dport 5190 \
      -j ACCEPT
```

Assuming your firewall is using eth0 for the external interface, you will want to modify the `-i` variable to be `-i eth0`. Further, if you are not supporting MSN traffic, remove the following line:

```
$IPTABLES -A INPUT -i eth0 -p tcp --dport 1863:1864 \
      -j ACCEPT
```

BLOCKING AOL INSTANT MESSENGER TRAFFIC

As we've discussed in reference to blocking other IM traffic, the number of servers and ports that these applications support generally involve multiple methods to consistently disable these services from the firewall. For AOL Instant Messenger, we use two separate rules—one to filter out the AIM traffic itself on port 5190

```
$IPTABLES -A FORWARD -p tcp -dport 5190 -m limit \
      --limit 1/second -j LOG  --log-level info \
      --log-prefix "Policy Violation: AIM "
$IPTABLES -A FORWARD -p tcp --dport 5190 -j DROP
```

and traffic going to the AOL login servers at login.oscar.aol.com. At the time of this writing, AOL only uses one hostname, login.oscar.aol.com. To determine the IP addresses for this server, we again use the host command, as in the preceding Yahoo example:

```
[user@firewall /tmp]$ host  login.oscar.aol.com
login.oscar.aol.com is an alias for login.login-grt.messaging.aol.com.
login.login-grt.messaging.aol.com has address 64.12.161.153
login.login-grt.messaging.aol.com has address 64.12.161.185
login.login-grt.messaging.aol.com has address 64.12.200.89
login.login-grt.messaging.aol.com has address 205.188.179.233
```

We can use the following rules to block those systems:

```
$IPTABLES   -A FORWARD -d 64.12.161.153 -j DROP
$IPTABLES   -A FORWARD -d  64.12.161.185 -j DROP
$IPTABLES   -A FORWARD -d  64.12.200.89 -j DROP
$IPTABLES   -A FORWARD -d  205.188.179.233 -j DROP
```

This is a much more manageable list than the Yahoo Messenger mentioned here, so automation probably isn't needed. However, the following script would automate this process:

```
#!/bin/sh

IPTABLES=/sbin/iptables
echo -n > /tmp/hosts

for i in login.oscar.aol.com; do
  host $i |grep address|awk -Faddress '{print $2  }'\
       >> /tmp/hosts
done
```

```
for i in `cat /tmp/hosts`; do
    $IPTABLES -A FORWARD -d $i -m limit \
        --limit 1/second -j LOG  --log-level info \
        --log-prefix "Policy Violation: AIM "
    $IPTABLES -A FORWARD -d  $i  -j DROP
done
```

ICQ

ICQ "I seek you" (http://www.icq.com) was created by the company, Mirabilis Ltd., in 1996 and was later acquired by AOL in 1998. In this regard, it is AOL's "other" instant messaging client, although it is maintained as a completely separate non-AOL branded company, ICQ Inc. ICQ supports text instant messaging, file transfers, as well as video and voice communications. More information on the ICQ protocol is available at http://www.icq.com/icqtour/firewall/netadmin.html.

CONNECTING TO ICQ

Much like AIM, ICQ uses TCP port 5190 to perform the basic client to server communications (login, etc.). Client to client communication is performed on TCP high ports from 1024-65535. This basically means that as long as you are running a standard NAT/Masquerading firewall and are not filtering out traffic on those ports, ICQ will work through your firewall with no issues.

The ICQ client documentation at http://www.icq.com/icqtour/firewall/other.html references reconfiguring your client specifically to deal with communicating to other hosts behind firewalls. However, the open source client we use, Gaim (one IM client to rule them all!), http://gaim.sourceforge.net, is compatible with NAT environments by default, so further configuration is not necessary.

BLOCKING ICQ

Blocking ICQ traffic is very similar to the methods used with AIM and MSN—primarily by blocking access to the login server at login.icq.com.

A deeper investigation of this server shows just how close AIM and ICQ are to one another:

```
[user@firewall /tmp]$ host  login.icq.com
login.icq.com is an alias for login.login-grt.messaging.aol.com.
login.login-grt.messaging.aol.com has address 64.12.161.153
login.login-grt.messaging.aol.com has address 64.12.161.185
login.login-grt.messaging.aol.com has address 64.12.200.89
login.login-grt.messaging.aol.com has address 205.188.179.233
```

These are, in fact, the same login servers used by AIM, so we can use the exact same rules for blocking AIM on ICQ:

This blocks specific ICQ/AIM traffic:

```
$IPTABLES -A FORWARD -dport 5190 -m limit \
        --limit 1/second -j LOG  --log-level info \
        --log-prefix "Policy Violation: AIM/ICQ "
$IPTABLES -A FORWARD --dport 5190 -j DROP
```

And this blocks access to the ICQ/AIM servers:

```
$IPTABLES -A FORWARD -d 64.12.161.153 -m limit \
        --limit 1/second -j LOG  --log-level info \
        --log-prefix "Policy Violation: AIM/ICQ "
$IPTABLES -A FORWARD -d 64.12.161.185 -m limit \
        --limit 1/second -j LOG  --log-level info \
        --log-prefix "Policy Violation: AIM/ICQ "
$IPTABLES -A FORWARD -d 64.12.200.89 -m limit \
        --limit 1/second -j LOG  --log-level info \
        --log-prefix "Policy Violation: AIM/ICQ "
$IPTABLES -A FORWARD -d 6205.188.179.233 -m limit \
        --limit 1/second -j LOG  --log-level info \
        --log-prefix "Policy Violation: AIM/ICQ "
$IPTABLES   -A FORWARD -d 64.12.161.153 -j DROP
$IPTABLES   -A FORWARD -d  64.12.161.185 -j DROP
$IPTABLES   -A FORWARD -d  64.12.200.89 -j DROP
$IPTABLES   -A FORWARD -d  205.188.179.233 -j DROP
```

SUMMARY

Instant messaging can be as dangerous as any other protocol on your network. It absolutely exposes you to an internal risk for a number of things including worms and viruses, litigation due to remarks or content shared over IM networks, leakage of sensitive information, and direct exploitation in the IM software itself.

RECALLING OUR METHODOLOGY

- **Define the Problem:** Are you trying to allow IM in or keep it from going out?
- **Gather Facts:** Fire up your sniffer or add logging rules to your firewall and see how many people and what IM protocols are being used. If this is to stop IM traffic, there could be quite a number of them, which means you will need to plan for blocking multiple protocols.
- **Define the End State:** What is the plan? Assuming we're blocking instant messaging, you will need to get a grip around what other requirements might be needed. Will there be exceptions? Do you need to log when it's attempted? Define this before you roll anything out.
- **Develop Possible Solutions and Create an Action Plan:** Some protocols will be easy; others like Yahoo will require upkeep to verify that it is still being effectively blocked. Don't forget to include this in your plan.
- **Analyze and Compare Possible Solutions:** Will your plan meet your goals? If this is for regulatory issues, then a failure in your plan could expose you or the business to legal liability. Don't forget to organize all the risks against the level of effort required to implement the plan.
- **Select and Implement the Solution:** Make your plan and implement your solution. Keep in mind that you might need to extend this plan at a later date due to the ever-changing nature of IM networks. IM systems are constantly being tweaked and manipulated to circumvent exactly what you are trying to do.
- **Critically Analyze the Solution for Effectiveness:** After implemented, measure the effectiveness. Test what you have changed, both against IM and your regular services. Blanket filtering against Yahoo servers, for example, might cause other legitimate outages.

The type of business you are in and the types of threats you have to protect yourself from will dictate if the risk of another service is acceptable to you or not. Measuring that risk is a difficult process and requires a great deal of insider information about a business to come up with a measured response.

DNS/DHCP

Name resolution and the dynamic assignment of IP addresses, whether from the perspective of the firewall as a dynamic device or as the DHCP address provider itself, poses several problems. These can include issues with updating firewall rules in a dynamic environment, such as cable modems and DSLs to DMZs for DHCP servers. In this chapter, we will cover some of the more common issues with getting DNS to work on or through firewalls as well as one more bizarre configuration involving getting console games to work over the Internet (we're not kidding).

COMMON QUESTIONS

Q: Can you use hostnames instead of IP addresses?

A: Yes, you can; however, when the rules are initially loaded, netfilter will perform a lookup on those names and use the IP address returned *at that time*. So any updates against the hostname made after the rules have been loaded will have no effect. The hard way to update this would be to write something using the **iptables** -R flag (replace). The -R flag, however, suffers from issues when the source and/or destination names resolved to multiple addresses. The low-tech approach to dealing with this problem is just to reload your rules.

Q: Can firewall rules direct traffic to different systems based on the domain name?

A: No—**iptables**/netfilter operates at too low of a level to do name-based rules like this. You would need to use an application layer proxy server or iproute2 to achieve this effect.

TOOLS DISCUSSED IN THIS CHAPTER

- **DNSMasq** (http://www.thekelleys.org.uk/dnsmasq/doc.html). The following is from the **DNSMasq** documentation:

    DNSMasq is lightweight, easy to configure DNS forwarder and DHCP server. It is designed to provide DNS and, optionally, DHCP, to a small network. It can serve the names of local machines which are not in the global DNS. The DHCP server integrates with the DNS server and allows machines with DHCP-allocated addresses to appear in the DNS with names configured either in each host or in a central configuration file. DNSMasq supports static and dynamic DHCP leases and BOOTP for network booting of diskless machines.

    DNSMasq is useful if you are in an environment where you need to provide an application layer DNS forwarding service but do not have the time or inclination to use a full-featured DNS server such as BIND.
- **DHCRelay** (http://www.isc.org) is part of the larger DHCP package from the Internet Software Consortium (ISC). We use it to provide an application layer proxy server for DHCP requests in a DMZ environment.

FORWARDING DNS QUERIES TO AN UPSTREAM/REMOTE DNS SERVER

In this configuration, you have a firewall, called Host-A (10.10.10.1), and an internal non-routable network (RFC1918) at 10.10.10.0/24. Currently this network either has no internal DNS servers or DNS servers serving queries for internal hosts. To provide DNS services for Internet addresses, these queries will have to be forwarded to an external DNS server that can do this. There are several methods to accomplish this...

1. The first method involves using application layer proxies, such as BIND or **DNSMasq**. Our first example involves using BIND, the Berkeley Internet Name Domain, from http://www.isc.org. BIND is the most commonly deployed

nameserver in existence and comes with most major Linux distributions. Install BIND on your firewall.

For Red Hat systems, a shortcut is to use the up2date (yum or redcarpet) service.

```
up2date -i bind
yum install bind
rug in bind
```

For other systems, consult your vendor's documentation or download and build your own nameserver from http://www.isc.org.

2. Configure your nameserver as a forwarder. For most systems, such as Red Hat/Fedora, this will be from the **/etc/named.conf** file; otherwise, this file will be located in **/usr/local/etc/named.conf**. Open this file in your preferred editor and change the following lines:

```
forwarders {
            11.22.33.44;
            11.22.33.45;
        };
```

Set these numerical IP addresses to correspond with your upstream Internet responding nameservers.

3. Configure your nameserver to listen only on your internal interface(s). By default, when you start the nameserver, it will bind to all your interfaces, including the external ones. Open the **named.conf** file with your preferred editor and modify/create the following lines in the Options section:

```
listen-on {
            10.10.10.1;
        };
```

Set these to numerical IP addresses that correspond to your firewall's internal interfaces.

4. Allow DNS requests to your firewall from hosts on your internal network. In our example, the internal network is 10.10.10.0/24 with the following rule:

```
$IPTABLES -A INPUT -p tcp --dport 53 -i eth1 -j ACCEPT
$IPTABLES -A INPUT -p udp --dport 53 -i eth1 -j ACCEPT
```

Optional Step: RedHat distributions also include the "caching-nameserver" rpm. This rpm will make your firewall a caching nameserver. This can accomplished with the following commands:

```
up2date -i caching-nameserver
yum install caching-nameserver
rug up caching-nameserver
```

The second method involves using **DNSMasq**, available from `http://www.thekelleys.org.uk/dnsmasq/doc.html`. **DNSMasq** is a much lighter weight DNS Forwarder/DHCP server suited for this type of task specifically.

1. Install **DNSMasq** (consult the **DNSMasq** documentation if you are not familiar with how to build or install this package). RPM shortcut: `rpmbuild -ta dnsmasq-2.6.tar.gz`.
2. Configure your firewall's **/etc/resolv.conf**. **DNSMasq** pulls the servers it will forward DNS queries to from the system wide **resolv.conf** file. If you want to configure **DNSMasq** to use a different list of nameservers, load up the **DNSMasq config** file, **/etc/dnsmasq.conf** in your favorite editor and change the following line:

```
resolv-file=/etc/somefile
```

where **/etc/somefile** is your file containing a list of nameservers, one per line, that **DNSMasq** will forward DNS queries to.

DNS Lookups Fail: Internal Hosts Communicating to an External Nameserver

In this configuration, hosts on the RFC1918 network, 10.10.10.0/24, behind the firewall (Host-A) cannot successfully make DNS lookups.

1. Before delving into deeper diagnostics, first verify that systems on the internal network can make connections through the firewall based on the IP address. Second, verify that you are using the correct IP address for the external DNS server(s)—and that they are actually active.
2. Assuming that both IP-based connections are successful and that the external DNS servers are active, this typically means two things: the NAT rules are not using connection tracking or that there are filters on TCP/UDP port 53. Step through your firewall rules and verify that these ports are not being blocked.

DNS LOOKUPS FAIL: SHORT DNS NAME LOOKUPS WORK—LONG NAME LOOKUPS DO NOT

This problem might also manifest itself as Unix hosts being able to perform short lookups only and Windows hosts not being able to perform any lookups at all. In general, DNS queries that are 512 bytes and below will use UDP port 53 and above that, TCP port 53. Windows systems will use both the TCP and UDP ports, regardless of size. (We've yet to fathom why it will use one over the other.)

The solution here is to ensure that your firewall rules are not blocking TCP port 53.

DNS LOOKUPS FAIL: NAMESERVER RUNNING ON THE FIREWALL

In this first configuration, the firewall Host-A is running a local DNS server, either handling requests for itself or for internal users on the network 10.10.10.0/24. Local zones contained on the server function correctly; lookups on Internet records fail.

Regardless of whether this server is acting as a forwarder or an authoritative nameserver—or even as a DNS proxy, all lookups to external zones will fail if the firewall does not a) have rules allowing it to make external connections and b) have connection tracking enabled.

In both cases, we can solve this issue with these rules:

```
$IPTABLES -A OUTPUT -m state --state NEW,ESTABLISHED,RELATED -j ACCEPT
$IPTABLES -A INPUT  -m state --state NEW,ESTABLISHED,RELATED -j ACCEPT
```

Note that this uses an OUTPUT rule. This is because the connection is originating on the firewall itself. This is a more general purpose rule that is going to allow *all* connections originating on the firewall outbound, which might not be what you want. An example of a more restrictive rule follows:

```
# where eth0 is the external interface on our firewall
$IPTABLES -A OUTPUT -o eth0 -p udp –dport 53 -m state –state NEW -j ACCEPT
$IPTABLES -A OUTPUT -o eth0 -p tcp –dport 53 -m state –state NEW -j ACCEPT
$IPTABLES -A INPUT -i eth0 -p udp –dport 53 -m state –state NEW,ESTABLISHED,RELATED -j
ACCEPT
$IPTABLES -A INPUT -i eth0 -p tcp –dport 53 -m state –state NEW,ESTABLISHED,RELATED -
j ACCEPT
```

DNS LOOKUPS FAIL: NAMESERVER RUNNING ON THE INTERNAL AND/OR DMZ NETWORK

In this configuration, the internal/DMZ nameserver Host-B (10.10.10.53) cannot make DNS lookups through firewall Host-A to root servers. Much like the example here, this is most likely being caused by two scenarios: a) there are no rules allowing this service to connect outbound or b) assuming this service is allowed to connect outbound, connection tracking is not enabled.

First, assuming that this firewall has a restrictive policy on what connections are allowed outbound, we ensure that the service is allowed through the firewall with these rules:

```
# where eth1 is the internal interface on the firewall
$IPTABLES -A FORWARD -p tcp -dport 53 -m state --state NEW,ESTABLISHED,RELATED -j
ACCEPT
$IPTABLES -A FORWARD -p udp -dport 53 -m state --state NEW,ESTABLISHED,RELATED -j
ACCEPT
$IPTABLES -A FORWARD -p udp -i eth1 -s 10.10.10.53 -d 0/0 -dport 53 -j ACCEPT
$IPTABLES -A FORWARD -p tcp -i eth1 -s 10.10.10.53 -d 0/0 -dport 53 -j ACCEPT
```

MISLEADING rDNS ISSUE: NEW MAIL, OR FTP CONNECTIONS TO REMOTE SYSTEMS TAKE 30 SECONDS OR MORE TO START

This is not actually a DNS issue at all, but enough people associate it with reverse DNS lookups that we decided to put it in this section. The extended description of this problem is that in general, other services such as web browsing or instant messaging are very responsive. Only connections that appear to involve reverse DNS lookups on your firewall, such as an FTP connection for example, take 30 seconds to start. What is probably going on here is that the server on the other side is making an identd (Auth) request to your server, and it's timing out waiting for a reply.

On a host-only firewall, there are three fixes for this. The first is the least favorable—to run an identd server on your host. This would both add a service that could be exploited and leak information about your system, which is not desirable. The second method of fixing this is to add in a rule to REJECT any identd requests to your system.

Following is an example:

```
# this will send an icmp response indicating that the identd/auth service is not
available
$IPTABLES -A INPUT -p tcp -dport 113 -j REJECT
```

The third option is to add in a connection tracking rule, which also works for firewalls handling NAT/MASQUERADED traffic:

```
$IPTABLES -A INPUT -m state -state ESTABLISHED,RELATED
```

DHCP: DYNAMICALLY UPDATING FIREWALL RULES WITH THE IP CHANGES

This is a fairly common scenario—you have a firewall with a dynamically assigned IP address, and when that IP address changes, you need to update your firewall rules accordingly. Most DHCP clients already have the hooks built in to call an external script when an IP address is renewed. We will cover two of the more popular clients, **DHClient**, and **DHCPcd** in the following examples:

DHClient is the default DHCP client for Red Hat and Fedora systems (this is generally already configured by default):

1. Create the file **/etc/dhclient-exit-hooks**.
2. Load this up in your favorite editor and add in the reference to your firewall script, example:

```
sh /etc/rc.d/rc.firewall
```

DHCPcd is another popular DHCP client, which you'll find on distributions such as Gentoo:

1. Load up **/etc/dhcpc/dhcpcd.exe** into your favorite editor
2. Locate the switch case at the end. In this you'll note several conditions on the state of the interface (Just activated/New IP, renewal with the same IP, and so on)
3. In the New IP case, insert a call to your firewall script. For example,

```
sh /etc/rc.d/rc.firewall
```

> **NOTE**
>
> Ensure that your firewall script(s) always flush their rules prior to reloading. Ensure something like the following is at the top of your firewall scripts.
>
> ```
> $IPTABLES -F
> $IPTABLES -X
> ```
>
> The first line will flush your tables; the second will delete the user-defined chains.

BLOCKING OUTBOUND DHCP

This question has been asked enough times that it warranted a response in this book. If you have read the Layer 2 chapter of this book already, you might already know a bit about the issues with blocking outbound DHCP in a bridging environment (or blocking DHCP responses by MAC address for example). This section assumes that you are posed with the problem of keeping DHCP requests confined to a physical segment, separated by a non-bridging firewall. Here's the good news—DHCP requests are not going to cross that firewall. If that's what you were worried about, you're done; worry no longer. If DHCP is running on the server itself, then all that is required is a simple reconfiguration of the DHCP daemon.

In the following example, our firewall, Host-A, has two interfaces eth0 (external), and eth1 (internal, 10.10.10.0/24). This configuration is using the ISC DHCP daemon (http://www.isc.org), which is commonly the default DHCP server in most Linux distributions. To restrict DHCP requests to the internal network, in this case interface eth1, you would start **dhcpd** with the interface name to which you want it to listen.

For example: /usr/sbin/dhcpd eth1

On some distributions, such as Red Hat systems, you can also set this as a configuration file:

1. Load up **/etc/sysconfig/dhcpd** in your favorite editor and set the following

    ```
    DHCPDARGS="eth1"
    ```

    where eth1 responds to the physical interface you want DHCP to listen on. If other interfaces were defined in this file, your job is finished at this point.

2. This is just an example of what the primary DHCP **config** file looks like:

```
subnet 10.10.10.0 netmask 255.255.255.0 {

        option routers                  10.10.10.1;
        option subnet-mask              255.255.255.0;
        range dynamic-bootp 10.10.10.100 10.10.10.200;


        option time-offset              -18000; # Eastern Standard Time
        option domain-name-servers       10.10.10.1;

        default-lease-time 21600;
        max-lease-time 43200;

}
```

The example here configures a DHCP range of 10.10.10.100-10.10.10.200 with a lease time of 12 hours. This also sets the default route to our firewall's internal interface, 10.10.10.1, and the default nameserver, 10.10.10.1.

DHCP: Two Addresses on One External Interface

This is a rather unique question. It was posted to the netfilter mailing list, and we felt that it was bizarre enough to require an honorable mention in the book. If this section is actually useful to you, and you actually did this, please drop us an email about it and why.

This being said, the topic of the post was about getting an additional DHCP address assigned to the external interface on his firewall to get this assigned to his gaming console. This device presumably needed a "clear shot" to the Internet to host games, and port forwarding these ports from the regular IP would have broken other services. Unfortunately not knowing what these ports were, it's hard to say if that was really as insurmountable a port forwarding problem or not, but that's neither here nor there. The initial attempt to lease a second IP by using an IP alias won't work because the IP aliased device (eth0:1) doesn't have a MAC address, which is what the DHCP server on the other end is looking for. According to the author, the following was the wrong way to do it:

The following works:

```
/sbin/dhcpcd -t 60 -h C0 -d eth0
```

The following, however, does not work because there's no MAC address for it:

```
/sbin/dhcpcd -t 60 -h C0 -d eth0:1
```

At this point, we're in the realm of "there's more than one way to do it." We could use **ebtables** (Chapter 15) and do some MAC layer NAT-ing of the device we'd like to get a DHCP address for. However, it turns out that the user space client itself can send the MAC address along with it.

```
/sbin/dhcpcd -R -N -t 60 -h C0 -I 00:11:22:33:44:55 eth0:1
```

00:11:22:33:44:55 is the MAC address you'd like to send out. The -I flag is the "Client Identifier," which is what tells the DHCP server on the other end the unique ID, typically the MAC address.

At this point you would need to customize the firewall rules based on IP address, using the IP alias, eth0:1, which is not going to work because **iptables**/netfilter uses the physical, rather than logical, device to match its rules against.

In general, this configuration is probably a bad idea. A safer setup would be to add a third interface and establish a DMZ for this device.

DHCP: REDIRECT DHCP REQUESTS TO DMZ

In this configuration we have a firewall (Host-A), a DHCP server (Host-B, 192.168.1.67), a DMZ segment (192.168.1.0/24), and an internal network 10.10.10.0/24. The strategy is to locate the DHCP server in the DMZ segment, potentially to provide some added security for this device or for some other infrastructure reason and to secure it from the hosts on the internal network. In this scenario, it is the "internal" hosts that are not to be trusted. This is *not* a safe configuration for an Internet-reachable DMZ. This is a DMZ against the internal network only.

There are numerous reasons for this sort of configuration—generally they stem from providing DHCP services for an untrusted network or perhaps to create some sort of fault tolerant DHCP cluster for a large network. Regardless, when we say DMZ, we aren't talking about something Internet hosts can reach. A DHCP server on such a DMZ, communicating to internal hosts, would make a fantastic vector for attack on internal systems.

Figure 18.1 should serve to illustrate the utility of this configuration.

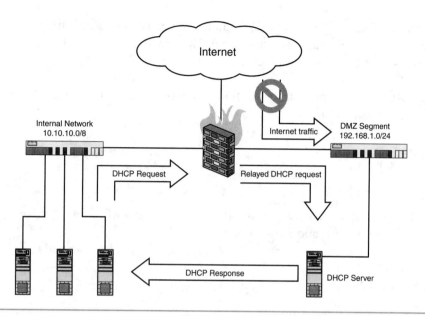

Figure 18.1 Redirect DHCP requests to DMZ.

While it is possible to use something such as **ebtables** (Chapter 15) to directly bridge in DHCP requests to our 192.168.1.0/24 network, it also would more or less open up the internal DMZ network to several vectors of attack. Instead, in this configuration we will use an application layer proxy server called **dhcrelay** to relay our client requests to the real DHCP server.

First, the proxy server, **dhcrelay**, is included in the DHCP package from the Internet Software Consortium (ISC).

From the ISC documentation on **dhcrelay**:

The DHCP Relay Agent listens for DHCP and BOOTP queries and responses. When a query is received from a client, dhcrelay forwards it to the list of DHCP servers specified on the command line. When a reply is received from a server, it is broadcast or unicast (according to the relay agent's ability or the client's request) on the network from which the original request came.

This is the standard DHCP server that comes with most Linux distributions, including Red Hat/Fedora, SuSE, Mandrake, and so on. The first step in this configuration is to ensure that this is installed on the server:

1. Red Hat/Mandrake/SuSE users will find this in the dhcp rpm (**yum, up2date**, and **redcarpet** shortcuts apply).

   ```
   up2date -i dhcp
   yum install dhcp
   rug in dhcp
   ```

2. For Red Hat users, load the configuration file, **/etc/sysconfig/dhcrelay**, into your preferred editor and modify the following:

   ```
   INTERFACES="eth1"
   DHCPSERVERS=""
   ```

   Where eth1 is the interface **dhcrelay** should listen for DHCP requests.
   For other operating systems, consult your documentation on where this is set, or start **dhcrelay** with the following example:

   ```
   dhcrelay -i eth1 192.168.1.67
   ```

3. Ensure that the firewall rules allow connections on the DHCP ports, 67 and 68.

   ```
   # where eth1 is your 10.10.10.0/24 network
   $IPTABLES -A INPUT -m state -state ESTABLISHED,RELATED -i eth1
   $IPTABLES -A INPUT -p tcp -dport 67:68 -i eth1 -j ACCEPT
   $IPTABLES -A INPUT -p udp -dport 67:68 -i eth1 -j ACCEPT
   ```

SUMMARY

This chapter, in combination with the Layer 2 firewalling chapter, should leave you equipped with a better toolbox, as it were, for dealing with protocols such as DHCP that span Layers 2 and 3. As the **perl** motto goes, "There's more than one way to do it," and hopefully this chapter has demonstrated this axiom.

- **Define the Problem:** What is happening, and whom is it affecting? For example, DNS lookups are failing. This manifests as some web browsers reporting that a site is not available.
- **Gather Facts:** Did anything change? Is this a DNS lookup issue? Are other systems on the internal network available that might indicate that this is a broader network outage? Don't forget to take a look with your sniffer!
- **Define the End State:** Now that you know what the symptoms and the facts are, what are you trying to accomplish? Restoring DNS or DHCP service?
- **Develop Possible Solutions and Create an Action Plan:** You know what the problems could be and whom they affect. Rough out your action plans and who should be involved.
- **Analyze and Compare Possible Solutions:** How long will it take to implement your plan, and will it solve the problem in the most efficient way? For example, it might be that your problem is that you had been using an upstream DNS server for internal DNS. When the outbound network is overloaded, DNS lookups fail frequently. You've determined you need an internal DNS—how long will it take you to deploy that and, in turn, reconfigure systems to use it? What is the cost in time and money, and will it break anything else?
- **Select and Implement the Solution:** Make your plan and implement your solution. DNS and DHCP changes on a live network can lead to some pretty hefty outages, so make sure you've got your bases covered in terms of back-up plans. Don't forget to notify your users and your Helpdesk!
- **Critically Analyze Solution for Effectiveness:** After implemented, measure the effectiveness. Especially with DHCP or DNS changes, your best bet is to test this from multiple locations. Last but not least, after it's verified, don't forget to document your changes in some way.

Virtual Private Networks

VPNs are becoming increasingly important as companies move away from using private WANs for intra-business communication or dial-up modem pools for remote access. More "road warriors" needing to access data on the corporate LAN from the road has driven a need for better approaches to security for wireless networking, the need to secure Voice-over IP connections between offices and homes, and ubiquitous security access from anywhere in the world to anywhere in the world. All of these demands and many others are driving the need for robust and sustainable VPNs between multiple locations and roving users. Depending on the VPN technology being used, this can be a simple project (openvpn, cipe, and so on) or an absolute nightmare (IPSEC!). In this chapter we will cover diagnostic procedures on some of the most common issues with two of the most popular VPNs, IPSEC, and PPTP.

THINGS TO CONSIDER WITH IPSEC

Having spent far too much time attempting to get the overly elaborate IPSEC VPNs working between our houses, businesses, and business partners (one of us has four separate VPNs—the other has five!), we can safely say...we hate IPSEC. Setting aside the firewall issues for a moment, IPSEC is less a standard and more a compilation of "shoulds." "Should" might even be too strong of a word...it's more like a lot of "yeah, kindas." Needless to say, before blaming your firewall for your VPN woes, it's important to dive into some of the very common issues with getting IPSEC to work.

First, IPSEC implementations are not always compatible. Even though IPSEC is supposed to be a standard, that does not mean that the implementations out there have to play nice with one another. Because of this, we tend to favor **openswan** (for the time being) for IPSEC VPNs. Even though 2.6 Linux kernels have native IPSEC support, we still prefer **openswan** because, for the most part, it just "works" with most of the IPSEC implementations out there. It's also relatively easy to set up on both 2.4 and 2.6 Linux systems, and standardizing it is a good thing. Further, **openswan** does use the native IPSEC support in 2.6 kernels; it just abstracts it away so you can use **openswan** configurations from 2.4 systems without any changes.

Nevertheless, you will still find that even something as old and robust as **openswan** might not work with the VPNs you need to support. For instance, one of our laptops has **openswan**, the Cisco IPSEC package, and (given that it doesn't work with Red Hat 9) Checkpoints VPN-1 IPSEC client running in a Red Hat 7.3 Vmware (www.vmware.com) image. The main issue we've run into on the compatibility front is that they use different authentication mechanisms—so always check your documentation first! Also some VPN software packages need to be configured to be NAT-aware, so to speak. They work perfectly outside of a firewall and not at all behind it. By default, IPSEC wasn't designed for NAT-ing, so more often than not, it won't work behind a firewall unless the implementation has been extended to work in NAT environments.

Network hardware matters! Specifically with IPSEC, you're going to have to worry about the Maximum Transmission Unit (MTU) size with DSL connections, some wireless cellular connections, or if you're doing any other tunneling such as Point to Point Protocol over Ethernet (PPPoE). We've found that you have to play with the MTU settings starting around 1470, dropping as low as 1300. We've even run into some cellular wireless services that required us to go even lower. It depends on your configuration, IPSEC implementation, and networking environment upstream. This is a critical issue with IPSEC—MTUs really do matter. If the VPN isn't working, check the MTU and try lowering. We recommend 1300 as a good starting point.

Another important step is to bind it to the right interface. This is more of a reminder of an embarrassing mistake made on another system and a warning on not to over-think the problem. Check the simple things first—like the network card...

COMMON QUESTIONS/PROBLEMS

When enabling a VPN, whether it's IPSEC or something in Layer 4, sometimes the VPN software will change your default route to the VPN. Keep an eye on your routes when starting to perform diagnostics.

Sometimes ISPs will implement no-VPN policies, so if your VPN stops working one day and you have literally changed nothing, check with your ISP to see if it has changed its VPN policy. A sniffer on both ends can help you to diagnose if the VPN packets are going out and if the destination is receiving them.

PPPoE, DSL, and other environments involving encapsulation suffer from issues with MTU path discovery (mentioned in previous chapters). This is a very common problem with VPNs and will manifest itself in all sorts of different ways: poor performance, large transfers of data failing where small ones succeed, a VPN "stalling" (working one minute and stopping suddenly) or authentication issues with VPN applications. The fix in nearly every occasion is to use PMTU and **iptables**/netfilter to manipulate the Maximum Segment Size (MSS) setting on your firewall with the following rule:

```
$IPTABLES -A FORWARD -p tcp --tcp-flags SYN,RST SYN -j TCPMSS  --clamp-mss-to-pmtu
```

In our testing of IPSEC implementations over the years traversing firewalls, we've generally had a relatively small number of specific problems that occur across multiple implementations. When dealing with IPSEC clients or servers, we've found a number of them have specific settings for traversing NAT environments. Always double-check your IPSEC documentation to see if you need to enable different settings for VPN environments.

The following is a sniffer trace of an IPSEC session not responding:

```
[root@minimoose root]# tethereal -i eth0 host 66.167.232.50
Capturing on eth0
  0.000000  68.98.150.6 -> 66.167.232.50 ISAKMP Identity Protection (Main Mode)
  9.994140  68.98.150.6 -> 66.167.232.50 ISAKMP Identity Protection (Main Mode)
 29.995130  68.98.150.6 -> 66.167.232.50 ISAKMP Identity Protection (Main Mode)
```

This is telling us that the originating system is sending out its authentication information, but the server on the other end is not responding for some reason. In this case, we are getting no response at all from the remote end. This could be because of any number of things, from the authentication information not being recognized, to filter rules, to IPSEC just not running on the remote system.

This is what it should look like:

```
[root@minimoose root]# tethereal -i eth0 host 68.100.73.75
274.959573 68.100.73.75 -> 68.98.150.6  ISAKMP Identity Protection (Main Mode)
274.960127  68.98.150.6 -> 68.100.73.75 ISAKMP Identity Protection (Main Mode)
275.006148 68.100.73.75 -> 68.98.150.6  ISAKMP Identity Protection (Main Mode)
275.045370  68.98.150.6 -> 68.100.73.75 ISAKMP Identity Protection (Main Mode)
```

```
275.196205 68.100.73.75 -> 68.98.150.6   ISAKMP Identity Protection (Main Mode)
275.287978  68.98.150.6 -> 68.100.73.75 ISAKMP Identity Protection (Main Mode)
275.430761 68.100.73.75 -> 68.98.150.6   ISAKMP Quick Mode
275.475328  68.98.150.6 -> 68.100.73.75 ISAKMP Quick Mode
275.581497 68.100.73.75 -> 68.98.150.6   ISAKMP Quick Mode
```

As you can see, both systems are exchanging information successfully. In this scenario, the problem was that IPSEC was not running on the remote server. It could have just as easily been filter rules in the ISP or on the remote system itself.

TOOLS DISCUSSED IN THIS CHAPTER

Sniffers:
Probably the most useful tool for us when diagnosing any type of tunneling or NAT-ing problems has been a really good sniffer. Personally we prefer **ethereal** (www.ethereal.com), which comes with most major Linux distributions and is available for just about every operating system under the sun (including Linux, Solaris, Windows, OSX, even BeOS). Another advantage to **ethereal** is that it has both a graphical and command line interface, and what is especially useful is that you can change the format of the command line interface to emulate the output from other sniffer software (**tcpdump** and **snoop**, among others).

In the case of VPN diagnostics, as long as the VPN creates a device, as **freeswan** creates the ipsec0 device, you can attach to that device and look at the kinds of traffic going through the VPN. This is imperative if you are attempting to NAT traffic into a VPN.

openswan, http://www.openswan.org, is an IPSEC implementation for Linux that includes support for numerous authentication mechanisms and is in general very compatible with the myriad IPSEC implementations from other open source and commercial vendors.

IPSEC: INTERNAL SYSTEMS—BEHIND A NAT/MASQ FIREWALL CANNOT CONNECT TO AN EXTERNAL IPSEC SERVER

Extended Description: You have an internal system (Host-A) that creates an IPSEC VPN to another system, for example a corporate VPN server (Host-B), through your firewall. Non-VPN traffic functions properly, however the VPN connection cannot be established. In this "road warrior" configuration, the internal system (laptop in diagram here) only connects to the remote system as an end-node; it does not perform any routing.

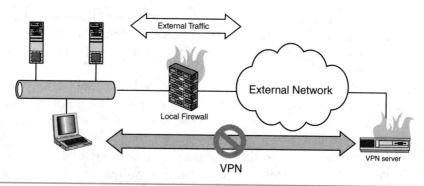

Figure 19.1 Internal systems cannot connect to external IPSEC server.

This is a pretty standard configuration with very common problems. In my experience with five separate VPN implementations, I've never had it be the same problem twice. Some clients are more sensitive to NAT scenarios than others, and some are just painfully slow when it comes to authentication. The first step is to ensure that you can reach the remote VPN server in the first place, as well as other sites on the Internet. Verify that you can access that system with **ping**, **traceroute**, and so on. I spent a whole afternoon tearing my hair out in frustration about a VPN not working, only to find out that they had changed IPs.

The next step is to get a sniffer running on the firewall itself and to look at the inbound and outbound traffic in each direction to verify that the traffic is traversing the firewall correctly (or at all!). One component to look into with VPN software is that you enable it to use NAT Traversal Mode. If traffic is not passing through the firewall, this is definitely the first place to start.

Assuming traffic is not passing through the firewall, this could be due to any number of issues, starting with the MTU settings mentioned earlier in this chapter. The following is a quick checklist of the more obvious problems that will cause a breakdown in this VPN configuration:

1. Are you running a DSL or PPPoE connection between Host-A and the VPN server, Host-B? If so, check the MTU settings on the firewall and Host-A. The default configurations can be as high as 1500, which will absolutely break your IPSEC VPN. Recommended configurations can back this off to as low as 1300 before you can get a successful connection working. We also have found that shutting down the interfaces and reloading the network card modules on the firewall are required to get this to go into effect 100% of the time—either that or a reboot.

2. Does your IPSEC client have a NAT traversal setting? Most of them do, as well as other encapsulation options. Enable these options first. If the IPSEC client requires these options to traverse NAT safely, no amount of tinkering on the firewall itself is going to help you.

3. Is another IPSEC VPN running to Host-B successfully? We have had the situation pop up on a very basic **iptables**/netfilter configuration where multiple systems behind the firewall were connecting to the same remote VPN server. Connection tracking was not enabled. Instead, it was using a very basic output rule, so only the first system to connect would work. The right answer here is to enable connection tracking! We also discovered on a 2.4 kernel that just adding the rules after the VPN connection was up didn't resolve the problem; even flushing the rules and clearing the connection tracking table didn't help. In the end, a reboot solved the problem. Later it was determined that this was an issue with the IPSEC VPN client itself.

Example Rules:

```
$IPTABLES -A INPUT   -m state --state ESTABLISHED,RELATED -j ACCEPT
$IPTABLES -A OUTPUT -m state --state NEW,ESTABLISHED,RELATED -j ACCEPT
$IPTABLES -A FORWARD -m state --state NEW,ESTABLISHED,RELATED -j ACCEPT
```

IPSEC: FIREWALL CANNOT ESTABLISH IPSEC VPNS

Extended Description: You have a NAT/MASQUERADING firewall that is IPSEC capable (**free/openswan**). This firewall acts as an end-node, NAT/MASQUERADING traffic into the VPN itself so all connections inside the VPN, as well as to the external network, appear to be coming from the firewall itself. The VPN will either not connect or when connected won't route correctly.

Generally you find this kind of configuration where you do not or cannot allow the remote network access to your network. I use this configuration personally because I do not trust the hosts on the other end of the VPN to be allowed to directly communicate with my network. This is also an optimal Extranet configuration.

As mentioned earlier in the chapter—and I cannot stress this enough with IPSEC—the MTU settings will cause issues here. This is generally the case when the VPN itself cannot be established with the remote system. In cases where the VPNs themselves are established and communicating successfully, routing to the remote network is the trouble. The next thing to check are the NAT rules.

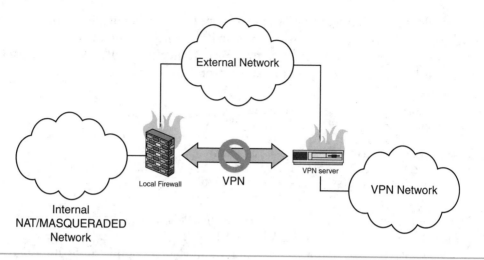

Figure 19.2 Firewall cannot establish IPSEC VPNs.

The great way to diagnose this type of problem is with a sniffer like **ethereal**. My method is to look at the ipsec interface itself, in the case of **free/openswan** this is ipsec0, ipsec1, ipsec2, and so on. The following output is from my home network through the firewall, minimoose, to a remote network showing a successful VPN tunnel:

```
[root@minimoose root]# tethereal -i ipsec0
107.113060 10.10.12.1 -> 10.10.11.102 TCP 58844 > ssh [SYN] Seq=2062573597 Ack=0
Win=5840 Len=0 MSS=1460 TSV=565962409 TSER=0 WS=0
107.175181 10.10.11.102 -> 10.10.12.1 TCP ssh > 58844 [SYN, ACK] Seq=2910414569
Ack=2062573598 Win=5792 Len=0 MSS=1460 TSV=90414655 TSER=565962409 WS=0
107.175746 10.10.12.1 -> 10.10.11.102 TCP 58844 > ssh [ACK] Seq=2062573598
Ack=2910414570 Win=5840 Len=0 TSV=565962416 TSER=90414655
```

This configuration consists of an internal host called winona (IP 10.10.12.100), SSH-ing through the firewall minimoose (10.10.12.1 internal IP, dynamic IP on the external interface), to the remote system 10.10.11.102. Connections from the 10.10.12.0/24 network have been NAT-ed to appear to come from the host minimoose using the following rules:

```
$IPTABLES -t nat -A POSTROUTING -o ipsec0  -s 10.10.12.0/24 -d 10.10.11.0/24 -j SNAT
--to-source 10.10.12.1
```

We would use this configuration where the remote network is only expecting to see a single source IP address for accessing hosts on its internal network. Otherwise the remote firewall would discard, or not know how to route the 10.10.12.0/24 traffic back to your network. Here is an example of what that would look like:

```
[root@minimoose root]# tethereal -i ipsec0
Capturing on ipsec0
  0.000000 10.10.12.198 -> 10.10.11.102 TCP 58845 > ssh [SYN] Seq=2724808935 Ack=0
Win=5840 Len=0 MSS=1460 TSV=566028529 TSER=0 WS=0
  0.000000 10.10.12.198 -> 10.10.11.102 TCP 58845 > ssh [SYN] Seq=2724808936 Ack=0
Win=5840 Len=0 MSS=1460 TSV=566028529 TSER=0 WS=0
```

Note that the host 10.10.11.102 isn't responding. This is due to the fact that 10.10.11.102 doesn't have a route back to the 10.10.12.0/24 network. Most likely it is responding out its default route. Another important element in this configuration to pay attention to is the -o flag, which in **iptables** designates the interface this rule is bound to. In multi-IPSEC configurations, this is an important rule to pay attention to, given that in general the default behavior is going to be to bind this to assume the external interface on the system. This would make the source for the packets be the external IP address for all your VPN traffic, thereby breaking your VPN connection.

IPSEC: FIREWALL CAN ESTABLISH CONNECTIONS TO A REMOTE VPN SERVER, BUT TRAFFIC DOES NOT ROUTE CORRECTLY INSIDE THE VPN

Extended Description: Two firewalls are configured to connect RFC 1918 networks to each other over a VPN. In the following example, the left side network 10.10.10.0/24 is attempting to be connected to the right side network 10.10.11.0/24 from the firewall, minimoose, to the firewall, jenner, over an IPSEC connection such as **free/openswan**.

This configuration is a true NAT to NAT VPN configuration that you would most likely be using in an environment where you are linking two corporate networks together, perhaps in the case of eliminating a legacy WAN connection.

As mentioned earlier in the chapter, not every IPSEC implementation is going to be compatible with every other. This is especially true when you get into the various authentication mechanisms used. We favor **openswan** (www.openswan.org), which for the most part handles all the standard authentication mechanisms. Assuming that the issue is with the initial connections themselves not working correctly, the MTU settings or an ISP policy that blocks IPSEC traffic could be the culprit. The best way to verify this is with a sniffer. If you can see your traffic outbound from one firewall but never see it arrive on the other, then the problem is most likely an upstream filter blocking your traffic. If the traffic arrives but is discarded, then the problem is likely MTU related.

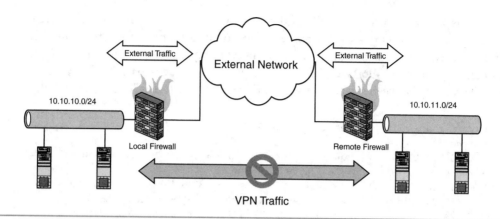

Figure 19.3 Traffic does not route through VPN.

Assuming that the VPN itself can be established, but the traffic is not routing between networks, set up sniffers on both sides to capture traffic between systems. Typically the issues in this area are related to the source and/or destination of the packets traversing the VPN. Like the section here, the systems on each end will get confused as to where to send the return traffic. The following is a basic working example of the preceding configuration using **freeswan/openswan** to link both sides. Keep in mind that this is a basic configuration and that you would not want to run this as it is in a production environment. Specifically, the FORWARD NEW rule should be more specific, covering traffic only from your trusted network to whatever destinations you want the firewall to forward traffic for:

```
#!/bin/sh

IPTABLES=/sbin/iptables

#Connection tracking rules
$IPTABLES -A INPUT   -m state –state ESTABLISHED,RELATED -j ACCEPT
$IPTABLES -A OUTPUT -m state –state NEW,ESTABLISHED,RELATED -j ACCEPT
$IPTABLES -A FORWARD -m state –state NEW,ESTABLISHED,RELATED -j ACCEPT

# eth0 is our external dynamic interface, eth1 is our internal interface
$IPTABLES -t nat -A POSTROUTING -o eth0 -j MASQUERADE

# enable IP Forwarding
echo 1 > /proc/sys/net/ipv4/ip_forward
```

This is a very simplistic example of the previous scenario. A major mistake here is where you bind the nat rule—the correct place to put it is on your external interface only. This way the address translation is limited to only the external interface and does not affect your other interfaces, ipsec0 or eth1. This allows the basic IP forwarding to handle routing between the two networks. Here's how the traffic looks in **ethereal**:

```
[root@minimoose root]# tethereal -i ipsec0
Capturing on ipsec0
  0.000000 10.10.10.198 -> 10.10.11.102 TCP 58845 > ssh [SYN] Seq=2724808935 Ack=0
Win=5840 Len=0 MSS=1460 TSV=566028529 TSER=0 WS=0
  0.068717 10.10.11.102 -> 10.10.10.198 TCP ssh > 58845 [SYN, ACK] Seq=3602031957
Ack=2724808936 Win=5792 Len=0 MSS=1460 TSV=90480758 TSER=566028529 WS=0
  0.069324 10.10.10.198 -> 10.10.11.102 TCP 58845 > ssh [ACK] Seq=2724808936
Ack=3602031958 Win=5840 Len=0 TSV=566028536 TSER=90480758
  0.128028 10.10.11.102 -> 10.10.10.198 SSH Server Protocol: SSH-2.0-NOYB
```

Here is the same configuration but with the nat rule bound to all the interfaces using the following rule:

```
$IPTABLES -t nat -A POSTROUTING -j MASQUERADE

[root@minimoose root]# tethereal -i ipsec0
Capturing on ipsec0
  0.000000 123.4.5.6 -> 10.10.11.102 TCP 58845 > ssh [SYN] Seq=2724808935 Ack=0
Win=5840 Len=0 MSS=1460 TSV=566028529 TSER=0 WS=0
  0.069324 123.4.5.6 -> 10.10.11.102 TCP 58845 > ssh [ACK] Seq=2724808936
Ack=3602031958 Win=5840 Len=0 TSV=566028536 TSER=90480758
```

In this case, the 10.10.11.0/24 network sees traffic coming over the VPN that has the wrong source address, specifically the masqueraded external IP from the firewall. Assuming an "unless allow, deny" model on the other side, a properly configured network is going to DROP or REJECT those packets because they are not matching the allowed rules on the other side.

This leads to the next scenario, assuming that the connections are being established, the routing is correct, and traffic still is not traversing the VPN successfully—it could be a DROP/REJECT rule blocking the traffic in or outbound. The best way to rule out that type of rule is to first test the configuration with no filtering. If things work, then you know it's a filter rule. You'll have to go through rule by rule to rule out which ones are being problematic, either by commenting out each filter or adding in diagnostic logging so you can see exactly which rules are being triggered and where.

PPTP: CANNOT ESTABLISH PPTP CONNECTIONS THROUGH THE FIREWALL

Extended Description: You have an internal system that creates a Point to Point Tunneling Protocol (PPTP) VPN to another system, for example a corporate VPN server, through your firewall. Non-VPN traffic functions properly; however, the PPTP VPN connection cannot be established. In this "road warrior" configuration, the internal system (laptop in diagram here) only connects to the remote system as an end-node; it does not perform any routing.

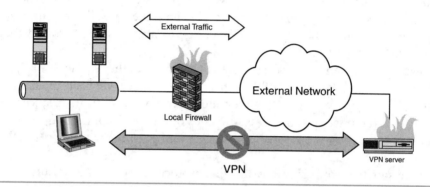

Figure 19.4 Internal systems cannot establish PPTP VPNs through firewall.

VPNs, like PPTP, suffer from problems seen in both Layer 3 and Layer 4 -based VPNs, given that it lives in both worlds—by using both a Layer 4 TCP control port, as well as a Layer 3 data protocol. This means that not only is a PPTP connection sensitive to MTU settings, it is also going to require a special connection tracking module as well as paying attention to filter rules on the Layer 4 traffic.

PPTP traffic uses protocol 47 (GRE), TCP port 1723, and requires some additional patches to be added into the Linux kernel to traverse NAT firewalls. Specifically, the kernel has to be patched with the `pptp-conntrak-nat.patch` from patch-o-matic and have the following options enabled:

```
Networking options
<*>    IP: GRE tunnels over IP
   [*]      IP: broadcast GRE over IP

Networking options ->
  -> IP: Netfilter Configuration
```

```
-> Connection tracking
  <*>   GRE protocol support
    <*>    PPTP protocol support
```

Without these modules and settings built into the kernel, PPTP connections will not work through the firewall. Furthermore, these are not set in default Red Hat kernels. So if you are running a Red Hat box and have not specifically rebuilt your system to support these options, then no amount of tinkering on the firewall is going to get this to work!

Just like IPSEC, PPTP is very sensitive to the MTU settings between endpoints. This is due to the fact that PPTP really uses PPP (Point to Point Protocol) inside the PPTP encapsulated session to handle the real network traffic. Because of the overhead involved in the encapsulation, you'll need to keep an eye on both the firewall and your client's MTU. In general, if you're having connection or performance issues, try setting both systems to the same MTU.

The next step is to verify that you can actually connect to the remote PPTP system. This is such a well-known service, ISPs with a no-VPN policy will likely block this PPTP connection. Verify with your ISPs that they allow this type of traffic in advance. If you have the capability to set up sniffers on both ends of the PPTP connection, verify that both endpoints are communicating both the TCP and protocol 47 traffic correctly. PPTP needs both!

Finally, ensure that your firewall is allowing protocol 47 (GRE) traffic outbound. The following example rules are from the **pptpclient** website (`http://pptpclient. sourceforge.net/howto-diagnosis.phtml`). Document the proper firewall rules to work with PPTP:

```
# eth0 is our external interface
$IPTABLES --insert OUTPUT 1 \
--source 0.0.0.0/0.0.0.0 \
--destination 0.0.0.0/0.0.0.0 \
--jump ACCEPT --protocol gre \
--out-interface eth0

$IPTABLES --insert INPUT 1 \
--source 0.0.0.0/0.0.0.0 \
--destination 0.0.0.0/0.0.0.0 \
--jump ACCEPT --protocol gre \
--in-interface eth0
```

RUNNING A PPTP SERVER BEHIND A NAT FIREWALL

For allowing PPTP access in the other direction where the remote system would need to connect to an internal PPTP server through a netfilter/**iptables** firewall, the following example DNAT rules should work:

```
# assuming eth0 is your external interface, and that you have a PPTP server at
10.10.10.5
$IPTABLES -t nat -A PREROUTING -i eth0 -p tcp --dport 1723 -j DNAT --to-destination
10.10.10.5
$IPTABLES-A FORWARD -i eth0 -m state --state NEW -p tcp -d 10.10.10.5 --dport 1723 -j
ACCEPT
$IPTABLES -A FORWARD -i eth0 -m state --state NEW -p 47 -d 10.10.10.5  -j ACCEPT
$IPTABLES -t nat -A PREROUTING -i eth0 -p 47 -j DNAT -to-destination 10.10.10.5
$IPTABLES -t nat -A POSTROUTING -o eth0 -j MASQUERADE
```

PPTP: FIREWALL CANNOT ESTABLISH PPTP VPNs

Extended Description: You have a NAT/MASQUERADING firewall that is PPTP-capable. This firewall acts as an end node, NAT/MASQUERADING traffic into the PPTP VPN itself so all connections inside the PPTP VPN, as well as to the external network, appear to be coming from the firewall.

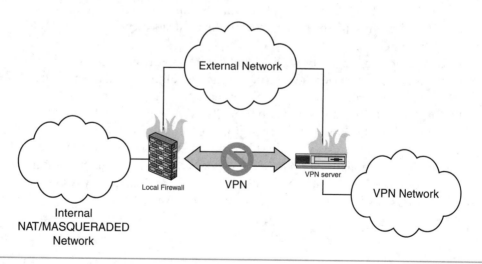

Figure 19.5   Firewall cannot establish PPTP VPNs.

This is a fairly basic configuration and in practice much more simple to implement than actually trying to NAT PPTP traffic through the firewall. In this configuration, the firewall needs only to establish a PPTP connection to the remote system and then using NAT rules, NAT/MASQUERADE the traffic from its internal systems into the PPTP VPN. For this type of setup, I cannot recommend the pptpclient project enough: http://pptp-client.sourceforge.net/. The documentation provided for numerous configurations just cannot be overlooked. They cover numerous scenarios dealing with the automatic establishment of the PPTP VPN, DSL issues, and installing the encryption modules required to secure the connection.

In this configuration you can borrow a rule right from the IPSEC section here dealing with masquerading traffic from one network across the VPN tunnel using an SNAT rule:

```
$IPTABLES -t nat -A POSTROUTING -o ppp0   \
-s 10.10.12.0/24 -d 10.10.11.0/24 -j SNAT \
--to-source 10.10.12.1
```

The primary difference between this rule and the IPSEC rule here is that PPTP encapsulates a PPP connection, so our device name is different.

PPTP: FIREWALL CAN ESTABLISH CONNECTIONS TO A REMOTE VPN SERVER, BUT TRAFFIC DOES NOT ROUTE CORRECTLY INSIDE THE VPN

Extended Description: Two firewalls are configured to connect RFC 1918 networks to each other over a PPTP VPN. In the following example, the left side network, 10.10.10.0/24, is attempting to be connected to the right side network, 10.10.11.0/24, over a PPTP connection.

This is the type of configuration you would use if you were attempting to join two remote networks together over the Internet, in the case of migrating from a legacy WAN to a VPN over the Internet. In this example, we have two RFC 1918 networks, 10.10.10.0/24 and 10.10.11.0/24, and two firewalls, Host-A and Host-B.

The first step into diagnosing problems with this configuration is to ensure that the VPN session itself is being established, which you can verify by monitoring the log files or using a sniffer like **ethereal**. In general, leaving out the obvious authentication or availability issues between Host-A and Host-B, the MTU path discovery issues are the first thing to look at when performing your PPTP diagnostics.

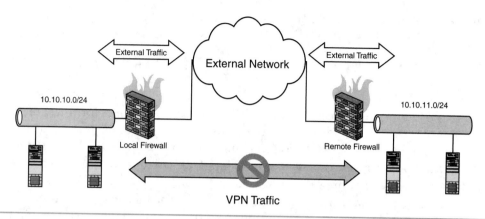

Figure 19.6   Traffic does not route through PPTP VPN.

As PPTP also uses GRE protocol 47, it is also necessary to build your kernel with GRE support, documented here, and if that support is modular, the `ip_gre` module is loaded in the kernel:

```
modprobe ip_gre
```

> **NOTE**
>
> Versions of pptpclient 1.2.0 and greater no longer require this.

A symptom of this not being loaded, aside from the obvious that the VPN isn't working, will be ICMP protocol unreachable reply messages in your sniffer dump on protocol 47.

Just like the IPSEC rules here, if your `NAT/MASQUERADING` rule is not bound to your external interface, you may be rewriting your VPN traffic so it appears to be coming from your external interface on your firewall. The following extremely simple example rule shows how to ensure that this traffic is not being NAT-ed:

```
#Connection tracking rules
$IPTABLES -A INPUT  -m state –state    \
  ESTABLISHED,RELATED -j ACCEPT
$IPTABLES -A OUTPUT -m state –state    \
  NEW,ESTABLISHED,RELATED -j ACCEPT
```

```
$IPTABLES -A FORWARD -m state -state       \
   NEW,ESTABLISHED,RELATED -j ACCEPT

# eth0 is our external dynamic interface, eth1 is our internal interface
$IPTABLES -t nat -A POSTROUTING -o eth0 -j MASQUERADE
```

Again, these are very simple rules and you should create specific rules for your firewall. The FORWARD rules here will forward any traffic, from either side of the firewall, which is *not* what you want. Make sure that you configure the sources, via -s, that you want to FORWARD NEW traffic for, and also use -i and -o interface settings to define the input and output interfaces on your firewall for that traffic.

Of course, there's always more than one way to do it. The following rules from the pptpclient website demonstrate a similar more elaborate configuration to route traffic between both networks:

Host-A configuration rules:

```
route add -net 192.168.0.0/16 netmask 255.255.0.0 dev ppp0


$IPTABLES --insert OUTPUT 1 --source 0.0.0.0/0.0.0.0  \
   --destination 192.168.0.0/16 --jump ACCEPT -o ppp0
$IPTABLES --insert INPUT 1 --source 192.168.0.0/16       \
--destination 0.0.0.0/0.0.0.0 --jump ACCEPT -i ppp0
$IPTABLES --insert FORWARD 1 --source 0.0.0.0/0.0.0.0 \
--destination 192.168.0.0/16 --jump ACCEPT -o ppp0
$IPTABLES --insert FORWARD 1 --source 192.168.0.0/16 \
--destination 0.0.0.0/0.0.0.0 --jump ACCEPT
$IPTABLES --table nat --append POSTROUTING -o ppp0 \
--jump MASQUERADE
$IPTABLES --append FORWARD --protocol tcp \
   --tcp-flags SYN,RST SYN --jump TCPMSS       \
   -clamp-mss-to-pmtu
```

Host-A

```
route add -net 10.10.11.0/24 netmask 255.255.0.0 dev ppp0
```

This first rule sets a static route to 10.10.11.0 network on Host-A.

```
$IPTABLES --insert OUTPUT 1 --source 10.10.10.0/24 \
   --destination 10.10.11.0/24 --jump ACCEPT -o ppp0
```

This second rule instructs **iptables** to redirect all outbound traffic from the 10.10.10.0/24 with the destination network 10.10.11.0/24 only out the ppp0 device.

```
$IPTABLES --insert INPUT 1 --source 10.10.11.0/24  \
  --destination 10.10.10.0/24 --jump ACCEPT -i ppp0
```

This third rule sets the INPUT policy that traffic on the ppp0 interface, from the 10.10.11.0/24 network destined to the 10.10.10.0/24 network, be accepted.

```
$IPTABLES --insert FORWARD 1 --source 10.10.10.0/24 \
  --destination 10.10.11.0/24 --jump ACCEPT -o ppp0
```

The fourth rule in this chain instructs netfilter to forward packets from the source network 10.10.10.0/24 and a destination of 10.10.11.0/24 out the ppp0 interface. Without this rule, only the Host-A firewall itself would be allowed to communicate with systems on the 10.10.11.0/24 network.

```
$IPTABLES --insert FORWARD 1 --source 10.10.11.0/24 \
  --destination 10.10.10.0/24 --jump ACCEPT -i ppp0
```

This fifth rule sets the FORWARD policy for traffic from the 10.10.11.0/24 network, destined to the 10.10.10.0/24 network, be accepted on the ppp0 interface.

```
$IPTABLES --append FORWARD --protocol tcp \
  --tcp-flags SYN,RST SYN --jump TCPMSS   \
  -clamp-mss-to-pmtu
```

This final rule is used on 2.4 kernels to deal with the oft-repeated MTU path discovery issue when dealing with DSL, PPPoE, and other situations where the MTU is causing problems with your connections.

USING A FREE/OPENSWAN VPN TO SECURE A WIRELESS NETWORK

This example is specifically for securing a wireless network, but it could just as easily be used to create a "road warrior" VPN configuration in conjunction with netfilter using this example.

In this scenario, we have a wireless segment (192.168.32.0/24) that we would like to secure using netfilter and an **openswan** IPSEC VPN. Our access point will act as a DHCP server, and we will configure our firewall (Firewall-A) to drop all traffic from the

192.168.32.0/24 network attempting to traverse the firewall. This is to ensure that if someone manages to hop on the wireless network by cracking the WEP or WAP keys, he or she still cannot access systems on the other side (internal network) of your firewall, or the Internet. Of course, they *will* be able to attack nodes on the wireless segment, so you might want to establish local firewall rules on all your hosts as shown in the example at the end of this section.

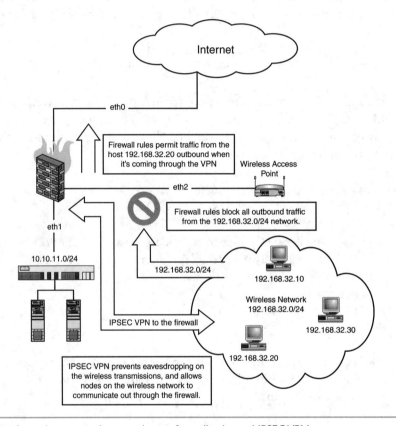

Figure 19.7   A wireless network secured using firewall rules and IPSEC VPNs.

The intent of this design is to

1. Secure your wireless communications from eavesdropping.
2. Secure your wireless network from becoming an open access point and prevent attackers from accessing your internal network or the Internet.

We will assume that you have configured your access point correctly and that the wireless network (192.168.32.0/24) is functioning properly. Our firewall (Firewall-A) is located at the IP address 192.168.32.1.

Configure your firewall for your "road warriors" using **openswan**. First we need to set up our ipsec mechanism. Consult the documentation for configuring **openswan** in your kernel. In this example, our firewall is running a 2.4.26 kernel and **openswan** 2.1.2. Firewall-A's **/etc/ipsec.conf**:

```
# Host-A is a firewall running redhat 9
config setup
        interfaces="ipsec0=eth0 ipsec1=eth1 ipsec2=eth2"
        # Debug-logging controls:  "none" for (almost) none, "all" for lots.
        # klipsdebug=all
        # plutodebug=dns

conn wireless
      left=192.168.32.1                    # Gateway's information
      leftid=@firewall-a
      leftsubnet=0.0.0.0/0       #
      #leftnexthop=%defaultroute     # correct in many situations
      leftrsasigkey=0sAQOF...
      right=%any                      # Wildcard: we don't know the laptop's IP
      rightid=@host-b
      rightrsasigkey=0sAQOit...
      auto=add                        # authorizes but doesn't start this
                                      # connection at startup
```

1. We configure our laptop to connect to the firewall. The key here is that the subnet for our VPN is 0.0.0.0/0, which is the world at large, as it were. Our laptop in this example is running a Red Hat 2.6.6 kernel, with **openswan** 2.1.3. The important difference between a 2.4 and a 2.6 kernel is that 2.6 comes with IPSEC by default. The **openswan** patches integrate with the existing IPSEC implementation in the 2.6.x kernel:

    Host-B's **/etc/ipsec.conf**:

```
# Host-B is a laptop running SuSE 9.1
# relevant section "road" is at the bottom. The rest is the SuSE default

version 2.0    # conforms to second version of ipsec.conf specification
```

```
# basic configuration
config setup
        # Debug-logging controls:  "none" for (almost) none, "all" for lots.
        #klipsdebug=all
        #plutodebug=all


# default settings for connections
conn %default
        # Default: %forever (try forever)
        #keyingtries=3
        # Sig keys (default: %dnsondemand)
        leftrsasigkey=%cert
        rightrsasigkey=%cert
        # Lifetimes, defaults are 1h/8hrs
        #ikelifetime=20m
        #keylife=1h
        #rekeymargin=8m

# OE policy groups are disabled by default
conn block
        auto=ignore

conn clear
        auto=ignore

conn private
        auto=ignore

conn private-or-clear
        auto=ignore

conn clear-or-private
        auto=ignore

conn packetdefault
        auto=ignore


conn road
    left=%defaultroute          # Picks up our dynamic IP
    leftid=@host-b                # Local information
    leftrsasigkey=0sAQOC....  # Local key
    right=192.168.32.1           # Remote information
    rightsubnet=0.0.0.0/0         # Remote subnet is set to "everything"
```

```
rightid=@firewall-a          # Remote information
rightrsasigkey=0sAQ0....   # Remote key
auto=add                     # authorizes but doesn't start this
```

2. Verify your configuration settings by running the command: ipsec auto status on both systems. If your systems are configured correctly, the output will look like the following:

Firewall-A (using the unsecured wireless IP of 192.168.32.1):

```
000 "wireless": 0.0.0.0/0===192.168.32.1[@firewall-a]...%any[@host-b]; unrouted;
eroute owner: #0
000 "wireless":   ike_life: 3600s; ipsec_life: 28800s; rekey_margin: 540s;
rekey_fuzz: 100%; keyingtries: 0
000 "wireless":   policy: RSASIG+ENCRYPT+TUNNEL+PFS; prio: 0,32; interface: eth2;
000 "wireless":   newest ISAKMP SA: #0; newest IPsec SA: #0;
```

Host-B (using the unsecured wireless IP of 192.168.32.190):

```
[root@host-b root]# ipsec auto status


000 "wireless": 192.168.32.190[@Host-B,S=C]...192.168.32.1[@Firewall-
A,S=C]===0.0.0.0/0; unrouted; eroute owner: #0
000 "wireless":   ike_life: 3600s; ipsec_life: 28800s; rekey_margin: 540s;
rekey_fuzz: 100%; keyingtries: 0
000 "wireless":   policy: RSASIG+ENCRYPT+TUNNEL+PFS; prio: 32,0; interface: eth1;
000 "wireless":   newest ISAKMP SA: #0; newest IPsec SA: #0;
```

If your system does not show the script here, then probably you have an error in your configuration files. **openswan** will log these messages to syslog. In the case of the systems in our example, this was to **/var/log/messages**.

3. Establish your firewall rules. We have two networks, an internal wired 10.10.10.0/24 network, and a wireless 192.168.32.0/24 network. In addition, our firewall runs a transparent **squid** proxy, a caching DNS server, and the **reaim** (http://reaim.sf.net) instant messaging proxy:

```
#!/bin/sh

IPTABLES="/sbin/iptables"
EXTERNAL="eth0"
```

```
INTERNAL="eth1"
WIRELESS="eth2"
VPN="ipsec0"

# clear our old firewall rules
$IPTABLES -F
$IPTABLES -X

echo "Setting default filter policy"
$IPTABLES -P INPUT    DROP
$IPTABLES -P OUTPUT   DROP
$IPTABLES -P FORWARD DROP



# Set our connection tracking rules
$IPTABLES -A INPUT   -m state -state \
  ESTABLISHED,RELATED -j ACCEPT
$IPTABLES -A OUTPUT -m state -state  \
  NEW,ESTABLISHED,RELATED -j ACCEPT
$IPTABLES -A FORWARD -m state -state \
  ESTABLISHED,RELATED -j ACCEPT

# For PPPoE, DSL, and other MTU sensitve connections
$IPTABLES -A OUTPUT -o $EXTERNAL -p tcp \
  --tcp-flags SYN,RST SYN -j TCPMSS -clamp-mss-to-pmtu

# Allow SSH on everything
$IPTABLES -A INPUT -p tcp --dport 22 -j ACCEPT


# internal rules
$IPTABLES -A INPUT -i $INTERNAL -p tcp \
  --dport 5190 -j ACCEPT
$IPTABLES -A INPUT -i $INTERNAL -p tcp \
  --dport 1863 -j ACCEPT
$IPTABLES -t nat -A PREROUTING -i $INTERNAL \
  -p tcp --dport 5190 -j REDIRECT --to-ports 5190
$IPTABLES -t nat -A PREROUTING -i $INTERNAL \
  -p tcp --dport 1863 -j REDIRECT --to-ports 1863

# A for loop to duplicate rules on trusted interfaces
INTERFACES="$INTERNAL $VPN"

for i in $INTERFACES; do
  #  Allow DNS traffic
```

```
    $IPTABLES -A INPUT -p tcp --dport 53 -i $i -j ACCEPT
    $IPTABLES -A INPUT -p udp --dport 53 -i $i -j ACCEPT

    # Allow SQUID connections
    $IPTABLES -A INPUT -p tcp --dport 3128 -i $i \
      -j ACCEPT
    $IPTABLES -t nat -A PREROUTING -i $i -p tcp  \
      --dport 80 -j REDIRECT --to-port 3128

    # Reaim connections
    $IPTABLES -A INPUT -i $i -p tcp --dport 5190 \
      -j ACCEPT
    $IPTABLES -A INPUT -i $i -p tcp --dport 1863 \
      -j ACCEPT
    $IPTABLES -t nat -A PREROUTING -i $i -p tcp  \
      --dport 5190 -j REDIRECT --to-ports 5190
    $IPTABLES -t nat -A PREROUTING -i $i -p tcp  \
      --dport 1863 -j REDIRECT --to-ports 1863
done

# IPSEC rules. This allows IPSEC traffic to be forwarded through the VPN
#
$IPTABLES -N IPSEC
$IPTABLES -A INPUT -j IPSEC
$IPTABLES -A FORWARD -i $VPN -j IPSEC
$IPTABLES -A IPSEC -i $WIRELESS -p udp --dport 500 \
  -j ACCEPT
$IPTABLES -A IPSEC -i $WIRELESS -p ESP -j ACCEPT

# Masquerading rules, we use this if we have a dynamic
# IP
$IPTABLES -t nat -A POSTROUTING -o $EXTERNAL -j MASQUERADE

# SNAT we would use this if we had a static IP
# $IPTABLES -t nat -A POSTROUTING -i eth1 \
#   -o $EXTERNAL -j SNAT --to $EXTERNALIP

# debugging rule, or for the paranoid. This will catch all dropped packets by the
firewall
$IPTABLES -A INPUT -p all  -m limit --limit 1/second \
  -j LOG  --log-level info --log-prefix "STEALTH -- \
  DROP "  --log-tcp-sequence  --log-tcp-options      \
  --log-ip-options

# Enable IP Forwarding in the kernel
echo "1" > /proc/sys/net/ipv4/ip_forward
```

The following is a sniffer dump of the 192.168.32.0/24 network from the firewall's eth2 interface, prior to the IPSEC tunnel being established to the host 192.168.32.190 (Host-B):

```
[root@firewall-a rc.d]# tethereal -i eth2 host 192.168.32.190
Capturing on eth0
   0.000000 192.168.32.190 -> 68.98.150.6   TCP 58862 > webcache [SYN, ECN, CWR]
Seq=3608226472 Ack=0 Win=5840 Len=0 MSS=1460 TSV=34015029 TSER=0 WS=0
   2.992793 192.168.32.190 -> 68.98.150.6   TCP 58862 > webcache [SYN, ECN, CWR]
Seq=3608226472 Ack=0 Win=5840 Len=0 MSS=1460 TSV=34015329 TSER=0 WS=0
   8.994929 192.168.32.190 -> 68.98.150.6   TCP 58862 > webcache [SYN, ECN, CWR]
Seq=3608226472 Ack=0 Win=5840 Len=0 MSS=1460 TSV=34015929 TSER=0 WS=0
  20.995165 192.168.32.190 -> 68.98.150.6   TCP 58862 > webcache [SYN, ECN, CWR]
Seq=3608226472 Ack=0 Win=5840 Len=0 MSS=1460 TSV=34017129 TSER=0 WS=0
  44.998586 192.168.32.190 -> 68.98.150.6   TCP 58862 > webcache [SYN, ECN, CWR]
Seq=3608226472 Ack=0 Win=5840 Len=0 MSS=1460 TSV=34019529 TSER=0 WS=0
```

And this is the sniffer dump after establishing the IPSEC VPN:

```
[root@firewall-a rc.d]# tethereal -i eth2 host 192.168.32.190
   1.019722 192.168.32.190 -> 192.168.32.1 ESP ESP (SPI=0x258d56d0)
   1.019830 192.168.32.190 -> 192.168.32.1 ESP ESP (SPI=0x258d56d0)
   1.020038 192.168.32.1 -> 192.168.32.190 ESP ESP (SPI=0xe180e07f)
   1.019921 192.168.32.190 -> 192.168.32.1 ESP ESP (SPI=0x258d56d0)
   1.020017 192.168.32.190 -> 192.168.32.1 ESP ESP (SPI=0x258d56d0)
   1.020111 192.168.32.190 -> 192.168.32.1 ESP ESP (SPI=0x258d56d0)
   1.020621 192.168.32.1 -> 192.168.32.190 ESP ESP (SPI=0xe180e07f)
```

SUMMARY

Implementing VPNs successfully across firewalls and to remote users can be a daunting task, and we have only covered two of the more common ones, IPSEC and PPTP. When troubleshooting VPN problems, recall our methodology section from previous chapters:

1. **Define the Problem:** Fire up your sniffer and see what's going on before you do anything else. Is the traffic leaving the host? Is it getting to the VPN server? Is it getting back?
2. **Gather Facts:** Did anything change? Did the client software or the server software get updated? Did firewall rules change? Did the topology between systems change?

3. **Define the End State:** Now that you know what the symptoms and the facts are, what are you trying to accomplish? Is this a road warrior that needs to access his e-mail? Or is this a site to site problem? Define the problem you are going to solve before ripping apart your network trying to solve symptoms that are not important to the problem.

4. **Develop Possible Solutions and Create an Action Plan:** You have determined that network topology has changed or that a new version of the client software has been installed. Come up with a plan to isolate the topology changes, perhaps by attempting the VPN connection from a location unaffected by the change—or collect older versions of the software.

5. **Analyze and Compare Possible Solutions:** Which solution is going to rule out the most variables? Running the old software? Or trying from a different location? What is the level of effort required to implement this solution?

6. **Select and Implement the Solution:** You determine trying the old software is the fastest method of ruling out the most problems, followed by attempting the connection from other locations.

7. **Critically Analyze Solution for Effectiveness:** Fire up the sniffer again and try your connection. Did it work? If so why, and can you apply this solution to solve the problem for everyone?

With these thoughts in mind, we hope that we have provided the granularity of solutions and methodology required to troubleshoot complex VPN problems. Keep in mind that this is a changing landscape of technology and implementations; the pace of development will often out-pace the quality of the documentation. Knowing how to figure out the answer is just as important as knowing the answer to a problem.

Index

A

-A switch (iptables), 111-112
ACCEPT rules, 106, 149-150
accepting only SMTP connections from specific hosts, 262-263
access
    filtering to forwarded servers, 278
    restricting with firewall rules (FTP), 291-292
action plans, creating, 67
adding rules, 112
AIDE (Advanced Intrusion Detection Environment), 60
AIM (AOL Instant Messenger), 314-317
ALLOW policy, 164
allowing MySQL connections, 253-255
analyzing
    risk management, 26-29
    solutions, 68
    traffic utilization, 157-158
AOL Instant Messenger (AIM), 314-317
application layers, troubleshooting OSI model, 91
application proxies, 17
apt-get, 49
arp cache, network diagnostics, 173-174
assets
    isolating, 36-37
    quantifying value of, 28
AUTH connections, TCP reset for, 146

B

bad flag rules (example firewall), 134-135
bad IP options rules (example firewall), 135
basic masquerading firewalls, 224-226
basic SNAT firewalls, 226-228

blocking
    AIM traffic, 315-317
    clients from accessing websites, 279
    ICQ, 318
    internal users from sending mail through firewalls, 261-262
    MSN messenger traffic at firewalls, 310
    outbound DHCP, 328-329
    outbound NetMeeting/GnomeMeeting traffic, 308
    Yahoo Messenger traffic, 311-314
bridging, 203
    building inline transparent bridging firewalls with ebtables, 207-210
    common questions, 205-206

C

catch all rule, diagnostic logging, 172
chains
    creating, 112
    default policy, 113
    deleting, 113
    order of rules, 121-122
    renaming, 113
    user-defined chains, 241
chkrootkit, 59
chroots, 56
CIA (confidentiality, integrity, and/or availability), 24
clients, blocking from accessing websites, 279
closing connections with TCP, 86
comparing solutions, 68
compatibility issues, IPSEC, 336
computer security, 12-14, 24
configuring software correctly, 60

congestion control, TCP, 84
connection tracking, 340
    engine, memory load diagnostics, 182-185
    fields, 102
connections
    accepting SMTP connections from specific hosts,
        262-263
    to AIM, 315
    closing with TCP, 86
    connections timeout, SSH, 253
    establishing with TCP, 84
    forwarding from firewalls to internal web servers,
        272-273
    FTP, troubleshooting, 299-300
    to ICQ, 317
    MySQL, allowing, 253-255
    to other MSN users, 309-310
    redirecting FTP connections to other ports on the
        server, 293
    to remote NetMeeting/GnomeMeeting clients, 304-307
    telnet, forwarding to other systems, 253
    to Yahoo Messenger, 311
control tools
    cutter, 160-161
    network probes, 161-162
counter measures, securing the enterprise, 35
countertrace, 146
cronjobs, 45, 49
cutter, 160-161

D

-D switch (iptables), 112
Debian, apt-get, 49
default policy, chains, 113
defense in depth (DID), 21, 31
defragmentation, 101
deleting
    chains, 113
    rules, 112, 119
denying large e-mails, 265
deploying security technology and counter measures, 35
DHClient, 327
DHCP
    blocking outbound, 328-329
    dynamically updating firewall rules with IP changes,
        327-328
    filtering with ebtables, 214-215
    redirecting requests to DMZ, 330-332
    two addresses on one external interfaces, 329-330
DHCPcd, 327
DHCRelay, 322, 331
diagnostics
    logging, 169-173, 219-220
    memory load, 182-185
    network problems, 173-179
    sniffers, 179-182

DID (defense in depth), 21, 31
disabling
    ICMP echo response, 126-127
    ICMP redirection, 124-125
    ip forwarding, 123
    proxyarp, 125
    source routing, 124
DMZ (DeMilitarized Zones), 217, 228-230
    cannot be reached from the outside, 236-239
    segments, forwarding to FTP servers, 293-296
    web servers, 245, 267
DNAT rules, PPTP connections, 347
DNS
    forwarding queries to upstream/remote DNS servers,
        322-324
    lookups fail, 324-326
    rDNS, misleading, 326-327
DNSMasq, 322-324
documentation
    iptables, 109-111
    risk management, 29-30
        creating plans, 30-32
        creating security policies, 33
        creating security procedures, 34
        holistic approach, 32-33
domains, 36
down stream liability, 29
drivers, troubleshooting OSI model, 89
dropping packets (example firewall), 143-144
dsniff, 202

E

-E switch (iptables), 113
ebtables, 206, 331
    building inline transparent bridging firewalls, 207-210
    filtering, 211, 214-215
ECN (Explicit Congestion Notification), 128, 278
ECN flag, diagnostics, 180-181
effective security, 9
egress filtering
    example firewall, 145
    securing the enterprise, 39
email. *See also* SMTP
    blocking internal users from sending mail through
        firewalls, 261-262
    large e-mail, deny, 265
    small e-mail, send/receive correctly, 265
    SMTP server timeouts/failures/numberous processes,
        264-265
emerge, 47-49
enabling
    ip dynaddr, 124
    ip forwarding, 150
enclaves, 36
end state, defining, 67
enforcement rules (example firewall), 144

ESTABLISHED (netfilter), 100
establishing connections with TCP, 84
eth0, 242
eth1, 242
etherape, 157-158
ethereal, 155, 304, 338
example firewall, 122-123
    ACCEPT rules, 149-150
    bad flag rules, 134-135
    bad IP options rules, 135
    egress filtering rules, 145
    enforcement rules, 144
    firewall rules, 130
    fragments rules, 140
    invalid packets rules, 139
    IP spoofing rules, 145
    iptables modules, loading, 129-130
    kernal options, 123-129
    odd port detection rules, 142-143
    polite rules, 142
    port scan rules, 132-134
    quality of service rules, 130-132
    shunning packets rules, 148-149
    silently dropping packets, 143-144
    small packets rules, 135-136
    state tracking rules, 147
    STEALTH rules, 147-148
    string-matching rules, 136-139
    SYN floods rules, 140-142
    TCP reset for AUTH connections, 146
    TTL values rules, 146-147
Explicit Congestion Notification (ECN), 128, 278
Explicit Congestion Notification (ECN) flag, diagnostics,
    180-181
external IPSEC servers, connections from internal
    systems, 338-340

F
-F switch (iptables), 119
facts, gathering, 66-67
failures, SMTP, 264-265
file services, 283. *See also* FTP; NFS
file systems, restricting, 56-57
File Transfer Protocol. *See* FTP
file transfers, troubleshooting, 240
filtering
    access to forwarded servers, 278
    DHCP with ebtables, 214-215
    incoming web servers to specific hosts, 270-271
    MAC addresses, 211-214
    port 80, 267
    securing the enterprise, 39
    specific ports with ebtables, 211
filtering tools, ebtables, 206
FIN scan, 198-199

Firewall Builder (fwbuilder), 165
firewall rules
    example firewall, 130
    protecting services, 51-55
firewalls, 189. *See also* example firewall; iptables firewalls
    DMZ, 228-230
    forwarding connections from firewalls to internal web
        servers, 272-273
    IP forwarding firewalls, 284-290
    local firewall security. *See* local firewall security
    managing building rules, 163-166
    masquerading firewalls, 224-226
    NAT, 284-290
    packet filtering firewalls, 190
    reasons for having, 16-17
    recommendations for, 15-16
    securing the enterprise, 36
    SMTP, allowing through firewalls, 258
    SNAT firewalls, 226-228
    stealth firewalls, 207-210
    testing, 190
    with three interfaces and corresponding devices, 242
    transparent firewalls, 203-204
    types of, 17-19
flow control, TCP, 83
forcing mail server traffic to use specific IP address with
        SNAT rule, 260
FORWARD, 98
forwarded servers
    filtering access to, 278
    restricting FTP access to, 298-299
forwarding
    connections from firewalls to internal web servers,
        272-273
    DNS queries to upstream/remote DNS servers, 322-324
    filtering access to forwarded servers, 278
    FTP servers
        behind firewalls on DMZ segments, 293-295
        from one Internet server to another Internet server,
            297-298
    local port 80 to local port 8080, 271-272
    to multiple FTP servers behind firewalls on DMZ
        segments, 295-296
    to multiple internal servers, 273-275
    packets from some other host to some other host, 96
    to remote servers on the Internet, 275-277
    restricting FTP access to forwarded servers, 298-299
    SMTP to internal mail servers, 258-260
    SSH to another system, 248-253
    telnet connections to other systems, 253
fragment reassembly, memory load diagnostics, 185
fragmentation, 101-102
fragments rules (example firewall), 140
fragrouter, testing firewalls, 200-201

FTP (File Transfer Protocol), 283
   forwarding
      from one Internet server to another Internet server,
         297-298
      FTP servers behind firewalls on DMZ segments,
         293-295
      to multiple FTP servers behind firewalls on DMZ
         segments, 295-296
      restricting FTP access to forwarded servers, 298-299
   redirecting connections to other ports on the
      server, 293
   restricting access with firewall rules, 291-292
   running local FTP servers (basic rules), 290-291
   troubleshooting, 299-300
full duplex, TCP, 83
fwbuilder (Firewall Builder), 165
fwsnort, 138

G

gathering facts, 66-67
Gentoo, emerge, 47-49
glibc, 45
GnomeMeeting, 304-308
GNU Gatekeeper, 304
grsecurity, 61

H

-h switch (iptables), 109-111
hardened kernels, 61
hardening, 62
highly structured threats, 10
holistic approach, documenting risk management, 32-33
host intrusion detection, 58-60
hostnames versus IP addresses, 321
hosts, filtering incoming web servers to specific hosts,
   270-271
hosts.allow, 52-53
hosts.deny, 52
hybrids, 18

I

-I switch (iptables), 111-112
ICMP (Internet Control Message Protocol), 79-80
   echo response, disabling, 126-127
   redirection, disabling, 124-125
ICQ, 317-318
identd, 264
iftop, 158
IM (Instant Messaging), 303
   AIM, 314-317
   GnomeMeeting, 304-308
   ICQ, 317-318
   MSN, 309-310
   NetMeeting, 304-308
   questions/problems, 303
   Yahoo Messenger, 311-314

improving risk management, 41
inaccessible websites, 278
inbound
   creating rules for new TCP services, 243-246
   filtering incoming web servers to specific hosts,
      270-271
   running local web servers, 269
   SSH as a local system, 246-248
incoming web servers, filtering to specific hosts, 270-271
ingress filtering, securing the enterprise, 39
inline transparent bridging firewalls
   building with iptables, 211-213
   creating with ebtables, 207-210
INPUT, 98
INSIDE-OUT test, 190
   interpreting from output, 194-195
   testing with nmap and iplog, 190-193
installing DNSMasq, 324
Instant Messaging. See IM
Integrated Secure Communications System (ISCS), 163
integration, risk management, 41
internal mail servers, forwarding SMTP, 258-260
internal systems
   communication with external systems, 236-240
   connections to external IPSEC servers, 338-340
internal users, blocking from sending mail through
   firewalls, 261-262
internal VPN routing, 342-344, 348-351
Internet, forwarding to remote servers on, 275-277
Internet Control Message Protocol. See ICMP
Internet protocol. See IP
interpreting output from INSIDE-OUT tests, 194-195
intrusion detection, snort signatures, 138
INVALID (netfilter), 100
invalid packets rules (example firewall), 139
inventory, analyzing risk management, 26-27
IP (Internet Protocol), 77. See also ICMP; TCP; UDP
   addresses, 211, 321
   packets, 78
   spoofing rules (example firewall), 145
ip dynaddr, enabling, 124
ip forwarding
   disabling, 123
   enabling, 150
   firewalls, troubleshooting, 284-290
iplog, testing, 190-193
IPSEC, 335-336
   common problems, 336-338
   connections to external IPSEC servers, 338-340
   internal VPN routing, 342-344
   NAT/MASQ firewall connections, 340-342
   securing wireless networks, 351-358
$IPTABLES, 241
iptables, 93, 241. See also rules
   building inline transparent bridging firewalls, 211-213
   filtering MAC addresses, 213-214

fragmentation, 101-102
listing current NAT entries, 221-222
syntax, 109-120
TRACE patch, 173
iptables firewalls, connecting to remote
    NetMeeting/GnomeMeeting clients, 304
iptables modules, loading (example firewall), 129-130
iptables policies, order of rules, 121-122
ip_conntrack, memory load diagnostics, 183-184
ip_conntrack_max, memory load diagnostics, 184
ISCS (Integrated Secure Communications System),
    163-165
isolating assets, securing the enterprise, 36-37

J-K-L

-j switch (iptables), 119-120

kernel options (example firewall), 123-129
kernels, 61, 294, 300

-L switch (iptables), 113-119
Layer 2 transparent firewalls. *See* transparent firewalls
length of names, DNS lookups, 325
liability, down stream liability, 29
libpcap library, 155
Linux, ECN, 278
loading iptables modules (example firewall), 129-130
local firewall security, 43-44
local systems, SSH, 246-248
local web servers, running, 269
log monitoring tools, 57-58
logcheck, 58
logging, diagnostic logging, 169-173, 219-220
logwatch, 58
lookup failures, DNS, 324-326

M

MAC addresses, filtering with iptables, 213-214
mail server traffic, forcing to use a specific IP address with
    SNAT rule, 260
managing firewalls, building rules, 163-166
martian addresses, detecting, 126
masquerading firewalls, 224-226
Maximum Transmission Unit. *See* MTU
memory load diagnostics, 182-183, 185
methodologies, 6-8, 64-66. *See also* troubleshooting,
    methodologies
misleading rDNS, 326-327
models. *See* OSI model
monitoring, implementing, 40
MSN, 309-310
MTU (Maximum Transmission Unit), 77
    path discovery and VPNs, 337
    settings
        IPSEC, 336, 340
        PPTP, 346

multiplexing, TCP, 83
MySQL, allowing connections, 253-255
myths, trustworthy or secure software, 19-20

N

-N switch (iptables), 112, 115
name length, DNS lookups, 325
name servers, running, 325-326
NAT (Network Address Translation), 217-218
    common questions about, 218-219
    connections, viewing with netstat-nat, 220-221
    current NAT and rule packet counters, listing, 222-224
    current NAT entries with iptables, listing, 221-222
    firewalls, troubleshooting, 284-290
    and IPSEC, 336
    rules, 340-342, 348-351
NAT Traversal Mode, 339
NAT/MASQ firewalls
    connections between internal systems and external
        IPSEC servers, 338-340
    IPSEC VPN connections, 340-342
    PPTP VPN connections, 347-348
netfilter, 93, 268
    firewalls, connecting to remote
        NetMeeting/GnomeMeeting clients, 305-307
    fragmentation, 101-102
    how it works, 93-94
    iptables. *See* iptables
    packets
        forwarding for some other host to some other host
            (FORWARD), 96
        sent by firewall from a local process to a remote
            system (OUTPUT), 96
        sent to service running on firewall from remote host
            (INPUT), 94
    parsing rules, 94-100
    states, 100-101
    TCP connections, 121
    UDP connections, 120
    website, 110
NetMeeting, 304-308
netstat-nat, viewing NAT connections, 220-221
Network Address Translation. *See* NAT
network diagnostics, 173-179
network performance settings (kernal options), 127-129
network traffic analyzers, 159-160
NEW, netfilter, 100
NFS (Network File System), 283-290
ngrep, 155
NIDS (Network Intrusion Detection System), 58
nmap, 162-163
    network diagnostics, 175-176
    reading output from, 197-198
    testing, INSIDE-OUT, 190-193

O

odd port detection rules (example firewall), 142-143
Open System Interconnection. *See* OSI model
openswan, 336-338, 351-358
order of rules, 121-122
OSI (Open System Interconnection) model, 75-76, 89-91
outbound
    blocking clients from accessing websites, 279
    blocking DHCP, 328-329
    FTP, troubleshooting, 299-300
    inaccessibility of websites, 278
    web traffic, transparent proxy servers, 279-281
OUTSIDE-IN tests, 190, 195-198

P

-P switch (iptables), 113
package management tools, 45-49
packet filtering, 17
packet filtering firewalls, 189-190
packet sniffers. *See* sniffers
packets
    forwarding for some other host to some other host
        (FORWARD), 96
    invalid packets rules (example firewall), 139
    IP packets, 78
    sent by firewall from a local process to a remote system
        (OUTPUT), 96
    sent to service running on firewall from remote host
        (INPUT), 94
    shunning (example firewall), 148-149
    silently dropping packets (example firewall), 143-144
    small packets rules (example firewall), 135-136
    string-matching rules (example firewall), 136-139
    TCP, 82
    troubleshooting packets that do not pass in or out of a
        firewall, 230-235
parsing rules, netfilter, 94-100
patch maintenance, 45
patching
    iptables, TRACE patch, 173
    reliance on, 50
physical connectivity, troubleshooting OSI model, 89
ping, 152-154, 174-175
PKI (Public Key Infrastructure), 163
plans, documenting risk management, 30-32
Point to Point Tunneling Protocol. *See* PPTP
policies, implementing, 35
polite rules (example firewall), 142
port 80, filtering out, 267
port scan rules (example firewall), 132-134
PORT STATE SERVICE, 199-200
POSTROUTING chains, 222
PPTP (Point to Point Tunneling Protocol), 345
    connections through firewall, 345-347
    internal VPN routing, 348-351
    NAT/MASQ firewall connections, 347-348

pptpclient, 346
PREROUTING, 98, 101
presentation layers, troubleshooting OSI model, 91
preventing networks from being added to routes, 243
privilege, running services with least privilege, 55-56
probing tools, 162-163
problem solving methodology, 64-65
/proc, 102
procedures, implementing, 35
processes, SMTP, 264-265
protecting services with TCP wrappers and firewall rules,
    51-55
protocols. *See* ICMP; IP; TCP; UDP
proxyarp, disabling, 125
proxys, 304, 307-308
Public Key Infrastructure (PKI), 163

Q-R

quality of service rules (example firewall), 130-132
quantifying value of assets, analyzing risk management, 28

-R switch
    iptables, 112
    ping, 174
Rash, Michael, 138
rDNS, misleading, 326-327
reading output from nmap, 197-198
ReAIM, 304
recognizing, defining, and isolating the problem, 65-66
red carpet, 46-47
redirecting
    DHCP requests to DMZ, 330-332
    disabling ICMP redirection, 124-125
    FTP connections to other ports on the server, 293
    local port 80 to local port 8080, 271-272
RELATED, netfilter, 100
reliability, TCP, 83
reliance on patching, 50
remote DNS servers, forwarding DNS queries to, 322-324
remote logging, 60
remote servers, forwarding to remote servers on the
        Internet, 275-277
renaming chains, 113
replacing rules, 112
restricting
    access with firewall rules (FTP), 291-292
    file systems, 56-57
    FTP access to forwarded servers, 298-299
risk, 8
risk management, 9-12, 23-24
    computer security, 12-14, 24
    elements of, 24-25
    steps for, 25
        analyze, 26-29
        documentation, 29-34
        implementing monitoring, 40

improving, 41
integration, 41
securing the enterprise, 34-39
testing, 40
rkhunter, 59
routers, 189
routing, internal VPN routing, 342-344, 348-351
Rowland, Craig, 58
RPC Bind, 197
rsync, 50
rule packet counters, listing, 222-224
rules. *See also* example firewall; iptables
adding, 112
building, 163-166
catch all, diagnostic logging, 172
creating for new TCP services, 243-246
deleting, 112, 119
internal VPN routing, 344, 349-351
IPSEC connections, 340-342
order of, 121-122
parsing with netfilter, 94-100
PPTP connections, 346-347
PPTP VPN connections, 348
replacing, 112
wireless network security, 355-357
running
local FTP servers (basic rules), 290-291
local web servers, 269
services with least privilege, 55-56

S

-s switch (ping), 175
samhain, 59
scripts, diagnostic logging, 170-172
search engines, troubleshooting methodologies, 69
Secondary Exploitation, 37
Secure Shell. *See* SSH
securing
enterprise, risk management, 34-39
wireless networks with openswan VPN, 351-358
security, 8-9, 17
computer security, 12-14
effective security, 9
security policies, 21, 33
security procedures, 34
security technology, securing the enterprise, 35
security tools, 57-60
selecting solutions, 68
SELinux, 45, 61
server timeouts, SMTP, 264-265
servers
DNS servers. *See* DNS
forwarded servers, filtering access to, 278
FTP servers, running local FTP servers (basic rules), 290-291
remote servers. *See* remote servers

transparent proxy servers, squid, 279-281
services
protecting with TCP wrappers and firewall rules, 51-55
running with least privilege, 55-56
turning off, 50
session layers, troubleshooting OSI model, 91
shunning packets rules (example firewall), 148-149
silently dropping packets (example firewall), 143-144
slabinfo, memory load diagnostics, 182-183
Small Office/Home Office (SOHO), 217
small packets rules (example firewall), 135-136
SMTP, 257
accepting SMTP connections from specific hosts, 262-263
allowing through firewalls, 258
forwarding to internal mail servers, 258-260
large email, deny, 265
questions about, 257
server timeouts/failures/numerous processes, 264-265
small e-mail send/receive correctly, 265
smurf attacks, detecting, 126-127
SNAT firewalls, 226-228
SNAT rule, forcing mail server traffic to use specific IP address, 260
sniffers, 155-156, 179-182, 304, 338
Snort, 258, 313
snort signatures, 138
software
configuring correctly, 60
importance of updating, 44-45
myths of trustworthy or secure software, 19-20
SOHO (Small Office/Home Office), 217
solutions
analyzing and comparing, 68
developing, 67
selecting and implementing, 68
source routing, disabling, 124
-sP switches (nmap), 175
spoof protection, 125
spoofing rules (example firewall), 145
squid, 268-269, 279-281
SSH (Secure Shell), 246
connections timeout, 253
forwarding to another system, 248-253
as local system, 246-248
ssh service, protecting, 54
SSLdump, 156
state engine, 102-106
state tracking rules (example firewall), 147
stateful inspection, 18
states of netfilter, 100-101
stealth firewalls, 207-210
STEALTH rules (example firewall), 147-148
steps for risk management. *See* risk management, steps for
Stevens, W. Richard, 76
string-matching rules (example firewall), 136-139

structured threats, 10
SYN cookies, 128
SYN flood attacks
    example firewall, 140-142
    preventing, 128
SYN scan, 198
syntax, iptables, 109-120

T

TCP (Transmission Control Protocol), 82-83
    closing connections, 86
    congestion control, 84
    creating rules for new TCP services, 243-246
    establishing connections, 84
    flow control, 83
    full duplex and multiplexing, 83
    reliability, 83
    TCP ABORT, 87-88
    TCP CLOSE, 86
TCP connections, netfilter engine, 121
TCP FIN timeout network setting, 127
TCP layers, troubleshooting OSI model, 90
TCP packets, 82
tcp ping, 176
TCP reset for AUTH connections (example firewall), 146
TCP wrappers, protecting services, 51-55
tcp-window-tracking modification, 106
tcpdump, 155-156, 179
tcptraceroute, 161-162, 178-179
telnet, 151, 253, 267
testing
    application layers, OSI model, 91
    drivers, OSI model, 89
    firewalls, 190-201
    presentation layers, OSI model, 91
    risk management, 40
    session layers, OSI model, 91
    TCP layers, OSI model, 90
tetheral, diagnostics, 179-180
threat analysis, analyzing risk management, 29
threats, 10
Three-Way Handshake (TWH), 85
TIGER, 59
TIME WAIT state, 104
timeouts, UDP connection timeout setting, 128
TITAN, 59
tools
    cutter, 160-161
    dsniff, 202
    ebtables, 206
    etherape, 157
    iftop, 158
    network traffic analyzers, 159-160
    nmap, 162-163
    package management tools, 45-49
    ping, 152-154

probing tools, 162-163
security tools, 57-60
sniffers, 155-156, 338
tcprack, 158
tcptraceroute, 161-162
telnet, 151
top, 158
vnstat, 159
top, 158
TRACE patch (iptables), 173
traceroute, 146-147, 154, 161-162, 176-179
traffic, analyzing utilization, 157-158
training, 21
Transmission Control Protocol. See TCP
transparent firewalls, 203-204
transparent proxy servers, 279-281
tripwire, 59
troubleshooting. See also diagnostics
    internal and external systems communication, 230-240
    large file transfer failures, 240
    methodologies, 63-64, 69
        analyzing and comparing solutions, 68
        defining end state, 67
        developing solutions and creating action plans, 67
        gathering facts, 66-67
        implementing solutions, 68
        problem solving methodology, 64-65
        recognizing, defining, and isolating the problem, 65-66
        websites for, 69-70
        with search engines, 69
    OSI model, 89-91
TTL values rules (example firewall), 146-147
tunneling. See VPNs
turning off services, 50
TWH (Three-Way Handshake), 85

U

UDP (User Datagram Protocol), 88
UDP connections, 120, 128
unstructured threats, 10
up2date, 47
updating
    firewall rules with IP changes, 327-328
    software, importance of, 44-45
upstream DNS servers, forwarding DNS queries to, 322-324
User Datagram Procol. See UDP
user-defined chains, 241

V

-v switch (iptables), 116
viewing NAT connections with netstat-nat, 220-221
VLANs, 201-202
vnstat, 159
VPNs (virtual private networks), 335

common problems, 336-338
IPSEC, 335-344
NAT/MASQ firewall connections, 340-342, 351-358
PPTP, 345-351
sniffers, 338
vulnerabilities, 20
-vv switch (iptables), 117

W

web servers
DMZ, 267
filtering incoming web servers to specific hosts,
    270-271
forwarding connections from firewalls to internal web
    servers, 272-273
forwarding to multiple internal servers, 273-275
local web servers, running, 269
redirecting local port 80 to local port 8080, 271-272
web services, squid. *See* squid
websites
blocking clients from accessing, 279
inaccessibility of, 278
for troubleshooting methodologies, 69-70
wireless networks, securing with openswan VPN, 351-358
wrenchin', 7
Wright, Gary R., 76

X-Z

-X switch (iptables), 113
xinetd, 51

Yahoo Messenger, 311-314
yum, 45-46

-Z switch (iptables), 113
Zeroconf route, 243